Guidance of Young Children

Eighth Edition

Marian Marion

Governors State University

Boston   Columbus   Indianapolis   New York   San Francisco   Upper Saddle River
Amsterdam   Cape Town   Dubai   London   Madrid   Milan   Munich   Paris   Montreal   Toronto
Delhi   Mexico City   São Paulo   Sydney   Hong Kong   Seoul   Singapore   Taipei   Tokyo

Vice President and Editor in Chief: Jeffery W. Johnston
Senior Acquisitions Editor: Julie Peters
Development Editor: Bryce Bell
Editorial Assistant: Tiffany Bitzel
Vice President, Director of Marketing: Quinn Perkson
Marketing Manager: Erica DeLuca
Senior Managing Editor: Pamela D. Bennett
Project Manager: Kerry J. Rubadue
Senior Operations Supervisor: Matthew Ottenweller
Operations Specialist: Laura Messerly
Senior Art Director: Diane Lorenzo

Text Designer: GGS Higher Education Resources, PMG
Photo Coordinator: Lori Whitley
Cover Art: Corbis
Cover Design: Kristina Holmes
Full-Service Project Management: GGS Higher
    Education Resources, PMG
Composition: GGS Book Services
Printer/Binder: STP Courier
Cover Printer: STP Courier
Text Font: Berkeley Book

Credits and acknowledgments borrowed from other sources and reproduced, with permission, in this textbook appear on appropriate page within text.

Every effort has been made to provide accurate and current Internet information in this book. However, the Internet and information posted on it are constantly changing, so it is inevitable that some of the Internet addresses listed in this textbook will change.

Photo Credits: Getty Images, Inc.–Photodisc/Royalty Free, p. 2; Anne Vega/Merrill, pp. 8, 21, 152, 160; David Mager/Pearson Learning Photo Studio, pp. 27, 216; Frank Siteman, pp. 32, 307; Image 100, p. 41; Kevin Fitzsimons/Merrill, p. 56; Todd Yarrington/Merrill, pp. 73, 323; Neo Edmund/Shutterstock, p. 79; Anthony Magnacca/Merrill, pp. 87, 93, 120, 133, 134, 256; Pearson Learning Photo Studio, pp. 89, 290; Krista Greco/Merrill, pp. 90, 233; Annie Pickert/ABMerrill, p. 100; Lloyd Lemmerman/Merrill, p. 112; Scott Cunningham/Merrill, pp. 147, 298 (bottom); Shutterstock, p. 167; Shirley Zeiberg/PH College, p. 175; Karen Mancinelli/Pearson Learning Photo Studio, p. 180; Silver Burdett Ginn, p. 189; Nancy Sheehan Photography, p. 193; Laura Bolesta/Merrill, pp. 204, 312; iStockphoto, p. 219; Valerie Schultz/Merrill, pp. 244, 254; Katelyn Metzger/Merrill, pp. 266, 298 (top); Barbara Schwartz/Merrill, p. 273.

Library of Congress Cataloging-in-Publication Data

Marion, Marian.
    Guidance of young children / Marian Marion.—8th ed.
       p. cm.
    ISBN-13: 978-0-13-703402-4
    ISBN-10: 0-13-703402-4
    1. Child psychology.   2. Child rearing.   I. Title.
HQ772.M255 2011
649'.1—dc22

                                                                                   2009049444

10 9 8 7 6 5 4 3 2 1

www.pearsonhighered.com

ISBN 10:   0-13-703402-4
ISBN 13: 978-0-13-703402-4

Dedication

For my "rescue" family members and companions in writing:

Lucy Ann, Rottweiler
Zoë-Grace, Golden Retriever
Nami Fiona, tuxedo cat
Leo Allesandro and Casper Mateo, tabby cats

Your woofs and purrs are like music to me.

Preface

Welcome to the eighth edition of *Guidance of Young Children*. My purpose in writing the eighth edition is the same as for earlier editions—to give students a book grounded in solid theory and research, a book that will help them understand the process of child guidance. This book is based on my beliefs about children, and these are stated near the end of this Preface.

▪▪ NEW TO THIS EDITION

The eighth edition retains features that have helped students construct a developmentally appropriate approach to guiding children. It also contains updated research throughout and new content and features designed to make the teaching and learning processes for instructors and students even more effective, efficient, and enjoyable. Following are some examples.

- **Expanded Content on *Bullying*** (Chapter 10) Students will understand the nature of bullying as a form of aggression. They will read about new research on an ecological approach to bullying, in which the bully, the victim, *and* bystanders are a part of the bullying. They will learn how to deal with bullying from an ecological perspective.
- **Expanded content on theories and the theory chapter moved to Part 1 of the book.** (Chapter 2) This chapter now explains the major theoretical perspectives shaping our views of guidance. The theories have been organized into a framework of three groupings: theories focusing on the ecology of children's development, theories focusing on how children construct knowledge, and theories explaining children's psychological, emotional, and social learning needs. All these placed at the beginning of the text will enable students to apply theory as they study the rest of the text.
- **New Chapter on Social and Emotional Competence** (Chapter 8) This new chapter emphasizes a teacher's role in supporting children's social and emotional learning. Students will learn how to create supportive social-emotional learning environments and how to teach the language and skills of social-emotional learning.
- **New Chapter on Guiding Children During Routines and Transitions** (Chapter 12) The focus is on *guiding* children during routines and transitions. Students will apply their knowledge about direct and indirect guidance to guiding children during arrival and departure, large groups, small groups, and transitions.
- **Revised Presentation of Child Development Chapter** (Chapter 3). This chapter now starts with information on basic cognitive developmental processes of perception and memory. Students will see how children depend on these parts of development to help them understand other people. Finally, how they understand other people forms a major part of their ability to act as kind and compassionate people.

Prepare with The Power of Classroom Practice

Register for **MyEducationLab** today at www.myeducationlab.com

What is MyEducationLab?

MyEducationLab is easy to use and integrate into this book.

Wherever you see the MyEducationLab logo in the margins or elsewhere in the text, follow the simple instructions to access the videos, strategies, cases, and artifacts associated with these assignments, activities, and learning units on MyEducationLab. MyEducationLab is organized topically to enhance the coverage of the core concepts discussed in the chapters of your book. For each topic on the course you will find most or all of the following resources:

Students:

• Take **Practice Tests** for each chapter of your text.
  – Completion of each practice test generates a **study plan** that is unique to you.
  – The study plan links to text excerpts, activities with feedback, and videos and other media that can help you master concepts covered in your text.

• Complete **Assignments and Activities** to apply text content to real classroom situations.

• Explore the **Building Teaching Skills and Dispositions** exercises to practice and strengthen the skills that are essential to teaching.

MyEducationLab offers:

• Authentic **classroom video** shows real teachers and students interacting, and helps prepare you for the classroom.

• **Case studies** offer real-life perspectives on common issues and challenges faced in the classroom.

• Authentic student and teacher **classroom artifacts** provide you with the actual types of materials encountered every day by teachers.

CONNECTION TO NATIONAL STANDARDS: Now it is easier than ever to see how coursework is connected to national standards. Each topic on MyEducationLab lists intended learning outcomes connected to the appropriate national standards. And all of the Assignments and Activities and all of the Building Teaching Skills and Dispositions in MyEducationLab are mapped to the appropriate national standards and learning outcomes.

ASSIGNMENTS AND ACTIVITIES: Designed to save instructors preparation time and enhance student understanding, these assignable exercises show concepts in action (through video, cases, and/or student and teacher artifacts). They help students synthesize and apply concepts and strategies they read about in the book.

Children: "Oo"
Teacher: Good job.

BUILDING TEACHING SKILLS AND DISPOSITIONS

These learning units help students practice and strengthen skills that are essential to quality teaching. Students are presented with the core skill or concept and then given an opportunity to practice their understanding of this concept multiple times by watching video footage (or interacting with other media) and then critically analyzing the strategy or skill presented.

STUDY PLAN

A MyEducationLab Study Plan is a multiple choice assessment tied to chapter objectives and supported by study material. A well-designed Study Plan offers multiple opportunities to fully master required course content as identified by the objectives in each chapter:

- **Chapter Objectives** identify the learning outcomes for the chapter and give students targets to shoot for as they read and study.
- **Multiple Choice Assessments** assess mastery of the content. These assessments are mapped to chapter objectives, and students can take the multiple choice quiz as many times as they want. Not only do these quizzes provide overall scores for each objective, but they also explain why responses to particular items are correct or incorrect.
- **Study Material: Review, Practice and Enrichment** give students a deeper understanding of what they do and do not know related to chapter content. This material includes text excerpts, activities that include hints and feedback, and interactive multi-media exercises built around videos, simulations, cases, or classroom artifacts.
- **Flashcards** help students study the definitions of the key terms within each chapter.

GENERAL RESOURCES ON YOUR MYEDUCATIONLAB COURSE

The Resources section on MyEducationLab is designed to help students pass their licensure exams, put together effective portfolios and lesson plans, prepare for and navigate the first year of their teaching careers, and understand key educational standards, policies, and laws. This section includes:

- **Licensure Exams:** Contains guidelines for passing the Praxis exam. **The Practice Test Exam** includes practice multiple-choice questions, case study questions, and video case studies with sample questions.
- **Lesson Plan Builder:** Helps students create and share lesson plans.
- **Licensure and Standards:** Provides links to state licensure standards and national standards.
- **Beginning Your Career:** Educate Offers tips, advice, and valuable information on:
    o Resume Writing and Interviewing: Expert advice on how to write impressive resumes and prepare for job interviews.
    o Your First Year of Teaching: Practical tips on setting up a classroom, managing student behavior, and planning for instruction and assessment.
    o Law and Public Policies: Includes specific directives and requirements educators need to understand under the No Child Left Behind Act and the Individuals with Disabilities Education Improvement Act of 2004.

What if I need help?

We've got you covered 24/7.
There is a wealth of helpful information on the site, under "Tours and Training "and" Support."
Technical support is available 24 hours a day, seven days a week, at http://247pearsoned.custhelp.com.

Visit **www.myeducationlab.com** for a demonstration of this exciting new online teaching resource.

- **Addition of Theory to Chapter on Physical Environment** (Chapter 4) Students will apply knowledge about theories to constructing the physical environment. They will see that the theories presented in Chapter 2 have real application to their teaching.
- **Expanded Content on Methods of Observing** (Chapter 6) Students will see that several practical methods for observing can help them make guidance decisions. They will see how a teacher uses different ways of observing the same behavior.
- **Expanded 'Milestones' Information** Several chapters now contain figures or tables with milestones of development. These should help students understand different aspects of child development and the change in different parts of development as children move through early childhood.
- **MyEducationLab** This is integrated into every chapter. Students will be able to work through video-based exercises and access other materials that will help them understand the concepts they are learning. Students will see margin notes about the assignments and activities for this feature, which is an online site requiring an access code.
- **Summary** Every chapter contains a summary. It briefly recaps the chapter's content, supporting a student's learning of the content.
- **Key Terms** Every chapter now has a list of key terms at the end of the chapter. Every key term is presented within the text in **bold font,** and then its definition is given.
- **Glossary** New to this edition is the glossary with all key terms presented in one place.

⠿ ANCILLARIES FOR THIS EDITION

- **Online Test Bank with answers, separate from the Instructor's Manual.** The test bank is easy to use and provides different types of questions. All online ancillaries can be downloaded from the Instructor Resource Center by adopting professors and instructors.
- **Online Instructor's Manual.** This manual has been updated and refined. I have retained the teaching objectives and suggestions for teaching each section. Handouts are included which support teaching and learning.
- **Online PowerPoint presentations.** There is one PowerPoint presentation for each chapter, including the new chapters. These are intended to decrease the time that you have to spend preparing materials for the class.
- **Pearson MyTest** is a powerful assessment generation program that helps instructors easily create and print quizzes and exams. Questions and tests are authored online, allowing ultimate flexibility and the ability to efficiently create and print assessments anytime, anywhere! Instructors can access Pearson MyTest and their test bank files by going to www.pearsonmytest.com to log in, register, or request access. Features of Pearson MyTest include:

    Premium assessment content

    - Draw from a rich library of assessments that complement your Pearson textbook and your course's learning objectives.
    - Edit questions or tests to fit your specific teaching needs.

Instructor-friendly resources

- Easily create and store your own questions, including images, diagrams, and charts using simple drag-and-drop and Word-like controls.
- Use additional information provided by Pearson, such as the question's difficulty level or learning objective, to help you quickly build your test.

Time-saving enhancements

- Add headers or footers and easily scramble questions and answer choices—all from one simple toolbar.
- Quickly create multiple versions of your test or answer key, and when ready, simply save to MS-Word or PDF format and print!
- Export your exams for import to Blackboard 6.0, CE (WebCT), or Vista (WebCT)!

▪▪ FEATURES RETAINED FROM THE PREVIOUS EDITION

My goal has always been to write a *student-friendly* textbook. Within that framework, I want students to see that a research- and theory-based textbook can challenge them to think critically about guiding children. These effective features from the last edition have been retained but have been refined to make them even more useful:

- **Writing style:** Conversational *and* informative.
- **Bold font:** Emphasizes definitions and terms seen for the first time.
- **Use of three teachers from the same school:** Mr. Bjornurd (infant-toddler), Mrs. Woodward (preschool), and Mr. Sanchez (K–2, multi-age, looping classroom) appear throughout the text and deal with guidance problems faced in real classrooms every day.
- **Chapter-opening vignettes:** Vignettes open every chapter and focus on children and teachers in early childhood classrooms. Students will read vignettes from the infant-toddler, preschool, and K-Primary classrooms. Occasionally, there is one longer vignette instead of three. The vignettes illustrate major points in each chapter.
- **Analyze vignettes:** Students apply newly acquired knowledge from the chapter to the chapter-opening case study. Students come full circle in each chapter.
- **Advance organizers:** A chapter outline and new guiding questions will help students get a good overall picture of the chapter prior to study.
- **Questions for Reflection:** An end of chapter feature, these are designed to encourage higher level thinking and analysis when reflecting on the chapter's main points.
- **Apply Your Knowledge:** An end-of-chapter feature focusing on the application level in the cognitive domain.
- **Examples:** Gleaned from real classrooms, these illustrate guidance in early childhood classrooms at all levels.
- **Appendix:** Summarizes major positive guidance strategies.

⠃⠃ THIS TEXTBOOK HAS EVOLVED FROM A SET OF BELIEFS

This edition continues to reflect my core beliefs about children and child guidance; it is these beliefs that I want to pass on to students.

- **I believe that protecting children is our most important role.** Students reading this text should understand that we teach and protect children most effectively by making active, conscious decisions about positive strategies. *We protect children when we refuse to use strategies that are degrading or hurtful or have the potential to harm or humiliate children.* Some strategies denigrate and dishonor children and should never be used, such as shaking, hitting, and other forms of physically hurtful interaction; hostile humor; embarrassment; ridicule; sarcasm; judging; manipulating; playing mind games; exerting hurtful punishment; ignoring; terrorizing; isolating; and violating boundaries. These are personality-numbing horrors. They are abusive and have no place in our lives with children.

  The National Association for the Education of Young Children (NAEYC), in its *Code of Ethics*, notes that the most important part of the code is that early childhood professionals never engage in any practice that hurts or degrades a child. Therefore, this textbook takes this approach: first of all, do no harm. Students who use this textbook will learn **only** positive strategies and a respectful approach to guiding children.

- **I believe that we have a choice about how we think about and behave with children.** John Steinbeck, in *East of Eden*, described the beauty inherent in the ability to make choices. Students need to know that what they choose to think about children, how they act with them, and the discipline strategies they use *do* matter. Using a positive, constructivist approach on a daily basis has a long-term impact on children—helping them become self-responsible, competent, independent, and cooperative people who like themselves and who have a strong core of values.

- **I believe that an adult's "style" of guiding children does affect children.** It affects several parts of their personality and their approach to life—for example, their moral compass, emotional intelligence, level of self-esteem, how they manage anger and aggression, how they handle stress, their willingness to cooperate with others, whether they can take another person's perspective, and their social skills.

  Therefore, the organizing force for this text is the concept of styles of caregiving—a concept presented right away in Chapter 1. Students should come away from that chapter with a clear idea of the authoritarian, authoritative, and permissive styles. They will learn about adult beliefs and behavior in each style and about the likely effect of that style on children. They will then encounter the concept of caregiving style woven into almost every chapter.

- **I believe that constructivist, positive, and effective child guidance is based on solid knowledge of child development.** Without this knowledge, adults might well have unrealistic expectations of children. Having this knowledge gives professionals a firm foundation on which to build child guidance skills.

- **I believe that there is no one right way to deal with any issue but that there are many good ways.** I do *not* give students a set of tricks to use with children. However, students will find numerous exercises and questions designed to help them construct basic concepts of child guidance. They might enjoy thinking critically about typical guidance issues and even more challenging behaviors.

■ **I believe that we should each develop a personal approach to guiding children, one built on theoretical eclecticism.** In this text, students will study and use the decision-making model of child guidance, a model that evolves from understanding various theoretical approaches to guiding children. Students will apply the major theories forming our beliefs and perspectives on guiding children.

myeducationlab

THE POWER OF CLASSROOM PRACTICE

"Teacher educators who are developing pedagogies for the analysis of teaching and learning contend that analyzing teaching artifacts has three advantages: it enables new teachers time for reflection while still using the real materials of practice; it provides new teachers with experience thinking about and approaching the complexity of the classroom; and in some cases, it can help new teachers and teacher educators develop a shared understanding and common language about teaching. . . ."[1]

As Linda Darling-Hammond and her colleagues point out, grounding teacher education in real classrooms—among real teachers and students and among actual examples of students' and teachers' work—is an important, and perhaps even an essential, part of training teachers for the complexities of teaching in today's classrooms. For this reason, we have created a valuable, time-saving website MyEducationLab that provides you with the context of real classrooms and artifacts that research on teacher education tells us is so important. The authentic in-class video footage, interactive skill-building exercises and other resources available on MyEducationLab offer you a uniquely valuable teacher education tool.

MyEducationLab is easy to use and integrate into both your assignments and your courses. Wherever you see the MyEducationLab logo in the margins or elsewhere in the text, follow the simple instructions to access the videos, strategies, cases, and artifacts associated with these assignments, activities, and learning units on MyEducationLab. MyEducationLab is organized topically to enhance the coverage of the core concepts discussed in the chapters of your book. For each topic on the course you will find most or all of the following resources:

CONNECTION TO NATIONAL STANDARDS

Now it is easier than ever to see how your coursework is connected to national standards. In each topic of MyEducationLab you will find intended learning outcomes connected to the appropriate national standards for your course. All of the Assignments and Activities and all of the Building Teaching Skills and Dispositions in MyEducationLab are mapped to the appropriate national standards and learning outcomes as well.

ASSIGNMENTS AND ACTIVITIES

Designed to save instructors preparation time, these assignable exercises show concepts in action (through video, cases, or student and teacher artifacts) and then offer thought-provoking questions that probe your understanding of theses concepts or strategies. (Feedback for these assignments is available to the instructor.)

---

[1] Darling-Hammond, l., & Bransford, J., Eds. (2005). *Preparing Teachers for a Changing World.* San Francisco: John Wiley & Sons

⠿ BUILDING TEACHING SKILLS AND DISPOSITIONS

These learning units help you practice and strengthen skills that are essential to quality teaching. First you are presented with the core skill or concept and then given an opportunity to practice your understanding of this concept multiple times by watching video footage (or interacting with other media) and then critically analyzing the strategy or skill presented.

⠿ GENERAL RESOURCES ON YOUR MYEDUCATIONLAB COURSE

The *Resources* section on your MyEducationLab course is designed to help you pass your licensure exam, put together an effective portfolio and lesson plan, prepare for and navigate the first year of your teaching career, and understand key educational standards, policies, and laws. This section includes:

- *Licensure Exams:* Access guidelines for passing the Praxis exam. The *Practice Test Exam* includes practice questions, *Case Histories,* and *Video Case Studies.*
- *Portfolio Builder and Lesson Plan Builder:* Create, update, and share portfolios and lesson plans.
- *Preparing a Portfolio:* Access guidelines for creating a high-quality teaching portfolio that will allow you to practice effective lesson planning.
- *Licensure and Standards:* Link to state licensure standards and national standards.
- *Beginning Your Career:* Educate yourself—access tips, advice, and valuable information on:

  o Resume Writing and Interviewing: Expert advice on how to write impressive resumes and prepare for job interviews.
  o Your First Year of Teaching: Practical tips to set up your classroom, manage student behavior, and learn to more easily organize for instruction and assessment.
  o Law and Public Policies: Specific directives and requirements you need to understand under the No Child Left Behind Act and the Individuals with Disabilities Education Improvement Act of 2004.

- *Special Education Interactive Timeline:* Build your own detailed timelines based on different facets of the history and evolution of special education.

⠿ BOOK-SPECIFIC RESOURCES

Study Plan

A MyEducationLab Study Plan is a multiple choice assessment tied to chapter objectives, supported by study material. A well-designed Study Plan offers multiple opportunities to fully master required course content as identified by the objectives in each chapter:

- *Chapter Objectives* identify the learning outcomes for the chapter and give you targets to shoot for as you read and study.

- *Multiple Choice Assessments* assess mastery of the content (tied to each chapter objective) by taking the multiple choice quiz as many times as needed. Not only do these quizzes provide overall scores for each objective, but they also explain why responses to particular items are correct or incorrect.
- *Study Material: Review, Practice and Enrichment* gives you a deeper understanding of what you do and do not know related to chapter content. This can be accessed through the Multiple Choice Assessment (after you take a quiz you receive information regarding the chapter content on which you still need practice and review) or through a self-directed method of study. This material includes text excerpts, activities that include hints and feedback, and media assets (video, simulations, cases, etc.).

Visit www.myeducationlab.com for a demonstration of this exciting new online teaching resource.

⠿ ACKNOWLEDGMENTS

I have been at Governors State University since 2006, and I am deeply appreciative of the time granted to me for writing. For this, I thank President Maimon, Dean Bordelon, and Colleen Sexton, my department chair. My early childhood colleagues—Jeannine Klomes, Ty Jiles, Evie Plofsky, and John Powers—are focused on helping students become effective teachers of young children. It is an honor to be a member of this group.

The professionals at Pearson/Merrill support authors as they write. I thank my editor Julie Peters; Bryce Bell, development editor; and Tiffany Bitzel, editorial assistant; Reviewers have been generous in offering ideas for enriching the content and structure of *Guidance of Young Children*. Several colleagues from around the country reviewed the material for the eighth edition: Vikki Boatman, Stephen F. Austin State University; Teresa Frazier, Thomas Nelson Community College; Jeanne Helm, Richland Community College; Sandra K. Regan, Middlesex Community College; Patrice Thatcher, College of the Siskiyous; and Elaine Wilkinson, Collin County Community College.

Their feedback was very helpful and constructively given. My guess is that their students receive the same type of helpful feedback. The reviewers made several specific suggestions that I have heeded. For example, I moved the theory chapter to Part 1 of the text and explained more theories and their relationship to guiding children. Their feedback has reshaped the structure of parts of this textbook.

Once again, I thank my husband Bill for his continued support and my animal friends Lucy Ann, Zoe-Gracie, Nami Fiona, Leo Allesandro, and Casper Matteo.

Please feel free to email me with questions, comments, or suggestions about *Guidance of Young Children*, Eighth Edition.

Marian Marion

Email: M-Marion@govst.edu

Brief Contents

Contents

Guiding Young Children

Three Essential Elements

Chapter 1   A Teacher's Role in Guiding Children

This chapter describes three adult caregiving styles: authoritarian, authoritative, and permissive. It explains the concept of developmentally appropriate practice as part of the authori*tative* style. It focuses on the processes that adults use to influence children.

Chapter 2   Theoretical Foundations of Child Guidance

Chapter 2 describes theory as a firm foundation on which to base decisions about guiding young children. The goal is *not* to memorize information about different theories but to understand that, without theory, we would not have a foundation for our profession. The chapter explains three categories of theories: theories explaining how children's behavior develops in different systems; theories focusing on how children construct ideas; and theories examining on children's psychological, emotional, and social learning needs.

Chapter 3   Understand Child Development: A Key to Guiding Children Effectively

Chapter 3 describes selected facets of child development. It starts with memory and perception, the basic building blocks of cognition. It also focuses on social cognition, which is children's understanding of other people, and it examines how children in different phases of early childhood show social cognition. The chapter focuses on how children develop self-control and how they become kind and compassionate people.

A Teacher's Role in Guiding Children

"Children of authoritative parents have proved to be more competent than the children of either authoritarian or permissive parents."

(Maccoby & Martin, 1983)

Chapter Contents

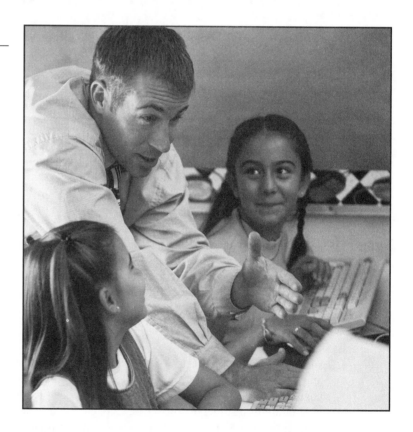

Guiding Questions

- How can I describe the two major dimensions of an adult's style of caregiving?
- What are the effects of different styles of caregiving on children's development and behavior?
- What are the basic processes through which I, as a teacher, influence children?

VIGNETTES

BLAKE IGNORES HIS MOTHER'S REQUEST

Blake left his scooter in the middle of the living room. His mother called out to him, "Put the scooter outside, Blake." Blake heard but ignored her as he walked away. "Blake, did you hear me? Put that scooter outside this instant. I mean it. No water park for you this afternoon if you don't put that scooter outside!" Blake shuffled down the hall to his room and Mom continued in an exasperated tone, "Blake, get back here. I want that scooter put away."

Finally, Mom just turned back to the kitchen. "That boy never listens to me."

Blake pays little attention to his mother's limits. He also knows that she hardly ever follows up on her threats. That afternoon, for example, Mom took Blake to the water park, after saying, "Next time, Blake, you'd better listen to me when I tell you to do something." Blake turned his head away from Mom and rolled his eyes.

DAVID DOES WHATEVER HE WANTS TO DO

At 18 months, David, when visiting a friend with his mother, banged on the friend's television screen and pushed at the door screen. His mom said nothing until the friend expressed concern for her property. Then she said, "David, do you think you should be doing that?" To the friend she said, "You know, I don't think I should order him around." When he was 4 years old, David stayed up until 11:30 when company was over. To the friend who inquired about his bedtime, Mom replied, "Oh, I let David make decisions on his own." David fell asleep in the book corner at his preschool the next day. At 6 years of age, David pushed ahead of others at a zoo exhibition. Mom ignored what had happened to the other children and said, "Go ahead. Can you see? Move up closer."

PATRICK'S PROBLEMS HAVE DEEP ROOTS

Patrick's father is irritable around his children. His sister-in-law has watched him for years and now thinks that he really dislikes being a father. He tells his three children, including Patrick, what he wants them to do by cursing at them and barking and snapping orders. He expects his children to obey immediately despite anything else they might be doing. He laughed when he recited his "motto" to one of the other men at work: "My kids know that I mean business! When I say jump, they know that they'd better say, 'how high?'" Patrick has watched as Dad used a belt on an older brother.

When Patrick was a toddler and learning how to use the toilet, Dad spanked him when he had an accident. When Patrick was 4 years old Dad grabbed one of his arms and yanked him to make Patrick move along at the store, saying, "#%&*#$# [curse word] I'm sick of you holding us up all the time." At preschool, Patrick had trouble with other children because he hit them when he was angry and the other children started to leave him out of activities.

LEAH BITES ROBERT

Leah's mother is a home day-care provider for Leah, 18 months old, and her friend's two children, Robert, aged 24 months, and Steven, aged 9 months. Steven's mother asked Leah's mom what to do when Steven bites her during feeding. "Quickly tell him no and pull his mouth off your breast. Don't make a joke of it, either, or he'll think you're playing a game." Leah wanted a toy that Robert had but did not seem to have the words for asking. She grew more agitated and then, even to her own surprise, she bit him! Leah's mother, also surprised, immediately took care of the bite on Robert's arm. Then, to her daughter, she said, "No, Leah. Biting is a no-no. Biting hurts Robert. If you need help, come to Mommy and I will help you get a toy."

:: INTRODUCTION

This entire textbook focuses on positive, authori*tative* child guidance, based on principles of developmentally appropriate practice. Many adults, like Leah's mother and many teachers, use developmentally appropriate, authoritative child guidance. They are warm, very responsive, and supportive, while they also have reasonable and high expectations of children. Their beliefs about discipline and guidance are developmentally appropriate. Their practices are also developmentally appropriate, with their beliefs "in sync" with their practices. This first chapter describes developmentally appropriate or authoritative child guidance. Other adults, like Patrick's father, use the developmentally *in*appropriate practices of the authoritarian. Still others, like David's and Blake's parents, use a developmentally inappropriate style of guidance known as permissiveness.

In this chapter, you will read about the authoritarian and permissive styles in this chapter as well, but the emphasis is on positive authoritative guidance. We will first examine each style of caregiving and its effect on children's development. Then we will focus on the ways in which all adults, whether they are authoritative, authoritarian, or permissive, influence children.

:: BEGINNING THE CIRCLE: OUR HOPE FOR CHILDREN

As teachers, we have a vision for our work and a hope for children. We hope to help them develop in all domains and to satisfy their inborn curiosity by learning eagerly and joyfully. Our vision is to help children, first, feel safe and secure, and to develop healthy self-esteem as well as a strong moral compass. We want them to honor and respect themselves and others and to learn how to deal with a variety of stressors. We can help children understand and deal effectively with an array of feelings, such as anger, sadness, love, and jealousy. Most of all, we can help children become compassionate individuals who can walk a mile in another person's shoes—or an animal's tracks. Thus, we help them to develop empathy, what every society needs for survival.

Bringing our vision to life takes some thinking and reflection. We as teachers need to acknowledge our role in the process. This book is about guiding children, but guidance starts with adult reflection, looking at oneself first in the guidance process. We are the ones responsible for constructing the interpersonal environment in which children develop. That is, we have a big part in setting the tone in a classroom and in how we interact with children. We are the adults. We have the life experience. We have the knowledge about children's development. We understand how to teach. Yes, children certainly have a part in interactions with us but we are the adults and have more responsibility in guiding children.

:: MAJOR DIMENSIONS OF CAREGIVING STYLES

Researchers have long been interested in how one parent or teacher differs from others. Researchers have also been interested in how these differences affect children. For example, almost 60 years ago, Becker (1954) analyzed several studies and classified a parent's style by looking at whether the parent was (a) hostile or warm and (b) restrictive or permissive. Then and now, we know that warmth is probably the single most important factor in an adult's relationship with a child.

Diana Baumrind (Baumrind, 1967, 1971, 1977, 1979, 1996; Baumrind & Black, 1967) built on the foundation of the earlier research. She is acknowledged as one of the most influential researchers in this area. She has found that two major factors—responsiveness and demandingness—determine an adult's style of caregiving. Some adults are highly responsive to children, whereas others are not very responsive. Some adults are high in demandingness, whereas others make very few demands. (See Figure 1.1.) Other researchers now use Baumrind's framework, examining the role of responsiveness and demandingness (Ciairano, Kliewer, Bonono, & Bosma, 2008; Mansager, 2004; Shek, 2007; Walker, 2008).

Responsiveness

Responsiveness is one of two major caregiving dimensions. It refers to the degree of adult supportiveness, the degree to which an adult is tuned in to a child's developmental level, and whether the adult meets a child's needs. Figure 1.1 shows that responsiveness is on a continuum. A person can exist anywhere along the continuum. Some adults are highly responsive to children, whereas others are not. This section and Figure 1.2 describes several important aspects of responsiveness, including warmth, whether an adult knows child development, whether he views children and adults as partners in interaction, communication style, and whether an adult uses good explanations along with guidance strategies (Baumrind, 1996).

Responsiveness
One of the elements of a person's caregiving style; whether an adult meets a child's needs and understands child development

FIGURE 1.1   **Two major dimensions of caregiving**

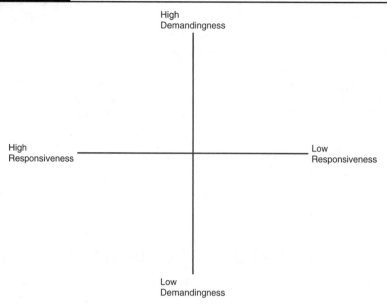

Warmth

Emotional expression of fondness

Warmth   **Warmth** is the emotional expression of liking or love. Observe a group of adults, either parents or teachers, as they interact with young children. You will observe differences in how warm they are toward children. Some teachers and parents are highly responsive: they show a high degree of sincere warmth. But others are low in responsiveness and do not express affection or love at all or do not express it appropriately.

There are many ways to show warmth; no one way is best because we each have our own approach. Whatever our culture or personal manner, however, the common thread in warmth is making it clear to a child through our interactions that we genuinely like or love him. Our warmth shows a genuine concern for that child's welfare, as shown in the next three examples.

EXAMPLE   Lev's father is not given to extravagant expressions of emotion. When Lev said before dinner, "Can I feed Sam [the cat] before we sit down to eat? He looks hungry," Dad thought that Lev had done a good thing but said little. He expressed his warmth, however, during the prayer before eating: "I am also thankful for a son who thinks about his cat first." Lev kept his head down but shifted his eyes to look quickly at his dad and then back at his plate. Lev is secure in his father's love and affection.

EXAMPLE   Jake's mother also loves her son but expresses her warmth differently, in a more unrestrained way. She tells Jake every night before he goes to sleep to remember that she "loves him right up to the moon and back again" (a statement from his favorite children's book). Jake always says, "Aw, Ma," but looks forward to hearing this affectionate close to his day.

EXAMPLE   Mr. Sanchez said to his first graders, who were sitting in a circle, "When I was driving to school this morning, I thought about how happy I was that I would see

FIGURE 1.2	What is responsiveness? What is demandingness?

Responsiveness

- **Warmth**
  Do I show that I like children? Do I show appropriate affection and support? Are my expressions of warmth sincere?
- **Child development knowledge**
  Do I have a good knowledge base in child development? Do I understand how families affect children? Do I understand how a child's culture affects him or her?
- **Children and adults as partners in interaction**
  Do I really understand that both adults and children have a part in any interaction? Do I also understand that my adult role carries greater responsibility?
- **Communication style**
  Do I communicate in an open and direct way? How do I send messages, especially limits?
- **Giving explanations**
  Do I use a reason along with a guidance strategy? Do I know how to state reasons well?

Demandingness

- **Boundaries, limits, and expectations**
  Do I have age- and individually appropriate expectations for behavior? Do I clearly state appropriate limits?
- **Monitoring and supervising**
  Do I know how to create an orderly, consistent environment? Do I monitor children and supervise them well?
- **Discipline strategies**
  Are my discipline strategies positive, age appropriate, individual appropriate, and culturally sensitive?
- **Style of confrontation**
  Am I willing to confront children when necessary? Do I confront in a firm yet kind way?

all the children in my class again." He then looked at each child, saying his or her name. "Susan, Tom, Vinnie, Sam, Reese . . . let's hold hands and make a circle of friends. This circle of friends is going to help each other to have a good week at school."

Warmth is an exceedingly important part of responsiveness (Belsky, Sligo, Jaffee, Woodward, & Silva, 2005). Children are often quite aggressive when their parents are not warm, when they are negative and irritable (Grusec & Lytton, 1988). These children act out in school when their parents are angry, nonaccepting, and disapproving. Baumrind (1996) cautions that warmth should be sincere. She believes that false expressions of affection prevent parents and teachers from appropriately managing discipline encounters when limits are necessary.

Child Development Knowledge Teachers using positive child guidance have usually taken formal course work in child development. Parents, too, can take formal course work, or they can acquire **child development knowledge** by reading and attending parent education classes (Patterson, Mockford, & Stewart-Brown, 2005). This knowledge base allows adults to have realistic expectations of children of different ages in terms of motor, physical, cognitive, social, and emotional development. It also enables adults to understand the role that families play in a young child's development.

> **Child development knowledge**
> Ability to describe and explain different aspects of children's growth

> **EXAMPLE** Mr. Sanchez, the primary grade teacher, realizes that his children feel emotions such as anger and that they express their angry feelings. He also knows that children do not understand anger. Nor can they manage their feelings on their own. Therefore, he helps them label feelings and he gives them the words to use for expressing feelings.

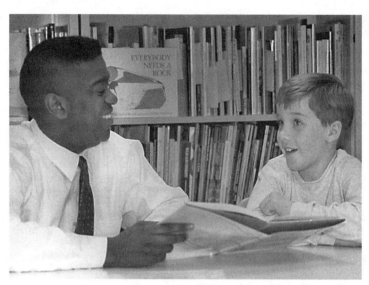

Highly responsive teachers convey warmth and understand child development.

Partners in Interaction   Researchers started to think about this concept in the late 1960s (Bell, 1968; Bell & Harper, 1977). We know that children are active partners in every interaction with other children or with adults. Adults who use developmentally appropriate child guidance believe that children have an important part in any interaction, but at the same time, they know that adults always have a greater responsibility (Maccoby & Martin, 1983).

> **EXAMPLE**   Mr. Sanchez has a right to expect his class to put things away after using them. The teacher also realizes that he has a greater responsibility in that he has to make the cleanup limit clear. He also has to teach children how to put things away, and he has to manage the classroom so that cleanup is simple. In addition, he has to pay attention to the children when they do put things away and acknowledge their efforts.

Communication style
Manner in which an adult delivers messages to children; indicative of the adult's view of children

Communication Style   Highly responsive adults communicate in an open, congruent, validating, and direct way. They deliver messages simply, kindly, firmly, and consistently. Children tend to accept this type of communication willingly because the adult uses persuasion, not force, to make a point. Children are socialized most effectively by adults who use this type of communication and who enforce their directives (Baumrind, 1993, 1996). Such a positive **communication style** indicates that they also see children as competent, as having choices, and as worthy of respect.

> **EXAMPLE**   Vinnie and Sam scooted off to the computer, leaving their library books on the table even though the classroom limit is that people put things away before they start a new activity. Mr. Sanchez, responsive in this discipline encounter, used a direct and validating style of communication: "I know that you've been waiting for your turn at the computer and I'll save your spot for you. First, though, I want you to put your library books in your cubbies."

Giving Explanations   Giving explanations to children is good for both children and adults. We all, and that includes children, tend to be more cooperative when we know why somebody wants us to do something or even to stop doing something. It is a sign of respect to give an explanation, and children deserve to know why we ask them to do something.

Giving explanations benefits adults, too. Already using positive guidance strategies, highly responsive adults are even more effective because they state a reason along with the guidance strategy. Discipline encounters usually deal with one specific act (a child leaving books strewn about the library). A good strategy—simply reminding the child to put the books away—helps a child understand what is appropriate for that incident. However, giving a reason along with the strategy paints a broader picture for the child. It tells him that the appropriate behavior would apply in many other cases, too (Baumrind, 1996).

> **EXAMPLE**   Mr. Sanchez says to Reese, one of his first graders, "Reese, I noticed that you left the library books on the floor near the beanbag chair. Please put the books back up on the shelf, standing up in their places. Then the other children can see them easily and the books won't get stepped on."

Demandingness

Demandingness is the other major caregiving dimension. The National Association of the Education of Young Children (NAEYC, no date, http://www.naeyc.org/research/using) urges teachers to use high-quality research in making decisions about children and families. This textbook uses research that shaped thinking about how we interact with young children and explains things using terms *from* that research. The word *demandingness* is the official term used in the caregiving style research, from Baumrind's earliest work to publications in 2009, as noted in the introduction. Demandingness, an off-putting word to some, merely refers to an adult's overall views on control and deals with the following elements (Baumrind, 1996):

> **Demandingness**
> One of the elements of a person's caregiving style: whether and how the person sets limits and monitors, supervises, and faces issues

Understanding and setting boundaries, limits, and expectations

How adults monitor and supervise

The type of discipline strategies used

An adult's style of confrontation

Adults differ in how demanding they are with children. Figure 1.1 shows that demandingness, like responsiveness, is on a continuum. A person can exist anywhere along the demandingness continuum. Some adults are on the higher end, whereas others tend to be at the lower end of the continuum—some are high, some lower in making expectations known to children. The following subsection and Figure 1.2 explain the elements of demandingness.

Boundaries, Limits, and Expectations   Adults differ in their ability and willingness to help children understand that there are boundaries, or limits, on behavior. They differ in how they state expectations (how they request or ask) for cooperative, helpful, appropriately self-controlled behavior from children. Demanding and responsive adults understand the importance of proper boundaries and appropriate limits in guiding young children. They develop and clearly communicate appropriate limits. The key is to combine high demandingness with warmth, understanding of child development, and giving explanations (high responsiveness).

Monitoring and Supervising   One part of demandingness is whether adults monitor and supervise children's activities and behavior and whether they provide an orderly and consistent physical environment and time schedule. Authoritative adults steadfastly believe that monitoring and supervising children is essential (Barnard & Solchany, 2002). Their actions or practices are in harmony with their beliefs because they are willing to commit themselves to the time necessary to monitor children in a classroom or at home. They fully understand that continuous but not annoying monitoring, combined with appropriate supervision, prevents or ends some inappropriate behavior in children (Baumrind, 1996). Early childhood students learn quickly that, when in a classroom with young children, they must be aware of the entire room or playground and what is going on. They learn that they must monitor all activities. It also takes time, effort, and skill to develop a responsive physical environment and time schedule (Haupt, Larsen, Robinson, & Hart, 1995; Ravid, 2003).

Guidance and Discipline Strategies   Adults believe in and use a variety of guidance or discipline strategies. Some adults use guidance strategies that are age, individually, and culturally appropriate. Other adults use strategies that are not appropriate for the age or individual needs of a child and very often focus on punishing a child. Other adults use unhelpful discipline strategies. The strategies are not hurtful but they do not help children, either. The strategies are simply confusing.

Age-appropriate guidance strategies are suitable for the general age group of the children being taught. For example, it would be age appropriate to teach all the children in a group of 3-year-olds to label feelings.

An individually appropriate strategy is suitable for a specific child, regardless of the child's age. It would be individually appropriate to teach David, one of the case study children and who is now 8 years old, how to put labels on his feeling of frustration when his dog does not sit on command. Why? David did not learn how to label feelings when he was a preschooler and he needs to learn the lesson now.

Style of confrontation
Facing something, often irritating or hurtful, and coping with it

Style of Confrontation   Style of confrontation refers to facing something and coping with it. In child guidance, confrontation deals with how an adult faces and copes with behavior that is clearly hurtful or inappropriate, such as name calling or physical aggression. Adults differ in how they face issues. Some adults are firm yet kind and are willing to take a stand even if doing so provokes a conflict.

> **EXAMPLE**   Mr. Sanchez heard Jack say to a child in a wheelchair, "We don't want you to play with us. Get that stupid chair out of here." He quietly asked Jack to come with him so that he could talk to (confront) him in private. Mr. Sanchez did not accuse him but dealt with this discipline encounter by using a discipline strategy called an I-message: "I heard you say . . . to Pippin. I was surprised to hear you say that because we have talked about kindness in our room and I know that you are usually very kind."

This teacher statement started a short conversation that gave Jack an opportunity to tell Mr. Sanchez that he was afraid of the wheelchair. He was also afraid that

Pippin would fall out of the wheelchair. Jack did not think that Pippin would be able to work very well with the science equipment while seated in the wheelchair. Mr. Sanchez then realized that Jack needed to know more about Pippin's wheelchair and that Pippin could do all the class activities, but that she had to do them sitting down.

:: STYLES OF CAREGIVING

Baumrind's longitudinal study is called the Family Socialization and Developmental Competence Project. The focus of this research, begun in the 1960s, is on the relation between adult authority and developmental outcomes for typically developing children. Over time, Baumrind has studied the effects of demandingness and responsiveness on the same children's development at three stages—preschool, school age, and adolescence. She assessed parents' specific discipline strategies but focused most pointedly on their overall levels of demandingness and responsiveness (Baumrind, 1996).

Baumrind identified and labeled several styles of parenting or caregiving based on the adult's level of demandingness and responsiveness, as shown in Figure 1.3. These caregiving styles are the authoritative, authoritarian, and permissive styles. For each, you will read about an adult's level of demandingness and responsiveness and the impact of the style on children. I will emphasize, though, the positive authoritative style.

The Authoritative Style

Authoritative caregivers possess qualities that help children develop equally positive qualities.

High Demandingness, High Responsiveness

Figures 1.1 and 1.3 show that authoritative caregivers are high in both demandingness and responsiveness. In terms of demandingness, they expect developmentally appropriate, mature behavior. They set and maintain reasonable, fair limits and closely supervise and monitor children's activities. They are willing to confront a child when necessary, but they confront in a respectful, kind way. In terms of responsiveness, authoritative adults are warm and nurturing. They understand child development and tend to have realistic expectations from children of different ages.

Authoritative adults have a clear communication style. They deliver messages simply, kindly, firmly, and consistently. They use persuasion, not force, to help children understand things. They use positive, developmentally appropriate discipline strategies. The strategies described and explained in detail in Chapter 5 focus on teaching and not on punishment. Authoritative adults believe in giving simple and clear reasons and explanations in discipline encounters. Recent research with families of Mexican descent in the United States found that parents in this group reported using authoritative practices more often than authoritarian strategies (Varela, Sanchez-Sosa, & Riveros, 2004).

Authoritative style of caregiving
Combination of high demandingness and high responsiveness; considered a positive approach

| FIGURE 1.3 | Authori*tative* caregivers combine high responsiveness with high demandingness |

Positive and Powerful Effect on Young Children's Development

The authoritative style helps children feel safe and secure   One of a child's most basic needs is for safety and security. Authoritative caregivers help children feel both psychologically and physically safe. They clearly communicate rules that say, "I will never hurt you and I expect you to treat others with respect." Adults who use positive discipline speak to children respectfully and refuse to degrade or demean children. Authoritative adults know that children control their own behavior best when they feel safe and secure (Baumrind, 1993).

The authoritative style encourages self-responsibility   Children learn to take responsibility for their own actions when they have good models of self-responsible behavior. Authoritative caregivers use positive discipline strategies such as I-messages that model self-responsible behavior. They accept responsibility for their actions and do not blame others for how they themselves feel or act. They are nonjudgmental as they explain the consequences of a child's choice of unsafe behaviors. They model self-responsible behavior.

The authoritative style fosters competence and healthy self-control Authoritative caregiving helps children become competent. Children of authoritative parents tended to be socially responsible and independent when they are first observed in preschool. When these same children were 8 and 9 years old, both boys and girls from authoritative families were still quite competent in the cognitive and social spheres (Baumrind, 1996; Baumrind & Black, 1967).

Our long-range goal in guiding children is to help them achieve healthy self-control. We want children to be able to regulate their own behavior and to want to behave appropriately in school as well as 5, 10, or 20 years from now. Children develop the ability to regulate or control their behavior when they interact with warm and supportive adults who use positive discipline (Hart, DeWolf, Wozniak, & Burts, 1992). Authoritative teachers and parents help children become self-controlled because they:

Model self-control.

Clearly communicate their expectation that children will show the level of self-control that they are capable of showing (Healy, 2004, 2005).

Give specific information on how children can control themselves.

Recognize and encourage children who act in an age-appropriate, self-controlled way.

The authoritative style helps children develop empathy. Piaget (1983) believed that there are classical factors of development—maturation, social interaction, physical activity. He noted that social interaction helps children gradually become less egocentric and more empathic because contact with other children and adults exposes children to ideas different from their own. Authoritative adults are themselves more empathic (Brems & Sohl, 1995). They model empathy and encourage children to look at things from someone else's perspective. Adults can guide children's understanding of that other viewpoint by taking the time to explain the other person's perspective.

> **EXAMPLE** Mr. Sanchez had playground duty and observed that one of the first graders hit a kindergarten child. Mr. Sanchez, after first helping the kindergarten child, said to the first grader, "I think that you hurt Cody when you hit him. I can tell because he is crying."

Mr. Sanchez's discipline strategy was developmentally appropriate. It will help the child understand how Cody seems to feel. The teacher has actually told the child how Cody feels and has avoided simply asking, "How do you think Cody feels?"

The authoritative style builds authentic self-esteem and a strong core of personal values. Competence, confidence, and a sense of worthiness are the cornerstones of positive self-esteem. One of our goals as early childhood educators is to help each child develop authentic self-esteem. Along with authentic self-esteem, we want to help children develop a strong core of personal values that guides them to believe in the rights of others to dignified, fair treatment.

Children are motivated by a need to be competent and to have confidence in their ability to do things well, whether it is identifying birds, finger painting, making and keeping friends, doing math problems, or taking care of a horse. The authoritative style helps children feel competent and confident enough to behave appropriately.

It takes time, effort, and creativity to use positive discipline strategies well, and children who experience positive discipline view themselves as worthy of an adult's time and effort. Adults who rely on positive discipline strategies also model, expect, teach, and encourage fair, dignified treatment of other people and animals.

> **EXAMPLE**   Mr. Sanchez quietly and calmly introduced the gerbils to his first graders during morning meeting. With the teacher's guidance, the entire group developed the kindness rules for dealing with the gerbils. They printed the kindness rules and posted them near the gerbil house. Mr. Sanchez reminded the children about the kindness rules at other group times and he pointed to the rule about being quiet around the gerbils when Jessie and Lee started talking too loudly near the gerbils' house.

The Authoritarian Style

Authoritarian style of caregiving
Combination of high demandingness and low responsiveness; considered a negative approach

The **authoritarian** style differs significantly from the more positive authoritative style just described. Authoritarian caregivers have a negative impact on children's development.

High Demandingness, Low Responsiveness

Figure 1.3 shows the authoritarian style in the upper right quadrant, where high demandingness meets low responsiveness—not a good combination.

Demandingness   Think about the differences between the high demandingness of an authoritative and an authoritarian caregiver. Both set limits, but authoritarians develop arbitrary limits and then state them poorly. Authoritarian caregivers do not monitor or supervise children's activities very well; then they punish when a child does something of which they disapprove. Smith and Farrington (2004) found that males who were poorly supervised by their parents were themselves poor supervisors as adults. When authoritarians confront children, they tend to do so in an inconsiderate, inept, or mean-spirited way. They try to exert a great deal of psychological control.

> **EXAMPLE**   Patrick and his family were eating at a buffet-style restaurant. Six-year-old Patrick ran to the serving area by himself, despite the rule requiring an adult to accompany children to the buffet. His father just kept on eating. After about 5 minutes, however, Dad sighed, got up, and went to the buffet to get Patrick. They came back, Dad belittling Patrick and Patrick carrying a dish overflowing with ice cream. Dad was furious because Patrick had slopped ice cream on the counter, himself, and the floor. (Patrick's father could easily have prevented this whole episode by monitoring his son's activity and by setting some limits.)

Authoritarian adults like Patrick's father rely on negative discipline strategies and equate discipline with punishment. Patrick's father does not use just one negative discipline strategy. He uses a combination of negative discipline strategies such as harsh corporal punishment, threats, lies, shame or ridicule or sarcasm, hostile humor, love withdrawal, and refusal or inability to teach a different way to behave. These negative discipline strategies reflect his need to control and blame, and he gets very frustrated and angry after his negative discipline strategies do not "work."

Responsiveness   Patrick's father is like many authoritarian parents—not very responsive to his children. He is often irritable and angry. He does not like being a parent and really does not know how to deal with the role of parent. He is rigid in his interactions with his children, and speaks negatively about them, especially Patrick. Parents who are unresponsive and who emotionally neglect their children set up their children for acting out types of problem behavior.

Patrick's father knows very little about child development. Consequently, he has unrealistic expectations of Patrick.

> **EXAMPLE**   Dad expects 6-year-old Patrick to sit quietly in a doctor's office or other public place, no matter how long they are there. Dad makes no attempt to help Patrick find something to read or to do while he waits. He does not know that young children are just developing self-control (Raffaelli, Crockett, & Shen, 2005). He does not attempt to talk to Patrick except to scold him.

Like many authoritarian adults, Patrick's dad rarely even thinks about how Patrick might feel, what Patrick might try to tell him, or what Patrick needs. He uses force (coercion) and places great value on unquestioning obedience. He punishes any attempt from his children at verbal give-and-take and suppresses any attempt at independence or autonomy.

Patrick's father also communicates in an unhelpful, hurtful way. He orders: "I said to get over here. Do it now." He blames: "I hope you're satisfied. You made a real mess at the ice cream machine." He distracts: He avoids issues and occasionally makes completely irrelevant statements. When Patrick complained that his brother had pinched him, Dad only said, "Patrick, pass the mustard." Dad criticizes by focusing on the negative. He criticizes even when Patrick does something Dad asked him to do: "Yeah, I see. You raked the leaves but you missed that whole pile!"

Patrick's father never thinks about the long-term effects of his authoritarian style; he is concerned only about short-term control. He does not know any good child guidance skills. He rarely gives a good reason to help Patrick understand a limit. The few reasons that he does give tend to be related to his adult power.

> **EXAMPLE**   When Patrick asked his father why his brother never had to empty the trash, Dad said, "I don't have to explain myself to you, boy. You hear me?"

Over the years, all of these negative interactions add up, making it difficult for children like Patrick to believe that their parents love them (see Figure 1.4).

Negative Effect on Young Children's Development

Authoritarian caregiving sets the stage for harm to children (Baumrind, 1996).

Authoritarian caregiving fosters negative self-esteem   Patrick experiences negative discipline and has developed negative self-esteem. He has not developed the competence, confidence, or sense of worthiness on which self-esteem is built. Instead, he mirrors the lack of trust that his parents communicate. He feels degraded by their authoritarian tactics.

Authoritarian caregiving results in poor self-control   Patrick's father, like many authoritarian adults, aims to control his children. He believes that he has to control Patrick (external control) and does not help Patrick learn to control himself

---

FIGURE 1.4   **Green jelly beans: authoritarian caregivers make it difficult for children to behave well**

Hurtful discipline strategies are a lot like green jelly beans. Yell at a child; drop a green jelly bean in his memory jar. Make fun of him; green jelly bean. Slap him; several green jelly beans. Therefore, it goes. Some children end up with a memory jar chock-full of green jelly beans.

The children with whom you work, from different backgrounds, will be affected by their culture's views on discipline and their family's caregiving style. Children who come from authoritarian homes will have hundreds or thousands of bad experiences with discipline. They will have experienced some or all of the situations listed below. Knowing this might help you understand that those children, when confronted with a problem, often reach into that jar of jelly beans and come up with a green jelly bean, a hurtful, unhelpful strategy, which they themselves then use.

Authoritarian adults often use:

- **Harsh physical punishment.** They use physical force to try to change a behavior. They do not understand or refuse to take a child's perspective and defend their right to use harsh punishment. They minimize the real harm that they do. Parents who, as children, experienced harsh physical discipline are at high risk for using harsh physical discipline with their children (Tajima & Harachi, 2006).

- **Threats.** Threats create fear and anxiety and are negative and harmful. Some children are terrorized through threats, a form of psychological abuse.

- **Lies.** We are talking here about a nasty pattern of lying to children, a form of manipulation aimed at changing or controlling a child's behavior.

- **Shaming, ridicule, sarcasm, humiliation.** Such strategies foster a negative view of the self and make unpleasant feelings and moods fester.

- **Hostile humor.** Patrick's father often cloaks his aggression as humor, but it is still aggression and is always disrespectful. **Example:** When Patrick had his first ice-skating lesson, he was afraid of falling down. His dad called him a sissy and made him get moving. At home that night, Dad cruelly imitated what he called "sissy-boy Patrick's" fearful approach to the ice and his wobbly start on skates. Patrick burned with embarrassment.

- **Disconnecting (clamming up).** They refuse to talk or listen to, threaten to leave or abandon, or glare at a child. **Example:** Patrick was slow in getting into Mom's car after Little League practice. Mom was angry and Patrick sensed it when she refused to talk to him and stared straight ahead. She looked at him a few times but only shook her head.

(self- or internal control). He does not teach Patrick about how his behavior affects others. Therefore, it is difficult for Patrick to act in a self-controlled way in school or anywhere else.

Authoritarian caregiving teaches and encourages aggression   Children who experience negative discipline tend to be more aggressive than children whose parents and teachers use discipline that is more positive. Either they aim their aggression toward the adult who hurt them or they recycle their anger and use the same degrading behavior with people or animals that had nothing to do with hurting the child.

> **EXAMPLE**   Dad, angry with 6-year-old Patrick for crying, said, "Cut the crying or you'll really get something to cry about." Patrick stopped crying and walked outside. His dog barked a greeting to him but Patrick threw a rock that smashed against his dog's kennel.

Authoritarian caregiving does not stop unacceptable behavior
Researchers have known for decades that high levels of punishment can restrain behavior only for a short time and, surprisingly, can make the undesired behavior even worse (Church, 1963; Rollins & Thomas, 1979). Undesired behavior seems to occur at a more intense level than it did before the punishment. This is a

phenomenon called response recovery. After the punishment is meted out, the behavior appears to cease. However, when the adult stops punishing, the behavior often recurs and is more intense.

Authoritarian caregiving negatively reinforces adults for using harsh discipline   Authoritarian adults who rely on negative discipline strategies wrongly believe that this sort of discipline works because they have been reinforced for using it. For example, when Patrick was a toddler and kicked his high chair, his teacher slapped Patrick's legs and Patrick stopped kicking. The teacher was reinforced for using slapping. The sequence went like this:

Patrick kicked his high chair (a behavior that annoyed the teacher).

Teacher slapped Patrick's legs (negative discipline strategy).

Patrick was surprised and stopped kicking—but only for the moment.

Teacher thought, "Hmm, that worked." (Teacher was reinforced because the negative discipline strategy of hitting seemed to work to stop an annoying behavior.)

The next day, Patrick kicked his high chair again. (Response recovery is operating. The negative discipline strategy stopped the behavior only temporarily.)

Teacher slapped Patrick again. (Remember, slapping seemed to work yesterday.)

The real problem here is that hitting Patrick became firmly entrenched in this caregiver's repertoire of disciplinary strategies. She had begun to believe that hitting was effective. It becomes easy for adults to rely on an ineffective discipline strategy, especially when they do not know or do not practice strategies that are more effective or when they rationalize their harsh behavior. Note also that Patrick's teacher used negative, hurtful discipline. She violated the National Association for the Education of Young Children (NAEYC) Code of Ethical Conduct.

In its extreme form, hitting is child abuse. First, we live in a society accepting of violent conflict resolution. Many parents reflect this idea by using violence to solve family problems; they use physical or psychological force as discipline and such discipline can easily injure a child. Second, negative discipline seems to work but really does not. Negative discipline is very ineffective. Third, adults are reinforced for using negative discipline and tend to use the same method again. Finally, an adult who relies on harsh negative discipline strategies soon discovers that she must increase the intensity of the punishment in order for it to be "effective." She must yell more loudly or hit harder, intensifying the strategy until it becomes abusive.

The Permissive Style
Low Demandingness

Figure 1.3 shows that *all* permissive adults are low in demandingness. They allow children to regulate their own behavior and to make their own decisions. They establish very few guidelines, even about when children eat, watch television, or go

Permissive style of caregiving
Low in demandingness

to bed. They make few demands for mature behavior, such as showing good manners or carrying out tasks. They avoid imposing any controls or restrictions and have a tolerant, accepting attitude toward the child's impulses, even aggressive ones.

Permissive adults are alike because they are all low in demandingness; they differ, however, in their degree of responsiveness. Some permissive adults are highly responsive to children, but others are quite low in responsiveness (Figure 1.3). Thus, there are two types of permissive adults—but both are low in demandingness.

Indulgent: Low Demandingness Plus High Responsiveness

Indulgent/permissive style of caregiving
Combination of low demandingness and high responsiveness; person chooses to be permissive

Indulgent caregivers are permissive by choice. They are low in demandingness and high in responsiveness. Members of this group are permissive because they choose to be permissive. Their view is part of their belief system about how to treat children. They firmly believe that children have rights with which adults should not interfere. These parents do not demand much from their children but they are highly responsive. They are warm and understand child development. They give their child much of what he needs, except for good limits.

Uninvolved: Low Demandingness Plus Low Responsiveness

Uninvolved/permissive style of caregiving
Combination of low demandingness and low responsiveness; also known as unengaged; person would rather not be permissive

Uninvolved or unengaged caregivers are also low in demandingness, which places them in the permissive category. The similarity ends here, however. Uninvolved, unengaged caregivers are also low in responsiveness. Members of this group have drifted into being permissive. They are permissive *not* because of a strong philosophical belief in a child's rights but because their method of discipline has been so ineffective. They would like to be able to set and maintain limits, but have been so ineffective in getting compliance from children that they have given up trying. They might even begin to see some behaviors, such as aggression, as normal.

Once on the slippery slope of permissiveness, these adults could not get off and have become unresponsive and indifferent toward children—they have become "permissive by default." Think about it this way: If you forget to set the margins on your word processor, the computer sets the margins by default. Similarly, a parent who does not consciously decide on and choose a style of caregiving has his style set by default.

Permissive adults tend to use ineffective discipline. They do not hurt children, but they are not very helpful, either. For example, permissive adults often fail to set appropriate limits, and even when they do set a limit, they frequently fail to maintain it.

> **EXAMPLE**   Liza's mother told Liza to clean up her space at the table. When Liza left the table without cleaning her space, Mom just shrugged her shoulders and walked away.

We guide children effectively by giving them enough of the right type of information so that they will be able to act appropriately under different conditions. Liza's mother did not follow through with her legitimate limit.

Permissive-by-default, uninvolved adults tend to natter and nag. These adults have tried to set limits but have been very ineffective. On occasion, they still try to set limits, but they tend to talk so much that the child ignores their limits.

Some permissive adults use inconsistent discipline, which is related to breaking rules, aggression, and defiance (Stanger, Dumenci, Kamon, & Burstein, 2004). There are two ways to be inconsistent:

Within-a-person inconsistency: This person deals differently with the same situation each time it occurs. Take biting as an example. Jared's father was inconsistent when he ignored Jared's biting one day and the next day told him, "No, no, Jared. Biting hurts." The third time he bit another child, Dad ignored him. This is inconsistency within the same individual.

Between-two-or-more-people inconsistency: Two adults deal with the same behavior differently. Parents might disagree about how they will deal with any number of issues. Patrick's parents, for example, inconsistently dealt with Patrick's biting when Patrick was a toddler. Dad hit him and Mom ignored the biting. Both techniques are ineffective and negative.

How Permissiveness Affects Young Children

Both children and adults pay a heavy price when adults refuse to make or give up making demands for maturity or to set clear, firm standards of behavior. Children from permissive systems tend to be low in impulse control. They are not very self-reliant or self-responsible. They tend to be dependent and are not very competent, either socially or cognitively. These results held when the children were 8 and 9 years old (Baumrind, 1967, 1971).

:: BASIC PROCESSES ADULTS USE TO INFLUENCE CHILDREN

All adults—authoritarian, authoritative, indulgent/permissive, or uninvolved/permissive—use these **basic processes of influencing** children directly and indirectly. In this section, you will read about each of the basic processes that are used by adults, whatever the caregiving style, to influence children. For example, all adults use the basic process of modeling, but an authoritarian adult demonstrates behavior that is very different from that modeled by an authoritative adult. The process is the same, but the content is different. The processes include:

Modeling (M)

Instruction and practice (I)

Feedback (F)

(Management of the) physical environment (P)

Expectations (E)

Change (help the child change understanding and attitude) (C)

Basic processes of influencing children Direct and indirect methods of persuasion used by any adult in an interaction with a child

Just as we help children learn memory skills, you can use a memory skill to remember this list. Use the mnemonic MIFPEC as an aid to fix the list in your memory

Modeling

Modeling
Performing an activity and having a child observe it

Much human behavior is learned simply by watching someone else perform the behavior. The other person is the model, and the basic process is **modeling**. Perhaps the best-known researcher to give us information about this process is Albert Bandura. His classic research (1971) demonstrates that children can effectively learn a behavior just by watching it. Although children can learn from several types of models (cartoon characters, pictures in books, and movie or video characters), Bandura's group showed just how powerful adult models are in demonstrating aggression. Adults can also model other behaviors such as kindness or fear.

Children learn undesirable behaviors—such as aggression or abusiveness—by observing models. An authoritarian parent or teacher who disciplines by hitting or by responding with sarcasm actually models (demonstrates) aggressive behavior. You will also see evidence throughout this book that children just as effectively learn more desirable and positive behaviors—such as generosity, cooperation, kindness, and helpfulness—through the same basic process. An authoritative adult who uses positive discipline teaches a different lesson than does the authoritarian adult.

Imitation
Performing an action modeled by someone else

Imitation is different from modeling. A child might learn, for example, how to be kind to animals by observing her teacher model the behavior. The child learns the behavior. There is no guarantee, though, that the child will also perform the behavior that she has learned. When she does perform a behavior learned via modeling, then she has imitated the behavior. Children in this country observe thousands of acts of violence on television and in video games before they enter first grade. Thus, they have several thousand sessions of modeling of aggression and violence. They learn the violence. Whether they imitate what they have observed is another story. Avoid saying, "She modeled after the television violence." Instead, consider saying, "She imitated the violence modeled in the television show."

Instruction and Practice

Direct instruction involves intentional and explicit teaching. There are many examples of adults influencing children through direct instruction. Teacher education students take curriculum courses so that they can learn developmentally appropriate methods of giving instruction in math, science, social studies, and language arts. Adults also instruct children in physical safety, such as traffic safety, safe use of toys, and how to recognize "good" and "bad" touches. We instruct children about so many things: the correct way to hold a baseball bat, build a campfire, ride a horse, or execute a figure 8 on skates.

Consider the benefits of instructing children in social skills—how to make and keep friends, how to take another person's perspective, how to work cooperatively with friends, and how to resolve conflicts (Lavallee, Bierman, & Nix, 2005).

The next step, after giving instruction, is to encourage a child to practice a new skill. It is very helpful to give on-the-spot guidance or coaching as the child practices.

EXAMPLE   Mr. Sanchez had taught Patrick how to wait for his turn at the computer (he is working on helping Patrick be more observant about approaching activities and other children because Patrick just barges right in). The teacher believes that Patrick will make changes, but Patrick is going to do so gradually. Now, he is at the computer with Patrick. He encourages Patrick to go through the steps that he has modeled and taught: First, check the list of names to see who is next. Second, put his name on the list, if necessary. Third, find something else to do while he waits for his turn and ask for help if he needs it. The teacher coached Patrick through each step. "What's the first thing to do, Patrick? Right! Look at the list." He continues this coaching. Mr. Sanchez believes that this is a much better approach than punishing Patrick for pushing ahead of others on the list to use the computer. It actually teaches something positive.

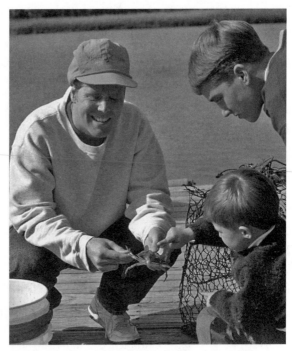
Adults influence children through direct instruction.

Feedback

It is important to give accurate feedback as children are learning and developing. Adults influence children by giving them feedback

Feedback is advice, pointers, and information from adults about how a child has done something. Feedback is critical to constructing skills and competencies as well as for making changes. Giving good feedback means that teachers give positive feedback as well as suggestions for change, when appropriate.

Feedback
Information that an adult gives to a child about how the child did something

Positive, unconditional feedback   This is positive information independent of anything that the child has done; the child does not have to earn the feedback. Examples include "I love you," or "I like being your teacher" (teacher to class).

Positive, conditional feedback   These are positive comments expressed after a child has done a specific task, for example, "Thank you, Reese, for showing Sam how to feed the gerbils without disturbing them" or "The fire alarm was very loud but everybody listened so carefully to my instructions." This is positive, meaningful feedback, not empty flattery. It should help children build a healthy view of their competence.

Feedback that helps children construct more helpful skills or competencies
Adults, with their expert knowledge and skills, can help children construct positive and satisfying interaction skills. For example, Mrs. Woodward, a preschool teacher, said to Jackie, "You look upset. Is that right?" Jackie told her yes and that Ralph would not give him the wagon. Mrs. Woodward had observed Jackie capture the wagon, pushing Ralph in the process. He needed to learn a better way to get what was rightfully his. "I see. Now, everybody is upset. Let's figure out how to use words to tell Ralph that it's your turn." The teacher expanded her feedback to include specific words: "You can say, 'It's my turn now, Ralph.'"

Feedback from computers   Interesting new research shows that children can get feedback from computers just as they can from teachers or parents. Bracken and Lombard's study (2004) examined the effect of praise from a computer on young children's learning. They found that children do have social responses to computer-generated praise and that their responses can lead to increases in recall and recognition in young children.

Physical Environment

Adults influence children by setting up the physical environment of the classroom well and by providing clean, safe, and appropriate learning materials. Teachers also influence children by developing an appropriate time schedule and by developing appropriate classroom routines and structures. It is possible, for example, for children to learn social skills such as conflict resolution through direct instruction—skits and scenarios. Learning the skill, however, does not guarantee that children will use the skills on the playground, in the cafeteria, or in other places outside the lessons directly focusing on specific skills (Johnson, Poliner, & Bonaiuto, 2005). Children need to practice their new skills throughout the school day.

Effective teachers manage the environment so that children have opportunities to practice skills. They often use a morning meeting (Kriete, 2002), a structured beginning to each day, for children to get to know one another, feel welcomed, shape the classroom culture, and practice social skills. They value social interaction in learning activities and use learning centers. They reflect on routines like recess and lunch, and decide to change them to meet the needs of the children. For example, they might decide to switch recess and lunch, now having recess first and then lunch, so that children might unwind and have a quiet transition to afternoon activities. They plan transitions, realizing that good transitions reduce stress for children.

Such developmentally appropriate practices can improve children's achievement in urban settings (Huffman & Speer, 2000). Fawcett and Garton (2005) found that both social interaction and children's explaining how they solved a problem helped children develop better problem-solving skills. At-risk 5- to 6-year-old children in Hamre and Pianta's study (2005) improved in achievement scores and their relationships with teachers when they were placed in classrooms with strong instructional and educational support.

Expectations

Teachers state expectations as part of scaffolding children's understanding of limits and interactions. Mr. Sanchez makes a conscious effort to define cooperative, helpful behavior. Authoritative adults like Patrick's teacher instruct by developing good rules or limits and then communicating them clearly to children. Authoritarian adults, on the other hand, tend to set too many arbitrary limits, and permissive adults may fail to communicate expectations at all.

Change

Change involves encouraging children to modify (change) their attitude or understanding about something. A young child's brain enables him to process information and make sense of the world. Children can act cooperatively when someone takes the time to present them with additional or different information in a way that is appropriate to the child's particular level of development. Focus on teaching children to understand why they should or should not do certain things. Be gently firm about the need for the children to act more appropriately, and make it clear that there is a reason for acting more appropriately. Be kind at the same time, though. Authoritative caregivers are firm and kind.

Go to the Assignments and Activities section of Topic 2: Guidance Theories in the MyEducationLab for your course and complete the activity entitled *Constructivism in Guiding Children*. Note how this supportive teacher helps the girls change their understanding of the conflict.

An effective way to do this is to help a child become more empathic. The goal is to help a child to understand gradually how her actions affect others and to be able to take somebody else's perspective. Like most learning, this occurs gradually over a period of years and begins in infancy. The goal here is not to induce excessive guilt or to shame a child. A good way to arouse empathy is to describe another's situation in an open, direct way that still validates the other person and that does not accuse her.

> **EXAMPLES**   Mrs. Woodward said to Ralph, "I see from the job chart that it's your day to feed the gerbils. I'll bet that they're hungry. So get the gerbil food and I'll help you put it in their house."
>
> Mr. Lee, the third-grade teacher, said to Rory, "Name-calling hurts feelings, Rory. Remember our class rules? That's right. Treat each other with respect."

Each adult avoided sarcasm, threats, and accusations while focusing on how the other person or animal might have felt. Arousing a child's empathy—having her "walk a mile in somebody else's shoes or tracks"—is a powerful technique because it encourages the child to examine and begin to understand how her behavior might well have affected someone else.

A common thread linking different forms of antisocial behavior, including child abuse, is the perpetrator's inability to take another person's perspective (Chalmers & Townsend, 1990). Preventing abuse involves helping abusive adults learn social perspective taking. Helping children become empathic, to take the perspective of others, then, is an important task for teachers and parents during early childhood.

WORKING *with* FAMILIES	**FIND YOUR PARENTING STYLE**

Help parents understand the concept of different styles of parenting. This topic lends itself to parent education's many formats, including the following.

Explain. Give a handout about styles of caregiving or give the links to web sites and handouts. One example is from Ianelli (2004) at http://pediatrics.about.com/od/infantparentingtips/a/04_pntg_styles.htm

Assess. Find out (assess) parents' needs. Ask them what they want or need to know about caregiving styles. For example, do they:

- Want to know more about setting effective limits?
- Need tips on monitoring and supervising children?
- Need help in facing difficult issues with their child?
- Want to know how to give better explanations to children?
- Need help with communicating in a more open and validating way?
- Need to know what to expect from children of different ages?
- Want to learn about different discipline and guidance strategies?

Plan. Once you know what parents need or want to know about caregiving styles, develop an efficient plan to deliver the information.

Deliver. Get the information to parents via meetings, newsletters, the school web site, handouts, and lists of resources.

ADDITIONAL RESOURCES FOR PARENTS

Brooks, R., & Goldstein, S. (2007). *Raising a self-disciplined child*. New York: McGraw Hill.
Parenting Style Quiz: http://pediatrics.about.com/cs/quizzes/l/bl_prnt_style.htm

---

myeducationlab

To check your comprehension on the content covered in Chapter 1, go to the Book Specific Resources in the MyEducationLab for your course, select your text, and complete the Study Plan. Here you will be able to take a chapter quiz, receive feedback on your answers, and then access review, practice, and enrichment activities to enhance your understanding of chapter content.

ANALYZE A VIGNETTE

Refer to the vignettes at the beginning of the chapter and analyze them by answering these questions.

1. Both Blake and David's parents are permissive. Which child's parent is the *indulgent* parent? Which child's parent is *uninvolved*? Name at least two things that led you to this conclusion.
2. Patrick's father is an author*itarian* caregiver.
   a. Cite at least three pieces of data that you can use to support this statement. Be sure to talk about this parent's demandingness and responsiveness.
   b. Then, from information in the chapter's examples, explain how the authoritarian style has affected Patrick.
   c. What do you think is the greatest obstacle standing in the way of Patrick's father making any significant changes in his style?
3. Leah's mother is an author*itative* caregiver. Explain why her way of dealing with Leah's biting Robert so clearly illustrates the authoritative style.

SUMMARY

Caregiving styles have two major components:

Responsiveness. This refers to how warm a person is and how he communicates and gives explanations as well as his knowledge of child development.

Demandingness. This involves how effectively and positively a person makes expectations clear to children and how she monitors and supervises children. It also refers to a person's way of facing issues with children.

The styles of caregiving include:

Author*itative***.** Positive and responsive; makes expectations clear; has a positive effect on children's development.

Author*itarian***.** Sets many rules but they are often unreasonable; communicates poorly; uses negative discipline strategies; often has a harmful effect on children's development.

Indulgent/permissive: Low in making expectations clear; highly responsive.

Uninvolved/permissive: Low in making expectations clear; low in responsiveness.

Adults use several methods to influence children's development and behavior:

Modeling desired behavior

Instructing and practice

Feedback

Physical environment: managing it well

Expectations: stating them clearly, kindly, and effectively

Change: refers to helping children look at things in a different way and build understanding of new ways of doing things.

QUESTIONS FOR REFLECTION

1. Think about an authoritarian caregiver you have observed. Avoid using his name or any identifying information about him. Describe the adult's behavior toward a child. Say how the adult's behavior was high in demandingness but low in responsiveness. Be specific and refer to elements of each (Figure 1.2).
2. Think back on your childhood and try to figure out the style of caregiving used by the people who were your main caregivers. Use the information from the text, including Figures 1.2 and 1.3, to do your

analysis. The idea here is to identify and describe, not judge, the style of caregiving used by your parents or caregivers.
3. Again, think about your past. Recall a couple of examples of when adults influenced you by modeling something. Recall a time when an adult gave you specific and direct instruction about something and then had you practice that skill. Did the adult do any coaching? Please describe it if she did. Recall the feedback that you received from adults. What was it like?

APPLY YOUR KNOWLEDGE

1. You have read several examples of Mr. Sanchez's authoritative style in this chapter. One morning, he had invited the director of the local humane society to talk with the children about kind treatment of animals. The director brought along Hannah, a mellow golden retriever who was accustomed to such presentations. Patrick, happy about the dog,

grew increasingly excited, causing Hannah to step away from Patrick and go to sit on the other side of the director.

Role-play how you think Mr. Sanchez would guide Patrick in this discipline encounter, using information from the chapter on how he manages his classroom and deals with Patrick. He will *not* punish

Patrick because you know already that he does not believe in punishment. What is he very likely to do instead?

2. Accentuate the positive! Do a real-world observation and find examples of positive authoritative caregiving. You should be able to see many good examples by visiting a variety of places in which you can observe adults and children interacting, for example, a grocery store, park, family reunion, laundromat, place of worship, or school. Briefly describe the setting and record the approximate age of the child(ren). Write a description of each interaction.

Describe why you think this was an example of authoritative caregiving.

3. You are the leader of a parent education group. A frustrated parent of a 5-year-old child asks you what she should do to get her child to put her tricycle away and not leave it in the driveway. Use one or two of the basic processes of influence (modeling, direct instruction, practice with coaching, and others described in the chapter) as you offer this mother some simple, practical, and realistic suggestions for guiding her child. Be prepared to present your suggestions to your class.

KEY TERMS

Authoritarian style of caregiving (14)
Authoritative style of caregiving (11)
Basic processes of influencing
    children (19)
Child development knowledge (7)
Communication style (8)

Demandingness (9)
Feedback (21)
Imitation (20)
Indulgent/permissive style of
    caregiving (18)
Modeling (20)

Permissive style of caregiving (18)
Responsiveness (5)
Style of confrontation (10)
Uninvolved/permissive style of
    caregiving (18)
Warmth (6)

WEB SITES

Center for Effective Parenting
http://www.parenting-ed.org

A collaborative project of the University of Arkansas for Medical Science, the Arkansas Children's Hospital, and the Jones Family Center. This site has numerous links for parents and teachers. Click on "Handouts" for excellent information in both English and Spanish.

Educational Resources Information Center (ERIC)
http://www.eric.ed.gov

This site is a digital library of education-related resources sponsored by the U.S. Department of Education. This is an excellent resource for teachers.

Theoretical Foundations of Child Guidance

"He who loves practice without theory is like the sailor who boards ship without a rudder and compass and never knows where he may cast."

Leonardo da Vinci

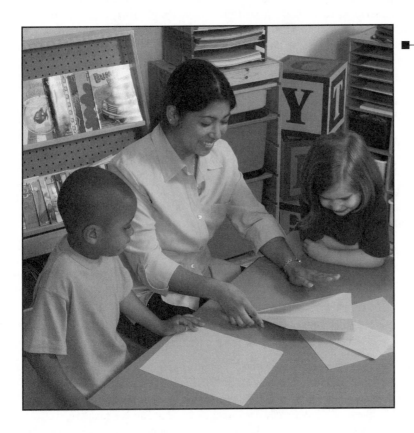

Chapter Contents

Guiding Questions

- How can theories about children's growth help me to guide children?
- What are the major theories that affect our understanding of guiding children?
- How can I use the theories to help me guide children effectively?

VIGNETTES

Toddler: Joseph Carries His Bowl

It was lunchtime and Mr. Bjornrud watched as Joseph, 2½ years old, finished lunch and then tried to pick up his bowl and spoon at the same time. When he could not seem to carry both, Joseph grew increasingly frustrated. "Here, Joseph, let's put the spoon in the bowl. Try holding the bowl like this" (the teacher demonstrated holding the bowl with two hands). He watched as Joseph started to the cart holding the bowl with the spoon in it. "Good, that's the way. Keep going."

Preschool: Emily Comes Up with an Idea

Mrs. Woodward, the teacher, observed that 4-year-old Emily grabbed things from other children several times every day, for example, at the water table, in the book area, at the puzzle table. The teacher then observed as Emily and Aaron sat facing each other on the carpet and played individually, each with a pile of small plastic snap-together blocks. Emily soon ran out of a favored color and stared directly at Aaron's pile. Then, without a word to the other child, she reached over and took several blocks. After Aaron squealed in protest, Mrs. Woodward said, "Emily, Aaron was playing with those blocks. I'm going to give them back to him. What else could we do instead of taking Aaron's blocks?" Emily, looking directly at the teacher, replied, "Well, you could take Aaron's blocks and give them to me!"

Primary: Lucy Changes Her Mind

Mr. Sanchez sat at one of the lunch tables with his class. Lucy, a first grader, sat across from him and announced, "I'm not going to eat!" The teacher replied, "Oh, you don't want to eat lunch today. That's okay. You can still have a good time talking with us." Lucy replied, "But, I really don't want to eat." Mr. Sanchez said, "So, you really don't want to eat." Lucy then stared at him, a look of surprise on her face. Lucy looked like she was trying to figure something out. The next day at lunch, Lucy started in on her "I-don't-want-to-eat" routine again but got quiet and looked at the teacher. Finally, she stopped talking and picked up her spoon, sighing audibly.

:: INTRODUCTION

Effective early childhood teachers, such as those in the chapter-opening vignettes, rely on **theory** to make decisions about guiding children. This theoretical foundation is based on observations, facts, and research directly related to child development and early childhood education. Theory is *not* a hunch or a guess. Theory is an explanation about something in the natural world. For example, years of observation and research from different types of studies show that children can learn aggression from watching it.

In this chapter, we will focus on the theories that form a firm foundation on which we base many decisions about children, including how we guide them. First, you will study the theories that explain how children's behavior develops in different systems. Then we will focus on theories focusing on how children construct ideas. Third, we will examine theories that focus on children's psychological, emotional, and social learning needs.

Theory
Not a hunch or a guess; an explanation about something in the natural world, substantiated by observations, facts, and research

:: THEORIES FOCUSING ON THE SYSTEMS IN WHICH CHILDREN DEVELOP

Some theories informing our work focus on children within larger systems. We will look at two of these theories as a starting point because children develop in systems. These systems affect both children's behavior and our decisions about guiding children.

Urie Bronfenbrenner

Urie Bronfenbrenner (1915–2005) was born in Moscow and moved to the United States when he was a child. He spent his career as a professor of human development at Cornell. We are indebted to him for his explanation of how children's families, homes, schools, and communities or societies affect their behavior and development. He also showed us that the economy, politics, and geography work together to influence children's families and neighborhoods and, by extension, children. This perspective was quite a departure from how researchers viewed human development. Until Bronfenbrenner disseminated this new perspective, researchers had studied each system's effect on children separately.

Ecology of human development   Urie Bronfenbrenner explained the **ecology of human development**, which refers to the idea that children exist in several environments nested within one another (Figure 2.1). The environments are the microsystem, mesosystem, exosystem, macrosystem, and chronosystem.

Ecology of human development
Concept that children grow up and develop in different systems, all nested within one another

- Microsystem: includes a child, her family, school, peer group, child-care center, and neighborhood. Relationships within families and the resources in a neighborhood all affect a child's development. Marta's parents, for example, get along well together and attend parent education classes at her school. The school believes that it has an obligation to develop partnerships with parents.

Children exist in several *systems*, nested within each other. All of these systems affect a child's development. Systems closest to the child, such as family, school, and the child's neighborhood, have a more direct effect. Systems on the outer rings have a somewhat more indirect effect. For example, the society's views about

FIGURE 2.1   children affect laws that are enacted, which, in turn, affect the child

- Mesosystem: the connected network formed by the different microsystems. Children benefit greatly when the different systems function harmoniously.
- Exosystem: the groups farther away from the child but still affecting his development. For example, Marta's family has access to very good parks; thus, she gets to play and explore this type of environment.
- Macrosystem: a larger system comprised of the values of the culture, type of government, social trends, and major events such as natural disasters. These values

and major events affect every other system. For example, societies valuing literacy will likely develop educational policies supporting literacy for all citizens.

■ Chronosystem: the degree of change or consistency of various systems over time that, ultimately, affects children's development. For example, if a society experiences major economic upheaval, it might need to decrease funding for health care or education.

Family Systems Theory

Family systems theory explains that families are groups of interrelated people. Each family member affects and is affected by others in the group in predictable ways. For example, families have set ways of communicating with each other and tend to repeat the patterns over time. Children learn their family's way of behaving and communicating and bring those patterns to school. Teachers can guide children more effectively if they understand how a family system operates and affects children.

Family systems have many characteristics (Christian, 2006). Features of family systems particularly relevant to early childhood teachers are:

Boundaries
Rules
Roles

Boundaries   Teachers can use the concept of boundaries within a family system to understand how a family makes decisions. Boundaries refer to a family's ideas about separateness and togetherness. Some families favor a sense of each individual's autonomy and value independence. Other families seem to prefer less autonomy and greater control over members. A teacher might find that one family makes decisions about children together, and another set of parents do not consult each other about such decisions.

Rules   Rules are the traditions that families use to guide their interactions with each other. Rules also tell families how to deal with persons and systems outside their family. Observant teachers understand that children's behavior has developed, in part, from their family rules. For example, some boys might not understand that they should participate in cleaning up because their family rule is that "women do the cleanup work." When you hear a child calling teachers "Mrs. _____" or "Mr. _____," you are really hearing their family rules that call for addressing adults with their social title and their last name.

Roles   A role is a responsibility or job that a family assigns to different members of the group. The roles include scapegoat (taking blame for things), peacemaker, helper, or savior. Families assign one of these roles to children and then encourage the child in that role. Some children are peacemakers, for example. They learn what the role entails and practice it in their family by trying to intervene when others are at odds. Their family system rewards them for acting out their assigned role. We should not be surprised, therefore, to see their assigned family role played out in our classrooms. The peacemaker might act as a mediator in classroom conflicts. Christian (2006) notes that such behavior might be commendable, but a peacemaker child also needs to know when *not* to act out their family's assigned role at school.

John Dewey believed that children find joy in constructing things.

:: THEORIES FOCUSING ON HOW CHILDREN CONSTRUCT KNOWLEDGE

Several theories on which we rely focus not on systems in which children exist but on how children themselves construct or build knowledge. You will notice great similarities among these theories. All emphasize that children learn through activity and that interaction between a child and others is important.

John Dewey

John Dewey, born in Vermont, lived from 1859 to 1952. As a teacher, philosopher, and social commentator, he committed himself to fostering the type of thinking that would help a democracy flourish. We in early childhood education are dedicated to many of the ideas that he put forward. Indeed, his influence has been as profound as Piaget's or Vygotsky's and we can use his ideas in guiding children.

Four primary interests of children   John Dewey identified four main interests of children. When we guide children, paying attention to these interests will help us be more effective.

- **Desire to investigate and discover things.** Children are interested in the process of inquiry to carry out investigations. Why, for instance, does Peter get so frustrated when he cannot find something in his locker?
- **Need to communicate.** Dewey believed that children are inclined to talk to teachers, to ask questions, and to discuss matters with other children. For example, a child called Joanne a "dummy" and she talked about it with another child.
- **Joy in construction.** Children find pleasure in making and building things. They work industriously, for example, in constructing models of buildings that they have seen or that they imagine.
- **Artistic expression.** Dewey observed that children enjoy expressing themselves through the arts, such as drama, dance, art, and music.

Education, including guidance, begins with the learner's curiosity
Children have questions about their world, including how to interact productively with others. Dewey believed that this curiosity is the sign of a child's intellectual power and increasing knowledge about the world. Observing children will give teachers clues about children's questions and interests, an idea from Dewey Pedagogical Creed (Dewey, 1897).

> **EXAMPLE**   Mrs. Woodward noticed that Jenna watched Paul cry after another child hit him. The watchful teacher concluded that Jenna was curious about other children's emotions. She can use this knowledge to help Jenna learn about feelings and to think about other people.

Creating classroom communities John Dewey had a vision about democracy and viewed schools as the places where children could develop the thinking skills necessary for creating and sustaining democratic governments (Dewey, 1938). Teachers can create classrooms in which democratic values thrive. This calls for respect for everyone, collaboration, and joint decision making. It requires that communication be open and courteous. Children need to learn to resolve conflicts, not hide from them. Most of all, Dewey believed that children need to learn that they are linked to others and that their individual actions affect others.

Jean Piaget

Jean Piaget was born in Switzerland in 1896 and died in 1980. He studied the natural sciences and published many papers in this area before concentrating on how children think and develop knowledge. Piaget's perspective on how children's knowledge develops is known as **constructivism**. Constructivism refers to how children build or construct knowledge and how they adapt to their environment.

Constructivism
Children's building or constructing knowledge

Processes involved in adapting Two processes help children to build knowledge and to adapt to different environments, both physical environments and interpersonal environments.

Interaction with people and objects. Like Dewey, Piaget believed that children are curious and learn most effectively when they are actively involved in building knowledge. They learn about the properties of objects by manipulating them. Rocks, for example, are heavy; sometimes smooth, sometimes rough; and sink when dropped in water.

Children also learn about people by interacting with them. Other children cry when somebody hits them. Somebody gets upset when you take her toys. Other children do not see things in quite the same way that he does; that is, they have a different perspective, which is puzzling to a young and egocentric child. Children must learn to listen to adults who tend to set and maintain limits.

Teachers have a major role in helping children adapt to interpersonal environments, the environment of relationships with others. Teachers do this with appropriate guidance, in which they help them make sense of things that puzzle them about other people.

myeducationlab

Go to the Assignments and Activities section of Topic 2: Guidance Theories in the MyEducationLab for your course and complete the activity entitled *Children Benefit from Working with Other Children*. Note that this strategy helps children construct knowledge about socially appropriate behavior.

Assimilation and Accommodation. **Assimilation** refers to *taking in* new information into an existing repository for such knowledge. The repository is a storage area for the child's ideas and grows over time as he takes in new information. For example, a child observes a butterfly and says, "Look, a birdie!" Why has he made such an obvious mistake? The child has an existing storage area or scheme for "things-that-fly." He puts anything that flies into this folder or scheme, even making mistakes upon encountering a new item, such as a butterfly. He has assimilated the butterfly into his things-that-fly scheme.

Assimilation
Process of incorporating new information into an existing concept

Accommodation
Process of changing an existing concept to include new information

Accommodation refers to the times when children *change* one of their existing ideas to make room for a brand new idea. In the butterfly example, the child observed something that did not fit easily into anything that he understood. It did not fit well with his existing ideas. His teacher explained that this thing was a butterfly and, yes, it does fly, but, no, it is not a bird. The child had to change his idea slightly to accommodate this new information. He formed a scheme (think of a scheme as a filing folder) for "things-that-fly-but-are-*not*-birds." He accommodated to this new information. He adapted.

Stages of Cognitive Development

Piaget was a stage theorist: He believed in stages of development. He believed that children adapt to their environments gradually, over several years. They adapt as they interact with other people in different systems and as they assimilate and accommodate new ideas. Specifically, Piaget explained that children's thinking is qualitatively different at each of four stages. Figure 2.2 gives a brief overview of the progression through the stages. A somewhat more detailed explanation follows.

One thing to remember about Piaget's stages is that there are no abrupt changes from one stage to the next. Instead, there is a gradual change as children's cognitive structures develop. You will see this in the three stages presented here. At the end of the first stage, for instance, we see a new ability in which a child *begins* to think about things instead of having to perform actions on things. This new ability carries over to the second stage, where it blossoms and continues to develop. The same thing happens between the second and third stages, when new abilities *begin* to emerge and then continue developing.

Sensorimotor Stage (Stage 1)   According to Piaget, there is a predictable and gradual change in how infants interact with their world. Their perceptual and memory abilities help them to move through the sensorimotor stage.

- **Birth to about 4 months.** Infants use reflexive actions and actions centered on their own bodies to find out about the world—opening and closing fists, kicking at mobiles, and watching people.
- **4 and 8 months.** Babies start to focus on things other than themselves, and they seem to observe how their actions affect other events, such as crying bringing help from mother.
- **8 months to 12 months.** A baby has noticed many times when he has had an effect on things, such as being able to get mother to notice and play with him. Now, he acquires two new abilities. One is object permanence, the knowledge that things do not disappear when they are no longer visible. Dad, for example, still exists in the infant's mind, even if Dad is not present. Similarly, the baby can remember a toy even when it is in another room. The other new skill is goal-directed behavior, which refers to an infant's new and deliberate attempts to cause certain things to happen. Now, he wants to make things happen and uses previously developed skills to that end. For example, he uses his old ability to grasp things. He might want to interact with his mother. Therefore, he grasps his mother's ear or nose to start the interaction.

FIGURE 2.2   Piaget's stages of cognitive development

Sensorimotor Stage (from Birth to About 2 Years)

- Babies center on their own bodies for the first 7 to 9 months.
- They gain information about the world mainly through motor activity and coordinating movements as well as through the senses.
- The ability to use *symbols* emerges at the end of this stage.

Preoperational Stage (from 2 Years to About 7 Years)

- Children can now use symbols to represent their experience and mental images: words, paintings, drawings, movements, deferred imitation (observing some action and imitating it later).
- They do not think as logically as they will in later stages.
- They are captured by how something *appears* and ignore other relevant information. For example, the same amount of water is poured into two glasses, one short and wide and the other tall and thin. The child will say that the tall, thin glass has more water because it appears that way to him. He cannot seem to take into account the idea that he watched you pour the same amount of water into each glass. This is called *conservation*.
- They cannot reverse things. They would not think about just pouring the water from our two different glasses into the original identical containers.

Concrete Operations Stage (from About 7 Years to About 11 Years)

- Children are no longer captured by the appearance in the conservation experiment.
- They can now reverse operations. They would say, "All you have to do is to pour that water from the tall glass and the short glass back into the first glasses. Then, you'd see that it's the same."
- They now think more logically but are limited to thinking about concrete objects.

Formal Operations Stage (from About 11 Years Through the Rest of One's Life)

- The child or adolescent can now apply logic to abstract ideas.
- They can now think through problems more efficiently.
- They can think about many possible reasons for an existing problem and many ways to solve problems.

- **12 months to 18 months.** Piaget believed that infants were innately curious. During this part of the sensorimotor stage, infants display this inquisitiveness and rapidly increase their experience base by experimenting with objects. They are curious about the physical properties of the objects (hard, soft, and scratchy, for example). They also experiment on familiar objects.

  > **EXAMPLE** A baby presses a familiar soft cube on its corner, then on one of the edges and finally right in the middle. She performs these actions repeatedly and this helps her figure out which of her actions causes changes in the cube, such as which action turns it over.

- **18 months to about 2 years.** There is a change in how children can operate on the world. Now, they *begin* to use mental operations on objects, such the baby thinking about what would happen to that soft cube if she were to drop it. Now, the action can come first in the child's mind before testing out the idea. This is actually a major cognitive shift, involving the ability to imitate something later and representing things in the mind. We see how children in the next stage build on this new ability.

Preoperational (Stage 2) This stage lasts from about 2 to about 7 years. The early childhood years are a time of positive intellectual accomplishment. Preoperational thinkers also have some major limitations on their ability to think. This section focuses on the major positive features and some of the limitations of preoperational thinking. These cognitive abilities and limitations influence the child's interactions with adults and the child's capacity for self-control.

Represent experiences
Major cognitive accomplishment of preoperational thinkers; ability to describe an experience using a variety of means

Deferred imitation
Observing an action but delaying imitating it until later

What children can do in this stage. One of the most significant changes in children's cognition from ages 2 to 6 years is the growing ability to **represent experiences**. That is, they can now use different types of symbols to represent or stand for an experience. Children symbolize their experiences, both good and bad, with deferred imitation, with language, and by using a variety of art media or technology.

Deferred imitation refers to delayed imitation Children observe an event; form and hold a visual image of the event; and then often defer, or delay, imitating the action. Recall from Chapter 1 that children learn by observing models. Each of the children in the following examples has observed models and imitates them now for the first time. The models can be real people, either adults or peers, in person or on a screen. They learn from models in audio recordings or on computers. Children also learn from models in reading material such as books, pamphlets, or even billboards.

> **EXAMPLES** Joseph swung his foot up martial arts style, and kicked another child. The model was an adult cartoon character in a video game. Sarah softly sang "Hush, little baby" as she cradled her doll in her arms. The models were Sarah's father and mother, who both sing to Sarah's new baby brother.

Talking about things or using language is one of the major ways that children represent their experiences. The major cognitive accomplishment of this stage is that children can use a symbol to represent something else; words are the symbols through which children represent experiences.

EXAMPLE   Justine used words to tell Mrs. Woodward about the car crash that she had seen.

Children also represent their experiences through art media such as painting, drawing, or play dough. They use chalk, paint, play dough, markers, pencils, computers, and other media or technology to create an artistic expression that symbolizes, represents, or stands for an experience that they have had.

Limitations of preoperational thinking   A 4-year-old's cognitive skills seem so much more advanced than the skills of an 18-month-old because the older child can represent experiences. Nevertheless, a 4-year-old preoperational thinker still has a limited ability to think logically. Preoperational thinkers tend to judge things by how they look, focus on the before and after and ignore how things change (transformations), and have trouble reversing a process.

Preoperational thinkers are somewhat **egocentric**, or focused on their own viewpoint. You will be puzzled and charmed by preoperational egocentricity, as I was, in the following conversation with my 5-year-old niece, who wanted me to take her to get ice cream:

Egocentric
Focused on one's own viewpoint

Marian (adult):	"Lisa, tell me how to get to the ice cream store."
Lisa:	"You go to the corner and then turn."
Marian:	"Which corner?"
Lisa:	"You know, the one with the trees."

At the time of our conversation, Lisa was egocentric and not very good at perspective taking. She did not give me all the necessary information, largely because she did not understand exactly what I needed to know. Preoperational thinkers tend to think that the other person has the same information they do.

Difficulty with perspective taking.   Egocentric thinkers center on what they want or need, but this is not the same thing as being selfish. A selfish person understands somebody else's perspective and chooses to ignore it, but an egocentric thinker cannot take the other person's perspective; there is a blurring of his or her own viewpoint with the perspective of the other person. A preoperational thinker, such as Lisa in the example above, believes that everyone thinks the same way she does.

Perspective taking is a cognitive developmental skill, the ability to understand how another person views a situation. It takes several years to develop and is first evident at the end of early childhood, as shown in Figure 2.3. We can expect that young children will not be able to take someone else's perspective.

Perspective taking
A basic cognitive developmental skill; ability to see things from another's perspective

Fooled by appearances.   Picture two containers—one short, one tall—and each holding an equal volume of water. Preoperational thinkers typically assert that the tall container has more water in it "because it looks like it has more." Appearances deceive them because they tend to judge something by how it appears on the surface.

Focusing on the before and after and ignoring how things change.
Preoperational thinkers ignore the process through which something is transformed

FIGURE 2.3	Levels in perspective-taking

Age in Years	Level	Perspective-Taking Ability
3 to 6	Level 0	• Egocentric perspective • No distinction between own and another's perspective
6–8	Level 1	• Still not able to take another's perspective • Believes that another, if in the same situation, will respond just as the target child would respond
8–10	Level 2	• Can take another's perspective • Sees self as others do • Not everyone reaches this level
10–12	Level 3	• Can take another's perspective but in a more sophisticated way than at level 2 • Now aware of recursive nature of different perspectives: "Mom thinks that I think she wants me to." Not everybody reaches this level
Adolescence and Adulthood	Level 4	• Very sophisticated in perspective-taking ability • Believes that different perspectives form a network • Has conceptualized society's viewpoints on legal and moral issues • Not everybody reaches this level

Source: Based on "Social-Cognitive Understanding," by R. L. Selman, in *Moral Development and Behavior*, by T. Lickona (Ed.), 1976, New York: Holt, Rinehart & Winston.

or changed. For example, you show two cups of sand to a child and he says that the cups have the same amount in them. Then you pour the sand in one of the cups onto a cookie sheet. You ask which has more sand, the other cup or the cookie sheet, or if both have the same. Preoperational thinkers usually say that the cookie sheet has more sand. A child at this stage usually says that it looks like it has more. What is the problem?

A preoperational thinker focuses first on the equal amounts of sand in the two small cups (the before state). Then she focuses on the sand in one short glass and on the cookie sheet (the after state). She tends to ignore the pouring of the sand from the small cup to the larger surface of the cookie sheet. The pouring is the transformation. An older child, adolescent, or adult, aware of the pouring, would explain things by saying, "All you did was pour sand from one container to another."

Difficulty reversing a process.   Preoperational thinkers focus on one thing at a time, either the before or the after in any action. An older child, who can think about a couple of things at once, is not deceived by how things look. Adults and older children realize that they could quickly show that the volume of sand on the cookie sheet is equivalent to that in the small cup. They would simply transfer the sand on the cookie sheet into the small cup. They can reverse the process; young children, however, do not think so logically.

Just as there was a gradual shift from the first to the second stage of cognitive development, children begin a gradual transition from the second to the third stage at approximately age 6.

Concrete Operations (Stage 3)   The new, concrete operations stage lasts until about age 11. This stage occurs at the end of the early childhood years and the beginning of middle childhood. Several major changes occur in children's thinking for this stage.

Children begin to think somewhat more logically.   They begin to pay attention to relevant dimensions in different conservation tasks. Changes in appearances deceive them less and less. They begin to pay attention to transformations in matter, such as pouring water from one container to another or squashing a ball of dough into a seemingly larger flat shape. They now begin to understand that the apparent changes really do not change the basic nature of the material because the child can reverse the process. The changes do not occur all at once but gradually (Gallagher & Reid, 2002).

Children classify things much more skillfully now. They use this cognitive skill in several ways. For example, children can understand that the category things-that-fly can be broken down into much more specific categories such as insects-that-fly or birds-that-fly. They can also seriate objects, meaning that they can arrange objects in a series.

> **EXAMPLE**   Mr. Sanchez put out 10 wooden dowel rods of varying lengths in the discovery/math center. He noticed that 8-year-old Celia easily put them in the correct order from the shortest to the longest.

A child who can classify, seriate, and reverse things can also learn mathematics.   The limitation for children in this stage is that they can apply their new abilities only to real objects; hence, the name *concrete operations*. They cannot deal effectively with abstract ideas or hypothetical problems.

Lev Vygotsky

Vygotsky, like Piaget, was born in 1896. Vygotsky was born in Byelorussia and graduated from Moscow University in 1917, just as the Russian revolution started. He died when he was only 37 years old.

Both Piaget and Vygotsky have had great influence on child development and education, although there are some central differences between their theories. Piaget lived much longer than did Vygotsky and Piaget's writing, unlike Vygotsky's, was widely disseminated. Eventually, translations of Vygotsky's work made it, along with Piaget's, available to child developmentalists and educators. Educators quickly saw the value in his views, and they used Vygotsky's theory to inform constructivist curriculum and instructional practice (Berk & Winsler, 1995).

Adults can use concepts from Vygotsky's theory to help them make wise child guidance decisions, including the following (Vygotsky, 1978):

- Scaffolding
- Zone of proximal development (ZPD)
- Adult–child dialogue or discourse

Scaffolding   **Scaffolding** refers to a teacher's changing support as a child develops a new competency or skill. Think of it like this: A building under construction usually

Scaffolding
An adult's modifying support as children develop new knowledge or skills

has a series of scaffolds, or platforms, that support construction workers. They are placed where the workers need them. Likewise, a child is like a building that constructs herself. Children are the main construction workers, constructing or building themselves, their knowledge, skills and competencies, views of morality, gender, the self, kindness, and compassion. Adults help children in their construction by serving as guides, by scaffolding the child's learning. Other children, as well as television, influence the strength of the child's construction. A child who has supportive guidance and a nurturing social environment can forge ahead and build strong social competencies (Berk & Winsler, 1995; Morrison, Brown, D'Incau, O'Farrell, & Furlong, 2005).

Scaffolding in child guidance is a teacher's changing support during a discipline encounter or series of interactions. For example, Mr. Sanchez notices that a child lacks a specific skill. He knows that the child could use support from somebody who possesses the skill (the teacher or a more skilled child). The more skilled partner provides help but tries to match the child's current level of ability.

Teachers usually offer more help when a guidance task is new. As the child gains skill in constructing the necessary knowledge, we can gradually step back, providing progressively less help. Scaffolding in child guidance helps children become autonomous and self-controlled. Here is an example of Mr. Sanchez scaffolding Rory's understanding of how speaking thoughtless words can hurt another person's feelings.

Zone of proximal development (ZPD)
Space in which learning and development occur

> **EXAMPLE**   Rory had told Ellen, a skillful reader, that he did not want to be in her reading group anymore because of how she stopped to look at every picture. Ellen looked dejected and withdrew from her group, refusing to read aloud.
>
> Mr. Sanchez noticed this interaction and talked with Rory in an effort to scaffold Rory's understanding of the effect of thoughtless statements on other people's feelings. Mr. Sanchez helped Rory by saying, "Sometimes people say things that make another person feel bad. They have not thought about how the other person will feel.

Zone of Proximal Development

The **zone of proximal development (ZPD)** is the space or zone where learning and development take place. At one end of the ZPD is a child's current ability, what he understands about some topic. At the other end of the ZPD is what the child can learn or accomplish with the help of an adult or more competent member of the culture. See Figure 2.4.

In the Rory–Ellen example, Rory at first did not really understand that thoughtless words born of frustration could hurt someone's feelings (Rory's current ability). Mr. Sanchez gave him some help, in a warm and supportive way (the expert help). Rory later demonstrated how much he had learned because of the dialogue with his teacher. He demonstrated the willingness and ability to acknowledge thoughtless behavior and its effect on another person.

Adult–Child Dialogue or Discourse

Any guidance strategy based on Vygotsky's theory relies heavily on adult–child dialogues, talking about tasks that a child can accomplish with adult help. Children gradually learn how to control their own behavior when adults scaffold their understanding of social interaction. This works by inducing children to use self-directed, private speech to guide their actions.

myeducationlab

Go to the Assignments and Activities section of Topic 2: Guidance Theories in the MyEducationLab for your course and complete the activity entitled *Teacher-Child Conversations*. Note the power of this strategy for helping children learn to get along with others.

FIGURE 2.4	Zone of proximal develoment (ZPD)

This end of of the ZPD is what she can accomplish in reading with the teacher's help.

This is this child's current ability in reading, without adult help.

EXAMPLE   Mr. Sanchez and Rory talked (engaged in discourse) about the effect of Rory's words on Ellen's feelings (Mr. Sanchez's scaffolding through talking). When he was later alone, Rory's private speech helped him work through the problem. Essentially his private speech stated, "I said something mean to Ellen. I need to tell Ellen that I'm sorry. I will write a note and leave it in her desk."

:: THEORIES FOCUSING ON PSYCHOLOGICAL, EMOTIONAL, AND SOCIAL LEARNING NEEDS

Some theories informing our guidance focus on children's emotional and social development and learning. You will see in each of the following theories that adults have an important role in guiding children's development and understanding of their world.

Erik Erikson

Erik Erikson was born in Germany but attained U.S. citizenship after moving to the United States in the 1930s. He was a professor and a therapist. He developed a theory of psychological development describing human psychological growth from birth through death, which is a life-span perspective. Erikson proposed eight stages of psychological development, each presenting humans with a **psychosocial crisis**. The person's interactions with the social environment affect whether she resolves the challenge of each stage in a positive or negative way.

Psychosocial crisis
Challenges presented at different ages and resolved in either a positive or negative way

Adult influence   Parents and teachers influence young children's resolution of the childhood challenges by using their knowledge of child development. For example, a toddler has new motor and language abilities and wants to establish herself as an independent person. We can use this information when working with toddlers by encouraging their independence within limits.

Erikson's theory guides our relationship building with children at all of their different stages. Forming good relationships with young children is one of an early childhood professional's main responsibilities and the base for all of our developmentally appropriate practices. Erikson's theory is also helpful as we strive to develop good relationships with parents and other professionals, each of whom is going through one of Erikson's stages.

Stages of psychosocial development   Erickson identified eight stages of psychosocial development.

- **Trust versus mistrust: Infancy, birth to 18 months.** Children develop the positive trait of trust when their needs are met consistently.
- **Autonomy versus shame or doubt: Toddlers, 18 months to 3 years.** Encourage toddlers to do things by and for themselves when such independence is possible and safe.
- **Initiative versus guilt: Preschool and kindergarten, 3 to 5 years.** Encourage children's growing desire to explore and make sense of their world. Recall that Dewey also views children as active, curious information seekers, as do most of the other theorists.
- **Industry versus inferiority: Primary grades and part of elementary school, 6 to 12 years.** Children now operate in at least a couple of different systems, such as school, religious institution, or recreational groups. They need support as they face new challenges.
- **Identity versus role confusion: Adolescence.** This is a time when children must deal with the world outside their family on their own. Help them learn to deal with pressure from their peer group and to make good decisions.
- **Intimacy versus isolation: Young adulthood.**
- **Generativity versus stagnation or self-absorption: Middle adulthood.**
- **Integrity versus despair: Late adulthood.**

Abraham Maslow

Abraham Maslow, born in New York in 1908, was one of several children born to his Russian immigrant parents. He earned all of his degrees from the University of Wisconsin—Madison and then taught in universities. He died in 1970. While a student at Madison, Wisconsin, Maslow had contact with Harry Harlow, who operated a research program with rhesus monkeys, which you probably studied in your basic psychology course. This work explained what happened when the baby monkeys were deprived of contact with and comfort from their mothers. Maslow noticed that some needs seemed to be very important.

Maslow (1954, revised 1987) went on to describe and explain a hierarchy of human needs. This ladder of needs, shown in Figure 2.5, has been very useful to a variety of professions. This figure shows that a child's most basic bodily or physiological needs, such as for sleep and food, must be met before we can attempt to help her learn in school. They must also be met before we can think about guiding her or helping her build ideas about getting along with others. Meeting needs for safety

FIGURE 2.5 Maslow's hierarchy of human needs

and security provides the foundation on which the social and esteem needs at the upper part of the illustration are met. Maslow's hierarchy is also useful in a teacher's work with colleagues and parents. We all have the same needs and have the right to feel like a valued member of a school or community.

Alfred Adler

Alfred Adler was born in Vienna, Austria, in 1870. He was a physician with an interest in psychiatry. He was a contemporary of Sigmund Freud but broke with some of Freud's main ideas. Adler believed that each person is primarily a *social* being. He maintained that a person's social environment and interactions, such as with teachers, heavily influence personality development. He believed that people actively, consciously direct and create their own growth. Notice that this is the same perspective that the constructivists hold—that we are active in building our ideas about the world.

This theory teaches us that children play a large role in their own development, that their interpretation or perception of their experiences is important. Adler thought that humans are social creatures who need to attain group membership. Children go about fitting into a group by following their own interpretations of the rules for group membership.

Some children are able to achieve a sense of belonging to their group by cooperating and making useful contributions. They make accurate interpretations of the rules of group member-ship. Other children have a pattern of misbehavior and noncooperation because they interpret events and people's intentions inaccurately. These children have a faulty perception, or mistaken goals, of how to fit into a group and use ineffective approaches to gain a place in it.

They base their behavior on their faulty perceptions of the world. To assist them, we must help them get a different perspective on things, to perceive events and people's intentions more accurately. Adlerians believe in thinking about what a child gets out of misbehavior, or what his mistaken goal is.

Table 2.1 explains the mistaken goals that drive some children's behavior. The faulty perceptions—mistaken goals—include the following:

Striving for undue attention from others
Seeking power over others
Hurting others through revenge
Displaying inadequacy or incompetence.

Carl Rogers

Carl Rogers was born in 1902 in Chicago. He was a teacher and an educational psychologist. Rogers counseled children and parents at the Child Study Department of the Society for the Prevention of Cruelty to Children. From 1940 to 1963, he developed and disseminated his views on counseling and therapy (Rogers, 1957). Rogers believed that individuals have the power within themselves to solve their own problems. A therapist or a teacher's job, therefore, is to help the person seek the answers.

Rogerian guidance strategies rest on the idea that children have the capacity for self-direction, that children can become increasingly able to control their own actions. Teachers and parents who use Rogerian guidance strategies believe that it is the adult's role to support children's efforts, to demonstrate acceptance and approval. Notice the fundamental similarity between Vygotsky's and Roger's theories. Both believed that children could develop or construct their own abilities and competencies. Both also believed that children need competent, warm adult support to do their constructing.

Carl Rogers had followers, professionals educated in his theory. One of these people, Thomas Gordon, developed a program of child guidance based on Rogerian theory. The program, Parent Effectiveness Training, is best known as

TABLE 2.1	Adler's Mistaken Goals			
Mistaken Goal	Child's Faulty perception	What the Child Does	How Adults Feel and Tend to React	A Better Approach: Ignore First Impulses and
Attention (child seeks *undue* attention)	Try to make themselves the center of attention	Keeps adults busy, some through mischief, others through passivity or idleness	Annoyed Gives in to demands Scolds	Show how to join group appropriately Gently insist that passive children do their assigned work
Power (child struggles to get power)	My personal value comes from showing you that I am in charge	Develops techniques for getting power: Tantrums, disobedience, arguing excessively, stubborn defiance	Threatened or angry Tends to get drawn into a power struggle	Tell child you do not want to fight Refuse to argue
Revenge (child seeks vengeance)	Hurt and angry, the child essentially says, "I will get my recognition by hurting you or others through revenge."	Expends much energy convincing others that he is *un*likeable; gets even	Feels hurt Might back away Might retaliate Feeds into child's mistaken ideas Not at all helpful	Do not take things personally Help child feel valued Teach how to manage anger and anxiety
Incompetence (child displays inadequacy)	Defeated, the child's message is, "I will be a member of this group by taking the role of someone who can't do things well."	Acts as though he cannot do something, often when this is not the case	Frustrated, annoyed, confused Tends to give in and do work for child, then does not expect much	Inform child that you expect her to do the job Show confidence in her ability Give instruction if necessary in how to do the work Gently insist if child does not, at first, change

P.E.T. (Gordon, 1978). He also developed a similar program for teachers, Teacher Effectiveness Training, or T.E.T. (Gordon Training International, 2005). Gordon's objective in starting the effectiveness training programs was to teach specific guidance skills to adults; these skills include the following:

Figuring out who owns a problem, adult or child.
Listening actively when a child owns a problem.
Delivering an I-message when the adult owns a problem.

Problem Ownership   Problems, issues, or conflicts arise in all relationships. The first step in solving any problem requires figuring out if a problem even exists and, if so, who owns the problem—**problem ownership**. Figure 2.6 shows that, at times, an adult owns the problem and at other times, the child owns the problem. At other times, there is no problem (Gordon Training International, 2005).

Problem ownership
Concept from Rogerian theory referring to deciding who in a relationship has the problem

FIGURE 2.6   Problem ownership

| Child owns the problem |
| Area of no problem |
| Teacher (or other adult) owns the problem |

Decide who owns the problem by looking at whose needs are thwarted. Who is upset? Who is afraid? Who is it that cannot do something? Who is frustrated?

EXAMPLE   Mr. Sanchez (the first-grade teacher) noticed Vinnie and Susan sitting on the floor, a large sheet of paper between them. They had written one sentence and seemed stuck in the middle of the second. "How is it going?" asked Mr. Sanchez. The children said that they were trying to figure out how to spell *the*. This problem, the teacher quickly concluded, belonged to the children. They were the ones who were at a loss about the spelling. He suggested that they consult the list of frequently used words.

EXAMPLE   Mr. Sanchez saw that Lucy was unusually quiet on Monday, hardly speaking the whole morning. He asked Lucy if she wanted to talk and found out that her grandpa had died. Lucy owned this problem.

It is important to decide on problem ownership because the guidance strategies that we choose depend largely on who owns the problem. Our goal is to *decrease* the number of problems owned by both adults and children and to *increase* the area of no problems.

Deliver I-Messages When an Adult Owns the Problem   Many questions raised in workshops on guidance and discipline center on problems in relationships with children, problems owned by the adults. Children sometimes behave in ways that interrupt an adult; cost the adult time, energy, or money; interfere with adult rights; or insult adults. For example, a child might consistently interrupt group time or might refuse to do an assigned job.

This theoretical approach advises adults to use I-messages when adults own a problem. The goal is to tell the child clearly that the adult has a problem with something that the child did. Another goal is to convey the adult's need for the child to do something to fix the problem. I-messages allow a child to make the change out of respect for the adult.

Good I-messages are simple statements of facts. A good I-message does not accuse a child of creating the adult's feeling (Gordon Training International, 2005). Good I-Messages include four elements:

- Give observable data (what you saw, heard, smelled, touched).
- State the tangible effects.
- Say how you felt.
- Focus on change. Give some ideas about how to change things or ask questions that prompt children to come up with solutions, a guidance strategy based on Vygotsky's theory, that will encourage the child to make a necessary change.

Here is an example of how the first-grade teacher delivered an I-message when Ryan destroyed property (the teacher's problem).

EXAMPLE Ryan used a pencil to rip a jagged hole in a bottle of glue, not by accident. At first, Mr. Sanchez felt very angry. He turned away, took some deep breaths to calm himself, and then turned back to Ryan. He picked up the bottle and handed a towel to Ryan. "Clean up the glue, Ryan, before it runs off the table and onto the floor." When he and Ryan had cleaned the sticky table, he took Ryan aside and calmly delivered his I-message.

- Give data: "I picked up the bottle of glue and saw that glue was flowing out of the hole in the bottle. I saw that you were laughing about it."
- State tangible effects: "You and I had to clean up all the spilled glue, which took quite a long time. I will also have to get a new bottle of glue." Ryan responded, "So?" Mr. Sanchez ignored the attempt to deflect the conversation.
- Say how you feel: "When I saw all the glue, I was startled and then I got angry because I saw that you were laughing about it."
- Focus on change: "I want you to help me figure out how to fix this problem. How will you replace the bottle of glue?" This is only the beginning of a conversation on how to replace the bottle of glue.

Practice delivering an I-message in Figure 2.7.

Listen Actively When a Child Owns the Problem Active listening is useful when children own a problem. (This process is similar to Vygotsky's idea of teacher–child discourse to solve problems.) Use this strategy when you want to help a child solve his own problem. In the example that follows, Jack, the child, makes a simple remark. The remark does not indicate that Jack has a problem, but Mr. Sanchez responds in a way that encourages Jack to get to the problem. Even

---

FIGURE 2.7 **Practice sending an I-message**

- **Situation.** Jessica, in Mr. Sanchez's kindergarten, played in the sandbox outside along with several other children. Jessica took a hefty amount of sand and threw it in the air with both hands. She did not seem to be aiming at anyone but the other children had to dodge the sand shower. Mr. Sanchez's delivered this I-message:

  Give data: _____

  State tangible effects: _____

  Say how you feel: _____

  Focus on change: _____

- **Situation.** A rescue worker brought her rescue dog, Sarah, to Mr. Sanchez's K–2 class. Michael and Willis interrupted the beginning of the presentation twice by barking and then laughing. Sarah, the dog, never flinched. The presenter appeared to be upset but went on with the presentation. Mr. Sanchez's called Willis and Michael aside.

  Give data: _____

  State tangible effects: _____

  Say how you feel: _____

  Focus on change: _____

when Jack first indicates that something is bothering him, Mr. Sanchez has no idea about what the real problem is. The teacher, however, communicates in a way that Jack felt safe enough to keep talking. He eventually gets to the real issue.

EXAMPLE   Six-year-old Jack was playing a card game with Vinnie, who said, "I like playing cards!"

Jack chimed in, "Me too! I like playing cards!" (At this point, the teacher did not see a problem at all.)

Teacher:	Good. I'll make sure we always have cards in the room.
Jack:	I like playing cards at school. (He emphasized *at school*.)
Mr. Sanchez:	(attending more closely now) You like playing cards at school.
Jack:	Yeah, but not at home.
Teacher:	. . . Not at home.
Jack:	Well . . . I like to play cards with my mom.
Mr. Sanchez:	(careful not to close down the conversation) You like to play cards with your mom at home.
Jack:	Yep, with my mom; not with Grandpa, though.
Teacher:	Playing cards with Mom is fun but playing cards with Grandpa isn't so much fun.
Jack:	Grandpa calls me a dummy if I count things wrong. (This is the real problem. Jack does not like it when Grandpa calls him names.)
Teacher:	When Grandpa calls you a name, you don't like it. Is that right?
Jack:	I don't like it. That's right. I don't want to play with him when he does that.

Mr. Sanchez used Vygotsky's approach, too, by asking a question that prompted Jack to come up with a solution. "How can you let your grandpa know that you don't like to be called names, Jack?" Mr. Sanchez urges Jack now to solve the problem. He does not give a solution. Figure 2.8 lists guidelines for listening actively.

Social Learning Theory

Social learning theory emphasizes social variables determining a child's behavior. It helps teachers understand that children are *not* just machines responding to stimuli. Social learning theorists believe that children are active in their own development, that they are affected by their environment, and that they contribute to producing their environment.

Social learning principles and child guidance

- **Principle 1: Social learning theorists do not emphasize stages of development.** Some theorists view development as a series of phases or

FIGURE 2.8	How to listen actively

Remember to	Avoid "roadblocks to communication"
<ul><li>Listen carefully.</li><li>Try to figure out what the message means.</li><li>Listen for what the child is feeling.</li><li>Suspend judgment (avoid judging anything about the situation).</li><li>Let the child finish speaking. Wait 1 or 2 seconds and then speak.</li><li>Merely reflect back your perception of the child's feelings with words or body language.</li></ul>	<ul><li>Avoid giving solutions.</li><li>Avoid interrupting the child.</li><li>Avoid preaching or ordering.</li><li>Avoid giving advice.</li><li>Avoid trying to persuade the child to feel something else.</li></ul> These things close down communication. A person is not listening actively when she, for example, interrupts the child.

stages, each stage being qualitatively different from the ones before and after. In learning theory, however, development is not viewed as a series of stages but rather as a gradual accumulation of knowledge. Even though social learning theorists do not emphasize stages of development, they do acknowledge that a child's level of development plays a part in learning from models. For example, a child must have good enough perceptual skills to enable her to pay attention to the model. Similarly, a child must have a good enough memory to allow her to remember the model's actions or words.

- **Principle 2: Development occurs because of learning from the environment.** The major belief common to all branches of behavioral or learning theory is that human behavior is learned. All learning theorists believe that a child's behavior is gradually shaped as he interacts with his environment. For example, learning theorists believe that an aggressive child has learned the aggression.

- **Principle 3: Modeling influences much of children's learning.** Social learning theorists believe that learning takes place in, and cannot be separated from, a child's social setting. Children can learn new behavior by observing another person perform the behavior. A child who cooperates with classmates, the social learning theorists would say, has learned this behavior by observing different models' actions and words about how to work with others.

- Children learn from a variety of models: a real person who is physically present; real persons on television, in movies, or in DVDs; cartoon characters; graphic representations of human figures in videogames; models in books; or audio models. Children become more and more accurate in their ability to imitate a model as they grow older.

The specific content that is demonstrated or modeled for a child depends on the child's social environment. All children learn simple things like vegetable preference, facial expression, and table manners by observing others. More complex social behaviors are also taught through modeling. Some social environments model behavior like respectful treatment of others and assertiveness, whereas other social environments model behaviors such as aggression and selfishness.

What accounts for a child's selectivity in what or whom they imitate? Children imitate models that are powerful, more skillful than the child, have a great deal of prestige, and who are nurturing and supportive.

■ **Principle 4: Children learn complex behaviors in big chunks rather than in tiny steps.** Some learning theorists believe that children learn things in tiny steps, with each reinforced. However, social learning theorists believe that children learn complex behaviors in big chunks.

> **EXAMPLE**   After a unit called "Showing Kindness to Animals," Nick demonstrated the kind behaviors that were shown on videos or demonstrated and described by Mr. Sanchez or by visitors to the classroom. He helped clean the hamster house, showing kindness to the hamster by handling it carefully.

■ **Principle 5: Behavior can be changed if a child's social environment is changed.** Social learning theorists believe that the most effective way to change (modify) a child's behavior is to alter the child's environment. Because they believe so strongly in the effect of the social environment, they emphasize changing the social environment. In practice, this means that teachers in classrooms might need to change how they respond to a child's behavior if they think the behavior needs to change.

■ **Principle 6: Children can learn behaviors without reinforcement.** Children can learn many behaviors simply by observing a model perform the behavior (e.g., using a napkin properly during a meal, raking leaves, feeding the class pet). The learner's success might well be acknowledged by a teacher, but the reinforcement can come after the learning took place. Teachers see the results of this type of learning in their classroom.

> **EXAMPLE**   Mr. Sanchez observed that three of the children were imitating the karate-chopping moves of the character they had watched on an action video. The character was the model, and they learned the movement simply by observing. Nobody reinforced them.

■ **Principle 7: Reinforcement gives information to children.**

> **EXAMPLE**   After Nick cleaned the hamster's house, Mr. Sanchez acknowledged the effort, "You were very kind to Sunshine, Nick. I'm sure that she appreciates it." Vanessa heard Mr. Sanchez's words of encouragement and thought, "Hmm, Mr. Sanchez liked the way Nick acted with Sunshine."

We see reinforcement operating in Vanessa's learning. She learned how to be kind to the hamster from watching Nick as a model. Whether she actually imitates (reproduces) the behavior depends on how she looks at the consequences of that activity for Nick. Vanessa is highly likely to treat Sunshine kindly because she heard and observed Mr. Sanchez's words of appreciation (positive consequences) to Nick. Recall from Chapter 1 that appropriate feedback gives information to children about their behavior. Words of appreciation (reinforcement) are a form of feedback and a basic process through which adults influence children.

Tokens: Tangible Positive Reinforcers   Recall that authoritative adults have reasonably high expectations for and are highly responsive to what children need. Some authoritative adults make a deliberate attempt to modify a child's environment and therefore to help a child modify his behavior by using tangible rewards, or tokens, as positive reinforcement.

FIGURE 2.9	Example of a token chart				
I want to remember to take things home!	**Monday**	**Tuesday**	**Wednesday**	**Thursday**	**Friday**
Week #1	XXXXXX	ΩΩΩΩΩ	ΔΔΔΔΔΔ	NO School	∞∞∞∞∞ΔΔΔ
Week #2	μμμμμμ	I forgot!	¿Ω£Δ≤>	±#£ΩΩ	≠≠≠≠

- What is a token? A **token** is an object, so the term *tangible* is applied. Some examples are a sticker, smiley face, photo, star, checkmark, or plastic chip. It is best to use nonfood items as tokens.

- An adult who decides to use a token system targets a specific behavior that he wants to see, such as cooperation or carrying out some routine activity, like cleanup or tooth brushing. The child earns a token for demonstrating the targeted behavior. The adult often uses a chart like the one in Figure 2.9 to display the token.

- Tokens are a means to an end, not the end in itself. They are *merely* a way to remind adults to give a child feedback for her efforts to live within limits, to act responsibly, and to be a productive group member. Tokens are gimmicks, and the stickers or photos must be combined with social reinforcement. Tokens must be used *ethically*.

- Figure 2.9 shows a chart that Mr. Sanchez used to help Nick remember routine tasks. Mr. Sanchez encouraged Nick to decide how to mark each day's space, and he *decided to* use different ink stamps each day.

- What if a child forgets to perform the agree-upon behavior? After the first week, Mr. Sanchez reviewed with Nick the things that were helping him remember. Nick forgot to take some items home on Tuesday, Week 2. Mr. Sanchez said on Wednesday morning, "You know, you've remembered every other day so far. You can go back to stamping tomorrow." Mr. Sanchez did *not* take away any stampings for the other days as punishment for forgetting. Ethically and competently done token systems or charts focus on teaching, not on punishing.

- Fading out using a token chart. Mr. Sanchez faded out using the chart. All along, he had made brief comments acknowledging Nick's effort to remember. This social encouragement or reinforcer, combined with the token (Nick's stamping), was what Mr. Sanchez needed to do to really help Nick. The chart was a good way to remind the teacher how he interacted with Nick in this case. Like Vygotsky, social learning theorists believe that adults can help children learn appropriate behaviors through adult–child talking. The tokens are merely reminders that the adult needs to do his part.

Token
An object that can be felt or held; therefore, it is tangible

Effective Praise: Intangible Positive Reinforcer

Early childhood educators raise some legitimate questions about using **praise**. Praise is an *in*tangible form of reinforcement—it is not a thing that we can see. Praise can be used quite *in*effectively. Some adults think that they can manipulate children with praise. Others think that praise is a good form of encouragement. There are some things to remember about praise in order to use it ethically and effectively.

Praise
A form of *in*tangible feedback for children

■ Be specific, descriptive, and appreciative but not gushy or mushy. When you praise, notice and then describe specifically what a child did. Describe what you saw, heard, tasted, or touched. Relate the praise directly to the event. Avoid judging (things such as the child's actions or character). Let the child know that you appreciate what she has done.

> **EXAMPLE**   Mr. Sanchez said to his class, which was assembled for a large-group lesson: "Thanks for putting all your writing notebooks in their bins with the spines facing out. That way, you can retrieve them easily tomorrow."

■ Give praise as soon as possible after the event. Praise is most effective given immediately after the event. This requires that a teacher concentrate and make an effort to watch for, notice, and then immediately give the feedback. There is a good reason for reinforcing as quickly as possible. Words of encouragement give children information about the consequences of their behavior. Children make more accurate connections between their behavior and your feedback if the two happen close together.

> **EXAMPLE**   After the all-school assembly, Mr. Sanchez said, "This class was a wonderful model for the younger children today. You listened to the speaker and showed respect."

■ Praise sincerely and reward effort and small steps. If you choose to praise, use honest and sincere praise. Your firmly grounded set of values and ethical standards and your respect for children will forbid you from giving insincere, phony, or perfunctory praise. When you think feedback would be helpful for a child, try to find something in a situation that you can praise sincerely and honestly.

You can foster persistence in children by giving feedback about a child's effort to complete difficult tasks. Children need to know that they control the effort that they put into a task. Teachers can help them increase their effort by giving feedback, specifically about effort.

> **EXAMPLE**   Several of the children seemed to be bored with the way they were practicing writing their weekly spelling words. Mr. Sanchez decided to use some different methods. One was for the children to write on a sheet of Plexiglas against a black background (like the menu boards in some restaurants).

myeducationlab

Go to the Building Teaching Skills and Dispositions section of Topic 2: Guidance Theories in the MyEducationLab for your course and complete the activity entitled *Use Guidance Practices Based on Child Guidance Theory*. Note how theory has helped the teachers choose developmentally appropriate guidance practices.

Pitfalls to Avoid: Ineffective Praise   Several factors make praise or any type of reward ineffective. Authoritative teachers make an effort to avoid the following forms of ineffective praise.

■ Avoid praising only perfection; do not combine praise with a negative comment. Some adults praise only perfection. Instead of noticing and praising a child's efforts to do something helpful, some adults attend only to something that the child is not doing.

> **EXAMPLE**   The playground aide said to Mr. Sanchez's class as they came in from recess, "You kids forgot again to put all the balls in the container." Rory, looking back at the playground said, "We put them in. Oh, there's one left." The aide replied, "That's what I mean. You left one out."

- Avoid praising only completion of a difficult task. Difficult tasks usually have a number of parts. Encourage children as they successfully complete each step in a difficult task. Some adults make the mistake of dismissing the effort it takes to do each part and to stay with a long-term task.

> **EXAMPLE**   Nick, bursting with pride about having written his first poem for a notebook of poetry, showed it to his grandfather. His grandfather responded, "Show it to me when you get all the poems written."

- Do not overdo praise. Children seem to adapt to a particular level of praise. An adult who uses praise indiscriminately will find it necessary to use even more praise because the child receiving such lavish praise becomes accustomed to it. Rewards given too frequently lose their value. Indiscriminately saying "Good job!" is an example.

- Do not give unnecessary praise. It is possible for praise and rewards to backfire and negatively affect a child's motivation. Children who are spontaneously interested in an activity but are then rewarded for practicing the activity might lose interest. They perceive the adult's praise as an attempt at control. The child's decreased interest is actually resistance to external control.

> **EXAMPLE**   The student teacher in Mr. Sanchez's classroom used praise with Nysha, who liked to read her math book and then do problems. Nysha made a face when she heard the praise, and the student teacher asked what was wrong. Nysha, not a shy child, said, "I like math and it makes me feel weird when you say 'Good job with the math, Nysha.'"

myeducationlab

To check your comprehension on the content covered in Chapter 2, go to the Book Specific Resources in the MyEducationLab for your course, select your text, and complete the Study Plan. Here you will be able to take a chapter quiz, receive feedback on your answers, and then access review, practice, and enrichment activities to enhance your understanding of chapter content.

ANALYZE A VIGNETTE

Refer to the chapter-opening vignettes, and then answer the following questions.

1. Joseph, the toddler in the vignette, is in the _____ of Erikson's stages of psychosocial development. How will the teacher's words and actions help Joseph resolve this crisis in a positive way?

2. Emily's preschool teacher used an appropriate guidance strategy. What is it about Emily's cognitive development that explains her solution to the teacher's question?

3. In the primary-grade vignette, how has the teacher demonstrated active listening?

4. In the primary-grade vignette, which mistaken goal does Lucy seem to be showing? Explain your response. Also explain why the teacher's response was so effective.

SUMMARY

Different theories inform our practice as teachers. Some focus on the systems in which young children develop and learn. These theories include the following:

- Urie Bronfenbrenner's ecology of human development, which describes the different systems in which a child and her family are nested.

- Family systems theory, which examines stable patterns of interaction and communication within children's families.

Other theories emphasize the processes that children go through in constructing knowledge. There are striking similarities among these theories, most notably the need for supportive interaction between adult and child and the need for active learning. We examined the theories of:

- John Dewey
- Jean Piaget
- Lev Vygotsky

Other theories helpful in guiding children are those focusing on their emotional and social learning needs. In this chapter, we have examined the theories of:

- Erik Erikson, who explained the stages of psychosocial development

- Abraham Maslow, who described and explained a hierarchy of needs that all humans have
- Alfred Adler, who identified mistaken goals that children might have as they seek group membership and acceptance
- Carl Rogers, who explained the concept of problem ownership and the guidance strategies to use when different people own a problem
- Social learning theory, which explains social variables determining a child's behavior.

QUESTIONS FOR REFLECTION

1. When you are a teacher, why would it be beneficial for you to understand some details about a child's neighborhood? That is, how might a child's neighborhood affect his or her behavior?
2. How does a young child's egocentricity often affect how she behaves with others?

3. Explain what scaffolding is in guiding children. Why is it so important for teachers to know about scaffolding and be able to do it?

APPLY YOUR KNOWLEDGE

1. **Observe.** Observe young children in a classroom or some other setting. Find examples of adults using praise with children. First, judge whether the praise was necessary. Then decide whether the praise was effectively stated.

2. **Observe.** Observe in a preschool classroom. Find examples of children using different ways to tell about or represent their experiences. The chapter section on Piaget would be helpful here.

KEY TERMS

Accommodation (34)
Assimilation (33)
Constructivism (33)
Deferred imitation (36)
Ecology of human development (29)
Egocentric (37)

Perspective taking (37)
Praise (52)
Problem ownership (45)
Psychosocial crisis (41)
Represent experiences (36)
Scaffolding (39)

Theory (29)
Token (51)
Zone of proximal development (ZPD) (40)

WEB SITES

Gordon Training International

http://www.gordontraining.com

Organization started by Thomas Gordon, who developed Parent Effectiveness Training (P.E.T.) and Teacher Effectiveness Training (T.E.T.). Based on Rogerian theory. Sign up for free tips and newsletters on the home page. Click on "What We Do." Then go to "T.E.T." and to "Our Classroom Philosophy" for a statement about the site's view of classroom management.

North American Reggio Emilia Alliance, Schools of Reggio Emilia, Italy

http://www.reggioalliance.org/reggio_emilia_italy/infant-toddler_centers_and_preschools.php

The schools of Reggio Emilia embody principles of constructivist theory, focus on systems in which children develop, and pay attention to theories focusing on emotional and psychological development.

Understand Child Development

A Key to Guiding Children Effectively

"We have made a commitment to . . . base our work on knowledge of how children develop and learn"
—National Association of the Education of Young Children (2005)

Chapter Contents

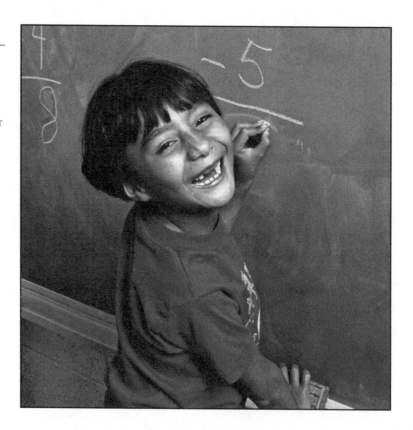

Guiding Questions

- Why is it important for teachers to understand perceptual and memory development in young children?
- How do preoperational and concrete operational thinkers differ in how they think about the behavior and motives of others?
- What is self-control and how does it evolve?
- What do children need to be able to do before they can help, cooperate with, or share things with others?

VIGNETTES

INFANT–TODDLER: PAUL REMEMBERS

Mr. Bjornrud planned some "memory" games for 6-month-old Paul. He showed Paul a plastic block and then slowly covered it with a cloth. Paul grabbed the cover and pulled it off. Mr. Bjornrud encouraged his effort by saying, "You found the toy!"

On another day, Paul smiled when his teacher showed him his favorite stuffed bear, which had been lost for about 2 weeks. Then Mr. Bjornrud turned Paul away so he could not see it. When Paul turned his head back to look for the bear, the teacher praised his effort and helped him retrieve the toy.

PRESCHOOL: MAYA DECIDES

Mrs. Woodward and a small group were preparing to make fruit salad. Maya's eyes gleamed at the sight of the starfruit, something that she had never seen before. She ran her fingers over the smooth exterior, smelled it, and then stared at the fruit after the teacher sliced it. Mrs. Woodward usually encouraged children to taste things when they cooked. Today, however, she had a different goal in mind and deliberately set a limit that they could eat the fruit for snack but that they would not sample the salad while making it. When the teacher turned aside to put the knife in a safe place, Maya stared into the bowl, at the starfruit. She reached for it, then hesitated, and finally pulled her hand away.

PRIMARY: THOMAS SHARES

Mr. Sanchez observed second graders Sean and Thomas in the coatroom getting ready for recess when Sean said, "Hey, where's my other glove? There's only one here." Thomas joined Sean in searching for the missing glove, but they did not find it.

Thomas, "I have an extra pair in my locker. Do you want to wear them?"

Sean took the gloves, saying, "Yeah, okay. Thanks, Thomas."

As the boys zoomed out to the playground, Mr. Sanchez said quietly to Thomas, "I appreciated what you just did, Thomas."

:: INTRODUCTION

All three teachers are warm, highly responsive, and supportive, and they also have high expectations of children. Skillful and kind teachers such as Woodward, Bjornrud, and Sanchez did not just pull their guidance strategies out of a hat. They do not do the first thing that pops into their heads. Instead, they make deliberate and intentional decisions about their guidance strategies. They use developmentally appropriate child guidance so effectively because they have a solid foundation in child development. Their child development knowledge is not the only thing that they need, but it is one of the major elements in effectively guiding children, as shown in Figure 3.1.

In this chapter, you will read about what to expect from children of different ages in selected areas of development. We start with perception and memory, two parts of a child's cognitive development that are important in how children take in, organize, and remember what they see and hear during interactions. Then, we will examine how children understand the behavior of others, how they view friendship, and how they understand accidental versus intentional behavior. Finally, we will look at how children build on perception, memory, and social cognition to develop self-control and to become compassionate and caring individuals. The rest of this book will help you understand how to use your knowledge of child development to guide children.

FIGURE 3.1   **Teachers need three things before they can guide children effectively**

Knowledge:
Understand characteristics of children's development

Guiding children effectively requires *three* things

Skills:
Need to know how to use a variety of positive guidance strategies

Attitude:
Willingness to use appropriate guidance strategies

:: PERCEPTION AND MEMORY

Many factors affect a teacher's guidance. Two such factors include how a child perceives things and whether he can remember what he perceives.

Perception: What to Expect

When teachers use guidance, they need children to take in what they say, and observe and pay attention to other signals and cues in the environment, such as the facial expression that somebody makes. With guidance, teachers help children concentrate on learning activities and make choices about many things. Our real goal is to have children eventually *think* about choices.

Perception is one part of the whole process of cognitive development. It is the process of organizing information obtained through seeing, listening, touching, and smelling. First, children sense things. Then they perceive or organize the information, and eventually they think about it.

Infants take in sensations with their eyes, ears, noses, mouths, and hands, and they can organize the sensations from birth. For example, infants perceive the discomfort of needing a diaper change, needing food or water, and needing comfort and cuddling. They also feel and express basic emotions such as anger and contentment, even though they cannot understand or talk about the feeling.

Children continue to develop and refine perceptual skills as they get older. A 2-year-old, with many perceptual skills, improves on these abilities by age 4 or 5. However, there is room for more improvement. What you can expect is that preschoolers and kindergarten children will have some perceptual problems that keep them from paying attention. You can also expect additional changes in children's perception during the school years that will help them pay attention better.

Problems affecting how children pay attention   The problems that young children experience with paying attention, which affect your guidance, fall into these areas.

- **Young children do not search or scan very well.** Young children can search for something, but they are not systematic in their search. Their search is not as accurate or efficient as an older child's, and some children do not seem to realize that they should stop searching at some point.

  > **EXAMPLE**   Robert watched Mrs. Woodward write his name on a nametag. Robert easily recognized his when the teacher showed Robert his nametag along with three others. The next day, however, Robert's nametag was on the chart with 22 others. Robert looked for a long time, but became frustrated when he could not find his nametag.

- **Young children have difficulty ignoring irrelevant information.** Young children have difficulty controlling their attention. They have difficulty tuning out (ignoring) meaningless information or stimulation. Their attention wanders when they hear or see some sudden, intense stimulus. Sudden changes or intense stimulation such as bright lights or loud noises will capture almost any person's attention for a short time. However, the issue with young children is that they have greater difficulty ignoring it.

Perception
Process that children use for organizing the information that they gain through sight, hearing, touch, smell

EXAMPLE   A new student teacher was frustrated when she read a story to a small group of 3-year-olds. A squealing sound from the parking lot and the squeaking from wheels on the lunch cart easily distracted them. Older children might also have noticed the noise, but they would have been better able to resume listening to the story.

■ **Young children tend to focus on only one thing at a time.** According to Piaget, young children cannot focus on two parts of a problem at the same time. For instance, show a 4-year-old two equally sized lumps of clay. Flatten one of the lumps in front of her. She will very likely say that the flattened mass has more clay. She cannot pay attention to two things at the same time—the equal amounts of clay in the lumps and now the flattened state. Similarly, she will not be able to pay attention to her own viewpoint and to somebody else's viewpoint at the same time when they have a disagreement.

EXAMPLE   Two of Mrs. Woodward's preschool children were playing at the sand table, constructing a tunnel. Then they had an argument about which way the tunnel should turn. Each child's focus was his own idea and neither could deal with the other child's suggestion.

■ **Impulsiveness affects perception.** Reflective children tend to be more accurate in their work because they proceed slowly enough to avoid major mistakes. Impulsive children tend to work too quickly, thereby missing important information and making unnecessary mistakes. Younger children tend to be impulsive, making it difficult for them to stop, look around, and think about choices.

■ **Some disabilities affect perception.** A characteristic of some disabilities, such as attention deficit hyperactivity disorder (ADHD) is impulsivity. ADHD is a problem with "inattentiveness, over-activity, impulsivity, or a combination to a degree that is not in the normal range of development for a child's age and development. Symptoms of impulsivity include shouting out answers before you finish a question, trouble waiting for a turn, and disturbing an ongoing activity or group, such as during a group time or when a teacher is talking to someone else (Ballas, 2009). Other factors place children with ADHD at even greater risk. For example, in one small study, abused children with ADHD had higher impulsivity scores than did children who were not abused but who did have ADHD (Becker-Blease & Freyd, 2008). Researchers also found that children with dyslexia were more impulsive, much faster in response time, during the testing phase of the research, than were children without dyslexia (Donfrancesco, Mugnaini, & Dell'Uomo, 2005).

Changes in perception help children pay attention better as they get older   Children in the primary grades have slightly more efficient memory, more mature language abilities, and more experiences to draw on. Listed below are three of the ways in which perception changes during the early childhood period. These changes will affect how you guide children.

■ **Children get better at selecting between what they ignore or what they pay attention to.** Child development researchers have known for over 40 years that even infants select—and seem to prefer—certain patterns (Fantz,

1966). A 2-year-old has the ability to attend selectively to stimuli, but this ability improves during childhood as she eventually learns to ignore distracting stimuli. Older children are much better than are younger children at selecting between what they prefer to attend to or what they ignore.

> **EXAMPLE**   Preschoolers in Mrs. Woodward's class looked up in surprise when they heard a helicopter flying over the school. Many jumped up from the group and ran to the window. The fourth graders in another part of the building heard the same noise. Several fourth graders simply said "Helicopter," and went right on with their work. The older children chose to ignore the intense, intrusive sound.

- **Children spend more time on task as they get older.** Older children are capable of controlling the time that they spend on a task; they tend to stay with a task longer than do younger children. However, children also consciously spend less time on an activity that they think is boring or uninteresting, such as workbook sheets. Many programs such as High Scope in Ypsilanti, Michigan, use this information and plan learning environments and activities that are activity-based and interesting to children because children are more likely to start an activity in the first place if it captures their interest in some way.

> **EXAMPLE**   Mr. Sanchez set out small plastic tubs filled with damp sand in the writing center. Larry, a second grader, had seen this activity on arrival and zoomed to it at work time. He practiced writing his spelling words in the sand and willingly practiced incorrectly spelled words until he got them right, working industriously at smoothing sand, writing words, then smoothing sand again.

- **Children are better able to redirect their attention as they get older.** Older children can more easily redirect their attention than can younger children. When a task has a number of parts, the older child has an advantage because she is able to shift her focus from one aspect to another quickly. These children are better able to say, for example, "Okay, I'm done with that part. I can start on the next part and then I can finish with the third part. Whoops! I forgot something in part one." The next examples are from Mr. Sanchez's second grade.

> **EXAMPLE**   Larry had to make a journal entry about the words he spelled correctly and incorrectly. After he finished with the sand, he started writing the list and then stopped suddenly. "I have to practice one more word," he said as he laid down his pencil and went back to the sand. After practicing, he went back to his list.

> **EXAMPLE**   Almost all of Mr. Sanchez's second graders worked with several specialists at different times each week. This resulted in many interruptions in class work for individuals. The teacher noted that some children had problems shifting gears and redirecting their attention to classroom work when they returned.

Memory: What to Expect

Memory is a basic cognitive process by which children store information and then later retrieve it. Children see and hear hundreds of bits of information each day, but they do not remember all of it. Their brain filters out some and stores only some in memory.

Memory
Process used to store information and later retrieve it

There are major and remarkable changes in how well children remember things during early childhood. Figure 3.2 shows the milestones in memory development, the slow and steady changes in the different types of memory. These changes allow a child to retain information pertaining to our guidance, such as the limit on staying inside the playground during recess or using words to tell somebody that you are irritated or upset.

Forms of memory   Different forms of memory are important for early childhood teachers to understand because they affect how well children can remember what we say to them or what they remember from interactions.

FIGURE 3.2   Milestones: memory development

Birth to 5 Months
- Recognition memory is good. Infants habituate to—become accustomed to or bored with—a toy put in front of him several times. This boredom indicates that a baby remembers or recognizes the object.
- Recall memory: Very young infants *can* recall a memory but need to get a cue or reminder. An adult can encourage a 2- to 3-month-old infant to kick a mobile, then remind the infant several days later about the mobile by moving it while she watches. The infant will recall having kicked the mobile. However, notice that the adult had to give the baby a cue; the baby could not actively recall kicking the mobile on her own.

Five Months to 1 Year
- Recognition memory improves. Classic research on infants' memory showed that infants could recognize objects after seeing them only a few times. They also seem to be able to remember the object for several weeks (Fagan, 1984).
- Recall memory also improves. After about 6 months, infants do not need cues as often to remember things.

One Year to 3 Years
- Recall memory improves even more (Howe & Courage, 1993; Perlmutter, 1986). After about age 2, children can recall exciting events that happened some time before and occasionally even tell about the memory in the form of a story. By the time a child is 3 years old, he might be able to recall something that happened to him 1 year previously.

Four Years to 12 Years
- Memory improves remarkably during the preschool and middle childhood years.
- Pure recall memory: Four-year-olds can remember without cues *some* of the time, but 8-year-olds are even better at remembering something without a reminder.

    EXAMPLE   Show a group of items to preschoolers. They will recognize almost all items but they would not be able simply to recall more than three or four. Third graders, on the other hand, would be able to recall about eight of the items (Baker-Ward, Gordon, Ornstein, Larus, & Clubb, 1993).

Disabilities Can Affect Memory (an example)
Recent research shows that the memory of children with autism is substantially different from the memory of children without autism. On one hand, children with autism had poor memory for complex verbal (stories) and visual (pictures) stimuli. On the other hand, recognition memory of children with and without autism was about the same (Williams, Goldstein, & Minshew, 2006).

- **Long-term memory** refers to storage for the information that we perceive and then store as a permanent record. Most of us can call up information from long-term memory because we often have the memory stored as a strong sensory image of places and events, sometimes from years or even decades ago. For instance, I remember one sunny afternoon in my grandfather's garden whenever I smell basil because he crushed some of the fragrant herb that day and let me sniff it. Do you have a pleasant event from your childhood stored in your long-term memory?

- **Short-term memory**, or working memory, is a storage site for temporarily placing new information or well-known information to which we need access. The lateral areas of the prefrontal cortex in a young child's brain are activated when she uses working memory, just as they are in an adult's brain (Tsujimoto, Yamamoto, Kawaguchi, Koizumi, & Sawaguchi, 2005). A child's space for short-term memory increases with age, allowing her to work with and process more information and to do so for longer periods (Eysenck, 2004).

   EXAMPLE   "Oh, no," thought Thomas as the class got to the playground, "There's Patrick! He corners me every time he gets a chance."

- **Recognition memory** refers to a feeling of familiarity with a stimulus that we have seen or experienced and that we encounter once again. Ask a child, for example, to pick out pictures of her dog and the cat who lives next door from a small group of photos of cats and dogs. She probably will easily recognize her pet and the pet from next door. Recognition tasks are easier than are recall tasks, which are described next.

- **Recall memory** refers to memories for which a child has to retrieve or call up some information. There are different types of recall memory, and they are important when we look at the memory capacity of infants and young children. Cued recall memory involves using a visual, auditory, or olfactory (odor/smell) sense to remind someone about a memory. Thus, children would get a cue or something else to remind them.

   EXAMPLE   Mr. Sanchez made a list of the names of trees that the children have studied. He posted the list (the cue) at the children's level in the area where they worked on the tree project.

Pure recall memory refers to remembering something *without* a reminder. A child actively retrieves information from memory with no cues involved, as David did when he listed the names of all of his cousins.

Explaining changes in memory   Listed below are the four main reasons for the dramatic improvement in memory from ages 3 to 12:

1. **Changes in basic capacities.** Older children process information more quickly and manipulate information better than younger children do because they have more working memory (short-term memory) space in their brains. Third graders, therefore, can keep more information in their minds and can perform mental operations much more rapidly than can younger children.

Long-term memory
Storage site for permanently stored information

Short-term memory
Temporary storage site for information with which a child needs to work. The child retrieves the information from long-term memory. Also called *working memory*

Recognition memory
Feeling of familiarity with something that we know about from our past and that we encounter again

Recall memory
Memories for which a child has to call forth information, either with or without a reminder or cue

2. **Changes in the strategies used for remembering things.** Older children will have learned a greater number of and more effective methods for getting information into their long-term memory and then for retrieving it later. Older children use memory strategies efficiently once they learn a strategy and understand why using it is helpful. A 12-year-old will rehearse something repeatedly until she remembers it. Preschool children generally do not use this strategy, and primary children use it but not very effectively—adults have to prompt them to rehearse things. Older elementary school children rehearse lists very effectively (Flavell, Miller, & Miller, 1993) *if* they have learned about rehearsal or other strategies. Older children also use another memory strategy called organization more effectively than do younger children. For example, when confronted with a group of 12 items to remember, the older child will organize it into four groups, such as vehicles, animals, food, and clothing. Young children do not organize groups of items to make recalling the items easier. Older children do make these logical groupings and are therefore much better at recalling such lists.

3. **Changes in knowledge about memory.** As an adult, you understand how and why memory strategies work and therefore perform memory tasks more effectively. This overall understanding of memory is metamemory. Children who are *at least* 10 years old seem to understand memory strategies, whereas younger children do not (Schneider & Pressley, 1989). Older children who understand why a memory strategy is helpful are much more likely to use such strategies in everyday life and in schoolwork (Brown & Campione, 1990).

4. **Changes in knowledge about the world.** Younger children simply have been on the earth for a shorter time than older children and have not had the opportunity to acquire the wealth of knowledge that an older child has. Older children, having learned more, are familiar with a greater amount of knowledge and therefore simply have more things *to* remember.

:: SOCIAL COGNITION: HOW CHILDREN THINK ABOUT OTHERS

Social cognition
How children think about how other people feel and about their motives, behavior, and feelings

Piaget's theory (see Chapter 2) described and explained the changes in children's cognitive development during childhood. Vygotsky's theory (1978), also discussed in Chapter 2, shows us that culture teaches children what to think and it affects how they think. **Social cognition** refers to how children think about the behavior, motives, feelings, or intentions of others.

Preoperational Thinkers: Ages 2 to 6 Years Old

Teachers can use information about cognitive development to understand other domains of development. For example, a child's stage of cognitive development affects his social development, such as how he describes how others behave, whether he understands the difference between accidental and intentional behavior, and how he looks at the concept of friendship.

Describing others   During the preoperational stage, children tend to describe another person by referring to the individual's physical qualities, such as "My Dad is big." They rarely describe abstract qualities, such as trustworthiness or honesty, because they are not cognitively equipped to deal with such abstract ideas. Occasionally, a young child will describe someone by using what seems to be an abstract term, such as "He's nice." Here, though, the child usually is describing something the other person has recently done rather than identifying a major psychological characteristic (Rholes, Jones, & Wade, 1988).

Understanding accidents or intentional behavior   Up to about the middle of the kindergarten year, preoperational thinkers do not understand the concept of intentionality. Recall that they do not take another's perspective. This affects their ability to distinguish between an accident and something done intentionally. They cannot see that the other person intended to hurt them. Near the end of the preoperational stage, they begin to understand the difference between accidental and intentional injury.

Viewing friendship   A child's level of development affects how she views friendship. Preoperational thinkers, somewhat egocentric, tend to describe a friend merely as someone who plays with her. Her egocentricity sets limits on how she sees the world in general, and the concept of friendship in particular.

Concrete Operational Thinkers: Ages 6 to 11 or 12 Years Old

Describing others   Children in this stage use fewer concrete terms and begin using broad psychological terms to describe other people. A young child in this stage might describe his friends by comparing their behaviors in some way: "Carl draws better than anybody in our class," or "Tyrone spells better than most of the class." Children usually use fewer and fewer such behavioral comparisons as they get older. Fifth graders—10-year-olds—would use broader psychological constructs in their descriptions: "Carl is very artistic"; "Cecil is one of the smartest people in class."

Understanding accidental or intentional behavior   Children, with their egocentricity diminishing, now understand intentional behavior. For some children, this occurs during kindergarten, but others might take longer to understand the concept. Children move toward greater understanding of the meaning of intentional behavior, however, during this stage. They get more accurate in detecting when someone did something on purpose.

Viewing friendship   As they mature, children's ideas about friendship change. They become less and less egocentric. Their sense of moral obligation blossoms, and they understand that they are responsible for themselves as they interact with others. Children become better at and more willing to share and take turns with age, and this enables them to bond with other children much more easily. Still later, in the next stage of cognition, a 14-year-old understands that friends support each other, a major shift in thinking about friendship. This is a more advanced view of friendship than the preoperational thinker's (young child's) observation that friends are merely momentary playmates.

:: SELF-CONTROL AND PROSOCIAL BEHAVIOR

As teachers or parents, we want to help children develop self-control and become compassionate and caring, to develop prosocial behavior. All of the changes in cognition, including memory and perception, and in social cognition form a foundation for a child's ability to regulate his or her own behavior—self-control. These changes also make it possible for children to become compassionate and caring individuals.

Self-Control: What to Expect

Self-control
Regulating behavior
internally and voluntarily

myeducationlab

Go to the Assignments
and Activities section of
Topic 1: Child
Development in the
MyEducationLab for your
course and complete the
activity entitled *Observing
Children's Self-Control.*
Note the strategies that
this teacher uses to
support the child in
building self-control.

Self-control is the voluntary, internal regulation of behavior. It might well be one of the most significant changes that takes place during early childhood. Also known as self-regulation, it is an essential part of how children learn, is important in a child's growth and development, and is fundamental in preserving social and moral order. Figure 3.3 shows the milestones in the development of self-control.

How children demonstrate self-control   Children show self-control when they do the following:

- **Control impulses, wait, and postpone action.** A child would step back, examine a situation, and then decide how to act. He resists reacting impulsively.

  > **EXAMPLE**   Larry took a block from Jordan's structure. Jordan resisted his usual urge to slug Larry and used words as his teacher suggested: "Larry, I was using that block. Give it back!"

- **Tolerate frustration.** A child would be able to endure disappointment, irritation, or aggravation. We can help children with this in many ways, by giving them guidance with seemingly small things such as not finding one's favorite ice cream flavor or having to wait for a turn at the computer.
- **Postpone immediate gratification.** This refers to putting off a pleasurable activity, such as having coffee with friends, until after completing an important task, such as studying for an exam. Children are simply not as skilled at delaying gratification as are adults. They have to learn how to do it and then must want to try it. Even older children need help figuring out when it is important to put off until later something that they want right now.
- **Set a plan in motion and carry it out.** David and Michael, second graders, planned how to build a model of a farm, drew the plans, and then built their model. It took them several days to complete their project.

How self-control evolves   Self-control emerges "from the outside to the inside," slowly, and haltingly.

| FIGURE 3.3 | Milestones: development of self-control |

Birth to approximately 12 months
- Infants are *not* capable of self-control (Kopp, 1981). The reflex movements of the first several months of life give way to voluntary motor acts such as reaching and grasping, but infants do not consciously control these movements.
- This is a time to learn that the self is separate from other people, the very first step on the road to self-control.

Between age 1 and age 2
- Children begin to be able to start, stop, change, or maintain motor acts or emotional signals.
- They demonstrate an emerging awareness of the demands made on children by caregivers.
- Communication skills become more sophisticated, enabling a child to understand another person's instructions and modeling.
- Caregivers usually discover that children this age are ready to follow an adult's lead.

At Approximately 24 Months
- Children can recall what someone has said or done.
- They can represent experiences.
- These new abilities help children make the transition to developing self-control.
- At this stage, however, children have only a limited ability to control themselves, that is, to wait for their turn or to delay gratification.

At About 3 Years
- Children can use strategies to help them delay gratification.
- These strategies set the stage for better self-control. Kopp (1981) did research with groups of 18-, 24-, and 36-month-old children to find out how they differ in their use of strategies to better tolerate delay. Researchers placed raisins under a cup, and the child being tested was told not to eat them. The older children spontaneously did things to distract themselves, such as singing, talking, sitting on their hands, or looking away. Younger children benefited from instructions on using delaying strategies, but they did not use them automatically.*

*Note: Some disabilities can affect self-control. In one study, children diagnosed with autism showed more problems with self-regulation in very early childhood than did children not diagnosed with autism (Gomez & Baird, 2005).

- **Self-control evolves "from the outside to the inside":** Responsible adults actually perform most of an infant's or toddler's ego functions, such as remembering things for the infant and reminding a toddler to hold the kitten gently, thereby regulating the young child's behavior for her. In this case, the adult greatly controls a very young child's actions. The control is outside the infant; it is external. The infant *cannot* control herself.

  Nevertheless, teachers realize that a child can, and should, take more responsibility for controlling herself as she grows older and acquires greater cognitive skills. They expect children to begin to internalize the control taught by the adult. Responsible adults communicate this expectation when they gradually transfer executive control to children. The adult might expect, for example, a child to try solving a problem, with the adult observing and offering advice or help only when necessary. This is scaffolding, a concept from Vygotsky's theory.

- **Self-control develops slowly.** Children begin to develop self-control around the age of 2 (Figure 3.3). It takes several more years before this emerging ability fully develops. Children are better able to control themselves as they get older for a number of reasons. First, their cognitive, perceptual, and linguistic systems have developed, allowing them to understand things from a different perspective and giving them access to better skills for dealing with impulses. Control of the self also implies that a child realizes that a self exists; this knowledge develops during late infancy and early childhood.

- **Self-control evolves haltingly, in a "sometimes you see it and sometimes you don't" fashion.** Preschool children often astonish adults with remarkable self-control, but they demonstrate considerable lack of control at other times. Jackie, for example, controlled himself in the block corner, but on the same day, he shoved someone out of the way while rushing to the swimming pool. You will see the same thing in older children who have never learned to control themselves. Young children have to practice self-control, just as musicians have to practice their instrument-playing skills. It is reasonable to expect some measure of self-control in young children, but it is usually a mistake to expect perfect control.

Prosocial Behavior: What to Expect

Prosocial behavior

Actions, such as sharing, helping, or cooperating, that promote the well-being of others

Prosocial behavior is an action that benefits another person or animal. Altruism refers to unselfish, benevolent behavior. True altruism means that the person shares, helps, or cooperates with no thought about what is in it for him. Prosocial behaviors are intended to meet someone's needs, either physical, psychological/emotional, or both. Sarah's mother demonstrated compassion toward the family's cat. She modeled how to meet a creature's physical and emotional needs.

> **EXAMPLE**   Sarah's mother attended to the cat's injured foot and cradled the cat, calming her down and telling her that she would be okay.

Forms of prosocial behavior   There are three major categories of prosocial behavior: sharing, helping, and cooperation (see Figure 3.4).

Sharing

Giving, donating; one type of prosocial behavior

- **Sharing** refers to dividing, giving, bestowing. A person owns something, or at least currently has possession of it, and decides to let somebody use the item or even gives ownership of the item to the other person. People can share or donate materials, information or time, as shown in Figure 3.4. Young children do share things with others. On some occasions, they share altruistically, such as moving over to make room at the lunchroom table, simply because they recognize that another person or animal needs something.

    On other occasions, children share something to initiate social contact and then keep the interaction going once it has started. Children might occasionally share as a way of meeting their own need for contact with others. Young children's sharing often takes the form of simply offering objects to other

FIGURE 3.4 **Prosocial behavior**

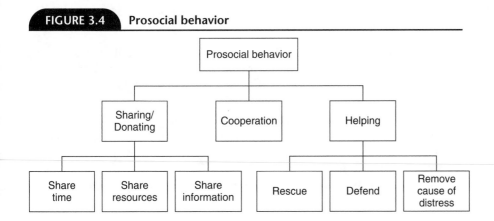

children or adults during social interaction (Eisenberg, Wolchik, Goldberg, & Engel, 1992).

> **EXAMPLE** Patrick asked Vinnie to join him in play on the playground like this: "I have a hoop, Vinnie. You can roll it and jump through it. Wanna try it?" He offered something to initiate an interaction.

Whatever a young child's reason for sharing, he is usually not highly self-sacrificing; that is, he takes little risk. There is little risk in sharing extra mittens, for example, or sharing information on how to do something.

We see sharing, helping, and cooperation frequently in young children, even in children who are aggressive. Teachers need to notice and encourage such behavior in *all* children, including those with different levels of aggression. Unfortunately, some preschool teachers do not pay attention to positive behaviors such as sharing or helping in aggressive preschoolers, even if the aggression is mild . (McComas, Johnson, & Simons, 2005). In this study, other children in the class paid positive attention to helping and sharing from their aggressive peers, but the teachers did not. Encouraging prosocial behavior is a good way to *decrease* aggressive behavior; therefore, a teacher who ignores a child who shares or helps misses an opportunity to support that child.

- **Helping** involves performing simple everyday acts of kindness and rescue (as did the rescue workers after Hurricane Katrina struck New Orleans in 2005). It also includes defending others, as when a bystander in a bullying incident intervenes and helps the victim. Helping also includes removing the cause of someone's distress, as when Sean's Dad removed a splinter from Sean's foot. All children are capable of sharing and helping, but a variety of factors influence their actual level of prosocial behavior. For example, children's willingness to help or share is heavily influenced by whether their teacher and parents value prosocial behavior (Eisenberg et al., 1992). A child might also share or help more easily if important adults have modeled the behaviors.

> **EXAMPLE** Thomas's father *helped* a neighbor fix the neighbor's gate. Thomas watched as his dad *shared* his tools.

Helping
Assisting, performing acts of kindness, rescuing; one type of prosocial behavior.

Cooperating
Working collaboratively to complete a job or task; one type of prosocial behavior

- **Cooperating** refers to working together willingly to accomplish a job or task. The motive for working together is altruistic.

  > **EXAMPLE**   Pippin, Tom, and Janet cooperated to clean the gerbil's house. Pippen cleaned and filled the food and water dishes, while Tom and Janet washed the inside of the house. Then, they all checked off completion of this task.

Many children play cooperatively (Anderson, Hilton, & Wouden-Miller, 2003; Parten, 1932). In cooperative play, children follow one another around and make mutual suggestions about what to do next. Such budding interest in others and in playing and working cooperatively is prosocial behavior when the cooperation benefits someone or a group, as Pippin, Tom, and Janet's cleaning the gerbil house did.

Children need specific competencies to act compassionately   Sharing or helping seems like such a simple thing. However, several events must occur during a child's first several years of life before he becomes capable of compassion and generosity. Most significantly, he needs to be securely attached to his parents, which boosts compassion as a child grows older (Mikulincer, Shaver, Gillath, & Nitzberg, 2005). He also needs a very specific set of competencies: cognitive and emotional. In addition, he needs specific skills (Zahn-Waxler, Radke-Yarrow, Wagner, & Chapman, 1992). A child can show compassion only when he has all three abilities (see Figure 3.5). Having one or two of these abilities is not enough.

Cognitive competencies   Children need specific cognitive competencies before they can share, help, or cooperate.

- **Sense of self.** A child needs to know that she is an individual and separate from other individuals (Bengtsson & Johnson, 1992). This occurs in infancy.
- **Identify needs.** The child must be able to recognize what somebody needs, such as understanding that a friend who lost some lunch money needs a small loan.
- **Make things happen.** A child must be able to see himself as a person who can make things happen (for example, "I can help John by sharing a little of my

---

FIGURE 3.5   **Three competencies children must have to act compassionately**

Cognitive Competencies
(e.g., I can make things happen.
"I can share my book.")

+

Emotional Competency
(e.g., I am *beginning* to understand what somebody needs.
"Jessie does not have his book. He needs a book.")

+

Specific Skills
(e.g., I have some "sharing" skills.
"I know how to ask Jessie if he would like to share my book.")

=

Prosocial Behavior
Ryan shares his book with Jessie.

lunch money with him"). This ability arises in infancy and continues to develop throughout childhood.

- **Language.** Children need good enough language skills to describe how others might be feeling and to describe how they themselves feel (for example, "John lost his lunch money and needs to eat").
- **Memory.** A child's memory has to be sophisticated enough to allow him to keep somebody's need in mind long enough to act on it.

All of these abilities have their roots in early childhood. Glimmers of these abilities appear in older infants and toddlers, allowing the youngest children to begin to act in ways that appear to be helpful or cooperative. These cognitive competencies are not fully developed, however, in very young children. For instance, young children can often tell that someone needs something, but they are not very good at reflecting on another person's or animal's inner experience based on the need. Recall that they tend to focus on people's readily observable, external characteristics. As they get older, children tend to focus more and more on another person's internal psychological perspective (Bengtsson & Johnson, 1992).

Emotional competencies   Children also need to have specific emotional competencies, which seem to develop quite slowly in order to respond to another's needs or distress.

- **Decoding emotion in another person's face.** This is the ability to look at a person's or animal's face and make sense of his or her facial expression. High-prosocial children seem to be much more accurate than are low-prosocial children in decoding emotion in other children's faces (Greener, 1998). This ability *begins* in infancy and continues to develop.

  Even adults can learn how to better read another person's emotions through training (Klinzing, 2003). Some children, as teachers quickly realize, are better at decoding emotion or "reading faces" than are other children. For example, children with Asperger's syndrome (AS) had more difficulty decoding facial expressions than did children without AS (Lindner & Rosen, 2006). A child who decodes emotion very well has a far better chance of understanding how another child might be feeling.

  > **EXAMPLE**   Mr. Sanchez discussed a playground incident with his class. Thomas said, "Jason was mad!" "How do you know he was angry?" asked the teacher. Thomas: "His face looked mad."

- **Responding to the emotions of others.** A very young baby responds to emotions in other people (Sagi & Hoffman, 1976) and seems to be able to discriminate among her mother's different emotions; in some cases, the baby can imitate these emotions (Cohn, Campbell, Matias, & Hopkins, 1990). Some children do not learn to read emotions very well and become adults who do not read or deal with emotions well. Hildyard (2005) found that mothers who neglected their children could not discriminate emotions in their children very well and did not know many labels for emotions. Recent research highlights the important influence that imitation plays in human development (Hurley & Chater, 2005).

FIGURE 3.6 Levels of perspective taking

Age in Years	Level	Perspective-Taking Ability
3 to 6	Level 0	• Egocentric perspective. • No distinction between own and another's perspective.
6–8	Level 1	• Still not able to take another's perspective. • Believes that another, if in the same situation, will respond just as the target child would respond.
8–10	Level 2	• Can take another's perspective. • Sees self as others do. • Not everyone reaches this level.
10–12	Level 3	• Can take another's perspective but in a more sophisticated way than at level 2. • Now aware of recursive nature of different perspectives: "Mom thinks that I think she wants me to." Not everybody reaches this level.
Adolescence and Adulthood	Level 4	• Very sophisticated in perspective-taking ability. • Believes that different perspectives form a network. • Has conceptualized society's viewpoints on legal and moral issues. • Not everybody reaches this level.

Source: Based on "Social-Cognitive Understanding," by R. L. Selman, in *Moral Development and Behavior*, by T. Lickona (Ed.), 1976, New York: Holt, Rinehart & Winston.

Empathy
Vicariously understanding the thoughts or feelings of another

myeducationlab

Go to the Assignments and Activities section of Topic 1: Child Development in the MyEducationLab for your course and complete the activity entitled *Children's Perspective-Taking Influences their Behavior.* Note how this strategy can support children in learning how to share.

■ **Demonstrating empathy. Empathy** is the ability to participate in another person's or animal's feelings; one person's emotional state is similar to the other person's emotional state. Hoffman (2005) calls empathy the "glue" that holds a society together.

> **EXAMPLE** Mr. Sanchez realized, on the first day of school for his first graders, that they would probably be anxious. He has good perspective-taking skills (Figure 3.6) and is able to feel what children might be feeling.

Like most other aspects of development, empathy develops slowly and starts in infancy (see Figure 3.7). Researchers have thought for a long time that human children are biologically prepared for empathy (Hoffman, 1975) because they respond to another person's emotional state. However, the budding ability to recognize another person's emotional state is not real empathy.

High-prosocial children score significantly higher on self-reports of empathic response (Greener, 1998). In a study of prosocial behavior in 10- and 11-year-olds, Bengtsson & Johnson (1992) found that some children had a high level of empathy for a victim. They were able to take both the victim's and the victimizer's point of view, as shown in the next example from the research.

A young girl was turned away by force when entering a room where her older sister and a friend were playing. Some children showed extended empathic reasoning by showing empathy for the little girl as well as understanding of the victimizer: "I didn't like the way they pushed the little girl out of the room, but I can also understand that they wanted to be left alone while playing."

| FIGURE 3.7 | How very young children are likely to show prosocial behavior |

Up to approximately 12 months
- Pats or rubs. Almost all babies will pat or rub a person who appears to be upset or hurt.
- Gives an object. Some young infants will try to offer an object to someone who appears to be upset.

14 to 20 months
- Kisses or hugs.
- Gives some object.
- Might try to protect someone.

20 months to 2½ years
- All of the above, plus the following:
  - Gives physical assistance.
  - Tries to get help from a third person.
  - Asks questions indicating concern (e.g., "Does your finger hurt?").
  - Gives advice to a person who is upset or hurt (e.g., "Tell your mommy").
  - Might offer reassurance to person or animal (e.g., "It's OK").

Source: Based on "Roots, Motives, and Patterns of Children's Prosocial Behavior," by M. Radke-Yarrow and C. Zahn-Waxler, in *Development and Maintenance of Prosocial Behavior*, by E. Staub, D. Bar-Tel, J. Karylowski, and J. Reykowski (Eds.), 1984, New York: Plenum Press.

Children who reasoned like this about another person's situation showed the highest levels of prosocial behavior. These were 10- and 11-year-olds, not young children. We know that children in the early childhood stage are not capable of reasoning like this. It takes several years to develop high-level empathy and the ability to think about the perspective of both a victim and a victimizer. Some children

It takes many years for children to develop empathy, to share another person or animal's emotional state.

PEARSON
myeducationlab

Go to the Building
Teaching Skills and
Dispositions section of
Topic 1: Child
Development in the
MyEducationLab for your
course and complete the
activity entitled *Helping
Children Develop Trust and
Autonomy.* Note the
importance of this strategy
in helping children become
independent
and trusting

WORKING *with* FAMILIES — RAISING A COMPASSIONATE CHILD

Here are some tips that you can give parents for encouraging kind and compassionate behavior in their child.

- Observe children sharing and helping. Encourage parents to watch their child closely, in school if necessary, for times when their child does share and help. Consider sitting with the parent during the observation.
- Provide cooperative games and play materials. Tell parents that these games, and not competitive games, encourage sharing, cooperation, and helping. Make children's books focusing on prosocial behavior available to parents and emphasize the value of such stories in developing sharing, helping, and cooperation.
- Encourage children to watch television shows and movies containing prosocial content. Label examples of sharing, helping, and cooperating (Rosenkoetter, 1999). Plan a parent meeting or write a brief handout on how to choose appropriate videos, show clips of good videos, and give parents a list of suggested movies and videos showing prosocial behavior. Encourage parents to look for advertising that emphasizes prosocial behavior and teach parents to make appropriate comments about the helping, sharing, and cooperation in such ads.
- Have children participate in prosocial behaviors. The idea here is not to force altruism but for the child just to observe and participate with a parent who shares, helps, or cooperates but does not preach. For example, encourage children to choose cans of food for a food pantry. Tell parents to make the whole process low key and tell them not to preach.
- Give children appropriate and manageable household responsibilities. Help parents understand how meaningful such work is in fostering sharing, helping, and cooperation. Immersion in a family in which everybody does their fair share of the work is an extremely effective strategy.
- Recognize and encourage the results of this teaching. Bolster a parent's confidence in encouraging kind, compassionate behavior. For example, give parents three specific ways of showing or telling their child that they recognize the child's efforts. "You were very helpful when we made cookies today, Amanda" or "It was kind of you to share your sand toys with Jess."

PEARSON
myeducationlab

To check your
comprehension on the
content covered in
Chapter 3, go to the Book
Specific Resources in the
MyEducationLab for your
course, select your text,
and complete the Study
Plan. Here you will be able
to take a chapter quiz,
receive feedback on your
answers, and then access
review, practice, and
enrichment activities to
enhance your
understanding of chapter
content.

never develop this high level of empathy. Growing older is an important element in developing empathy but growing older, by itself, is not enough.

Skill development   Children need to know how to help, share, or cooperate; they need specific skills. If Moua, for instance, wants to share something, he must have the social skill of approaching another child and must know what to say as he offers something. Zahn-Waxler et al. (1992) believe that young children have a better chance of developing such skills if they have a firm attachment to their primary caregivers and if their parents or caregivers shared, took turns, and cooperated with them.

ANALYZE A VIGNETTE

Referring to the chapter-opening vignettes.

1. The memory games that Mr. Bjornrud planned for 6-month-old Paul were appropriate for this age child because _____.
2. In the preschool vignette, the focus was on self-control. From your perspective, which aspect of self-control was the teacher working on? How do you think that the teacher's limit setting in this case would help a child develop self-control?
3. Explain the emotional competencies that Thomas needed before he was able to share his extra gloves with Sean.

SUMMARY

Knowing about perception and memory can help teachers choose appropriate guidance. Infants are born with perceptual abilities that continue to develop throughout childhood. For example, children spend more time working on tasks as they get older and can ignore intruding stimulation. However, we can expect that young children will have problems with perception that make paying attention difficult at times. Some of these problems include the following:

- Trouble ignoring extraneous information.
- Difficulty scanning and searching.

Children's memory improves significantly during childhood. For example, children need fewer cues or reminders in order to remember what they need. These changes are explained by

- growth in children's brains, which provides more storage.
- better methods for remembering things.
- more knowledge about the world.

As children get older and as their cognitive skills change, they also change *how* they think about and understand other people.

- Younger children tend to describe others in a very concrete way, while older children make a gradual transition to using psychological constructs.
- Younger children do not understand the difference between accidental or intentional behavior. Older children do understand the difference because they have developed the necessary cognitive skills.
- Somewhat egocentric young children view friendship quite differently than they do when they are older. An older child begins to understand the give-and-take nature of true friendship. Self-control evolves during early childhood. It develops slowly and allows a child to control impulses and to plan and carry out projects. Prosocial behavior is any action that benefits somebody else and includes sharing, helping, and cooperating.

QUESTIONS FOR REFLECTION

1. Explain to someone who has *not* read this chapter what "decoding emotions in another's face" means. Then explain why it is a good skill for a child to have if we want to help him act in a kind and helpful way.
2. True or false? Children develop self-control automatically, just by getting older. Justify your response.
3. In your own words, explain what this phrase means: Self-controls develops from the "outside to the inside."

APPLY YOUR KNOWLEDGE

1. **Self-control**: Observe how adults seem to behave in terms of expectations for self-control for children of three different ages.
   a. **Infants**: Observe an adult–infant interaction. Look for evidence that the adult does not expect the infant to control himself, For example, the adult does not expect the infant to remember things, to manage his emotions, or to complete tasks on his own. Describe specific things an adult does for the infant (rocks him to sleep, calms him down, burps him, wipes his mouth, and changes his diaper).
   b. **Toddlers–older preschoolers**: Now look for evidence that an adult expects these children to show some measure of self-control. For example, does the teacher expect the children to remember to wash their hands after using the bathroom, or to manage feelings by saying, "Use words to say that you are upset"?
   c. **Kindergarten and primary school children**: What evidence do you find in a classroom for 5- to 8-year-olds that teachers really do expect older early childhood children to be better able to control themselves?

2. **Sharing and helping:**
   a. Present this short puppet story about helping or cooperation. One puppet, Sam, has trouble placing paper on an easel.

Amanda:	What's the matter, Sam?
Sam:	I can't reach the clip for the paper.
Amanda:	Maybe I can reach it. (She clips the paper onto the easel.) There, it's done.
Sam:	Thanks for helping.

   b. Place the puppets in a learning center after this demonstration. Encourage children to practice what they observed. Encourage them to take both roles—helper and the one helped—so that each has a chance to practice helping.

KEY TERMS

Cooperating (70)
Empathy (72)
Helping (69)
Long-term memory (63)
Memory (61)

Perception (59)
Prosocial behavior (68)
Recall memory (63)
Recognition memory (63)
Self-control (66)

Sharing (68)
Short-term memory (63)
Social cognition (64)

WEB SITES

Center for Disease Control and Prevention
http://www.cdc.gov/ncbddd/child/development.htm

A division of a federal agency, Health and Human Services. Reliable and accurate information on child development. Many good links to information for yourself as well as for parents.

Child and Family Web Guide
http://www.cfw.tufts.edu/

An excellent site. It is ". . . a directory that evaluates, describes and provides links to hundreds of sites containing child development research and practical advice."

Compassionate Kids
http://www.compassionatekids.com

Nonprofit organization. Many links to activities and information on fostering compassion for the earth, people, and animals.

Educators for Social Responsibility
http://www.esrnational.org

Based in Cambridge, MA. Mission is to teach social responsibility in education.

"Direct" and "Indirect" Child Guidance

This book describes positive ways of guiding children, *only* positive approaches. The National Association of the Education of Young Children (NAEYC) Code of Ethics states that the most important part of the Code is that we do nothing to harm a child. To help you learn a positive constructivist approach, you will study three factors: the value of a well-constructed physical environment, how to use positive guidance strategies, and how to use observation in guiding children.

Chapter 4 Supportive Physical Environments: Indirect Guidance

This chapter explains the concept of indirect guidance, which can include any number of factors that an adult does to influence children indirectly. The adult might actually say little to the child; for example, the adult may simply hang a poster on how to wash hands over the sink to remind children about proper hand-washing technique. A classroom's physical layout and time schedule also indirectly and profoundly affect children's behavior.

You will read about the major indirect guidance strategies of designing and managing the physical environment effectively. You can minimize or even prevent problems by setting up your room well, by developing an appropriate curriculum and activities, and by competently managing materials. Chapter 4 gives several examples of practical ideas for indirect guidance that can be adapted for any early childhood setting.

Chapter 5   Positive Guidance and Discipline Strategies: Direct Guidance

Setting good limits, redirecting behavior, delivering an I-message: these are just a few examples of direct guidance in this chapter. These strategies involve a child or group of children directly. Your confidence in dealing with day-to-day discipline encounters will grow as you learn about, practice, and experience success in using these and other positive discipline strategies. After reading Chapter 5, you will know exactly how to use a great many positive, specific, and practical discipline strategies.

Chapter 6   Using Observation in Guiding Children

Children tell us what they need in so many ways—when they are charming, downright funny, and, on occasion, aggressive. Their behavior alone can communicate curiosity, excitement, happiness, or even heavy sadness or great anger. Behavior is a code, and only a person who knows the code can read it. Chapter 6 will help you understand the value of observation as the first step in cracking the code of children's behavior. You will learn some specific methods for observing children's behavior.

CHAPTER 4

Supportive Physical Environments

Indirect Guidance

"We organize our classrooms with an abundance of attractive and challenging materials and furniture that encourage individual and group study and interaction."

—(Bank Street, 2009)

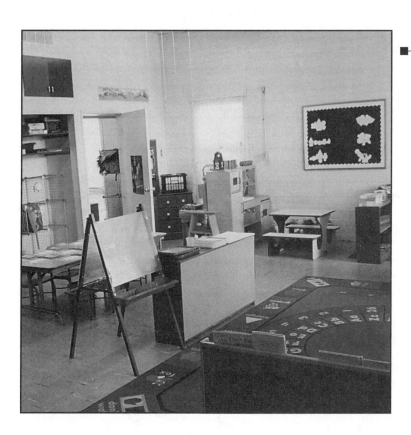

Chapter Contents

Guiding Questions

- How can early childhood theory help me arrange my classroom to support children's behavior?
- What are some guidelines for developmentally appropriate room design in an early childhood classroom?
- How do classrooms for infants and toddlers differ from classrooms for 3- to 8-year-old children?

VIGNETTE

PRESCHOOL: MRS. WOODWARD'S PRESCHOOL CLASSROOM

Mrs. Woodward, the preschool teacher, and her assistant teacher use the Project Approach (Helm & Katz, 2001) to curriculum development, working closely with the children, observing, and consulting with them, to determine children's interests. The current project started with a trip to the hardware store to get a gallon of paint mixed for the tricycle storage shed (the trip was a shared experience for every child in the class). Mrs. Woodward had visited the store ahead of time and talked with the person who would mix the paint, giving the store employee suggestions on what she might say to the children.

The "paint lady," as the children called her, opened the can and showed the light base color, almost white. She showed the paint chip with the color the school needed. Then she used the rotating device holding concentrated colors and carefully added the three different colors they needed to the base color, showing and naming each new concentrated color. "I need a teeny-tiny bit of black," she said, using her thumb and forefinger to illustrate such a tiny amount, "but we need a lot more blue (space measured by finger and thumb widened). Here's the gray—only four drops. Count with me!"

She showed them the base color, now with the dark spots of coloring agents. When she put the paint can on the shaker, she asked, "What do you think is happening to the little spots of paint now? Why do we need to shake the can?" In addition, she said, "What do you think the paint will look like after it has been shaken?" When she opened the can, the children confirmed their hypothesis about a new color, and she made a color chip for each child. The teachers decided that a project centering on color and color mixing was appropriate and practical, as well as interesting to the children.

Mrs. Woodward and her nineteen 4-year-olds investigate things from their classroom base, a busy but calm place. She has organized the classroom into activity areas. The activities in small-group learning centers, for example, reflect the principles of developmentally appropriate practice (DAP) and current projects under investigation. On arrival each day, children find areas ready for work and play, and Mrs. Woodward encourages each child to choose an area. On Monday, the children worked in different areas on the following activities.

Art Area

"Squish-squash, closely watch," said Mrs. Woodward as four children joined her around a small table. She had placed one lump of smooth, white play dough that the children had made on Friday in front of each child. Today's focus was to add one drop of blue food coloring to a little depression in each lump of white dough and to encourage squishing, squashing, predicting, observing, and describing color changes. Investigating color changes continued at the finger-painting table, where blue and yellow paints were available, and red and white paints waited at the easel. (The play dough, finger painting, and easel are all art and science activities in this integrated curriculum.)

Library Area

This is a serene, quiet, enticing area, with good lighting and high-quality books displayed on the rack. One of the books was about mixing colors, the current topic for the investigators of color in Mrs. Woodward's class. She put out the flannel board with figures for retelling the story of Little Blue and Little Yellow, and put out the tape recorder and headset, along with a set of pictures illustrating a story on the table.

Writing Area

This is also a high-interest area. Mrs. Woodward set out transparencies of the color of the paints mixed for the shed. Children placed the transparencies on top of each other to approximate the new color of the shed. Two children dictated a summary of that process just as the entire group had dictated a thank-you note to the paint lady at the store. Now, some of the children wrote notes to parents about the trip, attached their notes to the paint chip, and took the notes home. Two other children wrote in their trays of damp sand with a stick.

Science/Math Area

Today, the children made a graph showing the proportion of each color in the paint for the shed. Mrs. Woodward also placed three ice cube trays with clear water in each compartment on a separate table. Next to each tray were two eyedroppers, one with blue dye and one with yellow, for a color-mixing experiment. The parents have helped the teachers develop many homemade math materials (these items are packaged, labeled, and stored for easy retrieval). Two boys used some of the materials to work on the concept of larger and smaller "sets" on the table. Three other math-related games rested on shelves in the math area.

Dramatic Play Area

Dramatic play center activities usually stay set up for several days, depending on the children's needs. This week, girls and boys working in the "fix-it shop" wore special "inspector" shirts. They checked books and puzzles for needed repairs, inspected tricycles for squeaks needing oiling, examined dolls for necessary bathing and washing of clothing, determined whether blocks had splinters and needed light sanding, and inspected animal housing for required cleaning and repair. They dictated needed repairs to a teacher, who wrote them in a notebook. Then, over several days, with a student teacher's supervision, they completed one or two tasks per day from the notebook, checking off completed jobs.

Block Area

To follow up their one-half-block walk to watch the traffic signal change colors, Mrs. Woodward set out a model traffic signal the children could operate to change its colors. Several of the children worked on building a replica of the street outside the school, with their traffic light at the intersection.

Puzzle and Manipulatives Area

The school invests a little each year in small, manipulative toys and a good storage system, so Mrs. Woodward has access to a multitude of these items. On Monday, she placed three old, frequently used but well cared for puzzles on the table and set two tubs of small, interlocking blocks on the floor. The children could also choose from among seven or eight other manipulative toys stored neatly in clear plastic containers on low, open shelves.

:: INTRODUCTION

There are different phases of early childhood, and teachers need to know how to construct a classroom environment for their particular age group—infants and toddlers, preschool and kindergarten, or the primary grades. The preschool classroom in the chapter-opening vignette is appropriate for this age group—well designed and based on theory and research in child development and early childhood education. This type of environment sends messages to all who enter. It sends the following messages to children (Tarr, 2001):

You are *safe* here.

You can learn many things here.

You can play and work with other children in this room.

You can make many choices here.

You can work on many different projects.

When you finish your work in one area, you can go to a different spot and work there.

When you want to, you can work by yourself.

There is a good space where all the children in your class can gather.

Indirect guidance
Influencing children's behavior through environmental design, appropriate curriculum, activities, and materials management

We guide children both directly and indirectly. We focus in this chapter on **indirect guidance**. One of the elements of indirect guidance includes designing the physical environment in your classroom. We will start by using theory as a guide to room design. Then we will emphasize the process that you would follow in arranging a developmentally appropriate classroom for 3- to 8-year-olds. This will include an overview of developmentally appropriate room arrangements and their effects on children's development, and specific guidelines for designing good learning environments for young children. We will also examine, briefly, the role of appropriate curriculum, activities, and materials in guiding children. Finally, we will focus on designing environments for infants and toddlers.

:: THEORETICAL FOUNDATIONS FOR EARLY CHILDHOOD CLASSROOM DESIGN

Program models in early childhood education base their practices on accepted theories. The programs of Bank Street, High/Scope, Montessori, Reggio Emilia, and Responsive Classroom, for example, have some obvious differences but, more important, they share a theoretical orientation. Every one of these programs are premised on children's need for:

an active approach to learning
collaborating with others
working with real objects
talking with adults skilled in mediating learning

Chapter 2 described three categories of theory relevant to our practice as educators. We rely on these perspectives here to design physical environments that meet children's needs for activity and collaboration. A developmentally appropriate physical environment is a major—*indirect*—part of a teacher's guidance plan.

Theories Focusing on the Systems in Which Children Develop

Bronfenbrenner's theory explained the ecology of human development. It helped educators to understand that the many systems in which children exist affect their development, learning, and behavior. Classrooms are part of the microsystem of child, family, peers, and school in Bronfenbrenner's theory. This theory posits that every system, including a child's classroom, affects a child's behavior. The room's design, along with curriculum and instructional strategies, has an impact on how children behave and how they learn.

Theories Focusing on How Children Construct Knowledge

The theories of Dewey, Piaget, and Vygotsky have informed early childhood practice for many years. They focus not on systems in which children exist, but on how children themselves construct or build knowledge. There are differences, of course, among these theories. However, we find that the great similarities are very good guides to our practice. All emphasize that children learn through activity and that interaction between a child and others is important. Program models based on these constructivist theorists design classroom spaces so that children are active in their learning, can collaborate with others, work with real objects, and talk with teachers as they learn.

Theories Focusing on Psychological and Emotional Needs

Other theories focusing on children's psychological and emotional needs inform our practices. Erikson, for example, explained stages of psychosocial development; the first three or four stages are especially important in an early childhood teacher's work. Each of these stages can be resolved in either a positive or a negative way. Teachers who design developmentally appropriate classrooms help children develop trust during infancy; autonomy during toddlerhood; initiative during the preschool and kindergarten years; and a sense of industry during first, second, and third grades.

Maslow described and explained the human's hierarchy of needs (first shown in Chapter 2, Figure 2.5). Figure 4.1 further explains a teacher's role in helping children meet needs at each level. The classroom that you develop can help children feel safe and secure. It can also help children meet their needs for friendships and feeling confident and competent.

∷ DEVELOPMENTALLY APPROPRIATE PHYSICAL ENVIRONMENTS FOR 3- TO 8-YEAR-OLDS

The designs of the classrooms in Figures 4.2 and 4.3 are arranged appropriately for the age groups using them, and they have a positive impact on children's behavior and development.

Room Design Based on Theory

Both rooms in the figures are appropriate for young children because they demonstrate a teacher's respect for and knowledge of how children develop and learn. The teachers practice what they believe about children. The arrangements tell us that the teachers believe that children are curious, resourceful, and competent, just as John Dewey advised and as schools such as Reggio Emilia or the Bank Street programs for children put into action.

Sense of order   Each room conveys a sense of order and provides a comforting place for work and play (Greenman, 2005). The rooms are well arranged, tidy, and organized. Children know that items have their own place in the room and that the basic structure will be the same from day to day, even though the teacher might change materials and activities in centers.

myeducationlab

Go to the Assignments and Activities section of Topic 6: Physical Environment in the MyEducationLab for your course and complete the activity entitled *Maslow's Hierarchy of Needs and Early Childhood Classroom Design*. Notice how a well-designed classroom supports children's psychological and emotional needs.

FIGURE 4.1 Maslow's hierarchy of needs: Implications for teachers

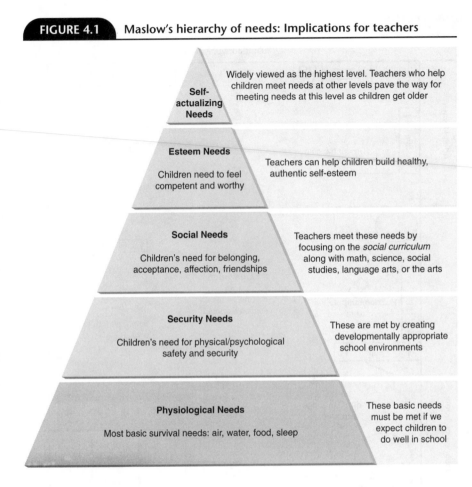

Self-actualizing Needs
Widely viewed as the highest level. Teachers who help children meet needs at other levels pave the way for meeting needs at this level as children get older

Esteem Needs
Children need to feel competent and worthy
Teachers can help children build healthy, authentic self-esteem

Social Needs
Children's need for belonging, acceptance, affection, friendships
Teachers meet these needs by focusing on the *social curriculum* along with math, science, social studies, language arts, or the arts

Security Needs
Children's need for physical/psychological safety and security
These are met by creating developmentally appropriate school environments

Physiological Needs
Most basic survival needs: air, water, food, sleep
These basic needs must be met if we expect children to do well in school

Social interaction Classrooms need to be set up so that children can interact easily with other children as well as with their teachers. Teachers have set up the learning centers deliberately and intentionally to foster working and playing together. Such interaction gives children the opportunity to confront other children's ideas and to clarify their own viewpoints.

Making choices Children need to learn how to make wise choices, and these rooms give them good practice. Consider the learning centers and materials. During choice time, children work alone or with other children. Each center has a variety of materials directly related to that center, and children choose from available materials. For example, children in the primary-grade classroom can write after choosing from among computers, small and large chalk or whiteboards, colored pencils, markers, or even trays of damp sand. Over time and in a supportive environment, children can learn to make wise decisions and choices.

Active learning Classrooms should encourage active learning. Whether in preschool, kindergarten, or the primary grades, children learn actively in centers,

myeducationlab

Go to the Assignments and Activities section of Topic 6: Physical Environment in the MyEducationLab for your course and complete the activity entitled *Constructivist Principles of Designing Early Childhood Classrooms*. Note that active learning, collaboration, and making choices benefit children's learning.

FIGURE 4.2 Floor plan of Mrs. Woodward's preschool classroom

FIGURE 4.3 | Children collaborate with others and learn actively in this classroom

through discovery and working with real objects. Children develop physical knowledge when they manipulate real objects such as blocks. Children can also learn actively when teachers initiate a learning activity, such as second graders working on simple machines. When children manipulate physical objects and gather data, they develop new ideas or deepen their understanding of older ideas. For example, preschool children can extend their understanding of colors in the art area by mixing two colors of paint. Second graders working with levers and pulleys can extend any existing knowledge about simple machines with their teacher's support.

Benefits of Well-Designed Spaces for Children

Children benefit in many ways when their teachers design developmentally appropriate classrooms such as those in Figures 4.2 and 4.3. They have lower levels of stress and far fewer discipline problems. They interact with other children in a more positive way than do children in inappropriately structured classrooms (Hart et al., 1998; Nicholson, 2005; Steinhauer, 2005).

Well-designed spaces help children to be more independent and self-controlled. They display greater feelings of competence and confidence, both of which are elements of positive and healthy self-esteem. Therefore, a well-designed physical environment supports children's efforts to meet the higher-order needs, such as the esteem needs, in Maslow's hierarchy. They also develop better decision-making skills and better ability to take initiative and engage in more sophisticated dramatic play than children do in poorly designed rooms. The research in these areas is not new. We have known about the benefits of good design for decades, and researchers of late have built on this base (Charlesworth, Hart, Burts, & DeWolf, 1993; Howes, 1991; Johnson & Duffek, 2008; Petrakos & Howe, 1996; Stallings, 1975).

The decade of the 1990s is viewed by many educators as the decade of the brain because of the tremendous amount of research on brain development and children's learning. Carrying on with that theme, research that is more recent describes the role of teachers who believe that brain development is an important factor in how they set up their classrooms. Rushton, Eitelgeorge, and Zickafoose (2003) describe the same sort of constructivist classroom environment needed to foster brain development, as did earlier researchers: well-structured, enriched environments that give children many chances to build their ideas as they work with interesting materials and with other children.

The schools of Reggio Emilia, Italy, citing children's need for beauty, simplicity, and challenge (Gandini; 1993; Reggio Emilia web site, 2009), have added to our renewed interest in classroom design. I participated in the Five State Study Tour (2008) in Reggio Emilia in May 2008 and was struck by the beauty of the classrooms. Children and teachers were calm and engaged. Children were busy learning through focused and enjoyable activities. They worked and played freely with other children. The room designs fostered their engagement.

Effects of poorly designed classrooms Poorly designed schools send quite a different message of expecting failure and lacking respect for children in the schools (Nicholson, 2005). A poorly designed space for children's classroom or program can contribute to poor academic achievement and behavioral problems. Higher levels of stress behavior occur in inappropriately versus appropriately designed preschool and kindergarten classrooms. The stress in poorly designed classrooms contributes to some of the discipline problems (Hart et al., 1998; Steinhauer, 2005).

:: GUIDELINES: DEVELOPMENTALLY APPROPRIATE ROOM DESIGN

A big part of early childhood classroom management is managing the physical environment of the classroom as well as the curriculum, activities, and materials. There are several practical things to consider when setting up or designing the physical environment in early childhood classrooms. We will consider the guidelines for designing a supportive physical environment, including the following:

> Organize the classroom into activity areas and develop enough of them.
> Arrange activity areas logically.
> Create attractive and sensory-rich areas.
> Use a variety of indirect strategies to make it easier for children to work and play in the classroom.

Organize the Classroom into Activity Areas

Appropriately designed classrooms are organized into areas or zones of activity. A good classroom arrangement of areas embodies the principles of movement, active learning, social interaction, and working with supportive adults. Effective teachers develop and arrange **activity areas** that support the overall curriculum goals for the children in that classroom (Bottini & Grossman, 2005; Bank Street, 2009).

There are several different types of classroom activity areas. Some of the areas are small, some large; some have seating, others do not. Specific materials are stored in some areas, but other areas have no materials stored there. Well-designed classrooms usually contain individual or small-group learning centers, a large-group area, and some sort of private area. A recent study (Clark & Kragler, 2005) examined the effect of providing writing materials in all centers on literacy development of children from low-income families. It found that having writing materials in not only the writing center but also the music, art, math, blocks, and other centers enhanced the children's literacy development.

Learning center: small group   A **small-group learning center** refers to a permanent or semipermanent space large enough for five or six children. Well-designed small-group learning centers serve a specific function reflecting the age of the children in that class as well as each school's curriculum goals. Examples of well-defined small-group areas include the following: math and science, manipulatives (puzzles and other small-muscle equipment), library and writing, dramatic play, block center, and creative arts (see Figures 4.4 and 4.5 for examples).

Teachers in developmentally appropriate classrooms create the types of centers that meet the needs of the children in that class. Therefore, *not* all classrooms will have the same small-group learning centers. One teacher might emphasize writing and math with permanent, well-stocked centers for each. Another teacher might provide those centers but with far less emphasis, stressing instead art, blocks, and music.

- **Seating arrangement.** The seating arrangement varies with the purpose of each center, making this type of center quite flexible. Some centers call for a table and

Activity areas
Zones designated for supporting children's development and learning

myeducationlab

Go to the Assignments and Activities section of Topic 6: Physical Environment in the MyEducationLab for your course and complete the activity entitled *Arrange an Early Childhood Classroom into Centers or Activity Areas.* Pay attention to how the different centers support learning in all content areas.

Small-group learning center
Space large enough for five or six children; center has a specific function, such as art or discovery

| FIGURE 4.4 | Dramatic play small-group area |

| FIGURE 4.5 | Puzzles and manipulatives area (a small-group learning center) |

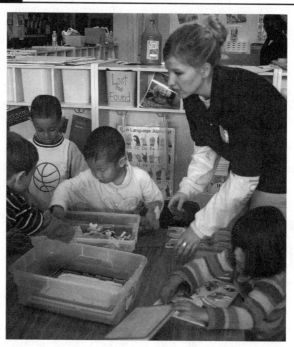

chairs, as in Figure 4.5. Some small-group learning centers do not require a table and chairs, such a preschool's block area. You may also decide to arrange a center so that children can work either at a table or on the floor, a good way to help children practice good decision making. Small-group learning centers should be well separated from other areas, which clearly communicate each area's function.

Bank Street's classrooms for primary grade and even the upper grades are arranged in activity areas. This program model encourages active learning at all levels. Children work with other children in classrooms set up to foster collaborative work and learning. Chang (2003) describes a primary-grade classroom's learning centers and routines set up to help children be responsible for themselves and to take good care of the classroom.

- **Materials for the center.** Store materials related to the activity in the area. Avoid storing materials not related to the function of the area in that location. Guide children indirectly by storing materials within their reach when you want them to have easy access to the materials; store other materials out of their reach.

Our goal in managing an early childhood classroom is to be helpful to children. One study (Cameron, Connor, & Morrison, 2005) examined the effect of good classroom organization and clear teacher instructions for activities. It found that children in well-organized classrooms could manage their own activities well as the year progressed. We can manage the classroom, for example, so children have an easier time cleaning up in any center. We can manage group time so that it is an

TABLE 4.1	Indirect guidance in the physical environment
Indirect Guidance Strategy	**What Is the Benefit to the Child?**
Paint block shapes on the shelf where blocks are stored.	
Music instrument shapes are painted on the pegboard for hanging instruments.	
Transparent storage tubs are used for art or writing materials.	
Attach a sample item from a box of art supplies to the end of the tub facing the room.	
Apron is placed on the back of a chair for messy activities.	
Picture choice cards are available for activities; they are used by the teacher in transitions or by children throughout work time.	
Day planner: index card on which a young child draws or writes a daily plan for activities.	
Carpet squares are arranged in a specific pattern before group activities: semicircle, cluster, lines, circle.	
Pictures of children properly washing hands is placed over the sink.	
Song about playground limits is provided.	

easier activity in which to participate. We can manage schedules so that all children can choose their next activity effortlessly. We can help children by using indirect guidance in the physical environment in many ways. Table 4.1 shows several ideas. For each suggestion, state the possible benefit to the child.

Learning centers for small groups change over time, as the needs, interests, and abilities of the children change and as they engage in different projects. In well-designed classrooms, teachers evaluate learning centers for needed modifications. They regularly add materials for new activities, rearrange the seating of a center as needed, reorganize materials as necessary, and remove materials no longer required.

EXAMPLE   At the beginning of the school year, Mrs. Woodward arranged a play sink, refrigerator, and stove along with a table and chairs and dress-up clothes in the dramatic play area. The children enthusiastically used the center for a while, but then Mrs. Woodward noticed less and less play there, even though she had added different items of interest. Mrs. Woodward concentrated on changing the area to rekindle interest in dramatic play.

She recruited parent volunteers to develop prop boxes (Barbour & Desjean-Perrotta, 2002; Bafile, 2004; Benson, 2004) and collected some great dress-up clothes. The "office," the "backyard," the "gardening center," and the "fix-it shop" were all hits. In the "backyard," children used a small picnic table, umbrella, toy lawn mower set on a green carpet, and hand gardening tools, along with a planting tray for starting plants from seeds in the outside garden.

**Individual learning
center**
Space for one child to
work

Learning center: individual   Figure 4.6 shows several examples for creating **individual learning centers** or work centers. This is a flexible area because the same comments about seating arrangements and materials for the small-group learning area also apply to individual learning centers. These centers block some stimulation, allowing a child to concentrate on a specific activity. They also give children a chance to work alone in a busy classroom.

| FIGURE 4.6 | Individual learning centers. There are many easy and inexpensive ways to create individual centers |

Source: Marion, 2007

EXAMPLE   Mr. Sanchez, the teacher in the mixed-age K–2 classroom, developed three individual learning spaces in one corner of his room. When children chose their activity, he often asked them where they would like to work. "Where would you like to write your story, Philip? You can sit at the big table with the other boys or you can pick one of the one-person workstations. There is still a space open in the one-person workstations. Which would you prefer today?"

Large-group area   A **large-group area** is a space large enough to accommodate most or all of the children for large-group activities or several children during a work period. This space should be large, open, and flexible to accommodate group activities such as music, language arts, creative dramatics, stories, nutrition education, dance, and other activities that a teacher thinks would be appropriate to do as a group. See Figure 4.7.

- **Seating arrangement.**   This depends entirely on the activity that takes place in the area. Some teachers have a permanent large-group area in their rooms. Some teachers move a table or two to make room for a large-group activity.
- **Materials for the center.**   The large-group area serves many purposes. Therefore, specific materials are not stored in the large-group area but are brought there by the teacher. Mrs. Woodward, the preschool teacher (see Figure 4.8), has brought items for an obstacle course to the large-group area.

Many teachers do store items in the large-group area that help them manage the space well. For example, individual pieces of carpeting can be arranged in seating patterns and indicate to children where they are to sit before group begins. Some teachers keep items in the large-group area that are used in transitions out of the large group (picture cue cards or printed names, for example, or the puppet that introduces the activity for the day).

Large-group area
A space in which a whole class can gather for a variety of learning activities

FIGURE 4.7   Early childhood classrooms have a large-group area where everyone can gather at one time

FIGURE 4.8   Large-group area in a preschool classroom

Private space

Place of refuge and relaxation, large enough for only one or at most two children; must be easily monitored by the teacher

Private space   A **private space** is a small, partially enclosed space with room for only one or two children. A teacher would be able to monitor and supervise this area easily, but it should be visually isolated from other children (Marion, 2007). There are no chairs, tables, or special materials in the private area. Figure 4.9 shows the private space for Mrs. Woodward's classroom. A teacher would follow the same principles for developing a private space for a kindergarten or primary classroom.

We provide a private space because healthy systems acknowledge the right to privacy and the right to choose or limit contact with others. Teachers in appropriately designed classrooms pay attention to the needs of both the entire class and of individuals. Like adults, children need breaks from large groups. Well-designed private spaces can help us make a special effort to teach children how to take these breaks and to pace their interactions.

Manage this part of your classroom well by clearly defining how everyone—teachers and children—may use the private space. Make sure that every adult who works in your room knows that the private space is a place of refuge and relaxation. Never use the private area as a punishment area. Make sure each child knows that she can retreat to this spot to be alone and will not be disturbed. Teach each child the strategies for politely telling another person that he does not wish to be disturbed when in the private area. Be sure to set limits about the number of children who may use the private space.

| FIGURE 4.9 | Private space in a preschool classroom |

Develop Enough Activity Areas

The principles of designing early childhood classrooms call for children to have choices; to move about the classroom; and to be actively involved with materials, other children, and adults. Thus, a classroom needs enough activity areas so that children do indeed have choices, are actively involved, and can easily move from one activity to another.

Age and number of children   Figure 4.10 shows how many of each type of space is useful. Consider two factors, the age and number of children when making decisions about the number of centers. Kantrowitz and Evans (2004) found that some classrooms do not provide enough centers for the number of children in a classroom, which led to discipline problems. Having enough centers, then, is important in helping children choose well and stay focused. Provide one-third more spaces than there are children so children can change activities without having to wait.

General formula   The general formula is $x = n + (n \div 3)$ where x = number of spaces needed and n = number of children in a classroom. A kindergarten classroom for 21 5-year-olds would need 28 workspaces: $x = 21 + (21 \div 3) = 21 + 7 = 28$ spaces, or one-third more spaces than children. This means that any child who completes a project in one area can move to another activity because there are always more workspaces in the classroom than there are children.

| FIGURE 4.10 | Number of areas needed based on ages and numbers of children in class |

Area	Ages of Children	Number of Children in Class		
		Up to 9	10–14	15–24
Private area	3–4	1	1	1
	5–6	1	1	1 or 2
	7–9	1	1	1 or 1
Small-group area	3–4	1	3	4 or 5
	5–6	2	3	4 or 5
	7–9	2	3	5
Large-group area	3–4	1	1	1
	5–6	1	1	1
	7–9	1	1	1

EXAMPLE   Mr. Sanchez's mixed-age class has 18 children. This classroom has six learning centers based on the needs of his children—reading, social studies, math, art, science, and writing. Applying the formula here, we have $x = 18 + (18 \div 3) = (18 + 6) = 24$ spaces.

It is possible to create a classroom that is too cluttered, so it is wise to avoid filling your classroom with so many activity areas that children are overstimulated, frustrated, and unable to move around easily.

Arrange Activity Areas Logically

Another important step in designing a supportive physical environment is to arrange activity areas logically. Do this by thinking about the type of work or play in each center, by separating centers from each other, and by regulating the flow of traffic in the classroom.

Type of work and play in each center   Design centers that are both stimulating and peaceful. Supportive classrooms contain quiet, purposeful, enthusiastic, and even vigorous interaction, but they are not excessively noisy.

- **"Quiet" learning centers.** Some learning and play centers lend themselves to relatively quiet, less vigorous work or play. Children tend to sit or stand and work quietly on projects or activities in these centers even if they work with several other children. This does not mean that children are silent in these centers. On the contrary, children in supportive classrooms talk quite a bit as they work together on math, at the computer, or on puzzles. The overall tone of these quiet centers is simply more subdued. The quiet centers typically include:

    private space

    library/writing centers (reading, writing, listening)

    science

    math

> puzzles and other small-table toys
>
> computer center

- **"Less quiet" learning centers.** Other learning and play centers lend themselves to somewhat noisier, more vigorous work or play. Children seem to move around more in certain centers because the nature of the work or play encourages a lot of movement. As they move around, children engaged in these centers tend to talk to each other. Activity in these centers is less subdued than in the quieter centers, but it is still not excessively noisy. This movement and talk is what makes certain centers into less quiet learning centers, and the activities there typically include:

> dramatic play
>
> blocks
>
> physical education
>
> music
>
> arts
>
> water or sand table
>
> play and/or work in a large-group area

Logically arrange areas so that quieter areas are placed near other quiet areas and so that they are well separated from areas encouraging active play.

EXAMPLE   Figure 4.2 shows how Mrs. Woodward appropriately placed the dramatic play area near the block area; both are high-activity areas, and dramatic play flows so easily from one to the other. She wisely placed the language arts center close to the puzzles/manipulatives toy center, with both of these centers well separated from the noisier areas.

She also developed and clearly stated limits on noise level. Children in her class work and play together without disrupting other people, and she emphasizes everyone's right to a quiet place in which to work. The children are learning that one of their basic classroom values is respect for the rights of others, including the classroom animals.

Create physical boundaries for areas   Supportive systems have appropriate boundaries. Here, you will learn why they are necessary and how to create good **physical boundaries for activity areas**. Creating proper physical limits for activity areas is not trivial. It is both age and individually appropriate. Creating good boundaries among areas is age appropriate because all children need to know how to function in the physical environment, and good boundaries give them useful cues. Creating good boundaries—with shelving and partitions of various types—is individually appropriate because some children especially need help understanding limits and boundaries.

Physical boundary for activity areas
Partition separating one activity area from another

Creating good boundaries may well be one of the most appropriate things you do for children from chaotic, disorganized homes. People in unhealthy systems tend to violate the psychological and physical boundaries of others. One of the clearest marks of a healthy system, however, including a developmentally appropriate classroom, is the idea of clear and distinct boundaries. These boundaries include psychological boundaries, such as keeping people safe through rules about no hitting and no name calling, and the physical boundaries within the classroom itself.

We teach the concept of boundaries by clearly separating one area from another. Children tend to be more cooperative and far less disruptive when they understand where one area ends and the next begins. Clear physical boundaries, along with well-organized materials, also help children know where each piece of equipment belongs and encourage them to put things in their proper areas. Figure 4.11 shows one idea for practical and efficient boundaries.

Create good traffic patterns in a classroom   Classrooms that have well-arranged activity areas and good physical boundaries give children cues about the traffic pattern in the room. The **traffic pattern** refers to the flow of movement in an early childhood classroom. Children should be able to move about the room through logical traffic patterns. Create good traffic patterns with open pathways that clearly lead to areas and that make it easy for children to move between areas (Colbert, 1997).

Traffic pattern
Flow of movement in an early childhood classroom

- Pathways should be wide enough for wheelchairs.
- Pathways should be long enough to make moving among areas easy.
- Pathways should not be so long that they encourage running—avoid zoom areas.
- Regulate traffic by making only one entrance to a center.
- Make sure that the circuit around the room allows children to stop off at each center if they wish.

FIGURE 4.11 **One example of how to create boundaries between activity areas**

Please Touch!

Burlap

Silk

Corrugated Cardboard

Sandpaper

Create Attractive, Sensory-Rich Activity Areas

Children need a clean, attractive, and sensory-rich space (Torelli & Durrett, no date). The design of the room does not have to be extravagant, and furnishings need not be expensive. However, a children's classroom should be aesthetically pleasing and serene. One good way to create such an environment is to pay attention to seemingly commonsense matters such as lighting and the sensory environment. Several specific and practical suggestions are discussed in the following subsections.

Strive for a sensory-rich but clean and uncluttered classroom   Many early childhood teachers do a good job of adding interesting items to the classroom, but it is also important to weed out items that have served their purpose. A cluttered, disorderly, or dirty room is unpleasant and distracting. Eliminating clutter helps children focus on new material because the number of stimuli to which they must attend is decreased (Alexander, 1996; Marion, 2007).

> **EXAMPLE**   For a project on butterflies, Mrs. Woodward added a book on butterflies, two large color photographs, and several real butterfly models to the science area. So she was puzzled by the children's lack of interest. A close look at the discovery area showed that it was cluttered with old cups of seeds, the rock collection, a magnet, and a magnifying glass. The pictures had been pinned to a somewhat cluttered bulletin board, the butterflies dwarfed by a large, green plant.

Mrs. Woodward cleared the table and the bulletin board, and then set out only "butterfly" things—the collection of butterflies, books, and the magnifying glass. She arranged the pictures of butterflies attractively on the bulletin board so that they were the central focus. She also placed a picture of butterflies on the door of the classroom with a note to parents to "join us in learning about butterflies."

Modify the lighting   Skillful use of lighting is an indirect method of guidance. Many schools are equipped with bright lights, and although it is desirable to have adequate lighting, it is boring, stressful, and overly stimulating to be in harsh bright light for an extended period. Classrooms are often equipped with only one or two light switches, giving adults only two options: all the harsh lights on or all off. Installing dimmer switches is quite inexpensive and enables teachers to control the intensity of lighting in different sections of the room.

Modify ceiling height or floor level   Create safe, cocoonlike spaces that define the areas in a classroom. Many schools, for example, build a safe, inexpensive platform (see Figure 4.12) to give some dimension to the room. Children use platforms for a variety of activities.

Consider defining an activity area by draping strips of cloth across and between dowels hung from the ceiling. This strategy softens an area and room and actually makes the ceiling appear to be lower, especially useful when children need a private, quiet, partially enclosed activity area. This idea can be applied to almost any area in the room.

FIGURE 4.12 Many schools place platforms in classrooms to give dimension to the room

EXAMPLE Mrs. Woodward, in her first year at her school, was disappointed that the children did not seem to enjoy the reading area. She assessed the area. She drew a floor plan of the reading area and decided that she needed to make some changes:

- Use bookshelves to better separate the reading area from other areas.
- Add a fluffy carpet.
- Place large pillows against a wall.
- Suspend cloth across two rods hanging from the ceiling.
- Occasionally, but not always, play soft classical music in the area.

The children loved their new area and reading activity soared. They even made special requests for specific music while they read.

Modify the sensory environment Well-designed classrooms are pleasant and attractive because the teacher has created visual, auditory, olfactory, and textural interest.

- **Create visual interest.** Enhance the aesthetic appeal of your early childhood classroom by keeping it clean and tidy. Make a real effort to keep clutter to a minimum. Judiciously add well-chosen, inexpensive items such as paintings; posters; safe, green plants; photographs of the children; cloth hangings; and artwork. Do not feel compelled to fill every square inch of wall space with these things, though. Leave some blank space where children get relief from stimulation.
- **Create auditory interest.** We have already discussed the importance of a calm and peaceful environment where children are free to move and to talk but not to make excessively loud noise. It is much easier to use sound to create a pleasant environment in such a calm environment. How pleasant and relaxing it is for children to be able to hear their favorite composer's music when they arrive at school. Other sounds help create this kind of atmosphere if the children are tuned in to the sounds and are not distracted by unnecessary noise. Here are some ideas:

New musical instruments.

The gerbil gnawing a box, scratching around in his bedding, running in his wheel.

A tinkling mobile.

The quiet hum of the computer.

- **Create olfactory interest.** Exquisite fragrances, such as lilac shrubs in bloom, the garden after a rainfall, homemade bread, and fresh oranges often call forth joyful memories. Other odors trigger unpleasant memories (the disinfectant odor of a hospital, the skunk odor reminding us that one of the critters sprayed the dog). Here are some easy ways to make a classroom pleasant through fragrance. First, eliminate unpleasant odors by maintaining cleanliness. Add pleasant aromas from safe sources:

  Bake bread, muffins, or cookies.

  Vary ingredients in baking, urging children to identify scents.

  Add food-grade extracts such as peppermint or orange to play dough.

  Place inexpensive scented soap in the bathroom on occasion. Introduce this at group time with reminders about hand-washing procedures.

  Occasionally place safe (real) flowers at the snack table or in the library (in a plastic vase).

  Place safe, fragrance-filled plants in the room or yard.

- **Create textural interest.**

  If appropriate, install carpet on selected sections of the floor. Carpet on certain sections of the wall is also a nice touch.

  Cover bulletin boards with cork or burlap.

  Hang a children-created large collage of cloth scraps.

  Create a touch wall with an expanse of corrugated paper and other materials. See Figure 4.11 for an example.

  Clear one wall of all signs and pictures and put up a fabric wall hanging.

  Make it a custom in your classroom to hang a differently textured fabric in a place where children are likely to see and want to touch it, for example, near lockers or cubbies. You will have created a way to start conversations with children who touch the fabric; you can ask, "How did the new fabric feel when you touched it? Did it feel the same as the strip of burlap we had up last week? How did it feel compared to the silk?"

:: ADDITIONAL CONSIDERATIONS IN A CLASSROOM FOR 3- TO 8-YEAR-OLDS

Curriculum

An appropriate curriculum for young children builds on how young children think and learn (Copple & Bredekamp, 2009). Hart, Burts, and Charlesworth (1997), in a chapter on integrated, developmentally appropriate curriculum, express concern about the emphasis on instruction for young children that is merely a copy of the type of formal instruction used in upper elementary grades. Several years ago,

Charlesworth (1985) warned that this type of skill-based instruction fails to meet the developmental needs of young children.

Children, then, are one source of appropriate curriculum. Effective teachers observe and assess children's needs, interests, and abilities. Then they develop activities that support children's development and learning (Helm & Katz, 2001; Marion, 2004; Williams, 1994). They *use* their knowledge about development and theory. They know that children learn in an active, not a passive, way. They believe that young children construct or build knowledge as they interact with people and things (Berk & Winsler, 1995; Piaget, 1952; Vygotsky, 1978).

Effective teachers offer options to children. They encourage children to participate in ways that best suit each child's learning style. They integrate the curriculum rather than chipping it into separate content areas such as math, science, and language arts. Teachers provide concrete experiences that actively involve children. They value play as an integral part of the curriculum as well as outside the classroom (Hart et al., 1997; National Association for the Education of Young Children, 2001).

EXAMPLE   Mrs. Woodward focuses on literacy in her integrated preschool curriculum. She wants her children to know that reading and writing, as well as listening and speaking, are useful. Her encouragement of literacy pervades the curriculum and is evident in every part of the room. Here are just a few examples:

- Large sheets of paper and pencils for writing and dictating stories about play are placed in block and dramatic play areas.
- Several types of paper, markers, and pencils are always available for drawing, writing, copying, inventing, and spelling.
- Charts, such as the arrival chart with the printed name of each child, are displayed and changed when appropriate. Next to the printed name is a space for a child to copy his or her name with a dry-erase marker. Parents sometimes help.
- Menus for each day's food (snack and lunch) are displayed near cubbies. Parents and children read the menus.
- Large recipe cards for one or two items are occasionally displayed during snack or lunch. Children and teachers read the recipes, and then recall the steps in preparing the food when they eat.
- A chart with pictures of all the new vegetables and fruits that the class has tried is displayed. Words describing each item are next to the picture, for example, for the raw carrot—*crunchy, orange, sweet, hard*, but for the cooked carrot—*soft, smooth, orange, sweet.*
- An "emotions" chart, with a drawing of a happy face on one side of the chart, is displayed. Children and teacher generate several synonyms for *happy* and list them on the other side of the chart.
- Tickets are issued to watch a video. Tickets display the name of the video.

Activities

Learning activities should support children as they search for answers to their questions. Developmentally appropriate activities help children investigate topics that interest them. Teachers assist children in identifying topics of interest and then develop activities that will help children investigate their topic. Teachers and children go through two phases in deciding on activities that will be part of the investigation (Helm & Katz, 2001).

Phase one of projects and investigations   The first step in developing a project is usually a common experience. This shared experience triggers interest in a topic and then becomes a project. Teachers lead children in asking questions about the event; that is, the children generate questions about "What we want to know." The teacher creates a web of the questions (Helm & Katz, 2001).

EXAMPLES   A kindergarten class generated questions about a recycling truck that they had seen when they were on the playground. Their teacher created a web of questions about the truck, as shown in Figure 4.13a.

Mrs. Woodward's preschool class generated questions about colors after the shared experience of the trip to the paint store (in the chapter-opening vignette). Mrs. Woodward created a web of their questions. See Figure 4.13b.

Phase two of projects and investigations   This step involves deciding on activities that help children answer their questions. The investigation of the topic with different activities spans several days (Helm & Katz, 2001).

EXAMPLE   The kindergarten teacher arranged the following activities to help the children answer some of their questions about the recycling truck:

■ **Day 1.** Visit from recycling truck and driver. Children observed, and asked questions of the driver. Back in the classroom, they dictated their observations to the teacher, who listed the observations on a chart.

FIGURE 4.13a   Web of questions about the recycling truck that the kindergartners created and the teacher recorded

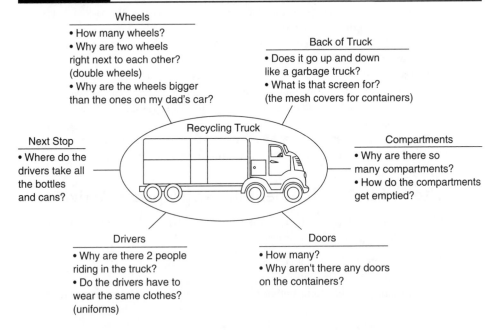

Wheels
• How many wheels?
• Why are two wheels right next to each other? (double wheels)
• Why are the wheels bigger than the ones on my dad's car?

Back of Truck
• Does it go up and down like a garbage truck?
• What is that screen for? (the mesh covers for containers)

Next Stop
• Where do the drivers take all the bottles and cans?

Recycling Truck

Compartments
• Why are there so many compartments?
• How do the compartments get emptied?

Drivers
• Why are there 2 people riding in the truck?
• Do the drivers have to wear the same clothes? (uniforms)

Doors
• How many?
• Why aren't there any doors on the containers?

FIGURE 4.13b Mrs. Woodward used the children's questions to create this web of questions about colors

Light and dark colors
- My mom said that my shirt is dark blue. What does that mean?
- Is the shed's paint color dark blue or light blue?

Eyes and hair
- Ralph's hair is black and my hair is black!
- Paul has green eyes, just like Harry Potter's.
- My dog has one blue eye and one brown eye. Why?

Effect of heat and light
- My dad cooked the green beans too long last night and he said the color turned "yucky." What does that mean?
- The church windows (stained glass) look pretty when the sun is shining.

Mixing
- How do you make brown?
- What would happen if we mixed a drop of color from every part of a rainbow into a tray of white paint?

Names of colors
- How do you say "red" in Spanish?
- Can a color have two names?
- If I add yellow to blue, does the name change?

- **Day 2.** Children began constructing their own recycling truck from cardboard and other safe recycled items. They put together a driver's uniform from clothing in the dramatic play area, and they printed a sign for their truck. The teacher showed a film about recycling trucks.
- **Day 3.** Construction of the recycling truck continued. One of the fathers brought his heavy-duty pickup truck to school to show the double wheels. Children asked questions about double wheels. They doubled the wheels on the back of their mock-up of the recycling truck.
- **Day 4.** Children collected classroom items for recycling, placing them in the recycling bins of their truck. They made up a recycling song to the tune of "Bingo."
- **Day 5.** The children dictated a letter to parents about their project in progress. The teacher documented the project with photos, which she placed on a photo board in the classroom. The teacher also printed and duplicated the children's letter and sent it home with each child.
- **Day 6.** The children invited the principal to see their truck and the photo display. They talked to him about their project, teaching him the recycling song.

Criteria for Developmentally Appropriate Activities

Early childhood activities, whatever the project and whatever the questions investigated, are developmentally appropriate when:

- There are many, but not an excessive number, of age-appropriate activities that occur throughout the day.
- Children know that some activities will occur at the same time each day.

- Children are actively involved and engage in concrete experiences.
- Children choose their own activities from among the large number of activities set up by the teacher.
- Children have options about when and how to complete activities.

Analyze the chapter-opening vignette using these criteria.

Materials: Choosing and Managing

Teachers in supportive environments provide appropriate materials with which children work and play. Appropriate materials refer to a moderately rich assortment of exploratory and safe items that encourage competent, independent behavior in children. These materials reflect the needs, interests, and abilities of the children. Figure 4.14 is a rating scale for managing classroom materials. Figure 4.15 presents ways to adapt curriculum and instruction for inclusive classrooms.

| FIGURE 4.14 | Rating scale: managing classroom materials |

Use this rating scale to evaluate classroom management of materials and equipment in this early childhood classroom. Rate each item using the scale. "1" indicates the lowest rating you can give. "5" is the highest rating you can give. A space is provided for comments.

	Lowest rating				Highest rating
The teacher has taken leadership in *gathering materials*.	1	2	3	4	5
All materials needed for an activity are there.	1	2	3	4	5
Materials appear to have been gathered well in advance of the activity.	1	2	3	4	5
Equipment is correctly sized for children using it.	1	2	3	4	5
Equipment works well.	1	2	3	4	5
Children will be able to use the materials without a lot of adult help.	1	2	3	4	5
Equipment is clean.	1	2	3	4	5
Materials are organized logically.	1	2	3	4	5
Items within centers are stored so that they are easy for children to get to and then to put away.	1	2	3	4	5
If children are expected to clean up after any activity, this teacher appears to have thought it through and has provided necessary items.	1	2	3	4	5
If children are expected to set up an activity, necessary materials are available.	1	2	3	4	5
Materials not intended for children's use are stored out of their reach.	1	2	3	4	5

Comments and suggestions:

FIGURE 4.15   **Ways to adapt curriculum and instruction for early childhood inclusive classrooms**

✓ **Environment:** Adapt materials for individual needs. Adapt the setup of the room or seating. Example: Siri has trouble grasping and then releasing things. You provide a variety of items in the small manipulatives area to allow for this difference.

✓ **Presenting Information:** Adapt the way that you present information and materials, including your language. Demonstrate instructions or simplify language.
Example: You have observed that several children, and not just those with special needs, have difficulty making transitions. You decide to use picture cues during transitions. When moving from large group to snack, you hold up a picture cue card, an actual photograph of snack time in your class while you **say** the words about going to snack.

✓ **Difficulty:** Adapt how a child might approach an activity.
Example: Laurie has difficulty cutting, so you encourage her to tear paper for her collage. You write the adaptation into the lesson plan.

✓ **Level of Support:** Observe to assess how much help a child needs and then vary the amount of help given.
Example: Luke does not need hand-over-hand assistance for playing outside but does seem to need it for brushing his teeth.

✓ **Alternative Goals:** Adapt goals and outcomes for children within the same lesson plan or learning activity.
Example: Suppose that your goal for a story is for children to see how to use words to express angry feelings. You have adapted goals for Jafar. He needs to understand the content of the story but you have adapted your guidance plan for him during the lesson so that he also learns how to listen without interrupting others when they are talking.

✓ **Participation:** Adapt activities for different levels of participation by children.
Example: Most of your children sit upright and respond to questions during a story or group lesson. You have noticed, however, that Aaron seems less distracted if he just leans against the wall and listens. You have adapted your guidance plan for Jafar, too. He also seems much more relaxed and attentive if he lies down and listens to a story. Yesterday, you noticed that he lay on his side, his head on one hand. For the first time ever, he just listened without interrupting others when they talked.

✓ **Time:** Adapt the amount of time for children to complete an activity or task. You can determine who might need more time for a variety of activities through careful observation.
Example: You have observed that Joshua needs a little more time, but not much more, to put away blocks. He uses the extra time to find the outline of the blocks on the shelves and then does a great job of putting away the blocks.

✓ **Child's Response:** This is really for the teacher. Adapt how much you expect children to accomplish. Be flexible in terms of how you expect a child to respond.
Example: You have noticed that Siri seems to like art and usually needs two sessions to complete art activities. For example, today she did part of a collage and you told her that you would put the collage materials out for her again in the afternoon. You have also noticed that Aaron will sometimes answer you by looking at something if you ask him to make a choice. Today you asked if he wanted grape or orange juice and he looked at the grape juice.

Source: Adapted from *Adapting Curriculum and Instruction in Inclusive Early Childhood Classrooms*, by A. F. Cross and S. D. Dixon, 1997, Bloomington, IN: Institute for the Study of Developmental Disabilities. Adapted by permission.

∷ DESIGNING SPACES FOR INFANTS AND TODDLERS

Infant/toddler teachers believe that the interpersonal and physical environments affect infants and toddlers.

Effect of Well-Designed Environments on Infant/Toddler Cognition

Effective teachers know that even the youngest infants are active information processers who need supportive and loving environments for optimal development. Consider the following ways in which an appropriate development environment enhances infant and toddler development.

Problem solving in infants and toddlers   Children's cognitive development is enhanced when they actively explore their surroundings. We want infants and toddlers to begin to be able to solve problems based on their safe explorations. Therefore, an infant or toddler's cognitive development is affected by how well teachers design and then manage the physical environment. For example, children in their second and third years have better problem-solving skills and engage in more exploratory behavior when teachers and parents provide safe objects for them to explore. An example is a set of soft cloth blocks.

Spatial relations and perspective taking   These skills have their roots in infancy and continue to develop over a period of years. Our goal is to create the type of environment in which the youngest children have a good chance of developing excellent spatial relations. We also want to help them begin to understand that they are separate from other people and that they can have an effect on their environment. Young children develop better spatial relations and perspective taking in well-organized and peaceful environments rather than in chaotic, stressful environments.

Learning to plan strategies   Play materials affect a very young child's ability to devise new ways of doing things and to plan effective strategies. Children are better able to figure out how to do things and to plan effective strategies when teachers provide play materials appropriate to their developmental needs, interests, and abilities.

Implications for teachers   The physical environment in an infant or toddler classroom should enhance the children's development. To do this, a teacher can do the following:

- Provide objects that are responsive to an infant's actions, such as busy boards, nesting blocks, and shape sorters.
- Avoid noise, confusion, and overcrowding in environments for infants and toddlers.
- Organize the physical environment well. Develop activity areas to meet the specific developmental needs of infants and toddlers.
- Provide age-appropriate play materials for infants and toddlers.
- Introduce certain forms of environmental stimulation at specific ages (see Figure 4.16).

FIGURE 4.16   Timing environmental stimulation for infants and toddlers

Birth to 6 Months	• Provide verbal stimulation • Provide a variety of things for baby to look at • Provide lots of physical contact. Some babies • Avoid overcrowding, excessive noise, and confusion • Pay attention to and respond to baby's social signals
6 to 12 Months (continue with above, emphasize the following)	• Plan a variety of appropriate activities • Ensure primary caregiver interaction with the infant • Give lots of 'floor time' • Provide a variety of safe objects • Place objects within reach and that 'respons' to baby's actions
12 to 24 Months (emphasize the following)	• Encourage exploration • Set reasonable limits for child's safety but encourage expploration • Ensure a predicable, flexible physical environment, and time schedule
24 to 36 Months (emphasize the following)	• Respond to the toddler's verbal signals • Expand and elaborate on the toddlers verbalizations

myeducationlab

Go to the Building
Teaching Skills and
Dispositions section of
Topic 6: Physical
Environment in the
MyEducationLab for your
course and complete the
activity entitled *Design a
Developmentally
Appropriate Early Childhood
Classroom*. Note how a
well-designed classroom
indirectly guides children.

myeducationlab

To check your
comprehension on the
content covered in
Chapter 4, go to the Book
Specific Resources in the
MyEducationLab for your
course, select your text,
and complete the Study
Plan. Here you will be able
to take a chapter quiz,
receive feedback on your
answers, and then access
review, practice, and
enrichment activities to
enhance your
understanding of chapter
content.

Physical Environments for Infants and Toddlers

Infants and toddlers are usually in Piaget's first stage of cognitive development, the sensorimotor stage. They are in the early stages of Erikson's and Maslow's respective frameworks and need safe and secure relationships. They take in information and act on their world through sensory and motor schemes. Very young children learn through experimentation and repetition, and teachers encourage learning by providing a safe and stimulating physical environment and **an emotionally supportive** caregiving environment.

The curriculum for the youngest children centers on routines. Sensitive teachers take advantage of routine situations such as eating, bathing, diapering, and dressing to help very young children feel safe and learn at the same time.

Well-organized infant and toddler rooms contain activity areas but are not just scaled-down versions of classrooms for children age 3 to 8 years old. Infants and toddlers should be able to practice sensorimotor activities in a well-designed space (Program for Infant/Toddler Care [PITC], 2007; Torelli & Durrett, 1996). A well-designed infant and toddler room is clean and has spacious bathing and dressing areas. It encourages crawling, scooting, and walking in safe, open areas; pushing, pulling, rolling, emptying, and filling safe, clean toys; and climbing on safe structures. An appropriate infant or toddler room encourages children to gaze at objects at their level and to do messy, active things such as finger painting or creating the swish-swish of a water table. Figure 4.16 suggests appropriate activity areas based on the infant or toddler's level of development. Also visit the web sites at the end of the chapter. The PITC site presents an excellent overview of one center's remodeling of their center.

ANALYZE A VIGNETTE

Refer to the chapter-opening vignette. Then answer these questions.

1. Mrs. Woodward has developed activities based on principles of developmentally appropriate practice. Find examples of how her preschool classroom meets the criteria for developmentally appropriate activities.
2. Explain how there is a wide, but not overwhelming, variety of age-appropriate activities that occur throughout the day.
3. Give examples of how Mrs. Woodward schedules activities so that they occur at the same time each day.
4. How does she emphasize concrete activities that actively involve the children?
5. Explain how she encourages children to choose their own activities.
6. How do the children have options about when and how to complete activities?

SUMMARY

Major theories of child development and early childhood education guide a teacher's practice in guiding children. We use theories from the following categories of perspectives:

- Theories that emphasize systems in which children's behavior develops.
- Theories emphasizing how children construct knowledge and skills about getting along with others.
- Theories focusing on children's psychological and emotional development.

Early childhood theories can guide teachers in designing classrooms that put theory into practice and that have clear benefits for children. Such classrooms convey or encourage:

- A sense of order
- Social interaction
- Making choices
- Active learning

Guidelines for designing supportive physical environments for young children include the following:

- Organize the classroom into activity areas and develop enough of them.
- Arrange activity areas logically.
- Create attractive and sensory-rich areas.
- Use a variety of indirect strategies to make it easier for children to work and play in the classroom.

Other indirect guidance includes the curriculum, activities, and materials in a classroom. Effective early childhood curriculum is integrated rather than segmented into separate curriculum areas. Effective learning activities indirectly guide children because of the following:

- How the activities are organized
- The number of activities
- Children's active involvement
- The choices offered to children

Physical environments for infants and toddlers are not just scaled-down versions of classrooms for older children. The curriculum for infants should be relationship-based centered on routines.

QUESTIONS FOR REFLECTION

1. Suppose that you are giving a tour of your preschool classroom for a parent who is thinking about enrolling his child in the school. You point out each small-group learning center, the individual learning centers, the large-group area, and the private space. Explain why you have organized the classroom into activity areas and tell the parent about what goes on in each area. The parent asks you why the block area is adjacent to the dramatic play area and why the books are next to the puzzle and writing areas. What would you say?

2. Name four of the most important things to remember about managing materials in an early childhood classroom. Why do these four seem most important to you?

3. Name the two main ways, in your view, that a classroom for infants and toddlers differs from classrooms for older early childhood children.

APPLY YOUR KNOWLEDGE

Observation: Recognizing Appropriate Practice in an Early Childhood Classroom

What you will be doing: Observing and suggesting change

Observing. Request permission to visit an early childhood classroom for preschool, kindergarten, or primary children. As a guest in the classroom, your goal is not to criticize; it is to look at how the teacher has designed activity areas, how the areas are bounded, the traffic patterns in the classroom, and the management of materials in the classroom.

Suggesting change. Practice professionalism by making suggestions for change after you leave the classroom. Keep information on the classroom confidential. If you share information in one of your courses, remove information that could identify the teacher, class, and school from your work. Present any suggestions in a positive way so that you are merely suggesting ideas that would make a good classroom even better.

1. Observing:

   Activity Areas

   Draw a simple floor plan of the classroom that you have observed. Include the toilet area for children, doors to the outside and to hallways, small-group learning centers, large-group area, private areas, and boundaries among areas. Label each area clearly. Use the floor plan in Figure 4.2 as a guide. Then analyze the activity areas in this room:

   - **Private area.** Explain whether and how the private space in this classroom meets the criteria for private spaces.
   - **Large-group area.** Explain whether and how the large-group area in this classroom meets the criteria for large-group areas.

   - **Small-group learning centers.** Number of centers: _____. Explain whether and how the small-group learning centers in this classroom meet criteria for this type of activity area.
   - **Individual learning center(s).** This classroom does (or does not) have individual learning centers. If it does, explain how these centers meet the criteria for this type of activity area.

   Boundaries

   Describe the boundaries used to separate activity areas from one another in this classroom.
   - Which areas were especially well bounded? Why?
   - Which areas would benefit from having more effective boundaries?

   Traffic Pattern

   Use a contrasting color and draw arrows from the entrance to the classroom and around the room to each center.
   - Describe the traffic pattern in this room using information on good traffic patterns from the chapter.
   - Suggest how to make the traffic pattern of this room even better.

   Management of Materials in the Classroom

   Use the rating scale (Figure 4.14) to evaluate classroom management of materials and equipment in this early childhood classroom. After you are done with the rating scale, name three ways in which this classroom's management of materials would most benefit from a change in how materials are managed.

2. Suggesting change: Working by yourself or with another student or even a small group, make suggestions for change based on your observation. Choose a method for presentation Here are a few suggestions:

   ■ Draw a second floor plan for this classroom. Clearly show your suggestions for change in your drawing. If, for example, you note that the classroom does not have quite enough small-group learning centers, decide where you would put them and draw them on your second floor plan. Indicate changes with a colored pencil or pen.

   ■ Make a table or chart listing the changes.

   ■ Prepare a PowerPoint set of slides on the changes needed.

   ■ Present your ideas verbally to your classmates.

KEY TERMS

Activity areas (89)
Indirect guidance (82)
Individual learning center (92)
Large-group area (93)

Physical boundary for activity areas (97)
Private space (94)
Small-group learning center (89)
Traffic pattern (98)

WEB SITES

Bank Street
http://www.bankstreet.edu

Home page for the Bank Street College of Education. The college has an old and respected children's program. Here is the site for the curriculum guide for the Children's School:
http://webstaging.bankstreet.edu/gems/sfc/CurriculumGuide.pdf

Program for Infant/Toddler Care
http://www.pitc.org/pub/pitc_docs/grossmont.html

State of California's concerted effort to attain high-quality care for infants and toddlers.

Grossmont College.
http://www.pitc.org/pub/pitc_docs/grossmont.html

Shows the infant and toddler center of Grossmont College, near San Diego. It is one of the sites designed to demonstrate a developmentally appropriate environment for infants and toddlers. This site shows before and after photos of the remodeling and its move to an even more developmentally appropriate physical environment for this age group.

Spaces for Children
http://www.spacesforchildren.com/

An architectural firm specializing in designing developmentally appropriate spaces for children's centers and schools sponsors this excellent site. You can view centers for infants and toddlers as well as schools for older early childhood children.

Positive Guidance and Discipline Strategies

Direct Guidance

"Above all, we shall not harm children. We shall not participate in practices that are disrespectful, degrading, dangerous, exploitative, intimidating, psychologically damaging, or physically harmful to children. This principle has precedence over all others in this code."

—(Code of Ethical Conduct and Statement of Commitment,
National Association of the Education of Young Children [NAEYC], 2006)

Chapter Contents

Guiding Questions

- How does your culture and what you believe about children affect how you will guide young children?
- What are the major *positive* guidance strategies and how can we explain why each is positive?
- How does using positive guidance strategies create a warm, supportive relationship between you and young children?

VIGNETTES

INFANTS AND TODDLERS: LOOKING AT BIRDS, SINGING ABOUT LUNCH, AND SPEAKING UP FOR BLUE

In the infant toddler room of a preschool, 11-month-old Paul grabbed his teacher's hair. Mr. Bjornrud, the teacher, removed Paul's hand, picked him up, and turning to the window, said, "O-o-o-h! Look at the birds, Paul." Paul brightened when he saw birds at the feeder.

Fifteen-month-old Jada scooted across the room toward the kitchen, and Mr. Bjornrud scooped her up and carried her back to a small table, singing, "Jada, Jada, lunchtime, lunchtime. Let's have lunch." "Lunch, lunch" returned Jada, in singsong style.

Alex, 2 years old, banged his hands on the playdough table while his teacher turned around to get the dough. The teacher placed his hands lightly on Alex's small hands, showed him two lumps of playdough, and said, "Listen carefully, Alex. Tell me whether you want white playdough or blue playdough." Alex piped up cheerfully, "I want BLUE!"

PRESCHOOL: JERRY DRIZZLES SAND

4-year-old Jerry stood at the sand table and scooped up a handful of sand. He looked at the sand and then at the floor. He then slowly drizzled sand onto the floor next to the sand table. He bent over to examine the little pile of sand on the floor. Mrs. Woodward watched for a few seconds and then decided that Jerry seemed to be doing an experiment with the sand. She said, "You're dropping the sand very carefully." Jerry replied, "Yeah. It goes straight down and doesn't fly around like snow." Mrs. Woodward said, "It's great to experiment but dangerous to put sand on the floor. I have an idea. Here is a towel to put on the floor to catch the sand. Then you can just lift the towel and put the sand right back in the sand table when you're done."

PRIMARY: HANNAH ASKS FOR A LUNCHBOX

Hannah, 6 years old, and Mom went to the store to buy a backpack for Hannah. They were in a hurry and had just enough time to pick out the backpack and still get to a doctor's appointment. Mom could afford to buy only a backpack. At the store, Hannah started the "Look-Mommy-I-want-that-WHY-can't-I-have-it" game. "Mom, can I get the lunchbox, too?" "No, Hannah. No lunchbox." "But Mom, I want the lunchbox. It's purple, just like my new backpack!" "Hannah, stop it. No lunchbox." "Why, Mom?"

:: INTRODUCTION

All of the adults in the vignettes faced typical interactions calling for guidance. The teachers have responded with positive guidance, and Hannah's mother has not fully responded. A chief part of your professional role lies in helping children acquire the values and beliefs of their culture and in becoming compassionate and competent people. You will do this by guiding children effectively.

Effective teachers use positive guidance strategies. This chapter's central focus is to describe and then to explain each of the major positive guidance strategies that teachers and parents have used successfully. We need to have access to many good strategies because we cannot rely on only one or two methods. You will learn about each strategy and read a number of real-life examples for each. Then you will have a chance to use and apply your knowledge to solve guidance dilemmas.

:: THE CONCEPT OF GUIDANCE AND DISCIPLINE
Culture, Socialization, Guidance, and Discipline

Culture
Beliefs, values, and traditions of a group of people; transmitted to the next generation through language, interactions, and relationships

How a society guides children reflects the values and beliefs of its **culture**. Culture refers to the beliefs or traditions of a group of people, which they give to the next generation through language, interactions, and relationships. Culture provides a setting or context in which the contacts with others, the relationships, take place. The members of the society gradually learn the culture's values and beliefs (Lewis & Ippen, 2007). Recall from Chapter 2 that different systems affect children's development, and children, families, schools, and communities reside in their culture, each system affected by the culture (Bronfenbrenner, 1979).

Each culture has values and beliefs about many things, including how it should take care of and socialize children. Suppose, for example, that one of a society's main values was the protection of children. Suppose that that democratic society also valued and believed in freedom of speech, which includes the freedom to make many types of movies, some of which contain violence. This free society would not ban unsavory movies. It would put its protection-of-children value into action in this case, however, by limiting access to such movies to older members of the society and by teaching parents how to minimize their children's exposure to the violence in movies.

Socialization refers to the process through which children acquire their culture and learn the values and habits that will help them adapt to it. Children acquire their culture's values through guidance and education, with adults and peers modeling and directly or indirectly teaching the culture's beliefs and values. Older members of the culture gradually lead a child to understand and accept culturally approved behaviors and values. A society believing that children should show respect for elders, for example, would transmit this belief to children in many ways, such as through words, interactions, books, and stories. Here is another example from Mr. Sanchez's primary classroom, this time with Caitlin, age 6½. The teacher helps Caitlin learn about the culture's value of treating other people with respect and *not* manipulating them.

Socialization
Process through which children learn the values and traditions of their culture

> **EXAMPLE**   Caitlin wanted a turn with the headphones and the story on tape, but it was near the end of choice time and Jerry had already sat down and started to put on the only remaining headset. Caitlin sidled up to him, a sad, sad look on her face. "I really wanted to listen to the story, Jerry—really, really," she whined as she started to gulp. Jerry looked startled by all of her emotion and handed over the headphone. As she put it on, she smirked to the others at the table, "Pretty good, huh?"

The next example illustrates the teacher's guidance, his deliberate and intentional teaching of the culture's belief in showing respect to others.

> **EXAMPLE**   Mr. Sanchez interrupted her, "Caitlin, put the headphone on the table and come with me." Away from the others, he said to her, "I watched you cry when you talked to Jerry and he let you take his place, which was a nice thing for him to do. However, I then saw you smile and make your eyes go like this (he demonstrated the smirk) and heard you say "Pretty good, huh?" That was a very mean thing to do to Jerry. We do *not* treat other people like that. It is not respectful and we've talked about showing respect to others. We have the headphones almost every day and you'll get a turn, but not today."

Teachers use guidance and discipline to teach the culture's beliefs directly, as Mr. Sanchez did with Caitlin, and indirectly. Their guidance is one part of the process of socialization. Many people are confused about the word **discipline**. It is derived from the Latin *disciplina*, "teaching, learning," and *discipulus*, "a pupil" (Merriam-Webster, no date). You can see, then, that *discipline* refers to guidance, *teaching, and learning*, not punishment. Discipline and punishment are *not* the same thing. In this book, discipline *always* refers to teaching.

Discipline
Teaching or learning

Guidance and Discipline Encounters

A **guidance or discipline encounter** is an interaction between an adult and child and often includes helping the child alter her behavior in some way. For example, the adult can help a child stop doing something harmful or destructive, treat someone with respect, or take responsibility for cleaning up. Mr. Sanchez stopped Caitlin from treating someone disrespectfully. Discipline encounters occur frequently in early childhood, even in classrooms and homes where adults are warm and supportive.

Guidance or discipline encounter
Interaction between a child and an adult in which the adult helps the child to alter his behavior

These interactions occur so that we can help children learn the culture's beliefs and values and to understand their obligation to respect the rights of others and to comply with legitimate authority (Baumrind, 1996). Each of the adults in the following examples faced typical discipline and guidance encounters.

EXAMPLES   Mrs. Woodward, the preschool teacher, watched as Calvin threw sand onto the tricycle path. She heard Nellie and Justine squabbling over the jar of paste at the collage table. She turned quickly when she heard someone banging on the hamster's house.

Several of the second graders in Mr. Sanchez's class left their backpacks on the floor instead of putting them in lockers.

The third-grade teacher noticed that two boys were bouncing their basketball on the wall right next to a classroom window.

Teachers deal with discipline encounters every day. Some include everyday concerns such as disturbing group time or not putting things away after using them. Others deal with serious issues, such as a child's endangering an animal or rude treatment of other children, as when Caitlin manipulated Jerry to get her turn with headphones. All, however, are discipline encounters.

Managing discipline encounters is a big part of a teacher or parent's role. First, adults have to help children learn to control their short-term behavior, for example, to stop banging on the hamster's house. Second, adults want to influence attitudes, values, and long-term behavior, which are part of the child's culture. They might want to help them understand, for example, about developing a humane attitude toward and kind, compassionate treatment of animals, a cultural value in many societies. They know, though, that they cannot fully determine attitudes or long-term behavior. They can only influence them.

EXAMPLE   Mrs. Woodward has faced several discipline encounters with Zeke over aggressive behavior. Because she is responsible for the safety of all the children in her class, she must help Zeke control his aggression for the short term—stop him from threatening or hurting other children and the classroom animals. She is also concerned about Zeke's long-term attitude and behavior. She knows that he will have an increasingly difficult time getting along with other children if he is aggressive, so she wants to help him willingly learn better social skills.

Guidance Strategies

Guidance strategies
The actions that we use in managing guidance encounters

Positive guidance strategies
Methods that rely on teaching

Guidance strategies refer to specific actions that adults use in managing guidance encounters. This chapter explains the major *positive* guidance strategies. Authoritative, trust-building adults use positive strategies, focusing on teaching and not on punishment. For example, they explain limits, redirect behavior, and teach behaviors that are more helpful. They give information that children need for learning and practicing behavior beneficial to the child.

EXAMPLE   Mr. Lee managed the discipline encounter with the boys who were bouncing the basketball on the wall near the window by reminding them firmly but kindly to throw the ball only at the basketball backboard. His action, restating a limit, was positive and gave information while maintaining a limit.

Other adults use negative strategies, focusing more on punishment. They might write the names of children on the board when children have violated a limit, which is public humiliation. Some adults isolate children, use physical punishment, are sarcastic, or even refuse to speak to a child (love withdrawal). Still other adults use strategies that are simply unhelpful, such as nattering and nagging. The idea of even thinking about negative or harsh discipline strategies repulses some early childhood teachers because they know that negative discipline harms children.

However, our goal is to guide all children effectively. All in this case means *all,* including children whose families use negative, harsh discipline. Our practices must be individually appropriate and we need to acknowledge that some children experience harsh discipline at home. This will help us understand their experience and then to use this information to develop appropriate guidance plans. All children benefit from positive discipline strategies, but children who have experienced harsh discipline at home need these strategies most desperately.

PEARSON
myeducationlab

Go to the Assignments and Activities section of Topic 4: Guidance Techniques/Strategies in the MyEducationLab for your course and complete the activity entitled *Characteristics of a Positive Guidance Strategy.* Note that positive guidance strategies are beneficial for *all* children.

:: POSITIVE GUIDANCE STRATEGIES: DESCRIPTION AND EXPLANATION

This chapter describes and explains the major positive guidance strategies (Figure 5.1). Learning how to use these strategies makes it possible for you to meet the needs of individual children. You will be able to choose the most effective strategy in a variety of discipline encounters. The appendix also lists these strategies and outlines how to use each.

Positive discipline strategies begin with adult behaviors: good limit setting, clearly communicating limits. They include teaching more appropriate behavior, giving cues for the new behavior, giving choices, and supporting children in their new behavior. Positive guidance and discipline also include changing something about a situation, and ignoring behavior when it is appropriate to do so.

Positive guidance and discipline continue when adults manage typical discipline encounters with positive, helpful strategies. These strategies include redirection, active listening, I-messages, conflict resolution, and recognizing and dealing with strong emotions.

Finally, helpful adults learn to recognize signs of stress, anxiety, and strong emotion. They try to prevent overstimulation, and they teach calming techniques. The core of positive discipline strategies, however, is the last section in this chapter. Helping children save face and preserve their dignity in discipline encounters is the most important and essential element in child guidance.

Use Limits Effectively

Adults spend a lot of time helping children understand boundaries or limits. Doing this effectively involves four factors:

Developing reasonable limits that focus on important things.
Stating limits effectively.

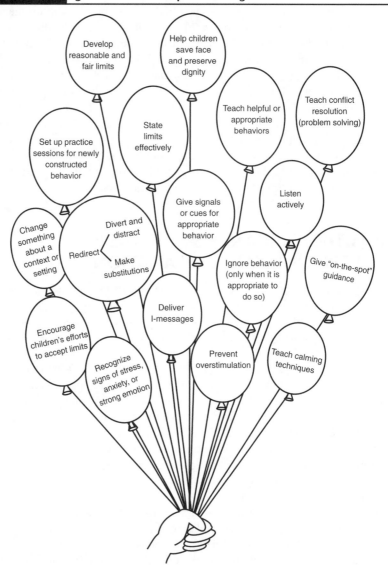

FIGURE 5.1 Authoritative adults know how to use many positive guidance and discipline strategies

Limits
Boundaries; in guiding children, refers to boundaries on children's behavior communicated by a teacher or parent

Helping children accept limits.

Communicating limits to others and reviewing limits periodically.

Develop reasonable limits that focus on important things Adults influence children by stating their expectations for desired behavior and helping children understand that there are boundaries, or **limits**, on behavior. Authoritative caregivers understand the importance of proper boundaries in relationships in general, and appropriate limits in an adult–child relationship in particular. They figure out and clearly communicate limits that will be most helpful in encouraging children to behave appropriately. They understand what a good limit is and what benefits appropriate limits have for children (Marion, Swim, & Jenner, 2000).

Authoritative adults work with children in developing some, but not all, limits. For example, Mr. Sanchez, the first-grade teacher, led a discussion about classroom limits at the beginning of the school year.

> **EXAMPLE**   Mr. Sanchez started by first stating, "The most important rule in our classroom is that we treat each other and our animals with respect," as he wrote on a large sheet of paper. Mr. Sanchez then described what that might mean and elicited the children's contributions; for example, "The gerbils get scared when they hear loud noises. What would be a good rule about noise around the gerbils?" He printed limits and posted them as a reminder.

Mr. Sanchez's class is much more likely to take ownership of limits because the children have helped to develop them. Highly responsive, authoritative adults set and maintain reasonable, fair, developmentally appropriate limits. Their limits focus on important, not trivial, factors, as explained in Figure 5.2.

State Limits Effectively   Authoritative caregivers have a clear, direct, and validating communication style. If a goal in guiding children is to help children, we can best help them understand necessary limits by stating these limits effectively.

Speak naturally, but speak slowly enough that the child hears everything you say; use concrete words and short sentences when stating limits   "Put your puzzle in this first slot of the puzzle rack." This limit tells a child exactly where the finished puzzle goes. It is more effective than saying, "Put it over there." Avoid using abstract words or phrases such as "in a little while," "be a good boy," or "knock it off."

Go to the Assignments and Activities section of Topic 4: Guidance Techniques/Strategies in the MyEducationLab for your course and complete the activity entitled *Identifying Positive Guidance Strategies*. Note that effective teachers need to know a variety of guidance strategies.

FIGURE 5.2	Classroom limits: focus on significant things	
Reasonable Limits	**How Limits Can Help**	**Example**
Help children learn self-control	Limits clearly communicate appropriate behavior and reasons for the behavior	"Scoot back to your spot on the carpet, Jack. Vinnie can't see if you sit in front of him."
Protect physical health	Limits specify procedures that keep disease from spreading	Limits about thorough hand washing or sanitizing toys, using tissues, proper toileting and diapering routines
Ensure physical safety	Limits govern safe use of equipment and physical space	"You can pour and dump sand in the sand box, but not on the tricycle path."
Ensure psychological safety	Good rules let everyone know that they are safe	Teacher to second-grade child, "You are angry, and that's ok, but I want you to tell Ryan that you are upset. Use words to tell him that you want your book back."
Help make the classroom a caring community	Focuses on respect for others and on humane treatment of animals	"Hold the kitten gently, like this." (teacher demonstrates). "Mitchell's name is on the list before your name. He goes first."

Good limits, such as telling the children, "Be quiet around the gerbils," teach them about respectful treatment of other people and animals.

Tell a child exactly what to do rather than what not to do, and be as positive as possible   It is more helpful to say, "Use this tissue to clean your nose" rather than "Don't pick your nose!" We do need to be clear about what children may not do, but it is most helpful to focus on what we want children to do.

Go to the Assignments and Activities section of Topic 4: Guidance Techniques/Strategies in the MyEducationLab for your course and complete the activity entitled *Was this Limit Communicated Clearly?* Note that it is essential to use this strategy in matters of health and safety.

Use suggestions whenever possible   Suggestions are persuasive statements. Suggestions describe an acceptable behavior to a child in an appealing way; they do not order a child to do anything. Children cooperate more frequently and willingly when adults use suggestions (Baumrind, 1996). Ty's teacher makes a suggestion in the next example.

EXAMPLE   Ty and Daniela's teacher said to the two 4-year-olds, "Hmm, two children and one rocking chair (adult-size chair). I wonder if you could figure out how two children could sit on that chair at the same time."

Use direct, self-responsible statements when you think it is necessary to make a reasonable request

Authoritative adults do occasionally have to state a very direct request, but their style is highly responsive.

EXAMPLE   Mrs. Woodward had given an appropriate warning about cleanup on the playground, but Jackie was still zipping around on his tricycle. "Whoa, there!" said the teacher as she signaled Jackie to stop. "I gave the signal for cleanup and now I want you to park the tricycle." Then she put her hand on the handlebars, pointed to the row of tricycles parked against the shed, turned Jackie in that direction, and said, "There's a spot for your tricycle right next to the yellow tricycle. Let's go and fit it in that space."

This limit is stated directly, firmly, and kindly. This authoritative teacher relies on persuasion, not force. She has acted self-responsibly, and the child is very likely to cooperate. Consider how a different, more authoritarian teacher would have stated the limit—by ordering, "Jackie, put that tricycle away now!" Ordering others around is a power-based way of speaking and it stirs up anger and resistance, not cooperation (Baumrind, 1996).

Give choices whenever possible   Children face so many important choices as they grow up. One of our goals, then, is to help children learn to make wise choices, a skill that we have to teach. A good way to start is by offering manageable choices to children.

> **EXAMPLE**   Mrs. Woodward first used a when-then statement to communicate clearly that the limit was that children had to wear paint aprons when painting, "When you put on your paint apron, then you may paint at the easel."

Then she gave Ralph a choice: "Do you want to wear the green or yellow paint apron?" Alternatively, she could have given a different choice: "Would you like to snap the Velcro pieces together yourself or do you want me to help you?"

Avoid giving a choice when the child really has no choice   For example, avoid saying "Do you want to wear a paint apron?" or "Do you want to go home now?" A logical response from a child to these questions is a yes or no answer because this is a closed type of question. It is unfair and confusing to give a child a choice when she really does not have one. You also set yourself up for an argument with a child who says no to such questions because then you must backtrack and tell her why she really has no choice.

Issue only a few suggestions at a time; avoid giving a chain of limits   It is difficult for children to keep a string of limits or suggestions in their minds. If a child cannot remember part of your string of limits, chances are good that he will not comply with all of the limits. Children comply more easily with limits when we state them in small chunks, small enough for children to remember. For example, "Use the clothespins to hang your painting." "Good, it will dry nicely. Now, wash the part of the table where you worked with this sponge." "Okay, nice and clean. Now, wash your hands and hang up your apron."

Avoid rushing   Allow time for the child to process information and complete a task before issuing another suggestion (Schaffer & Crook, 1980); repeat a limit if necessary, but do it effectively.

Suppose that a child ignores your request. Frustrating? Yes, but do not take it personally. Avoid getting angry and remember that your job is to help this child accept a simple limit. You will be most effective if you manage your emotions well, repeat the limit calmly and with goodwill, call the child's name again, pick up the item, and hand the item to the child. Repeat the request. Avoid simply

FIGURE 5.3	Guidelines for limit setting

Things to Remember about Stating Limits

- Involve children in developing some limits in a classroom or other setting.
- Tune in, help children focus on the task, and give good cues.
- Speak naturally but slowly enough that a child hears the limit clearly.
- Use concrete words and short sentences.
- Use natural, normal sentences, for example, "It's time to put away the teacups."
- Tell a child exactly what to do, for example, "Take small bites of your bread."
- Be as positive as possible and give choices when appropriate.
- Give short, clear, fair reasons for limits.
- Issue only one or two suggestions at a time.
- Give a child enough time to carry out the limit or to complete something else before she carries out the limit.
- Restate limits appropriately. Restate limits when it is necessary to do so.

Avoid These Behaviors When Stating Limits

- Avoid giving choices when children really do not have a choice, for example, "Do you want to go to the library?" when the whole class goes to the library.
- Avoid giving a chain of limits.
- Avoid using "cute" reasons; for example, avoid saying things such as, "I think that the teacups want to be put away now." This makes a teacher sound silly.
- Avoid telling children only what not to do, for example, "Don't take such big bites of your bread!"
- Avoid vague limits, for example, "I'm not sure that you should be doing that."
- Avoid stating arbitrary or trivial limits.
- Avoid arguing or playing the "why game" about limits.
- Avoid complex or excessive reasoning about limits.

restating the limit in a snappish, peeved way because your irritation will show and will likely bring out anger and stubbornness from the child; then you will have a full-blown argument on your hands. See Figure 5.3 for guidelines on setting limits.

Help Children Accept Limits   Authoritative caregivers and teachers help children willingly accept good limits. They do several things to set the stage so that children will accept legitimate boundaries on behavior. Here are some practical ways to get you started on helping children willingly accept limits.

Researchers demonstrated many years ago how important it is to set the stage so that children can accept a limit (Schaffer & Crook, 1980; Stayton, Hogan, & Ainsworth, 1971). Adults who effectively help children accept limits believe that children are naturally compliant (Haswell, Hock, & Wenar, 1981). Authoritative adults tune in to a situation, help children focus on the task at hand, and give good cues.

Tune in to the Context.   Effective teachers pay attention to the context or setting. They focus on what children are doing and what is going on in the setting before telling or asking a child to do something. Here are some specific and practical things to remember about tuning in to the context.

***Observe* what the child is doing before stating a limit**   Be responsive and take into account what a child is doing because her activity is important to her. If

Moua is putting together her favorite puzzle when the cleanup signal is first given, she will very likely try to finish her work before putting materials away.

Give **children a reasonable amount of time to complete their work**
Consider cleanup in a classroom. Before officially beginning to clean up, announce cleanup quietly to the whole group, to small groups, or to individuals, and then allow the children a bit of time to finish their work.

Decrease distance between you and a child. Avoid calling out limits from across the room. Decrease horizontal distance by walking toward a child. Decrease vertical distance by bending or stooping so that you can talk directly to a child.

Get a child's attention politely. Touch a child on the arm or say her name quietly. Using nonthreatening verbal or nonverbal cues and appropriate physical contact is essential with toddlers and is highly recommended with preschoolers, especially those who have not learned to live with reasonable boundaries and limits at home.

Help children focus on the task at hand and give cues. Direct a child's visual attention to a specific object or task. "Here's one of the puzzles that you worked on, Moua," you say as you show her the puzzle you are holding and then point to the puzzle table. This is orientation compliance; its purpose is to orient the child properly (direct her attention toward something) before stating a limit or making a request.

Have the child make contact with a specific object. For example, place a puzzle with which a child has worked in her hands and say, "Please hold the puzzle while we walk over to the puzzle table." This is contact compliance; its purpose is to help the child tune in to the task at hand before she is asked to do anything specific.

Make your specific request (ask for task compliance). A child is much more likely to comply with your request when you have properly oriented her. It is much easier for a child to accept the cleanup limit when she is at the puzzle table holding the puzzle rather than when she is sitting in another area listening to a story when you announce cleanup.

Give reasons for rules and limits. Children accept limits much more readily when they understand the rationale behind them (Baumrind, 1996). Three practical suggestions will help you use reasons well.

- Give short, simple, concrete reasons along with a limit An example is "Put the lid on the paint cups" (the limit). "It will keep the paint fresh" (the reason).
- Decide when to state the reasons. One choice is to state the rationale *before you give the limit*: "We need tables cleared of toys before we can have guided reading" (the reason). "Put each puzzle back in the rack" (the limit). Some children

tend to argue less about a rule if they hear the reason first and the limit second. Another choice is to state the reason *after you state the limit*. "I want you to put the puzzles away" (the limit). "Then the table is clear for snack" (the reason). A third option is to state the rationale *after the child complies with the limit*: "The puzzle table is clear! Now we can do guided reading there."

- Decide whether you need to repeat the rationale if you restate the limit. Repeating the rationale is a good idea when you want to emphasize the reason for the limit, perhaps when children are first learning a limit.

> **EXAMPLE**   Mrs. Woodward said before going out to the playground on the second day of school, "Tell me our safety rule about how many children are allowed on the sliding board at one time. . . . That's right, only one at a time so that nobody gets hurt." She also showed a picture of one child on the slide.

Be aware, however, that some children might try to distract you from carrying through with a limit by playing the why game, repeatedly asking, "Why?" Ignoring their "Why?" is one of the most helpful things you can do for them. You can also say, "I think you're having fun asking me why and I'll tell you why one more time and then the game is over" (Seefeldt, 1993).

Communicate Limits to Others; Review Limits Periodically

It is important that everyone who works in your classroom, however short the time, understands and uses the same limits. This includes but is not limited to parents, other volunteers, specialists, the principal or director, children from upper grades, college students in a practicum, and persons invited to do a presentation. Some children are confused when adults in the same classroom use different limits.

> **EXAMPLE**   Mrs. Woodward forgot to tell a new volunteer about some of the classroom rules. The volunteer told two boys that they could just leave the blocks out and that she would put them away. The classroom rule is that children put away things that they have used.

Communicate classroom limits by posting them conspicuously. Point out the list when a visitor first comes to the classroom. Or have a number of copies of a handout titled "Classroom Limits" ready to give to anyone who works in the room. Talk with all classroom workers and visitors about how important it is for all adults to use the same limits. Demonstrate limits when necessary, as with proper hand washing.

You can make classroom limits even more effective by telling parents about the limits. First, this highlights limits for parents and reassures them. Second, communicating effectively with parents tells them that you think they are worthy of your time. This will help you develop a good working partnership with parents. Third, talking with parents about limits might help some parents ask questions about limit setting at home.

Parents like the topic of how to set and maintain reasonable limits when offered as a parent education topic. Communicate information to parents about setting limits in a variety of ways: with handouts, newsletter write-ups, appropriate articles, formal parent meetings, and videos/DVDs either used in meetings or borrowed by parents. See the Working with Families feature and the list of web sites at the end of this chapter. You will find many handouts and other free or inexpensive material about guidance and discipline to use with parents.

WORKING *with* FAMILIES — COMMUNICATING WITH FAMILIES ABOUT GUIDANCE STRATEGIES

Teachers must clearly communicate school or center policies, including discipline policies and strategies, to parents. You will have to think through this issue and be able to articulate the policy without insulting parents who, according to Socolar (1995), believe in using physical punishment such as hitting (spanking). Your goal is to establish rapport and then maintain a good relationship with parents so that you can work effectively with each family and child. You can take several steps to explain school policies about positive discipline strategies to parents.

Write It Down!

Let parents know about the child guidance policies of the school. Use the NAEYC Code of Ethical Conduct and Statement of Commitment (National Association for the Education of Young Children [NAEYC], 2006) as a base and draw your own center or school policies from that. Incorporate your guidance policies in a policy manual written just for parents. Then it will be clear to parents that the school has a guidance policy, that it is based on a professional group's guidelines, and that it is positive in nature.

Focus on Teaching

If you plan to do home visits, you can, as a small part of your visit, talk with each parent about a few of the specific positive strategies that you use. Does your school have a newsletter? Write a brief article explaining a specific discipline strategy. Does your school have a parent's bulletin board? Use this space to display information about a specific strategy. Are you having a group parent meeting? Explain the guidance policy along with all the other policies and highlight one or two positive discipline strategies.

For example, explain how you set limits and how you restate them if a child does not seem to listen the first time. Many parents react almost reflexively with spanking when their children do not obey immediately. Explain how you use redirection.

Do a Needs Assessment

Effective teachers work as partners with parents. Make a list of the many positive discipline strategies that your school uses and ask parents to check off the ones about which they would like to know more. Work with parents by giving them information on the strategies that they have identified as areas of need. Do this through an early childhood family education program that includes one-on-one interaction with parents as well as more formal methods such as group meetings.

Listen With Respect, Avoid Being Judgmental, and Don't Argue

Some parents ask questions that simply call for clarification of a specific policy. A few parents challenge a policy. Some might even want to engage you in a protracted debate about controversial discipline strategies such as spanking that they see as acceptable. In all cases, you help parents best by remaining calm and professional; do not argue with a parent.

Suppose a father says, "I was spanked when I was a kid and it never hurt me!" You can neutralize such a statement and avoid arguing by not taking his statement as an attack and by saying respectfully, "Yes, lots of people were spanked and believe in spanking. Our school does not want to force ideas on anybody. But we do want parents to know that we guide children with positive discipline strategies."

Teach Helpful or Appropriate Behavior

Help children build self-control by teaching them about helpful behaviors. Children must learn so many behaviors that they do not know automatically. Here are just a few examples:

How to ask for something.
How to listen when others talk, and not interrupt them.

How to join a play or work group.

How to put things away when children complete a project.

How to participate in a group, such as where and how to sit, how to listen, how to offer an idea, and how to get the teacher's attention.

Mealtime manners, such as passing items and waiting their turn.

Plan lessons to teach the skills. Choose from your large collection of teaching strategies and incorporate them into your regular teaching plan. Teach individuals, small groups, or large groups. Use songs, stories, finger plays, flannel boards, demonstrations, films, DVDs, guest speakers, or other methods.

EXAMPLE   At the beginning of the school year, Mrs. Woodward observed that several of the children did not understand the concept of passing items. For instance, the children seemed confused about how to pass baskets with snacks, and they did not know how to pass pitchers with juice or milk. Here are two examples of the lessons through which she taught the children how to pass things.

- Lesson 1: Large group. Mrs. Woodward held a basket filled with colored squares of paper. She said, "I'm going to take one of these squares from the basket. Then I'm going to pass the basket to Nellie" (who sat next to the teacher). Nellie takes the basket. "Now, Nellie will take one square out of the basket and pass the basket to Ralph. Ralph takes a square and passes it to Justine." After all the children had a chance to pass the basket, Mrs. Woodward showed them a basket used at snack time. She said, "We will pass baskets like this one when we eat snack."
- Lesson 2: Snack time. "Here's the basket that we will pass! I'll start today." Mrs. Woodward softly chanted as she took a cracker and then passed the basket,

> "Mrs. Woodward takes a cracker and passes them to Jerry.
> Jerry takes a cracker and passes them to Chelsea.
> Chelsea takes a cracker and passes them to Ralph."

They continued singing until every child had passed the basket.

Determine which skill you need to teach by observing. Consider using checklists, anecdotal records, or rating scales to assess the needs and abilities of children in your class as described in Chapter 6 of this text. Then, observe again to assess a child's understanding after you have taught a skill. Mrs. Woodward noted that Calvin had learned how to pass the basket from the demonstration.

Set up Practice Sessions and Give "On-the-Spot" Guidance

Give children a chance to practice what you show or tell them, as Mrs. Woodward did when they practiced passing baskets. Mr. Sanchez had observed that Willis did not wait his turn for the computer stations in the K–2 classroom. Consequently, he had taught Willis the steps in getting a turn (putting his name on the list if necessary, checking the list and waiting, and working somewhere else until his name was next). He knows how important it is for children to practice what they have learned, and so he planned a simple practice session for Willis about waiting for a turn.

Mr. Sanchez started the practice session (Mr. Sanchez worked with Willis individually) by saying, "Let's practice waiting for a turn at the computer, Willis. You already know the main things that you have to do. Please tell me the first thing."

Willis:	I have to put my name on the list.
Mr. Sanchez:	That's right. Write your name now on this list. (Willis prints his name at the bottom of the list.) Good. Now, check to see how many children are ahead of you.
Willis:	Sandi and Michael. That's two.
Mr. Sanchez:	Right again! You won't have to wait very long at all. What would you like to do while you wait?
Willis:	Work on my math.

The next day, Mr. Sanchez introduced a new math game to use at the computer, and Willis was eager to get a turn. Mr. Sanchez gave **on-the-spot guidance** to Willis. He quietly reminded him about how to get a turn and used this real-life situation as another practice session. Willis did very well. He had learned the steps, had practiced them with the teacher individually, and finally had practiced them in the classroom.

On-the-spot guidance
Helping children through direct coaching in daily guidance situations

Give Signals or Cues for Appropriate Behavior

Cues are hints or suggestions that remind children about a limit in a low-key way. The signals or cues can be verbal, nonverbal, pictorial, or written (for older children). Good cues are developmentally appropriate; they are age- and individually appropriate for a variety of children—typically developing children, children with disabilities, and a child who is learning English. Recent research with a child with autism used pictorial cues or symbols to help him understand words that a teacher used in describing an action. Supporting this child with visual cues resulted in fewer behavior problems (Mirenda, MacGregor, & Kelly-Keough, 2002).

Cues
Verbal, nonverbal, pictorial, or written reminders about limits

EXAMPLE At the end of group time, Mrs. Woodward verbally reminded the children to wash their hands for snack time. The group sang the action song, and then she sent them to the bathroom (the song was the cue or reminder).

EXAMPLE Shortly after the children went to the bathroom, she showed one of the pictures of a child washing her hands to the group. "Where can we hang this picture so that it reminds us to always wash our hands after going into the bathroom?" (The picture is the cue.)

Cues are helpful to all children, but some children might benefit from them even more. For example, many children in classrooms are learning English, and using cues is one of the research-based methods found to help them in literacy instruction (Linan-Thompson & Vaughn, 2007). Visual types of support are also useful in guiding English language learners. Picture cues can help children with limited English understand limits, schedules, and transitions.

Visual support

Pictures, photographs, drawings intended to help children remember the messages implied in the image

EXAMPLE   At transition from work and play time to large group, for instance, Mr. Sanchez showed each child two picture cues, one of a child playing and the other of the child in a circle with other children. At the same time, the teacher described moving from play to large group. (The pictures are cues.)

Children with an autism spectrum disorder (ASD) tend to have well-developed visual skills, while their skills related to hearing are less well developed. A problem arises for children with ASD when we guide them. We tend to set limits and give other guidance suggestions with words, which often makes it difficult for a child with ASD to remember and comply. Supporting this child with a **visual support**, such as pictures, in the environment keeps the limit and/or guidance fresh for the child long after you have stated a limit or suggestion with words (Illinois State University, no date).

Encourage Children's Efforts to Accept Limits

Children need more than limits—they also need encouragement for their efforts to accept limits and to behave in a prosocial way, cooperatively or helpfully. There are many ways to encourage children's efforts.

Promote new behavior that is "self-encouraging." Think of ways to set things up so that a child will find a new behavior so attractive that he will eagerly comply.

EXAMPLE   Larry did not wash his paint smock when he painted. Mrs. Woodward made a new job for the job chart and assigned that job to Larry for 2 days. The new job entailed being the person who ran the paint smock wash. This person wore a special hat and smock, was in charge of checking all the smocks to make sure they were clean, and was responsible for the new sponge and bucket.

Observe children to determine whether they have learned what they need to learn and whether they have complied with a limit. For example, Mr. Sanchez wanted all children to use a tissue when sneezing and wiping their noses. He taught them how to use the tissue with a demonstration. Then he used a simple checklist to document learning.

In another example, the principal visited Mr. Sanchez's room to read a story for the class. The children had just cleaned up after their morning work period and they sat on the floor for the story time. Mr. Sanchez introduced the principal. He showed a large photo of the entire class with the label "We are good helpers!" He said to the principal, "We have lots of children in this class and we are all good helpers." He then noted how every child had helped during cleanup.

Change Something about a Context or Setting

Behavior communicates. Behavior does not occur in a vacuum—it happens in a context or setting. The context of a behavior has an effect on that behavior. With these statements in mind, consider reframing or rethinking the concept of a discipline encounter by asking a question. "What can I do about this context, this situation that will help this child be safe or help her choose a different behavior more helpful to her?" For example, "Do I want to keep telling these two children to stop arguing over the blocks, or can I change something to help them accept the idea of cooperating?"

Three major ways to change a situation to be helpful and to prevent or stop potentially dangerous or inappropriate behavior include changing the physical environment or the time schedule, increasing options, and decreasing options.

Change the physical environment and/or time schedule if necessary

You can easily change something about a situation by evaluating how you have structured the physical environment. You can then decide that a slight change might be very helpful to children. Do children run, not walk, from one center to another? Then check for zoom areas, which are tunnel-like spaces that invite running. If any exist in the classroom layout, then rearrange the room to eliminate the zoom area(s). You can also adjust the schedule to help children, as Mr. Sanchez has done for his large-group time.

> **EXAMPLE** Mr. Sanchez's student teacher found that his opening large-group time was almost unpleasant because of all the talking and squirming. Mr. Sanchez, during the evaluation of group time, asked the student teacher to reflect on how long the lesson had been. The student teacher discovered that the group time was too long and made a simple adjustment. The adjusted schedule resulted in a much shorter, more productive, and more peaceful group activity.

Increase options available to a child

Authoritative adults closely supervise and monitor activities. They recognize when children need more options from which to choose. They realize that children might be stuck on a nonproductive course of action and require additional information or choices. Here are three practical ways to increase options for children.

Prevent predictable problems.

Prevent problems whenever possible. Young children have a difficult time controlling themselves. Observe the group for signs that adult intervention is necessary. One way to do this is to identify the times in a group's schedule when things could go wrong and prevent these problems. Transitions are troublesome and stress-inducing for children. Prevent problems by having as few transitions as possible in the schedule. Observe and identify the times when transitions are difficult for children, for example, nap to waking activities or from large group to outside play. Reflect on the transitions and alter them to make them more appropriate.

> **EXAMPLES** Transition from nap to waking activities: Some children awoke from nap before the others but still had to be quiet. Instead of just asking them to sit quietly, she prevented the potential problem by using toys and books for quiet play. This was a special group of items used only after nap and before everyone was awake.
>
> Transition from large group to outside play: The teacher cut out and laminated simple squares of different-colored construction paper and kept them in a basket in the large-group area. At the end of the activity, each child took one square from the basket. She then sent the five children with blue squares to put on coats, and continued with the other colors in turn. This simple method helped children focus on the transition and seemed to decrease anxiety about it.

Introduce new ideas to children engaged in an activity. Our goal is to let play sessions unfold and not to dominate play. Occasionally, however, children benefit from getting ideas from adults. Offer a new idea when it would extend the play or help children get beyond an argument. Sometimes children will use the idea, and sometimes they will not.

> **EXAMPLE** Mrs. Woodward noticed that some of the children had worked cooperatively on building a train from large blocks for about 10 minutes. When she heard an argument about who would be the driver of the train, she said, "Here is that book about trains. Look here [points to passengers]. We do need a conductor but we need passengers, too. The conductor helps passengers find a seat on the train." Ralph immediately shouted, "I want to be the passenger!"

Introduce new materials into an activity. Assess the situation and decide whether new materials would be helpful. Then decide how to present the new materials to the children. One way is to add the new item, simply and quietly, without comment. Another way is to introduce the new materials in work sessions as needed.

> **EXAMPLES** Mrs. Woodward gave red or blue tickets and small suitcases to the train "passengers." She also gave the conductor a hat and a hole puncher with which to punch one hole in each passenger's ticket. Another time, she brought out plastic farm animals and placed them near the children working on building a farm. A final example took place at the play dough table. After children had worked with dough for one day, she brought out new rolling pins, taught them the term *rolling pin*, and asked them how they might use the new item with play dough.

Decrease options available to a child Occasionally, the problem is not that children need new ideas or materials but that they need fewer options. Too many choices can easily overwhelm children, especially impulsive children. Guide children effectively by limiting choices or changing activities.

Limit choices. Making wise choices is a skill that develops over time. Helpful adults teach young children how to make choices from only a few alternatives.

> **EXAMPLE** Mr. Sanchez knew that Pae (pronounced "pay") had great difficulty zeroing in on one activity. He helped Pae focus attention and he limited his choices by asking, "You said yesterday that you wanted to write a story about your kitten and you wanted to make labels for your leaf collection. Which of those two things would you like to do first today?"

Change activities. Authoritative caregivers understand that a variety of things might affect children's attention or behavior. They are skillful enough and have enough confidence in their ability to modify plans or to abandon a plan if necessary.

> **EXAMPLES** Mr. Sanchez had just gathered the entire group for story time when the roaring noise started. The earthmovers had come onto the school grounds to start digging the swimming pool. "There goes group time," he thought, but he

remained calm. To the children he said, "Let's walk outside and stand out of the way so that we can watch for a little while. Then I'm going to tell you the story of an earthmover!'"

Ignore Behavior (Only When It Is Appropriate to Do So)

Teachers **ignore behavior** when they stop paying attention to a specific action. You can safely ignore some behaviors but not others. The ignore strategy is appropriate for the following categories of behavior:

Whining or arguing about limits.
Any other effort to distract you from following through on a limit.
Efforts to pull you into an argument.
A child's efforts to make you angry.

It is safe to ignore these behaviors because they are not hurtful, not destructive, not disrespectful, and not dangerous. In fact, it is a good idea to ignore them because paying attention makes them worse. Giving attention to whining, for example, rewards the child's whining. The following guidelines will help you use the ignore strategy effectively.

Guidelines for using the ignore strategy

- Tell the child that you will ignore a specific, targeted behavior. Suppose that you decide to use the ignore strategy when a child argues about limits. You know that telling the child about the strategy will make things easier. Therefore, you politely but clearly tell the child that you will stop paying attention to her when she argues about something that she has to do: "Nellie, I've made a mistake and paid attention to you when you argue about some things, such as cleaning up. From now on, I will not pay attention when you argue with me. I won't look at you, and I won't talk to you when you argue about cleanup."
- Take enough time to use the ignore strategy effectively. Adults usually give a lot of attention when they need to ignore. Paying attention has caused problems for the child. When an adult decides to use the ignore strategy, a child who has received so much attention for unhelpful behavior, such as arguing or whining, will be surprised and is likely to increase the intensity of the arguing or whining. Essentially, her behavior says, "Look here, you've always argued back when I argue. Now you're ignoring me. Looks to me like I have to argue more loudly. Maybe that will get your attention!"

  Consider how you are now ignoring Nellie's arguing. She will not stop after you first ignore her, even though you have politely alerted her. Like most children whose irritating behavior is ignored for the first time, she will try even harder to recapture your attention by arguing even more insistently. You should expect and be prepared for the "bigger and better" arguments. You will have to carry out the procedure at least one or two more times before Nellie finally realizes that you have resolved to stop paying attention to her arguing.

- Decide to ignore the behavior completely.

   Give *no* attention. This is difficult because the adult has decided to change her own customary behavior. To refrain from paying attention to and encouraging the arguing, the teacher wrote the following list of prompts:

   "Resist the urge to mutter to myself under my breath."

   "Resist the urge to make eye contact."

   "Resist the urge to communicate with this child, either with words or gestures."

- Teach and encourage more acceptable behavior.

   Go beyond ignoring a behavior to teaching children some other, more appropriate behavior. Mr. Sanchez ignored Vinnie's whining but also remembered to teach Vinnie how to ask for things in a normal voice. Mr. Sanchez modeled the "normal" voice.

Do Not Ignore These Behaviors   Figure 5.4 explains the types of behaviors that we should *not* ignore because they are clearly dangerous, destructive, or hurtful. Ignoring some behaviors endangers people or animals. This figure also illustrates an appropriate teacher response to the behavior.

Redirect Children's Behavior—Divert and Distract the Youngest Children

Diverting and distracting
Useful with toddlers; redirection in which an adult sidetracks a toddler from one activity and steers him to a safer activity

Diverting and distracting is a form of redirection in which an adult immediately does something to distract a child from the forbidden or dangerous activity. The adult then gets the very young child involved in a different activity.

Authoritative, responsible caregivers perform most of an infant's or young toddler's ego functions. For example, they remember things for the child and keep him safe because an infant's or young toddler's concept of danger is just emerging.

FIGURE 5.4	Do not ignore these behaviors	
Do *Not* Ignore These Types of Behaviors	**Example and/or Comment**	**Teacher Responds**
Treats someone rudely; embarrasses someone; is intrusive and/or disrespectful; causes an undue disruption	Tyler said to a volunteer, "You're not the teacher. I don't have to listen to you." Teachers can help children learn civility. Teach specific skills and state expectations."	"It is disrespectful to speak to a helper like that. It was his job to remind you about lunch."
Endangers anyone, including herself, as well as animals	Jack poked a stick into the rabbit's house. Ignoring dangerous behavior gives approval for it; increases it.	"In this classroom, we take care of the rabbits. They were afraid when you poked the stick into their house."
Damages or destroys property or acts in a way that *could* damage something	Lori jams her binder into the storage shelf forcefully because the shelf is full. Ignoring it conveys approval.	"That will damage binders. What can you do to store your binder without damaging it or the others?"

Authoritative adults accept responsibility for stopping very young children from doing something by setting limits that discourage certain behaviors, but they do so in a helpful way.

Diverting or distracting the youngest children accomplishes both of these tasks. An adult can be most helpful by immediately doing something to distract the child from the forbidden activity and steering her toward a different activity.

EXAMPLE   Mary, 16 months old, walked over to the bowl of cat food, picked up a piece, and started to place it in her mouth. Her father said, "Put the cat food back in the bowl, Mary" (a short, clear, specific limit). Then he picked up Mary and said, "You know, I think it's time for us to take a walk!"

Redirect Children's Behavior—Make Substitutions with Older Children

Substitution is a form of redirection in which an adult shows a child how to perform an activity or type of activity in a more acceptable and perhaps safer way. Substitution is an excellent strategy to use with children who are at least older toddlers or young preschoolers. Substitution is a good strategy to use with older children because it acknowledges the child's desire to plan and engage in a specific activity. The adult must accept the responsibility of developing safe substitutions to demonstrate the first step of problem solving.

> **Substitution**
> Useful with preschoolers and older children; redirection in which a child learns how to do an activity in a safer, more acceptable way

EXAMPLE   Mrs. Woodward saw Justine aim her paintbrush at Calvin's picture. The teacher stepped in and said, "Paint on one of these pieces of paper, Justine, not on Calvin's. Which size do you want to use?" She then led Justine to the other side of the easel.

Children may test adult commitment to substitution by trying the inappropriate activity again—later in the day, the next day, or with a different person.

The teacher on the left used diversion and distraction when she scooped up Sam to get him away from the outside door. "Look, Sam, I have a toy!"

Redirect by using substitution. "Reach in and get the spoon, Jacqie. You can use that instead."

EXAMPLE Justine swung around from her side of the easel to try to paint on Calvin's paper. The teacher stayed calm and simply said, "Paint on your paper, Justine." Justine eventually accepted the substitution because the teacher resisted the power struggle that would have occurred had she become angry about Justine's challenge. She continued to make the substitution quietly and with goodwill.

ANALYZE A VIGNETTE: REDIRECTION

Redirect by Diverting or Distracting

The teacher in the infant and toddler room redirected by diverting or distracting (see the chapter-opening vignette). Answer the following questions about his strategy.

1. Focus on the child's actions. Which behavior did Mr. Bjornrud need to stop for Paul; for Jada; and for Alex, the toddler?
2. The teacher used diversion and distraction three times. From your perspective, was he effective all three times? If he was, explain your reasoning for your decision. If he was not in any of the three situations, state why.
3. Suppose that Mr. Bjornrud used diversion and/or distraction effectively. Explain what you would do to make the strategy even more effective in one or more examples.

4. Explain how redirecting with diversion and/or distraction is developmentally appropriate for infants and toddlers.

Redirect with Substitution

1. Explain how Mrs. Woodward redirected Jerry successfully. Consider noting when she showed Jerry how to perform the same activity in a more acceptable way. Did Jerry test this substitution? If he did, explain how the teacher effectively dealt with Jerry's testing of the substitution.
2. Think about the differences between diversion/distraction and substitution. Why do you think that substitution is especially appropriate for preschoolers and older children?

Listen Actively

Active listening is a positive strategy that is useful when a child "owns" a problem. The adult focuses on what the child says, not interrupting, not offering solutions, but listening for the feelings in the words, suspending judgment, avoiding preaching, and then feeding back perception of the feelings. Mrs. Woodward watched Ralph try to mix colors to get orange paint. He forcefully jammed one brush in the cup, clenching his jaw at the same time, twisted his face in a frown, and blew out a deep breath.

> **Active listening**
> An adult listens reflectively and carefully to a child; does not offer solutions and does not criticize; useful when the problem belongs to the child

Mrs. Woodward:	Looks like you might be tired of dealing with that paintbrush!
Ralph:	Yeah, I want to make orange.
Mrs. Woodward:	You want orange but could not get orange?
Ralph:	I got pink!
Mrs. Woodward:	I see that you mixed red and white and got pink. (Ralph turned back to the easel and looked at the two paint cups. Mrs. Woodward continues.) So, those two colors together don't make orange.
Ralph:	Can I get another cup of paint? (He points to different colors.)
Mrs. Woodward:	Sure. Here's an idea. Keep your red paint and put the white away. Get one different color to mix with red. (Ralph got blue paint. When that did not work, he tried yellow with the red.)

Ralph had a problem and the teacher used active listening to help him work through it. An authoritarian caregiver would have dealt with Ralph's rough use of a paintbrush differently, very likely by punishing Ralph. Authoritarian teachers do not take the time to find out what a child is feeling and thinking, or what is bothering the child. They miss the chance to "hear" what a child's behavior says. Children often communicate their deepest fears or try to tell adults through their behavior that something is wrong. Adults discover what is wrong only if they take the time to listen actively.

Active listening, then, is the skill that responsible adults use when something is troubling a child—the child is afraid, is angry, is jealous, cannot do something, or is frustrated. The adult can best help a child by listening actively and responding to the feelings implied in the child's words or actions.

Deliver I-Messages

An **I-message** is a positive, self-responsible strategy useful when the *adult* "owns" the problem in a relationship with a child. An adult owns the problem when a child has done something that interferes in some way with that adult's needs. Here are some examples:

> **I-message**
> Self-responsible adult behavior useful when the problem belongs to the adult

The child does not clean up after an activity.
The child interrupts group time frequently.
The child curses at the teacher.

The child takes scissors and cuts into the glue bottle.
The child tosses library books on the floor.

Adults who see these kinds of behaviors usually feel afraid, irritated, or annoyed—all normal, natural feelings because the behavior usually tangibly affects the adult in some way. For example, a teacher would have to spend her time cleaning brushes and aprons left by a child; the teacher would have to use her own money to replace the ruined glue bottle.

I-messages are easy to learn to use. It is difficult, however, to use an I-message if an adult has not experienced hearing them. The key to using I-messages well is to acknowledge the feelings of irritation, annoyance, sadness, anger, or fear. Adults who use I-messages well fully realize that a child has done something annoying that has cost them time, energy, or money, but they know that they are the ones experiencing the feelings. They avoid accusing the child of causing these feelings. They simply take responsibility for communicating the feelings to the child in a firm but respectful and nonaccusatory way.

> **EXAMPLE** Mrs. Woodward had a discipline encounter with Madelyn, who immediately left a center when the signal for cleanup was given and left whatever she had been working on to somebody else (usually the teacher) to put away. Mrs. Woodward knew that she owned the problem, that she was annoyed, and that she should tell Madelyn in a nonaccusatory way. She used an I-message.

I-messages have four parts.

Give data I-messages give data about the child's behavior but avoid accusing the child. The message tells the child what the adult saw, heard, smelled, touched, or tasted. These are facts, not opinions, and are stated as facts.

Mrs. Woodward:	Madelyn, when I gave the signal for cleanup, I saw you leave the block area and go to another center. (Data: Teacher saw something; the child left the area without cleaning up. Mrs. Woodward told Madelyn what she saw; but did not accuse.)

Describe the tangible effect I-messages tell the child how his behavior tangibly affects the adult, such as how the child's behavior has cost the adult time, effort, and/or money.

Mrs. Woodward:	That means that I would have to pick up the blocks. (Madelyn's behavior tangibly affected the teacher because the teacher would have to do the extra work of straightening the block area.)

Communicate feelings I-messages tell the child how the adult feels.

Mrs. Woodward:	I get frustrated when I have to pick up things that somebody else has worked with. (Teacher states the feeling but clearly says that she has the feeling. Mrs. Woodward did not accuse Madelyn of causing that feeling.)

FIGURE 5.5	Practice delivering an I-message

Discipline encounter: Mr. Sanchez observed Reese walk away from the writing center, having left markers, paper, pencils, and rulers strewn over the table. Moua wanted to use Reese's spot at the table but would have to straighten up first. Mr. Sanchez decided to use an I-message with Reese. Practice writing an I-message by filling in each part.

Give data: (what did you see, hear, touch, taste, smell?)

Describe the tangible effect: (avoid telling about your feelings here)

State feelings: _____

Tell how to change things: _____

Reflection: Adults are important models for children. What has Mr. Sanchez modeled for Moua by delivering an I-message to Reese?

Tell how to change things   If you, an adult, heard an I-message, you would likely know what to do to change things. A child, however, most often does not know how to do this. In the example above, a child would hear that her teacher was irritated and that the teacher had to do some extra work. The child would not necessarily know what to do to correct the situation. The teacher can follow up an I-message with a simple statement telling a child how to change things: "I want you to come with me to the block area and put away the blocks." Practice writing an I-message in Figure 5.5.

Teach Conflict Resolution (Problem Solving)

Madelyn and Ralph had been working in the block corner, building a road and a yard with a large building. Then Mrs. Woodward heard the shouting.

Madelyn:	It's a barn!
Ralph:	No! It's my garage!
Madelyn:	It's a barn! It's for the tractor.
Ralph:	It's for the cars!

Madelyn stuck the tractor into the building and Ralph thrust it aside, putting his cars into the building. Madelyn, face red, grabbed one of the cars. Ralph grabbed it back and shouted loudly.

Ralph:	Put it back, Madelyn!

Treat conflict as an opportunity to teach a skill to children   This teacher knows that conflict is inevitable and not necessarily bad. She believes that relationships can become even stronger when people resolve conflicts peacefully and with goodwill. She believes in supporting children in learning how to recognize and manage conflict. She takes the stand that everybody in the conflict can "win," that there do not have to be any "losers."

Some teachers might simply punish Madelyn and Ralph by taking away all the blocks or by placing each child in time-out. Teachers who use the red light–green light strategy would probably change each child's light to yellow or red. All of these strategies are forms of punishment and do not teach anything positive. The bickering might irritate the teacher, but she realizes that her job is to support children in learning a brand-new skill—conflict resolution (Clark, 1999).

You will find that you use other guidance strategies along with the steps described for conflict resolution. For example, you will very likely use calming techniques, active listening, or I-messages when you teach children how to resolve conflict.

Adults who teach conflict resolution acknowledge that children's needs are important, and they communicate trust in their ability to construct and carry out decisions. Using this method, therefore, requires that adults truly accept the child's feelings and needs as valid and important. This is not a strategy that an adult can fake.

Teaching conflict resolution   Mrs. Woodward heard the argument and walked quickly to the block corner. "We need to talk, but first, let me just move the car and tractor over here for a minute." She unobtrusively took the car and the tractor and set them aside, then turned to both children. "It sounds as though you have a problem. Two children, one building."

Madelyn:	It's a barn!
Ralph:	No, a garage!
Mrs. Woodward:	First, let's take a slow breath. (She does deep breathing with them, a calming technique. She then continued, after checking to see that both children were calm enough to talk.) Okay. Listen carefully. You have one building. Madelyn, you want it to be a barn. Ralph, you want it to be a garage. Is that right? (The children nod.) I see. We do have a problem then. Two children and one building. (She then looked at both children.) Let's think for a minute about how to fix the problem. Do you have an idea?
Madelyn:	Make another building?
Ralph:	Make this building bigger!
Mrs. Woodward:	Two ideas! Do you have any other ideas?
Ralph:	Make a wall right here. (points to the middle of the building) Then we can have a garage and a barn together. (The children had generated these three ideas.)
Mrs. Woodward:	Good ideas. Do you have enough blocks for another whole building? (The children decide that they do not have enough blocks.)
Madelyn:	We can't make another building, huh?
Mrs. Woodward:	Probably not. Do you think that there are enough blocks to make the building bigger?
Ralph:	(looking at the supply of blocks.) Yes.

Mrs. Woodward:	How about enough blocks to make a wall to divide the building? (Both children vigorously nodded.)
Mrs. Woodward:	Which idea do you want to try—making the building bigger or dividing it to make two parts?
Ralph:	Let's make it bigger!
Mrs. Woodward:	Is that okay with you, Madelyn?
Madelyn:	Uh-huh. If we make it bigger, then we can have a wall, too.
Mrs. Woodward:	What do you think about that, Ralph? We could use two of your ideas together. (Ralph nodded, indicating that he agreed.) Tell me the first thing that you can do to get started on making your building bigger. (They discuss this a bit more.) Okay. Start making the building bigger. Then make the wall and we'll look at how things work out when you are done. We will check to see how this works.

Figure 5.6 shows the steps in teaching conflict resolution.

FIGURE 5.6   Steps in teaching children conflict resolution

✓ **Identify the problem and define it as a shared problem.**
Young children do not take the perspective of others very well. Adults have to help them understand that they can share a problem with someone else. Children will likely see the problem mainly in terms of what they want (Ralph wanted a garage, Madelyn a barn). How has the teacher carried out this step?

✓ **Invite children to participate in fixing the problem.**
Children think about what they want, not about solutions. Teachers or parents must get and keep them focused on moving toward solving the problem together. A good, constructivist approach is to invite their participation. How did Mrs. Woodward do this?

✓ **Generate possible solutions as a group.**
This is brainstorming. Encourage a variety of solutions. Do not evaluate solutions at this stage. You might have to teach children not to evaluate now. When did Mrs. Woodward do this?

✓ **Examine each idea for its merits or drawbacks. Decide which idea to try.**
Encourage children to think through each idea. Facilitate an evaluation of each idea and let the children decide which idea to try. Acknowledge the children's participation and thank them for working together. How did Mrs. Woodward do this?

✓ **Work out ways of putting the plan into action.**
Children need help in taking action after coming up with ideas. They do not automatically move from the problem to working on a solution. How did Mrs. Woodward help Madelyn and Ralph start to put their plan into action?

✓ **Follow up. Evaluate how well the plan worked.**
Children need to learn that some plans work nicely and some do not work at all. Teachers have to help them through this process. Children who are just learning how to resolve conflicts might get frustrated when a new idea does not work for some reason. Teachers can then step in and help them figure out why the plan did not work and anything else they might do to create a better plan. The children learn about fine-tuning a plan. When did the teacher do this?

Source: Based on *Before Push Comes to Shove: Building Conflict Resolution Skills with Children,* by N. Carlsson-Paige and D. Levin, 1998, St. Paul, MN: Redleaf Press.

Prevent Overstimulation and Teach Calming Techniques

Many times, the best thing that we can do for children is to look beyond the behavior that we see. Children often have difficulty controlling themselves when they are under stress or when they are anxious. Children often lose control because they are under so much stress (Goleman, 1995). At these times, children have difficulty thinking clearly, and adults need to help them. We help them best, not by punishing, but by doing the following:

Recognizing signs of anxiety and stress.
Preventing overstimulation.
Teaching calming techniques.

EXAMPLE Mr. Sanchez noticed right away that first grader Gene was acting differently as they talked about the visit from the firefighter. Gene bit his lip and was very agitated. Mr. Sanchez recognized the signs of anxiety and stopped talking about the visit. Instead, Mr. Sanchez and the children did their favorite "rubber-band" exercise. They stretched out both arms and stretched one as far as they could. Then they slowly brought the arm back to its original position. After this, they did slow, deep breathing with their eyes closed. Only then did the teacher proceed with talking about the firefighter's visit. Later, Mr. Sanchez discovered that Gene's family home had burned the year before and that several fire engines had responded to the fire.

Mrs. Woodward knew that some holidays are stressful for many people and wanted to prevent overstimulation (Greenberg & Berktold, 2006). She realized that many of the children would become overstimulated if she stressed the holiday too much, and the effect would last for several hours or days. She approached holiday seasons carefully. She did nothing to whip the children into a holiday frenzy. They proceeded with the curriculum, bringing in the holiday only when it seemed relevant to a project at hand, and then in a low-key way.

EXAMPLE One of the few things that the children did for Valentine's Day was to bake a heart-shaped cake with red frosting. This was part of an ongoing project about creating colors and color mixing, and was done to focus on helping the children remember the list of ingredients and the steps in preparing the cake.

Help Children Save Face and Preserve Their Dignity

Our culture values children, and one of its beliefs is that adults should protect children. The quote that opens this chapter is from the early childhood educator's code of ethics. This quote tells teachers that their most important professional obligation is to protect children from harm. We are obligated to *reject* any strategy that is "disrespectful, degrading, dangerous, exploitative, intimidating, psychologically damaging, or physically harmful to children."

Our responsibility, then, is to examine, critically and unemotionally, any strategy that somebody tries to get us to use. Some strategies that you will see on the Internet or in a teacher workshop come complete with teacher recommendations, but you still need to ask yourself, "Is this disrespectful or psychologically harmful to children?" Consider, for example, something called the red light–green light strategy. This strategy is *not* recommended.) A child starts the day with a green light. His first or second infraction earns him a warning and a yellow light. Still another infraction earns him a red light and he loses 5 minutes of recess (This is a form of punishment. It is response cost—your inappropriate behavior will cost you 5 minutes of recess). Still another infraction earns a *double* red light. The child also loses the entire recess and teacher sends a note home.

Think critically. Be compassionate. Put yourself in the child's place. How would *you* feel if your instructors used the red light–green light method in your classes? What if you turn in a paper late? How would you *feel* if the teacher used this system and changed your light to yellow? I would feel humiliated if my dean or department chair used such an outrageous method. Children have the same feelings that we have, and so it would undoubtedly be degrading and humiliating to them as well. This system and others like it should be rejected. *We should not use them.*

This chapter presents so many positive strategies. We do not need punishment such as the red light–green light strategy. We reject such strategies because our ultimate responsibility is to help children save face and preserve their sense of dignity, no matter what positive guidance or discipline strategy we use. Authoritarian adults degrade children by using negative discipline strategies. Some continue to humiliate a child; they might tell others about what the child did in front of her (double red light), or they might humiliate her by saying "I told you so," or "No recess for you" to the child.

Use your perspective-taking skills and put yourself in a child's place. Think about how it would feel to have an adult changing that light from green to yellow, and then to red. *You,* an adult would probably not like it at all and would demand that the other person treat you in a dignified way. Children also deserve dignified treatment.

:: BELIEFS ABOUT DISCIPLINE INFLUENCE CHOICES ABOUT DISCIPLINE STRATEGIES

"Memory believes before knowing remembers."
        —(William Faulkner)

Beliefs and Practices

Early childhood professionals study developmentally appropriate practices. They must examine their own practices and their beliefs about those practices. For example, a teacher attends a series of workshops on appropriate guidance and discipline. She learns the strategies. She does not use the new strategies in her classroom, however. In this case, the teacher's past experiences and beliefs about discipline more strongly affect her practices than anything that she learned in formal classes. She strongly believes, for example, that time-out is acceptable and uses it even after learning that it is a form of punishment.

This teacher's "memory" of past experiences, then, "believes" some things about inappropriate discipline; these inappropriate beliefs will be difficult to modify. To make any real changes, this teacher will have to examine her beliefs about discipline before she thinks about specific strategies (Haupt, Larsen, Robinson, & Hart, 1995).

An Opportunity to Examine Your Beliefs about Discipline

Take the time to examine what you really believe about discipline. What did you experience as a child? If you are already a parent, what have you tried with your own children? Which strategies have you used as a teacher? It is important to reflect because your experiences so strongly affect what you believe about discipline. One of my students had, as a child-care aide, been told to use the "sad pad." The sad pad is a carpet square with a sad face drawn on it. A child is sent there when she is angry. This is *not* a very good strategy because it confuses two emotions and is often used in place of a time-out chair. Whether one uses a sad pad or time-out chair, it is still a form of punishment and *not* a positive form of discipline. We should question any form of discipline that comes our way.

This chapter described many positive discipline strategies. When a person is confronted with such a large number of possibilities, there is a tendency to feel overwhelmed. Avoid this feeling by looking at things differently. Adopt an optimistic perspective by keeping three things in mind.

Knowledge base   At this point in the book you should be able to describe each strategy and state why it would be effective in some cases. That is a knowledge base, the beginning of expertise.

Skill building   Second, you will have a chance at the end of this chapter to build your professional self-esteem by doing some skill development in the Apply Your Knowledge section. You will have an opportunity to use several positive guidance strategies. Then, as you work with children in classrooms, you will practice using these strategies: You will become more skillful over time.

Decision-making approach   Third, this book teaches the decision-making model of child guidance (Chapters 11 and 13). It teaches how to make decisions about which strategy to use in specific discipline encounters. You will be able to do this because you have learned and practiced the strategies. Chapter 11 takes you through the decision-making model of child guidance and shows you, in a systematic fashion, how to make wise decisions about which strategy to use.

ANALYZE A VIGNETTE

Hannah's mother (in the chapter-opening vignette) was embarrassed and angry and used a negative discipline strategy. Boost her confidence as a parent by teaching her more positive ways to deal with the same discipline encounter. Teach the skills that will enable her to use positive strategies.

1. Set Limits
   - Show Hannah's mother how to set a limit, before going to the store, on what they will buy. (Be specific and follow the guidelines for limit setting.)
   - Suppose that Hannah's mother simply forgot to state a limit. Then, in the store, Hannah started

whining. Tell Mom how she could state the limit in a direct, nonaggressive way by saying:

2. Teach and Cue More Appropriate Behavior
   - Show Hannah's mother how to teach Hannah a new behavior that is different from whining, such as asking for things in a normal, conversational tone of voice. Show her how to model and give direct instruction.
   - Show Hannah's mother how to use a cue to remind Hannah about the limit. Explain why it is best to cue her daughter in a matter-of-fact,

low-key way in a public place. Be prepared to role-play what this would look like.

3. Ignore Behavior
   - Demonstrate how to use the ignore strategy effectively in this case. List the essential things that you would tell Hannah's mother to do—or not to do.
   - How do you think Hannah's mother might feel when Hannah reacts with a bigger and better whine? Give her some hints on how to cope with the feeling and with other adults in the store who say, "She should do something to that kid to stop her squealing!"

SUMMARY

How we guide children is based on what we value and believe as a culture. A culture has specific beliefs about how it should care for children. We help children acquire the beliefs of their culture through the process of socialization. We adults help children understand what the culture values through our teaching and our interaction with them.

- Discipline refers to guidance and teaching, *not* punishment. Adults help children make better choices about behavior through guidance and discipline encounters, and dealing with guidance or discipline encounters is a big part of a teacher's professional role.
- We use *positive* guidance strategies in guidance or discipline encounters. The strategies are the actions that we use in managing the encounter.

- There are many positive guidance strategies, and it is a good idea to know about all of them. Knowing about and being able to use a group or cluster of positive strategies allows teachers to meet the individual needs of children. Table 5.1 summarizes the major positive guidance strategies.

Our beliefs about guidance grow out of our experiences in our culture. Believing that positive guidance is preferable to punishment makes it easier for teachers to learn and then use positive strategies presented in this text.

QUESTIONS FOR REFLECTION

1. What do you see as the main focus of a positive, as opposed to a negative, discipline strategy? What is the major difference between the two?
2. Authoritative adults know how to use many different positive discipline strategies. Explain to someone who has not read this chapter why it is so important for teachers and parents to understand and know

how to use many, and not just one or two, positive discipline strategies.

3. Describe at least three practical and time-efficient ways in which teachers can help parents understand the child guidance policies of the school, including the use of positive guidance strategies.

APPLY YOUR KNOWLEDGE

Discipline Encounters and Appropriate Solutions
Each adult in the following vignettes faces a discipline encounter. Help the adult deal effectively by offering advice on how to use the specific strategy mentioned. Refer to information in this chapter when writing your solution.

1. **Discipline encounter:** Maricela walked over to the piano and started to bang on the keys. Her teacher called out, "Stop banging on the piano!"

   Appropriate strategy
   I think that this teacher would be helpful and effective by telling Maricela what *to* do instead of

TABLE 5.1	Summary of major positive guidance strategies
Guidance Strategy	**Purpose or Benefit of This Strategy**
Use limits effectively	Helps children understand boundaries
Teach helpful or appropriate behavior	Fosters children's self-control
Set up practice sessions and give on-the-spot guidance	Practicing new behaviors and skills is important for children
Give signals or cues for appropriate behavior	Reminds children about appropriate behavior
Encourage children's efforts	Lets children know that you appreciate their effort to behave prosocially
Change something about the context	Context affects behavior; changing context helps children choose a different behavior
Ignore behavior (only when it is appropriate to do so)	Decreasing our attention for a behavior helps children decrease that behavior
Redirect with diversion and distraction or with substitution	Diversion and distraction is helpful for younger children; substitution is beneficial for older children
Use I-messages	Useful when the adult "owns" the problem
Teach conflict resolution	Teaches skills for solving interpersonal problems
Prevent overstimulation; teach calming techniques	Children need to learn to deal with stress and to calm themselves
Help children save face and preserve their dignity	Children have the right to dignified treatment, even as we use positive guidance strategies

what not to do. The teacher can be positive, polite, and firm as she says, "＿＿＿＿＿＿＿."

2. **Discipline encounter:** Ed and Jim rode their tricycles at breakneck speed and their teacher said, "Stop driving so fast!"

   Appropriate strategy
   This teacher would be more helpful and effective by telling the boys what to do rather than what not to do. I would advise that she say, "＿＿＿＿＿＿＿."

3. **Discipline encounter:** Tim's parents had been sitting in the booth at a fast-food restaurant for 15 minutes. They had finished eating and were talking to each other. Three-year-old Tim wiggled off the bench, ran around, and then crawled under the table. His dad scooped him up and told him, "Now, you sit here and be quiet." Five minutes passed, and Tim, who had missed his morning nap, started screaming in frustration. His dad grabbed Tim's arm to try to quiet him, but Tim continued screaming.

   Appropriate strategy
   I would change this situation by ＿＿＿＿. (Note: Tim must be supervised constantly, so sending him to the restaurant's playground is not an option unless the parent goes with him.) Start your solution by stating whether you would increase options, decrease options, or change the physical environment or time schedule, and then state exactly how you would proceed.

4. **Discipline encounter:** Dad was frustrated when 10-month-old Richard kept crawling right to the uncovered electrical outlets. He said "No-no" every time his son approached an outlet.

   Appropriate strategy
   I suggest that Dad change this situation by
   ＿＿＿＿＿＿＿.

5. **Discipline encounter:** John, 4 years old, has been working for 20 minutes in the sand pile constructing a "canal" for water (he has no water yet). You glance over and notice that he is tossing sand into the air.

   Appropriate strategy
   In addition to stating a safety rule, I would change this situation by   .

6. **Discipline encounter:** Sylvia finger-painted on the window because she likes how the sun shines on the colors.

   Appropriate strategy
   I would use this substitution: .
   (*Note:* The substitution must be appropriate and safe for the child and acceptable to you.)

7. **Appropriate strategy:** I would use this substitution: .

8. **Discipline encounter:** Pat wiped his nose on his sleeve.

   Appropriate strategy
   I would use this substitution: .

Should I Ignore This Behavior?

Look over this list and decide which of the behaviors you should *not* ignore. Which could you safely ignore? Give a rationale for your choices.

- One child tells another child, "You're stupid!" Ignore?

  Yes   No   Reason:

- A 3-year-old girl smashes her play dough creation. Ignore?

  Yes   No   Reason:

- The same child smashes another child's play dough structure. Ignore?

  Yes   No   Reason:

- One of the children in your group forcefully splashes water from the water table onto the floor. Ignore?

  Yes   No   Reason:

- Josie shoves Kyle as they walk to the bathroom. Ignore?

  Yes   No   Reason:

- "You clean up! I don't want to clean up. Why do I have to clean up?" a 7-year-old said argumentatively to her teacher. Ignore?

  Yes   No   Reason:

KEY TERMS

Active listening (*135*)	Guidance or discipline encounter (*115*)	On-the-spot guidance (*127*)
Cues (*127*)		Positive guidance strategies (*116*)
Culture (*114*)	Guidance strategies (*116*)	Socialization (*115*)
Discipline (*115*)	I-message (*135*)	Substitution (*133*)
Diverting or distracting (*132*)	Limits (*118*)	Visual support (*128*)

WEB SITES

Adults and Children Against Violence
http://actagainstviolence.apa.org/index.html

Organization's mission is to prevent violence through publishing information on discipline, resolving conflict, managing anger, and other related topics. Printable handouts and other resources useful to teachers and parents are available.

Association of Professional Humane Educators (APHE)
http://aphe.org

Main web site for the organization. Good materials for helping children learn about humane treatment of animals. Helps teachers state limits about treatment of animals to children.

Division of Early Childhood (DEC)

http://www.dec-sped.org/index.aspx/About_DEC/
Who_We_Are

The early childhood branch of the Council for
Exceptional Children (CEC). Major professional
organization focusing on children with special needs. See
the paper "Responsiveness to Family, Culture, Values, and
Education" in the Concept Papers link.

Second Step

http://www.cfchildren.org/about/

The organization's mission is to foster social and
emotional development. Excellent programs for very
young children and grades 1 to 5.

National Association for the Education of Young Children (NAEYC)

http://www.naeyc.org

Web site of the national professional association for early
childhood researchers and practitioners. Go to the catalog
or resources link. Look for publications or posters on
guidance and discipline. Find the Code of Ethics.

CHAPTER 6

Using Observation in Guiding Children

"To be effective, teachers must get to know each child in the group well. They do this using a variety of methods—such as observation . . . ."

—National Association of the Education of Young Children (2009)

Chapter Contents

Assessment in Early Childhood Education

Reasons for Observing Children's Behavior

Practical Methods for Observing Children's Behavior

Guiding Questions

- What is assessment and what are the goals of assessment in early childhood education?
- Why should teachers observe children's behavior?
- What are the major effective methods that teachers find useful in observing children?

VIGNETTES

INFANT-TODDLER: ENRIQUE TRIES MITTENS FIRST

Mr. Bjornrud recorded this observation of Enrique, 2½ years old, as the toddlers prepared to go outside.

E. shook his head vigorously, saying, "No!" as his teacher took his coat off the hook. Instead, Enrique put his hat and gloves on first and only then picked up his coat. He struggled to get the coat on over the gloves, then took off his gloves, and finally put on the coat.

PRESCHOOL: JERRY MAKES AN OFFER

Mrs. Woodward has been observing how Jerry works with other children. Today in the discovery/science center, she watched as Jerry and Sarah, both almost 5 years old, collaborated on making shapes with rubber bands stretched around nails, which were hammered into squares of wood. Sarah needed another big rubber band and Jerry responded, "Here, I have one," and offered it to Sarah. Later, at story time, the teacher noticed that Sarah made room next to her on the carpet for Jerry.

PRIMARY: SANDI FINDS A SOLUTION

Mr. Sanchez assessed each child's social skills. Here is one of his notes about Sandi's interaction with three other children in a small, first-grade reading group. Bert finished reading; Alicia started her turn. Dave yelled, "It's my turn!" Sandi looked at each child in the group as if figuring out something and then said, pointing at Bert, "Uh-oh! Bert just read. Alicia is sitting next to him, so she goes next." Then Sandi beamed at Dave and chirped, "You go right after Alicia!" Dave said, "Oh, yeah. Okay."

:: INTRODUCTION

All three of the teachers in the chapter-opening vignettes are committed to using constructive guidance. As described in Chapter 1, they have an *authoritative* trust-building style of interacting with children. They are warm and they genuinely like children; understand child development; and deliver messages simply, kindly, firmly, and consistently. They also use positive discipline strategies, set reasonable fair limits, monitor and supervise children well, and give reasons for limits. Combining responsiveness and reasonable expectations is the key to the positive, powerful, long-lasting effect of the authoritative style on children's behavior and development (Baumrind, 1996).

Effective teachers monitor and supervise children well, which implies that they *observe* children's behavior. Their proficiency at observation and their willingness to observe do not provide easy answers, but they do yield information they can use for making sound decisions about how to support children. Effective teachers use observation to crack the code, or unravel the meaning of Enrique's, Jerry's, and Sandi's behavior. This will make it possible for them to guide the children. In this chapter, we will briefly examine the meaning of assessment in early childhood education. The focus, however, is on the role of **observation** in guiding children. First, we will examine the role of assessment, and then we will focus on reasons for observing children's behavior. A major part of the chapter emphasizes practical methods for observing young children.

Observation
Systematic study; in guidance refers to watching, recording, and reflecting on children's behavior

:: ASSESSMENT IN EARLY CHILDHOOD EDUCATION

Assessment involves gathering and recording information about young children's development and learning appropriately and ethically. Teachers use assessment to make a variety of decisions affecting children, such as developing plans for individual children or for groups of children. Appropriate assessment involves many sources of information about young children's development and it is appropriate for *all* children, including those with disabilities or children from diverse backgrounds (National Association of the Education of Young Children 2009; Wilson, 2009).

The major overall goal of assessment is to identify and build on children's strengths; appropriate assessment, therefore, is strength-based. It is important to assess all domains of development because we take a whole-child approach and because all domains are the basis of state learning standards. In addition, how a child develops in the domains, including the social and emotional, is related to outcomes such as school success. Social and emotional competence includes skills such as regulating emotions and getting along well with others. Assessing children's social and emotional strengths yields information teachers can use to support development in these domains (Kozey, Merkel, & Ford, 2006; Scott-Little, Kagan, & Frelow, 2006; Snow & Van Hemel, 2008).

Appropriate assessment benefits children, teachers, administrators, and parents. Parents benefit because ethically done assessment gives them a full, rich picture of their child's development and learning. They also benefit from being a member of the assessment team. Children benefit when teachers use assessment to plan effective environments and curriculum. Children also gain when they learn how to evaluate and reflect on their own work. Teachers and administrators benefit from

Assessment
Systematic procedure for obtaining information from observations, interviews, portfolios, projects, tests, and other sources that can be used to make judgments about characteristics of children or programs

effective assessment because they get a good picture of a child's development, which helps them perform their roles more effectively.

> **EXAMPLE**   Mr. Sanchez observed how a second-grade child new to the classroom reacted to the morning meeting. He recorded the child's ability to join the group on the very first day, not seeming to be afraid at all. He noted, however, that she did not know the greeting. This reminded him to make sure that she had a friend to help her learn the greetings used in their meetings.

Assessment in early childhood education has several purposes. It allows teachers to plan so that they can meet *all* children's developmental and learning needs. For the National Association of the Education of Young Children (2007), *all* means all, or each and every child, including, for example, children with disabilities and those who are homeless as well as young children who are learning English. First, young English language learners have a right to be assessed so that teachers can make informed decisions about how to assist them. Second, they have a right to be assessed in ways that support their development (National Association of the Education of Young Children, 2003; 2005). Good assessment also allows teachers to identify individual children who might need focused programs or interventions. A third purpose for assessment is to evaluate the effectiveness of programs and services (Shepard, Kagan, & Wurtz, 1998).

There are many good ways to assess young children (National Association of the Education of Young Children, 2009). **Authentic assessment** is performance-based, with children applying their skills and knowledge in a real-world setting. Examples include their work samples, interviews with children, and *teacher observation* (National Association of the Education of Young Children, 2009). This chapter emphasizes observation, an essential part of effectively guiding children. We will examine reasons for observing and will look at what we can learn about children's behavior with systematic study. You will also learn about several practical and efficient methods for observing children's behavior and development.

Authentic assessment
Children apply their skills and knowledge in a real-world setting

myeducationlab

:: REASONS FOR OBSERVING CHILDREN'S BEHAVIOR

Observation helps teachers gather information that they need in planning for children. In guiding children, the major reasons for observing are that they communicate with behavior, we can discover and build on their strengths, and we can assess individual needs.

Children Communicate with Behavior

Perceptive teachers know that behavior has meaning, that it is a code. For example, a 3-year-old whirls with delight, trying to catch snowflakes. Another child's face turns red with anger as he strikes out at a classmate. A 5-year-old twirls her hair tightly around her finger as she sits hunched over a workbook page. A boy in the same class lowers his head until it nearly touches his workbook and turns his head from side to side, eyes darting to the other children's pages. Finally, a tear drops onto his page. A first grader, head thrust forward slightly, one hand scratching his head, eyes open wide in wonder and mouth making a little O-shape, stares at the gorilla mother and her baby in the zoo.

Head scratching, wide eyes, worried looks, tears, twirling, smiling, a red face, and a fist that smashes—not one of these children uttered a word, but they all communicated eloquently. Their hands, feet, facial expressions, and body movements communicated just as well as words could. Of course, young children *do* communicate with words. They are just as likely, though, to tell us what they are experiencing, how they feel, and what they think through their behavior.

Their words and behavior give clues about what happened, who was involved, when things happen, and where things take place. Reflecting on these "W" questions often helps teachers to figure out the final "W" question, which is *why* some behaviors occur. See Table 6.1 for an explanation of the five **"W" questions about behavior**.

Discover and Build on Children's Strengths

Ethical professionals observe behavior to discover children's preferences and what they can do successfully. We also use observations as a logical step in helping children with challenging behaviors and identifying strong points, as well as areas in which the child needs help. For example, a teacher might observe that a child,

"W" questions about behavior:
Questions that observers can answer with well-planned observations. They include What? Who? When? Where? and Why?

TABLE 6.1	The 5 "W" questions about children's behavior
The Question	**Ask Yourself**
Who was involved?	Was only the one child involved, or were others involved? If there were others, were they adults, children, or both? Did the behavior involve animals? If this is a recurring behavior, are the same children, adults, or animals generally involved?
What happened?	Note the *precise* nature of the behavior. Record what happened before and after the behavior. Note how long the behavior went on.
When did the behavior occur?	Does it occur at the same times during the day or at different times? Only on certain days of the week or every day? What type of activity is going on at the time—for example, is the child arriving at school; is it naptime, large-group time, during transitions or throughout the day? Be specific.
Where did the behavior take place?	Does it happen only in certain areas of the classroom or school, or just about anywhere?
Why did the child behave this way?	This requires you to reflect and interpret the behavior, which is difficult. Reflect on answers to the other four questions. Decide if you have enough information for interpreting. Do you even need to interpret this behavior? Do you need more information before you can make an accurate conclusion?

Mr. Sanchez has observed that the children in his class seem to prefer working with other children.

cheerful and well liked, does have some trouble when interacting with others because he occasionally interrupts them. Teachers observe a child alone or as she works with others. See the examples below.

> **EXAMPLES**   Mr. Sanchez discovered that Jim often took on a leadership role when he collaborated with other children in small-group activities, which is a strength.
>
> Mrs. Woodward observed Jerry's social skills because some of the children had been rejecting his bids to play with them (he needed help with some social skills).

Review Individual Needs

Teachers also use observation to contribute to a team that assesses individual and special needs. They would not be responsible for making an official diagnosis, but they would participate in a larger plan to arrive at a diagnosis. It is important that special needs such as autism spectrum disorder (ASD) be diagnosed as early as possible. Parents and teachers, in spite of not making a formal diagnosis, are invited and often expected to observe early symptoms of ASD in young children (Filipek, 2008; National Institute of Mental Health, 2009).

Figure 6.1a lists the three major categories of indicators of ASD. Towle (2009) has developed a video through which teachers directly observe core indicators of this disability in children who are between 12 and 48 months old. The link is in the References section at the end of this book. Determining whether a child has attention deficit disorder (ADD) or attention deficit hyperactivity disorder (ADHD) also requires observation as one part of the diagnosis (American Academy of Child & Adolescent Psychiatry [AACAP], 2008; Smith, Jaffe-Gill, Segal, & Segal, 2008). Figure 6.1b shows behavioral indicators of ADHD.

FIGURE 6.1a — Indicators of autism spectrum disorders

Social skill
- Content being alone
- Ignores a teacher or parent's bid for attention
- Seldom makes or asks for eye contact
- Does not respond when someone calls his name
- Problems with joint attention or sharing interest in an object or event with someone and looking back and forth between the other person and the object (seen very early, at about 10 to 12 months)
- Problems making friends

Communication deficits
- Lacks speech, important when coupled with
  - No apparent desire to talk
  - No compensatory skills such as using gestures
  - Parroting of speech of others; should not be confused with advanced speech

Repetitive patterns of behavior
- Non-functional and recurring behaviors such as twirling, rocking, hand flapping
- Might not advance beyond a sensory motor type of play with objects, such as repeatedly opening and closing snaps on a doll's dress, rather than playing with the doll

Source: Based on Johnson, Myers, & Council on Children with Disabilities (2007).

FIGURE 6.1b — Behavioral indicators of ADHD

ADHD is seen in 3 to 5% of school-age children. The following are some of the behaviors that children with ADHD typically display. Many young children have difficulty paying attention or are easily distracted. Children with ADHD, however, show these behaviors **much more frequently and much more severely than do other children of the same age and developmental level.**

- Blurts out answers
- Very easily distracted
- Fidgets or squirms
- Talks too much and has difficulty playing quietly
- Has trouble paying attention
- Makes careless mistakes; does not pay attention to details
- Has trouble listening and following directions
- Interrupts others or intrudes on others
- Impatient

Source: Based upon material developed by the American Academy of Child & Adolescent Psychiatry, "Children Who Cannot Pay Attention," 2008, *AACAP Facts for Families*, No. 6. Adapted by permission.

:: PRACTICAL METHODS FOR OBSERVING CHILDREN'S BEHAVIOR

Constructive positive guidance rests on observing, reflecting on what you see, and then wisely using the information to guide children. This part of the chapter focuses on practical information that teachers need to observe well. There are several major methods for observing, and you will learn how to choose the format best suited to your needs.

Choosing the most helpful format for observing depends on whether you need to tell or narrate a story. If you need to tell or narrate a story, then you would choose a **narrative method**, such as anecdotal or running records. If you do not need to write an account, then you would choose a **non-narrative method**, such as a checklist or rating scale. You could also choose a sampling format such as time sampling or event sampling.

Anecdotal Records

An **anecdotal record** allows a teacher to observe an incident and then to tell about it in brief notes that form a snapshot of the incident. There is just enough detail to describe the incident accurately and to recall it later. Teachers can use this method to observe a variety of behaviors or any aspect of children's development or learning. The observations can be spontaneous or planned. For example, a primary-grade teacher might plan to record anecdotal records on every child's social skills. He might then make a few unplanned entries about how other children react to a child's improved social skills.

Using anecdotal records provides clear advantages. Teachers write anecdotal records while they teach; therefore, they do not have to take time away from the children. Anecdotal records are easy to learn to use and take very little of a teacher's time. Anecdotal records also have two disadvantages. The first is that there is very little information given—an anecdotal record is, after all, a snapshot, a very short story. Another is that an observer might come up with conclusions unsupported by data presented in the notes.

Figure 6.2 shows the format for anecdotal records. Some teachers duplicate the form and make several copies readily available. They file completed forms in a child's folder. Some teachers use sticky notes instead of the form and place these

Narrative method
Observation that tells a story

Non-narrative method
Observation method that does not tell a story

Anecdotal record
Brief written notes about an incident; like a snapshot; gives less information that the longer running record

---

FIGURE 6.2 Anecdotal record format

Goal for this observation: Jerry's social development

Date/day: Thursday, May 20

Time of day: 8:00 a.m.

Focus child, if appropriate: Jerry (J)

Other children involved? Sarah (S)

The anecdote: S had gone to the art center immediately after putting things in her cubby. She asked Jerry to play there, too. He walked over to the center but just stood, watching as Sarah chose a marker. She turned to him, offering a marker. He smiled and took it, and then they worked on drawing together.

Reflections/interpretations: Jerry often, but certainly not always, hesitates before beginning to play, even when another child has issued a clear invitation. He seems to be very cautious but also seems to enjoy playing with others, and he usually responds in a very positive way.

very brief entries in the file. Still other teachers prefer to use a digital voice recorder, with a file for each child, or they like recording anecdotal records on a computer or other electronic device. Taking a digital photograph of a child during an episode about which one is writing is an effective addition to the file. Whichever format they choose, teachers are responsible for maintaining files in a confidential manner and guarding the child's privacy.

Running Record

A **running record** is like the anecdotal record in that it tells a story, but it is also different because it gives more detail. Greater detail gives more information that should help a teacher understand some developmental issue, such as how a child expresses feelings. Having a clear focus is important here. For instance, a teacher might focus on one child's attempt to enter an ongoing work group, or on the class's general reaction to a new learning center or a change in an existing center.

Running record
A longer narrative method for observing; tells a longer story; gives more detail than an anecdotal record

Running records take only about 5 to 10 minutes. They allow a teacher to see an incident in detail. For example, in a 5-minute segment of observing on the playground, Mr. Sanchez watched Hector as he was greeted by four other children and all five approached the climbing wall. Mr. Sanchez documented Hector's continued positive interaction with the others. A clear drawback is that a teacher cannot interact with the children in his class while observing.

Figure 6.3 shows the format for running records. There are three columns. Use the Context/Background/Time column to record brief notes on the setting: Where did the incident take place? Was there something going on that affected the context? For instance, were there sirens blaring outside? Did the mood of the group seem important for this observation? It is a good idea to record the time you begin to take notes and the time you end.

Most of the writing takes place in the second, the Intensive Observation, column. Here, a teacher gives an objective and somewhat detailed account of the episode and records both the child's speech and action. It is important to record only observable data—facts, what you saw and heard—not your opinion. In the next example, the observer has stated an opinion that cannot be backed up by what she has recorded. Teachers should refrain from making such judgments.

EXAMPLE   "Sammy was selfish. He took the last piece of fruit." This is an opinion.

First, we do not have the right to judge others and there simply is not enough information presented for the teacher to conclude that Sammy needs help with the idea of sharing. This is one observation, and it is not ethical to draw conclusions on such an unconvincing amount of data.

It is advisable to record only what you see or hear, as the next example shows.

EXAMPLE   "Sammy had eaten two apple slices already when John joined the group. There was one slice left, Sammy watching it closely. Just as John reached for the plate, Sammy swept the plate over to his spot at the table, seized the remaining fruit, popped it into his mouth, and turned to John, grinning. He said, "Two points!""

FIGURE 6.3	Running record format

Focus: Jerry/social development S = Sarah
Date: May 15 J = Jerry

Context/Background/Time	Intensive Observation	Comments/Reflections
8:00 a.m. Arrival time: children arrive, put things in cubbies, and then go right to a chosen center. Today, the teacher had placed a very large piece of paper on a wall—a mural-size piece of paper. Sarah's mother drove both Jerry and Sarah to school. Jerry and Sarah live next door to each other and have a good relationship. She has helped Jerry gain new social skills, but they occasionally have arguments.	S & J put things in cubbies, S surveying the room. J continued to organize his cubby.	
	S, "O-o-o . . . look, J! A BIG piece of paper. J glanced at the paper as S speed-walked to the paper, set up for mural drawing. S looked at the baskets on the floor, picked up a marker, and ran her hands over it, smiling. S dropped the marker, and scurried back to Jerry.	S indicates that she wants to play with J.
	S whispered to J, "I saw *new* markers in the art center. They're big and fat! Let's go *there*." S hurried back and grabbed a marker.	J seems curious. As usual, is cautious. Other observations reveal his trust in S.
	J walked slowly to the mural, watching S for about 15 seconds. He moved closer and looked in the basket of markers.	J's smile/nod: nonverbal positive interaction. Tentative in accepting even S's offer.
	S looked up at him, "See? Really fat markers!" She held one out to him. J *smiled at her, nodded,* and then slowly folded a hand around the marker.	S responds positively. Issues another invitation to work together.
	S smiled back, relinquished the marker, picked up another, saying, "Come on. Let's draw!" (Observation lasted 5 minutes)	

This anecdotal record gives better data. We have a better picture of Sammy's actions and words. The observer has not stated an opinion. However, we still do not have enough data to make conclusions. We would need more data, such as what happened before snack time, whether John had done something that upset Sammy before snack, and whether Sammy does this sort of thing with other children and in different places. One observation, however clearly written, is not enough data for making judgments.

The third column, Comments/Reflections, is for brief comments and reflections after completing the intensive observation. Regarding Hector, Mr. Sanchez commented, "Same thing yesterday . . . lots of children greeted him (Hector) . . . good social skills." For the apple episode, the teacher simply said, "Have not seen Sammy act this way before . . . will observe further." It is not necessary to comment on or interpret every observation, but it is when we have detected a pattern.

Checklists

A **checklist** is a list of characteristics or behaviors. A teacher observes an individual child or a group of children and notes whether each child does or does not show that behavior. The teacher records a check if a child shows the behavior or leaves a blank space if a child does not show the behavior. Checklists are an efficient way to determine the presence or absence of behaviors. For example, which children wash their hands correctly? How do children react to anger-arousing interactions? What social skills does the child demonstrate most of the time?

A checklist is a shortcut method because so little detail is given and it takes so little of a teacher's time. The teacher does not need to tell or narrate a story; thus, a checklist, like rating scales, and the sampling methods described in this chapter, is a non-narrative method. For a hand-washing checklist, for example, a teacher would know only whether a child had demonstrated the skill but would not know if he had to be reminded to wash his hands. You would choose a checklist approach if you only needed to know whether a child can or cannot do something. You would choose another method if you needed more detail.

Figure 6.4 shows the format for one type of checklist. It is McClellan and Katz's (2001) Social Attributes Checklist, which assesses social development. This checklist should be used several times to get as accurate an idea as possible. The developers of this checklist believe that a child's social development is adequate if he *usually* shows many of the attributes in the checklist.

Checklists have several benefits or advantages. They are extremely easy and quick to use for behaviors requiring only a check to determine their presence or absence. Checklists are flexible, meaning that teachers can choose when to complete the checklists and can use them to observe a wide array of behaviors. The drawbacks for checklists include lack of information about the quality of the behavior or the *how* of the behavior. It tells an observer whether a child approaches a group, for instance, but does not indicate *how* she approached: fearfully? joyfully? cautiously? Checklists give no information on how frequently a child shows a behavior. Does the child who approached a work group do this every day? Only when encouraged by the teacher? Only when specific children are in that group?

Increase the power of any of the non-narrative methods by combining them with anecdotal or running records, thus giving the detail missing in checklists. Some teachers insert a comment section on a checklist so that they can record their reflections or comments. This allows the teacher to give a bit more detail on the checklist.

Rating Scales

Teachers use a **rating scale** to summarize observations and to make a judgment about a child's performance. This implies that the teacher has already been observing with some other method. A rating scale is a shortcut method because the teacher does not present the original data, but it does allow teachers to organize information quickly and in an easy-to-read format.

Teachers can develop rating scales that give them information for making guidance decisions. Figure 6.5 is a rating scale on Jerry's peer relationship attributes.

Checklist
Non-narrative method for observing; an inventory of characteristics or behaviors that can be checked as observed

Rating scale
Non-narrative method for observing, a listing of activities or characteristics, calls for a summary judgment

---

FIGURE 6.4 A sample checklist

Social Attributes Checklist

Child's Name: _____ Date:

Observation number (circle one): 1   2   3   4

I. INDIVIDUAL ATTRIBUTES
The child:
____ Is *usually* in a positive mood
____ Is not *excessively* dependent on the teacher, assistant, or other adults
____ Usually comes to the program or setting willingly
____ Usually copes with rebuffs adequately
____ Shows the capacity to empathize
____ Has positive relationships with one or two peers; shows capacity to really care about them, miss them if they are absent
____ Displays the capacity for humor
____ Does not seem to be acutely lonely

II. SOCIAL SKILLS ATTRIBUTES
The child *usually:*
____ Approaches others positively
____ Expresses wishes and preferences clearly; gives reasons for actions and positions
____ Asserts own rights and needs appropriately
____ Is not easily intimidated by bullies
____ Expresses frustrations and anger effectively and without escalating disagreements or harming others
____ Gains access to ongoing groups at play and work
____ Enters ongoing discussion on the subject; makes relevant contributions to ongoing activities
____ Takes turns fairly easily
____ Shows interest in others; exchanges information with and requests information from others appropriately
____ Negotiates and compromises with others appropriately
____ Does not draw inappropriate attention to self
____ Accepts and enjoys peers and adults of ethnic groups other than his or her own
____ Interacts nonverbally with other children with smiles, waves, nods, and so forth

III. PEER RELATIONSHIP ATTRIBUTES
The child:
____ Is usually accepted versus neglected or rejected by other children
____ Is sometimes invited by other children to join them in play, friendship, and work
____ Is named by other children as someone they are friends with or like to play and work with

Source: This is from an ERIC DIGEST. You may duplicate it without permission but must give credit to the developers: McClellan & Katz (2001, March).

---

myeducation**lab**)

Go to the Assignments and Activities section of Topic 3: Observation in the MyEducationLab for your course and complete the activity entitled *Methods for Observing Children's Behavior.* Note that each strategy is useful for teachers.

These attributes were also checked in the sample checklist, but they are now evaluated using a rating scale instead. Note the section for comments, which allows a teacher to add brief notes on how she arrived at the judgment shown in the rating scale. The teacher has also added a section on how she intends to use the information to guide the child.

Some of the same advantages found in checklists exist in rating scales, too. Rating scales are easy to use and do not require much training. Observers tend to

---

| **FIGURE 6.5** | A sample rating scale |

Rating Scale: Peer Relationship Attributes

Reflect on your observations of this child, and rate his or her peer relationship characteristics. For each statement, choose the rating that best describes this child and circle the appropriate spot on the scale. Write a brief narrative in the Comments section. Use this information when you think about how to guide this child's peer relationships.

Child's Name: Jerry

Date: May 20

	Usually	Only Occasionally	Never
Accepted by other children	⊖		
Neglected or rejected by other children			⊖
Invited by other children to join them in play, friendship, and work	⊖		
Named by other children as a friend	⊖		
Named by other children as someone they like to play and work with	⊖		

Comments: Jerry is well liked and, like all the children his age, has learned quite a lot about managing emotions and about social skills this year.

How I will use this information in guiding this child:

_____

---

like using rating scales because they get to make a judgment and do not record raw data. Disadvantages include the possibility of personal bias because the observer does not give supporting data. Many observers tend to rate every child at the middle of a rating scale, effectively rendering it useless.

Teachers use rating scales only after they have observed a child in some other way and then want to make an overall statement about some aspect of guidance. For example, if a teacher has completed several objectively written anecdotal records about a child's peer relationship attributes, then a rating scale on the same topic would be a good way to present the data. The teacher could use the rating scale when talking with parents.

Event Sampling

Event sampling is a good way to observe one particular aspect of a child's development or learning. An observer identifies a specific target, such as "positive nonverbal interaction with other children." An important step is to define the category precisely. For instance, the teacher defines *positive nonverbal interaction* as "nodding; smiling; waving; or giving a thumbs-up, a high-five, or other positive gesture of greeting." Then the teacher observes the child and records instances only of the defined behavior, nothing else.

Event sampling
Formal method for identifying specific categories of behavior

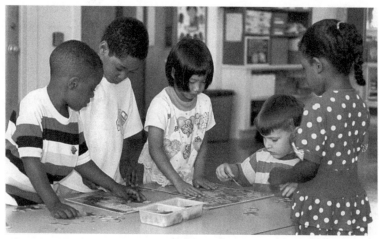

Mrs. Woodard has concluded, after several observations, that Brian (far left) works very well with other children.

Event sampling is a very focused type of observation and is quite useful (Brassard & Boehm, 2007). Suppose that a teacher, when using the Social Attributes Checklist, did not check an item such as "usually approaches others positively." The teacher wants to know more about this social skill for the child and decides to do an event sampling, which would zero in on that aspect of behavior. The major advantages of event sampling are that the focus is on something so specific and that a bit of detail is encouraged. A potential drawback would arise if the teacher did not define the behavior well.

Figure 6.6 is an example of an event sampling form. In addition to the information about the date and child's name, you will see that there are three essential

---

FIGURE 6.6   **Event sampling form**

Focus of the observation: Social skills, positive nonverbal interaction

The event that I am looking for is as follows: Interacts nonverbally with other children with smiles, waves, nods, a thumbs-up, a pat on the back

Day of week/date: Thursday, May 20

Time: 8:00 a.m.

Child: Jerry

Antecedent event: What happened before the event?	Sarah whispered to Jerry, "I saw *new* markers in the art center. They're big and fat!"
Describe the event	Sarah went to the art center and stood at the mural paper on the wall. Jerry watched for about 15 seconds and then approached Sarah. She looked up at him and said, "See? Really fat markers!" and held one up for him to see. *He smiled at her and nodded.*
Results: What happened after the event?	Sarah smiled back and said, "Come on. Let's draw."

things to record. First is what happened right before the event, such as Sarah's observation told to Jerry that there were brand new markers in the writing center. Second is the event itself. Third is what happened after the event, such as Sarah's statement that there were many markers.

Time Sampling

Time sampling allows teachers to observe small samples of a child's behavior. It is useful in guiding children because teachers often use it for recording children's interactions. Time sampling is different from event sampling because it doesn't record every instance of a behavior, such as positive interaction with other children, only a *sampling* of the behavior.

Time sampling
Observes for a limited time period; focuses on a precisely defined behavior; records whether that behavior occurred

Figure 6.7 shows a time sampling form. The observer has to choose the total amount of time for observing and then divides the total time into equal intervals. The observer also decides the length of each interval. Finally, the observer chooses how long he will observe during the interval, for example, the first or last minute of a 3-minute interval.

There are benefits in time sampling. It requires observers to write less than in anecdotal or running records or even event sampling. Observers do not have to record every example of the behavior, only those behaviors that occur in the designated interval. A disadvantage is that some of the target behaviors do occur but outside the interval designated for monitoring.

| FIGURE 6.7 | Time sampling form |

Observer's name: C Woodward

Child's name: Jerry

Date: May 20

Start time: 8:00, beginning of center time

Behavior observed: Positive nonverbal interactions with another child, for example, smiles, nods, thumbs-up, waves

Total Observation Time: 20 min.	How long is each interval? 4 minutes	When and for how long will I observe in the interval? 1½ minutes at the beginning of the interval
Interval	Did the behavior occur (yes if the behavior occurs; no if it does not); number of times that it occurred	Total number of times that the behavior occurred for this observation time period
1	Yes, one time in the 1½-minute interval	
2	Yes, one time	Jerry showed positive nonverbal interaction with another child 4 times during the first 20 minutes of center time.
3	No	
4	Yes, two times	
5	No	

PEARSON
myeducationlab

Go to the Building
Teaching Skills and
Dispositions section of
Topic 3: Observation in the
MyEducationLab for your
course and complete the
activity entitled *Practicing
Observation Skills*. Notice
how useful anecdotal
records are to early
childhood teachers.

PEARSON
myeducationlab

To check your
comprehension on the
content covered in
Chapter 6, go to the Book
Specific Resources in the
MyEducationLab for your
course, select your text,
and complete the Study
Plan. Here you will be able
to take a chapter quiz,
receive feedback on your
answers, and then access
review, practice, and
enrichment activities to
enhance your
understanding of chapter
content.

WORKING *with* FAMILIES   FAMILIES AS PARTNERS IN OBSERVING

Invite parents to form a partnership with you. Working together, you and the parents will guide children in your class even more effectively. Here are some ideas for helping parents understand the importance of observation.

- **Explain.** Give a handout or a web site about why it is important to observe (see the Resources for Parents below). Tell parents that you will be observing in the classroom to learn more about their child. Explain that you will use your observations to better plan for individual children.
- **Illustrate.** Show an example of a real observation form (one that is blank) and describe how you will complete it. Mrs. Woodward showed an anecdotal record form to a group of parents.
- **Request.** Tell parents that you will be observing emotional and social development, and request examples of their child's reaction to a happy emotion. Ask that they write this down or simply verbalize it. Tell them that you will be looking for similar examples of this and other parts of emotional development or social skills.
- **Invite.** Give parents two or three anecdotal record forms and urge them to observe how their child gets along with other children over the next couple of days. Request that they let you know about their observations.
- **Report.** Merge your and the parents' observations for your final report. Discuss both sets of observations with parents when you meet with them.

RESOURCES FOR PARENTS

Davis, L., & Keyser, J. (no date). *Learning to observe children*. Online. Retrieved on May 16, 2009, from http://www.canadianparents.com/article/learning-to-observe-children. This is a very brief article listing good reasons for observing for parents.

Grumbach, G. (2007). *Developing emotionally skilled children*. Online. Retrieved on May 16, 2009, from http://parenting247.org/article.cfm?ContentID=1180&strategy=6&AgeGroup=3. This article describes observing children as the first step in helping them develop emotional competence.

ANALYZE A VIGNETTE

Refer to the chapter-opening vignettes and to Table 6.1. Answer the following questions.

1. Answer as many of the first four "W" questions (Who, What, Where, When) as possible for each vignette.
2. The "Why" question—Toddlers: Enrique insisted on putting on mittens before his coat. Why might such a young child behave in this way? What does it tell us about normal toddler development?
3. The "Why" question—Preschool: Jerry shared something with Sarah and later she made room for him in group time. In your view, is it possible that the two events are connected? If so, how?
4. The "Why" question—Primary: Sandi had a positive approach and was cheerful. Why does this sort of interaction usually work for children? What do you think would have happened if she had *ordered* Dave to wait his turn?

SUMMARY

Assessment involves using a variety of methods to gather and record information about young children's development and learning. Appropriate assessment is done ethically, and teachers use assessment to make many different decisions that affect young children. Observation is one method of assessment. Key ideas about assessment include the following:

- Appropriate assessment is strength-based, which means that it focuses on children's strong points, not their weaknesses.
- Appropriate assessment benefits children, teachers, parents, and administrators.
- One of the major purposes of assessment is for teachers to plan for meeting children's individual needs.

Observation, a form of authentic assessment, helps teachers plan for children. There are three main reasons for observing children's behavior:

- Children communicate with behavior. Observing helps teachers answer the 5 "W" questions about children's behavior.
- To discover and build on what children know and can do well.
- To assess individual needs.

Teachers have access to several realistic and efficient methods for observing. Some of these tell a story and other methods do not. Teachers choose the method best suited to their needs. The methods include the following:

- Anecdotal and running records.
- Checklists and rating scales.
- Event sampling and time sampling.

QUESTIONS FOR REFLECTION

1. True or False? Observing a child's behavior always gives teachers the answer to a discipline dilemma or a child guidance issue. Explain your reasoning.
2. All of the examples for observation forms used the same behavior for illustration—Jerry's social skill development.

   a. How was the running record different from the time sampling?
   b. What were the major differences between the anecdotal record and the running record?
   c. How were the anecdotal record and the event sampling similar?

APPLY YOUR KNOWLEDGE

1. Suppose that you wanted to know more about the social skills, particularly turn taking, of the children in your kindergarten. Which of the following observational methods do you think would be the most powerful for getting this information? Why?
   a. Anecdotal records alone.
   b. Checklist alone.
   c. Anecdotal records plus checklist.

2. You decide to observe how a child reacts to anger-arousing events. Which of the formats for observing described in the chapter would work best for you in this case? Why?

KEY TERMS

Anecdotal record (*154*)
Assessment (*149*)
Authentic assessment (*150*)
Checklist (*157*)

Event sampling (*159*)
Narrative method (*154*)
Non-narrative method (*154*)
Observation (*149*)

Rating scale (*157*)
Running record (*155*)
Time sampling (*161*)
"W" questions about behavior (*160*)

WEB SITES

Center on the Social and Emotional Foundations
for Early Learning (CSEFEL)
http://www.vanderbilt.edu/csefel

A federally funded, national resources center. Excellent resources in general, and on using observation in particular. For example, type in *observation* in the site's search box. Look for the *What Works Brief, Number 9*, which is one example of how observation is used, along with other sources of information to help children with challenging behaviors.

High Scope Foundation
http://www.highscope.org

Several good links. See the link for the Child Observation Record (COR). There is an Infant-Toddler COR and a Preschool COR. These are excellent observational assessment tools that chart a child's development and progress over time. Combines rating scales with anecdotal records. Highly recommended.

Special Topics in Child Guidance

Each of the five chapters in this part of the book is designed to help you apply your knowledge to a specific special topic in guiding children.

Chapter 7   Self-Esteem and Moral Identity

Developmentally appropriate child guidance helps children develop a healthy and balanced sense of self and self-esteem that is firmly rooted in a strong set of personal values. Chapter 7 gives you several practical suggestions on how to use guidance to support children in developing healthy self-esteem and a moral identity.

Chapter 8   Feelings and Friends: Emotional and Social Competence

Effective teachers support children's social and emotional competence. Children begin to develop these competencies in infancy and contine to develop them through childhood. We will explore what it means to be emotionally intelligent and how this relates to specific emotional competencies. You will also be able to describe social competence and examine some of the factors affecting emotional as well as social competence. You will then learn about practical strategies for helping children deal with their feelings well and get along with others.

Chapter 9   Resilience and Stress in Childhood

Chapter 9 explains the concept of resilience and concentrates on the positive when describing children and stress. You will read about the nature of stress and how stress affects children. The main focus in this chapter is to help you develop knowledge and skills for assisting children in coping with specific stressful events.

Chapter 10 Aggression and Bullying in Young Children

You will study two topics in Chapter 10: aggression and bullying. The chapter describes and explains different forms and purposes or goals of aggression. The focus then shifts to a topic of great concern to teachers—bullying, which is a type of aggression. The chapter explains how children gather information on how to be aggressive from different systems. You will learn specific strategies for dealing effectively with bullying and other forms of aggression.

Chapter 11 Minimizing Challenging Behavior

All teachers are puzzled at times by some behaviors in children. We feel frustrated or even annoyed when our positive strategies do not seem to work. Chapter 11 will help you understand challenging behaviors, including persistent difficult behavior. You will learn about the roots of challenging behavior and about specific information on how to deal with challenging behaviors like biting, teasing, and disrespectful language. This chapter introduces the decision-making model of child guidance, a framework for making decisions about guiding children deliberately and intentionally.

Self-Esteem and Moral Identity

"Someday, maybe, there will exist a well-informed, well-considered and yet fervent public conviction that the most deadly of all possible sins is the mutilation of a child's spirit . . . ."

—Erik Erikson (1958, p. 70)

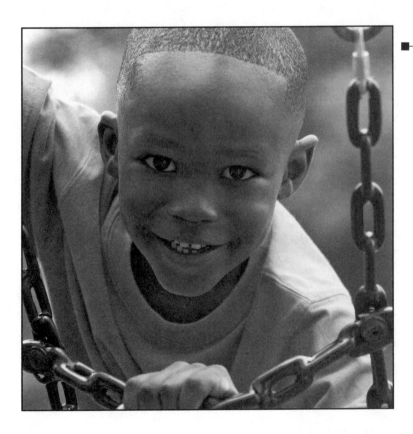

Chapter Contents

Guiding Questions

- What are the parts of the self and why are they important in children's development?
- What are the building blocks of self-esteem; how does it develop and how can I help children develop authentic self-esteem?
- Why do children need to develop a moral identity?

VIGNETTES

INFANT-TODDLER: PLAYING THE "POINT TO" GAME

Mr. Bjornrud sat facing 15-month-old Jamal, who had just pointed to his nose. The teacher said, "Now, point to your arm." "Arm!" squealed Jamal. They continued Jamal's favorite game, with the toddler pointing to his feet, legs, head, and eyes.

PRESCHOOL: SHOWING KINDNESS TO SQUEAK

Mrs. Woodward, the teacher, was leading a discussion on making rules for the classroom and wanted the children to help design the limits. "We need a rule about how to show kindness to Squeak, our hamster. What do you think that we should say?" Sarah said, "Don't drop Squeak. Don't squeeze him. Hold him like this." She demonstrated gentle holding and stroking. Jerry added, "Yeah, and be quiet when you're near his house."

PRIMARY: GRAPHING GROUP INFORMATION

Instead of doing an "all about me" chart for each child, Mr. Sanchez's class did an "all about us" chart. He explained this different approach. "I was trying out this idea to get the children away from focusing so much on themselves as individuals. It's Katz's (1993) idea, really. We gathered information about each child: number of teeth, eye color, number of lost teeth, shoe size, current weight, birth weight. Then we pooled all the information on each item and made graphs. What you see on the wall chart is information, for example, on how many children in the class have brown, blue, or green eyes or the average weight of first graders in our room. This way, we did not single out any one child."

:: INTRODUCTION

The children in the chapter-opening vignettes are learning about themselves and will eventually develop self-esteem and a moral identity. Building self-esteem is an active process that continues throughout a lifetime (Mruk, 2006). The wonderful thing about working with children is that we are present as children start to evaluate themselves, and we can help them construct a healthy and balanced view of themselves. Children's initial self-esteem develops slowly in early childhood and tends to be positive and stable (Robins & Trzesniewski, 2005). Authentic self-esteem—positive, healthy, earned, and balanced—provides a secure foundation for further growth and development. Negative, unhealthy, unbalanced self-esteem, on the other hand, provides a shaky foundation for a child's development. Some children with damaged self-esteem make a negative evaluation of their competence, control, or worth. This negative evaluation stays with a person for many years or even decades and affects many aspects of a person's life. Others have a positive view of their abilities but are conceited, arrogant, self-absorbed, and egotistical at the same time (Baumeister, Campbell, Kreuger, & Vohs, 2003; Katz, 1993). An excellent but arrogant skater, for example, might sneer at anybody with less skill.

In this chapter you will learn about the four parts of the self. We will then focus on the building blocks of self-esteem and how self-esteem develops. Then, because children need a strong moral compass as much as they need positive self-esteem, we will examine moral identity and what it means to a child's sense of self. Then you will study practices that help children develop positive, authentic, earned self-esteem.

:: PARTS OF THE SELF

The **self** is a mental structure, a set of ideas that humans gradually construct or build (Curry & Johnson, 1990; Harter, 2006; Mruk, 2006). Children need to develop a stable sense of self so that they understand themselves. Like all humans, they need to set goals, regulate thoughts and emotions, find out what they enjoy doing, and be able to persevere in meeting goals. Knowing one's self is the starting point to this understanding (Brown, Mangelsdorf, Neff, Schoppe-Sullivan, & Frosch, 2009).

Children begin to construct their sense of self during infancy and continue to develop this concept throughout their lives. The four parts or components making up a child's self are:

Self-awareness
Self-concept
Self-control
Self-esteem

Self
A concept that a child produces in his or her mind; ideas are constructed gradually; consists of four components: self-awareness, self-concept, self-control, and self-esteem

Figure 7.1 illustrates each of the four parts and Figure 7.2 gives examples of each.

Self-Awareness

Self-awareness refers to the idea that a child views himself as separate from others. For example, a child might say that his mother is a person and that he is separate from her. Infants gradually learn that they are separate from other people as the perceptual system develops during the first year of life. Self-awareness emerges during infancy and toddlerhood and continues to develop during early childhood. Self-awareness also means that a child realizes that he can make things happen. For example, an infant learns that when he cries, someone will pick him up. A preschool child knows that he can get the teacher's attention by asking for help.

Self-awareness
Child sees himself as separate from others

FIGURE 7.1   There are four parts to a child's self

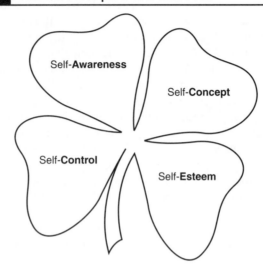

Self-**Awareness**

Self-**Concept**

Self-**Control**

Self-**Esteem**

FIGURE 7.2   Observe to discover what children are constructing about the parts of the self

Children gradually build ideas about the self and their current knowledge reveals itself in simple everyday statements that they make to other children or teachers. They also reveal their current knowledge about their self through behavior. Here are a few examples.

Self-awareness (child knows he is an individual and can influence events)

> "Mommy! (toddler points to his mother). "José!" (toddler points to himself).
> "When I curse, everybody looks at me and then they giggle or laugh" (preschool child's behavior indicates this).
> "We have five people in my family: Mommy, Dad, John, Sarah, and me" (kindergarten child says this when he and Mr. Nellis looked at pictures of families).
> "When I call my dog, she trots over to me and then I pet her or give her a treat" (primary child).
> "I swing at the mobile and it moves" (infant's behavior).

Self-concept (child learns things about herself)

> "My grandma told me that I look like my aunt Gail."
> "Sam and Ralph like me" (child learns that others like him).
> "I am a girl" (child learns that her gender is female).

> "I can run fast. I'm still learning how to swim" (child learns about athletic ability).
> "I can speak Spanish and English!" (child learns about ability to speak languages).

Self-control (children use these behaviors to regulate impulses, tolerate frustration, and delay immediate gratification)

> "I used WORDS to tell Pete that I wanted my book back."
> "I wanted to tell the teacher something, but he was talking with Susan, so I waited."
> "I'd better look at the list to see who is next at the computer."

Self-esteem (child evaluates the "self" she has come to know)

> "My dad called me a dummy this morning. I feel bad."
> "My uncle helped me with my math last night and said that I'm a 'natural-born' mathematician."
> "My brother and I finally figured out how to attach the wheels to the car. Mom said that we are persistent and that is a good way to be."
> "My teacher told the class that we work well together. We are a class full of helpers."

A child must be aware of her self as separate from others and as capable of causing things to happen before she can develop self-esteem.

Self-Concept

Self-concept is the knowledge that a child acquires about her self. Children go through a long process of learning about the self. They gradually gather information about their physical appearance, physical abilities, gender, intellectual abilities, and interpersonal skills. Gathering such knowledge occurs at about the same time as more general changes in cognitive development, as shown in the next examples.

Self-concept
The accumulation of knowledge that a child gathers about herself

> **EXAMPLE** Six-year-old Quang participated in one of the classic Piagetian conser-
> vation experiments with Mr. Sanchez and said, "You have the same amount of water
> in that short glass as you have in that tall glass because the short glass is so wide that
> it holds just as much as the tall glass." Conservation is one of the general changes in
> cognitive development).

During that same week the teacher heard Quang say to his friend Reese, "Yeah! We're boys and we'll always be boys. They're girls (pointing to a group of girls) and they're always going to be girls." This is called gender constancy, and children understand that gender remains the same when they understand the concept that some things remain the same despite apparent changes.

A child's set of ideas about himself affects how he behaves. Because 7-year-old Mi-Cha thinks that she can run fast, for example, she is much more likely to enter races than her friend who does not think that she can run fast.

Self-Control

Self-control, also called self-regulation, refers to controlling impulses, tolerating frustration, and delaying immediate gratification. The means of this control lies deep within us and is the basis of our intentional and deliberate behavior. In acquiring self-control, children must learn how to *stop* a behavior, such as blurting out questions during a large group. They have to be able, then, to inhibit a behavior. They must also be able to *do* something that they are supposed to do even if they do not want to comply. Therefore, they must be able to initiate or start a behavior (Bedrova & Leong, 2005).

Self-control
A child's ability to put off gratification until later, to put up with some frustration, and to keep impulses under control

Poverty affects young children in countless ways, one of which is its influence on self-control. A child's environment has a strong effect on how his or her brain develops and functions. Recent research shows that socioeconomic status (SES) affects children's brains. For example, there are disparities between low and high SES children in terms of how their brains process information (Hackman & Farah, 2009).

Other researchers measured 26 children's responses to a simple visual stimulus that changed. Half of the children were low SES and half were high SES. None of the children had brain damage and none had been exposed to prenatal drugs or alcohol. Low SES children's brains showed a dramatic difference in detecting changes in pictures of triangles. Their responses were similar to an adult who has had a stroke that affects the prefrontal cortex. The researchers concluded that the chronic stress of poverty alters children's brains but that the damage can be lessened (Kishiyama, Boyce, Jiminez, & Knight, 2009). One of the best things that teachers can do to help low SES children is to provide high-quality imaginative play in which they have to develop props and stop and think. Imaginative role playing requires that children begin to think about the roles involved and adjust to the "twists and turns" of such play (Valentine, 2008).

Chapter 3 lists milestones in self-regulation or self-control, and we see that children who are about 24 months old show the beginnings of self-regulation. Children become better able to use certain strategies to regulate their own behavior as they get older. Self-control or regulation enables children to stop themselves from hurting somebody, to think before acting, and to use words instead of hitting. Parents and teachers can choose guidance strategies that help children learn to regulate their own behavior. In the next example, Mr. Sanchez helps Chayton with inhibiting or stopping a behavior and then intentionally doing something more productive instead.

EXAMPLE   "Remember what we practiced yesterday?" Mr. Sanchez asked Chayton when he greeted him in the morning. "That's right. Listen to others during large-group lessons."

Self-Esteem

Self-esteem
A child's overall judgment of the self about which he is aware, knows about, and regulates

myeducationlab

Go to the Assignments and Activities section of Topic 1: Child Development in the MyEducationLab for your course and complete the activitiy entitled *Physical Activity and Development can Influence Children's Self-Esteem*. Note how play can have a positive influence on how children form self-esteem

Self-esteem refers to how a child evaluates the self about whom she has learned (Coopersmith, 1967; Harter, 2006; Mruk, 2006). A child pays attention to information that she has gathered about herself and judges the self. A child who evaluates her self as competent, in control, and worthy will likely develop healthy, balanced judgment; she is likely to have predominately positive self-esteem. A child who evaluates her self as unworthy, unloved, and not competent will likely develop a negative view of the self; she will very likely have predominately negative self-esteem.

A brief note on the term *high self-esteem*, which is a heterogenous term consisting of varied parts. We get an interesting picture when we examine the term *high self-esteem* more closely. Some people with high self-esteem simply and gratefully acknowledge their abilities, which is one type of person with high self-esteem. High self-esteem people can also include another type, however, such as those who are narcissistic and arrogant (Baumeister et al., 2003).

:: BUILDING BLOCKS OF SELF-ESTEEM

What is it in the self that a child examines and evaluates so that she can develop her self-esteem? Self-esteem is not just one overall global concept; it can be broken down into distinct parts (Coopersmith, 1967; Harter, 2006; Mruk, 2006). As shown in Figure 7.3, the parts or dimensions of self-esteem are:

Competence
Control
Worth

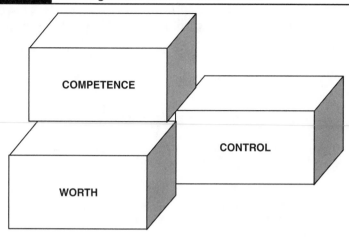

FIGURE 7.3 Competence, control, and a feeling of worthiness are the building blocks of a child's self-esteem

Competence

Competence is the ability to meet demands for achievement, and it grows over time and with effort (Tafarodi & Swarm, 1995; Dweck & Molden, 2005). Children earn authentic, healthy self-esteem. People with healthy self-esteem have learned that they cannot just wish for competence but that they must work for it. They understand that they have to make things happen through their own effort rather than trying to force or manipulate others into doing things for them. People with healthy self-esteem have earned a positive self-evaluation through hard work, which increases feelings of competence and results in earned self-esteem.

Children congratulated for mediocre work do not develop healthy, earned self-esteem. Giving good feedback means that teachers give positive feedback, as well as suggestions for change when appropriate. Failing to give suggestions for change or implying that everything a child does is excellent is highly inappropriate.

It is important to help children develop self-esteem that is realistic, positive, and healthy. It is highly *in*appropriate to boost children's view of themselves artificially. Artificially boosting self-esteem gives children inflated self-esteem and an unrealistically positive view about the self (Baumeister et al., 2003). Children who have a balanced sense of self can look at themselves in several dimensions and make realistic judgments about how they are doing in a particular area. It is possible to feel extremely competent in one area and only moderately competent in another, and still have positive self-esteem.

EXAMPLE Sandi, a child in Mr. Sanchez's first grade, is 6 years old and is very competent socially; she gets along well with adults and other children. She makes friends easily and knows how to get her parent or teacher's attention without whining. She deals with angry feelings in a positive way. She is only moderately competent in physical skills but seems to enjoy them anyway because her mother and father have never made physical skills an issue.

Competence
A child's ability to meet the culture's and her family's demands for success

Other children have a far less balanced view of themselves. They might not recognize their competence in an area and might even dwell on poor performance in some other area. Children with a negative view of their competence might have had their lack of ability pointed out by adults. Some children are humiliated for being competent.

EXAMPLE   Celia, 5 years old, likes and is very good at physical activities. Her mother, however, teases Celia about "turning into a boy" when she runs and climbs. Celia has begun to think about her physical abilities in a negative way, even though she is skillful.

A child's motivation affects how she achieves. Some children are primarily interested in understanding something new or in acquiring some new skill. They are oriented toward learning (Elliott & Dweck, 1988). They will fail at some tasks or make mistakes, but they will not just give up; they will try to overcome the problem.

EXAMPLE   Pete, a third grader in Mr. Sanchez's class, realized that he did not understand the new science concept about a pulley as a simple machine. He seemed puzzled but not upset about his confusion and said to his teacher, "I don't understand this. Can you help me?"

Other children, motivated differently, go to great lengths to avoid unfavorable judgments about their competence. They dread mistakes and often react to them by giving up a project instead of trying again, practicing, and overcoming the difficulty.

EXAMPLE   Eight-year-old Karim went to a day camp during the summer and one of the projects was to collect, preserve, and identify a variety of leaves. Karim forgot to press the leaves and ended up with crinkled, dry leaves that cracked when he put them in his book. When the camp counselor offered to help Karim gather new leaves, Karim started crying. He refused to go back to camp the next day.

Some children have confidence that they can achieve their goals, whereas others expect that they will not be able to achieve their goals even when they have the capacity to do so. Children who expect to perform well on challenging tasks are able to analyze the skills needed for effective performance. Children who expect to be able to perform well realistically analyze tasks. They are not overly optimistic, but they do not overestimate the difficulty of a task or say, "I can't do it" (Dweck & Leggett, 1988; Elliott & Dweck, 1988). They also tend to deal well with failure or minor setbacks.

Control

Control
The extent to which a child thinks that he can influence outcomes of events

Control is the degree to which a child thinks that he is responsible for how things turn out. Control is a lifelong issue, and a child's sense of control is a critical aspect of self-esteem. Some children believe that they do have a measure of control, that they can "get things done," and that their actions influence whether they achieve a goal. They also believe that they can decide how much effort to expend in achieving goals—that they have control over their effort. They have a positive and healthy view of control, as 4-year-old Nellie does in the next example.

EXAMPLE   Nellie was doing a science experiment—adding food coloring to white play dough to change the color of the dough. She tried to match a light blue color on a chart but added far too much coloring. Her teacher said, "You have a problem. What do you think would happen if you took this big glob of white dough and mixed it with your small glob of dark blue dough? It will take a lot of squishing and squashing!" Nellie pummeled and pushed the dough until she got the light color that she wanted and said, "Look! I made the color of the sky!"

Nellie had had a minor setback. Something had not gone well for her and she essentially failed at what she had set out to do. It is important for children to learn to deal with such minor setbacks if they are to develop authentic self-esteem (Katz, 1993). Hundreds of such interactions with adults who help them deal with setbacks teach children that they can control many of the outcomes in their lives.

Many children have been discouraged from viewing themselves as "in control." Authoritarian teachers and parents, for example, exert a great deal of arbitrary control over children, discouraging them from making decisions and from engaging in appropriate verbal give-and-take with adults. Some parents are abusive or neglectful, which very possibly has long-term negative effects on children's development (Child Welfare Information Gateway, 2008). For example, some abusive parents model an extremely rigid, external type of control. It is difficult for children from these types of families to evaluate themselves as controlling anything that happens to them. The children tend not to think that their own actions influence whether they achieve goals, and this contributes to negative self-esteem.

Worth
A child's view about how significant he is to others

Worth

Worth refers to a child's general sense of his own social value, of his significance to others (Tafarodi & Swarm, 1995). He evaluates how much he likes himself and whether he thinks that others like or love him. Whether a child judges himself worthy also grows from feeling accepted by and deserving of attention from others. Children who feel accepted, well liked, and deserving of others' attention are likely to evaluate themselves as worthy. Others see themselves as unloved and unworthy of attention and are likely to evaluate themselves as unworthy.

:: SELF-ESTEEM DEVELOPS IN A SOCIAL CONTEXT

Any child's view of herself develops in a social context or setting. Infants are born with a basic temperamental style and certain physical, psychological, and emotional characteristics. These characteristics influence that baby's behavior as well as adults' reactions to the

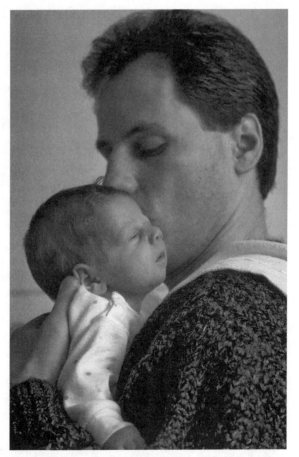

The "self" that an infant comes to know depends on the infant's characteristics *and* the behavior of other people.

infant. An infant's self depends on both factors—the child's characteristics and interaction behavior with other people (Kernis, Brown, & Brody, 2000; Mruk, 2006). This implies that both the child and the adult have an active role in a child's developing sense of self; a child's sense of self is not just a mirror image of the adult's attitude toward that child. However, *adults always have a greater share of responsibility in any interaction with a child.*

> **EXAMPLE**   Mr. Bjornrud, the infant teacher, noticed that Amelia, 5 months old, cried a lot in spite of loving and appropriate caregiving. The teacher thought that something was bothering Amelia, that Amelia needed something. The caregiver thought, "Hmm, how can I help Amelia?"

To this caregiver's credit, he recognized his responsibility to figure out how to mesh his responses with the baby's style.

Adults Influence a Child's Self-Esteem: Garbage In, Garbage Out (GIGO)

Teachers, parents, grandparents, brothers, sisters, and others make up a child's social environment; a child's opinion about her competence, control, and worth develops out of close involvement with them. Adults observe children, have attitudes about them, interact with them, and interpret a child's behavior and characteristics. Adults reflect their attitudes about children to children. Children evaluate the self and develop self-esteem, to some extent, because of the attitudes of others important to them. Parents and teachers affect children's self-esteem because young children believe that adults possess a superior wisdom and because children tend to rely on adult judgments.

Computer programmers use an unusual term, garbage in, garbage out, to describe the effect of feeding nonsensical or invalid data into a computer. What comes out is often a huge pile of equally nonsensical or invalid output. The process that adults use to influence children's self-esteem is similar to the process that a computer programmer employs to develop information "output."

Significant adults feed data to the child through words, facial expressions, and actions, which essentially outline the adult's attitude toward the child. The adult "data" say things such as:

> "You sure have lots of friends!"
>
> "You're so gentle with Sam [the puppy]. I'll bet he feels safe with you."
>
> "I like being with you."
>
> "It's okay to feel angry when somebody takes something that belongs to you and you remembered to use words to tell him that you were upset."
>
> "It was thoughtful of you to whisper when you walked past the baby's crib when she was sleeping."
>
> "It was fun to play the video game with you. Let's do that again sometime."
>
> "This class really works well together on projects."
>
> "You tell funny jokes. Let's call Grandma so that you can tell her!"

Unfortunately, adult data can also bruise self-esteem with hurtful statements such as these:

"No wonder nobody plays with you!"

"You're really a lazy person."

"Yuck! What muddy colors you used for painting."

"Don't bother me. Play by yourself."

"Grow up! Stop whining because she took your puzzle."

"Why don't you stop cramming food into your face? You're fat enough already."

"You know something? I wish you'd never been born."

Computer scientists emphasize that if input is garbage (harmful data), then we can expect output to be garbage as well. Adults who degrade a child with garbage messages should realize the harmful effects of their practice: garbage in, garbage out.

Other relationships, such as those with other children, can also affect children's self-esteem.

Bullying: Effect on Self-Esteem

Bronfenbrenner's theory reminds us that the systems in which children live include other children, for example, a child's peers and siblings. Interactions and relationships with other children can affect a child's self-esteem. Some interactions, such as bullying, are problemmatic.

Bullying is a form of aggression in which a child intends to humiliate or hurt the victim. Bullying involves repeated negative acts in which the bully enjoys hurting the victim and the victim feels oppressed. Bullying can be verbal, psychological, or physical. For example, a bully might hit or punch his victim or might call him names. The bully might tease his victim or spread rumors. Bullying is done in person or through some form of technology, such as cell phones, the Internet, or interactive and digital devices. Some children are pure bullies who bully others but have never been bullied themselves. Other children are pure victims. They have been bullied but have never bullied others. Other children bully and are bullied.

Bullying
Intentionally and repeatedly hurting or humiliating someone. Bullying takes different forms and is done in different ways

Bullying seems to have a negative effect on children's self-esteem, whether they are the bullies, victims, or both bully and victim. The children in O'Moore and Kirkham's study (2001) had lower overall self-esteem than children who had neither been a bully or a victim. Victims had the lowest scores on self-esteem. Helping children develop a positive view of themselves has the potential for protecting them from bullyng. We will examine bullying more closely in Chapter 10.

:: MORAL IDENTITY

It is not enough to help children develop knowledge about themselves and positive self-esteem. Children certainly need positive self-esteem, but each child also needs to embed his or her self in a strong ethical and moral framework. A child needs to develop a moral identity.

What Is Moral Identity?

Moral identity
Describing oneself by
using moral principles
such as honesty, kindness,
fairness

A person may define and describe him- or herself in many ways. One way is to use concepts such as honesty, kindness, or fairness, which are *moral principles*. Thus, a person who uses moral principles is referring to his **moral identity**. His view of himself focuses closely on the ethical and moral self. It involves the person's willingness to see things from another's perspective as well as behaving compassionately (Coles, 1986; 1997; Damon, 2009; Lapsley, 2008). While every person has a moral identity, people differ in the degree to which they use moral principles to define the self. Words used to describe oneself give clues about that person's moral identity.

> **EXAMPLE**   Alberto uses words such as "fair when I work as an umpire" and "kind to my pets" to describe himself. Alberto's friends use words such as "nice" and "kind" to describe him because he will help anybody with math.

Just as a compass indicates direction, Alberto has a strong *moral compass* guiding his behavior. Suppose that he did not have such a guide and approached things differently, such as refusing to help others or even laughing at them. With such egotistic, arrogant behavior, it would be unlikely that he would describe himself as kind. While children need to feel good about themselves, they also need a strong, objective moral compass to help them acquire a stable sense of right and wrong.

A child's moral identity takes shape in later childhood and governs his view of the right thing to do. Alberto, 16 years old, knows that the right thing to do is to help others, whether it is his pets or other students needing help with math. Second, moral identity also determines *why* a child should take a specific course of action (Damon, 2004). Alberto takes his friends' perspective and understands their frustration when they have trouble with math because he also experiences frustration. He reasons that he can and should help them learn math, just as others have helped him.

Theoretical Perspectives on Moral Identity

Many theorists have contributed to understanding moral and character development. Lawrence Kolhberg's cognitive developmental approach described a lifespan view of moral development. He named six stages in moral development and maintained that the stages were universal. Each stage, he believed, was qualitatively different from stages either before or after it (Kohlberg, 1958; 1981; Power, Higgins, & Kohlberg, 1989). However, Carol Gilligan noted that Kohlberg's work was based on research involving boys only, not girls. She believes that his work, therefore, was fundamentally flawed. Her research went beyond that of Kohlberg to describe and explain girls' moral development (Gilligan, 1993; 2008; Snall, 2007).

Robert Coles, a child psychiatrist, wrote extensively about the moral life of children (Coles, 1986; 1997). He was particularly interested in how some children living under the most extreme stress could show grace, psychological strength, and moral clarity. He described the experience of Ruby, an African American child who integrated a school in the American South in the early 1960s and who displayed a remarkably calm approach to dealing with her harrassers.

John Dewey, a philosopher whose theory was explained in Chapter 3, believed that children, such as Ruby in Robert Coles's work, gradually understand the moral resources of the culture. Dewey also believed that schools should work with parents in terms of moral education. He believed that children develop moral understanding as they work and learn with others in school (Dewey, 1897).

Constructivist theorists, such as DeVries and Zan (1994) or Hildebrandt and Zan (2008), believe, as Dewey did, that teachers can help children build their own ideas about the right thing to do. Among the many strategies that they advocate is discussing moral issues. Children can, for example, come up with classroom rules or limits. Many of these are based on moral principles and topics about which children care, such as how animals are treated or how we treat others in embarrassing situations. Note this classroom rule suggested by a first grader and reported by Hildebrantd and Zan (2008): "Don't laugh when people pass gas. It might hurt their feelings." Even though this child was only 6 years old, he was concerned about the possibility of causing embarrassment to others.

:: PRACTICES THAT HELP CHILDREN DEVELOP AUTHENTIC SELF-ESTEEM

Adults use specific practices that affect a child's self-esteem. Authori*tative*, supportive adults use strategies that help children develop authentic—healthy, positive, earned, and realistic—self-esteem. Nonsupportive adults use strategies that degrade or humiliate children, thus contributing to the development of negative self-esteem (Pawlak & Klein, 1997). Other adults focus on activities that ultimately foster narcissism or excessively self-centered views of the self.

Believe in and Adopt an Authoritative, Caregiving Style

Authoritative caregivers are demanding in an appropriate way. They are also highly responsive to what children need. The authoritative style helps children comply with (obey) reasonable limits and assists them to be more helpful and cooperative and less aggressive.

Authoritative adults also help children develop positive self-esteem (Kernis et al., 2000; Pawlak & Klein, 1997). Parents and teachers are most likely to help children develop healthy self-esteem by combining acceptance, affection, high but reasonable expectations, and limits on children's behavior and effort. Children also have a better chance of developing healthy self-esteem when parents have little conflict in their marriages (Pawlak & Klein, 1997).

Plan Appropriate Activities That Are Deserving of Children's Time

You really do not need to plan "cute activities" intended to boost self-esteem. In fact, cute activities are frequently developmentally *in*appropriate. One of the leaders in our field explained quite awhile ago that children are most likely to develop authentic self-esteem when they participate in activities for which they can make real decisions and contributions, such as the graphing of information in the chapter-opening vignette for the primary grade (Katz, 1993). The project approach, for example, helps children focus on real topics, environments, events, and objects that are deserving of a young child's time and effort. Developmentally appropriate activities help a child see herself as connected to others, as a hard worker, as kind and helpful, and as a problem solver. These are enduring traits that will help children develop a healthy sense of self and self-esteem.

Organize a classroom so that children play and work collaboratively, which allows for the give and take that helps children understand that others have ideas, too. Self-esteem and moral identity grow in classrooms where children take responsibility for keeping the room tidy, for how they speak to others, for how they work with others and for how they treat animals.

Express Genuine Interest in Children and Their Activities

Engage in joint activities willingly. Adults who show an interest in children believe that a child's activities—whether playing with measuring cups, finger painting, playing computer games, building a campsite, or playing in sand—are valid and interesting. An adult communicates belief that the child is a person worthy of the adult's

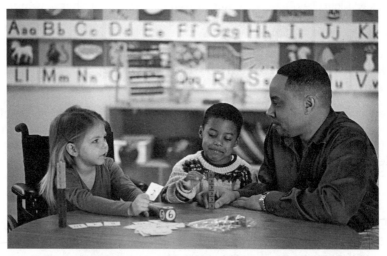

Developmentally appropriate activities help children build competence and confidence.

attention by demonstrating concern about a child's welfare, activities, and friends. Children tend to be competent, both academically and interpersonally, when significant adults communicate genuine interest in them (Heyman, Dweck, & Cain, 1992).

Several decades ago, Coopersmith (1967) found that parents of children with both high and low self-esteem spent the same amount of time with their children. He explained this puzzling finding by stating that the mothers of children with high self-esteem spent time willingly with their children and seemed to enjoy the interaction. Mothers of children with low self-esteem, on the other hand, appeared to spend time with their children grudgingly.

Give Meaningful Feedback to Children

Giving feedback is one of the basic ways through which adults influence children. Information from adults about how a child has performed a task is an important source of information about the child's competence. Kernis, Brown, and Brophy (2000) found that children with unstable self-esteem had fathers who were critical, such as giving unhelpful feedback.

We can help children learn to acknowledge what they do well without bragging— to take credit gracefully. Adults who encourage humility focus on what a child has done well, thereby helping her recognize her competence, one of the dimensions of self-esteem.

> **EXAMPLE**   Mrs. Woodward knew that Justine recognized and could name a square and a circle. From her checklist she also realized that Justine did not know the name for a triangle. Consequently, she placed a large square, circle, and triangle on a bulletin board and had the same shapes in a box. "You know the names of some shapes, Justine. Please reach into this box, take out one shape, and put it on top of the same shape on the board." When Justine correctly matched squares, the teacher said, "You're right! This is called a square." When Justine matched the triangular shapes, Mrs. Woodward simply said, "You've matched the triangles!"

Use Encouragement and Avoid Empty Praise

Some people use empty praise (constantly saying, "Good job!") (Kohn, 2001) and flattery, thinking that such information will boost self-esteem. We are most likely to help children develop a healthy sense of self and self-esteem when we use what Katz (1993) calls **appreciation**. Think of this as encouragement. This is meaningful positive feedback directly related to a child's effort or interest. Expressing encouragement or appreciation is an appropriate practice that will help a child build a healthy view of her competence.

Appreciation
Encouraging children with appropriate comments based on a child's effort

> **EXAMPLE**   Bennie was working on a project about mammals and had a specific question. Mr. Sanchez had a book at home with some information in it that Bennie needed. The teacher brought the book to school the next day so that Bennie would have a good reference.

This teacher was helping Bennie develop healthy self-esteem based on increased understanding of a specific concept. It is also possible that Bennie would view himself as worthy of the teacher's time because Mr. Sanchez took the trouble to search for the book.

> **EXAMPLE**   Carl, a third grader, finished his homework. His grandmother said to him, "You really concentrate well, Carl. You had homework to do and did it in spite of all the noise outside."

What about praise? Is it okay to use praise occasionally? Should we never use it? As with most things, a measured, reasoned approach is appropriate. Strive for effective praise if you choose praise. Avoid empty praise. Aim for encouragement and expressing appreciation most of the time.

myeducationlab

Go to the Assignments and Activities section of Topic 8: Challenging Behavior in the MyEducationLab for your course and complete the activity entitled *A Teacher's Role in Helping Children with Challenging Behavior.* Note how this strategy can help young children deal with unpleasant or confusing emotions.

Acknowledge Both Pleasant and Unpleasant Feelings

A child is jealous of a new baby brother. Another child feels guilty about having hit someone. Another feels great anger when an older child takes his lunch money. A primary-grade child envies the children who belong to the country club. A preschooler is sad about his puppy who had to have surgery. Still another child is angry with a grandfather who makes fun of him. These children are all experiencing unpleasant emotions or feelings.

The real test of support for children comes when they are sick, hurt, unhappy, angry, jealous, fearful, or anxious—when they have unpleasant feelings. It is difficult at times for adults to acknowledge unpleasant feelings. Some adults tend to focus on a young child's behavior that often results from these feelings. They become so upset themselves with the child's behavior that they forget how to or refuse to deal with whatever brought on the guilt, anger, or sadness.

Demonstrate Respect for All Family Groups and Cultures; Avoid Sexism and Judging Physical Attributes

Convey, with words and actions, your abiding belief that all children are valuable, *all* children. It is important that children observe adults demonstrating authentic respect for both genders, for children with different abilities, and for various family groups and different cultures.

> **EXAMPLE**   Mr. Sanchez knows his class well. Several children live in single-parent families, and one child lives with her grandmother. When discussing the topic of families, he showed digital photographs on a large screen of each child's family taken at the school picnic. He acknowledged that each group was indeed a family. He said, "We all live in families. Some families have lots of people in them and some families are small."

> **EXAMPLE**   Moua's mother and aunt do intricate embroidery on cloth, producing beautiful and complex geometric designs. The children, other faculty members, and administrators have admired the wall hanging that they produced and that Mr. Sanchez placed in the classroom.

Teach Specific Social Skills

Some children have poor social skills; for example, they might interrupt others, hit when angry, tattle, refuse to help others, call others names, or not know how to join others in play. Children with serious deficits in social skills are likely to view themselves as incompetent with others and in many social situations. They are also likely to evaluate themselves as having little control over anything. Consequently, they are likely to develop negative self-esteem.

Avoid artificially boosting self-esteem. Instead, consider teaching children real skills as a way of giving them positive social experiences with others. For example, they might need to learn how to take turns, how to ask for something, how to enter a group, or how to respond to someone's anger. Mr. Sanchez, in the next example teaches a 7-year-old how to wait his turn.

> **EXAMPLE** Mr. Sanchez observed one of the second-grade children trying to push his way into the line at the slide, only to hear other children shout, "Hey, wait your turn!" The teacher walked over and asked the child in private, "Would you like to take a turn on the slide? . . . Okay, I guess that you've noticed that others don't like it much when somebody crashes into the line. If you want a turn, go to the end of the line and wait until it's time for you to go up the ladder."

To summarize, many appropriate practices are available for you to use to guide children toward a healthy and balanced sense of themselves and self-esteem. Many children, however, come from families using inappropriate and even hurtful practices. Such practices do *not* help children gain accurate self-knowledge or self-control. Hurtful, inappropriate practices batter and bruise children's self-esteem by degrading and demeaning them.

:: PRACTICES CONTRIBUTING TO UNHEALTHY SELF-ESTEEM

This brief section describes these degrading practices so that you will know just how some of the children you teach have been treated. Children incorporate negative adult opinions into their sense of self; you will likely see a child's negative view of herself reflected in her behavior. Your job with these children will be to keep this in mind as you reflect a more positive view.

Child Abuse or Harsh Discipline

There are several forms of child abuse. Child abuse can be mild, moderate, or severe. It can be a one-time event or the abuse can be chronic, a continuous assault on the child. When abuse is severe and ongoing, a child's self-esteem is likely to be damaged (Bolger, Patterson, & Kupersmidt, 1998). Harsh discipline, even when it is not physical—for example, sarcasm, threats, and humiliation—hurts and degrades children. Harsh discipline has a negative effect on self-esteem. It leaves children lacking in self-confidence, feeling inadequate and incompetent, and belittling themselves.

Failure to Emphasize Self-Responsibility

Some parents do not take the time necessary to help children assume responsibility. Chores are not specified, or if they are, there is no penalty for failing to do them. Nonsupportive adults also often fail to require children to take responsibility when they have hurt another person or an animal, or damaged property.

Unhelpful, Overly Critical, Negative Style of Communication

Constant negative feedback is degrading because it communicates the adult's belief that the child is incompetent and unworthy of better feedback. Younger children, who rely heavily on adult opinion, feel incompetent when they are constantly criticized. Children who are criticized by adults and who live in a negative verbal environment tend to judge themselves negatively, including judgments of their goodness (Kernis et al., 2000).

Denying Unpleasant Feelings

Denying feelings is akin to denying a child's self because even unpleasant feelings are real and are part of the child. The implication is that "if my feelings are bad, then maybe I'm bad, too."

EXAMPLE   "Lily! You're not angry. You really like the new game, don't you?"

Lily obviously did not like the game and was angry, but this adult is denying her the right to her feelings.

Ignoring Children or Spending Time with Them Grudgingly

myeducationlab

To check your comprehension on the content covered in Chapter 7, go to the Book Specific Resources in the MyEducationLab for your course, select your text, and complete the Study Plan. Here you will be able to take a chapter quiz, receive feedback on your answers, and then access review, practice, and enrichment activities to enhance your understanding of chapter content.

Ignoring children is one of the classic forms of psychological child abuse. Ignoring children sends them the message that they are essentially unlovable and unloved, that they are not worthy of an adult's time. Some adults do not ignore children, but they are irritable when they interact with their children. They give their time grudgingly.

EXAMPLE   Marty asked his father to show him how to dribble a basketball. Feeling obligated, Dad did teach him. However, he clearly communicated resentment, annoyance, and irritability by talking quickly and answering Marty's questions abruptly. It is quite possible that Marty will conclude that he cannot be very likable because his own father does not like to do things with him.

Acting in a Judgmental or Sexist Way, or Showing Contempt for Some Families or Cultural Groups

Judging, such as "You are so stupid," violates the guidelines for effective communication. When we judge someone, the person is very likely to stop talking because we have offended him and have made a degrading comment. The same holds for sexist comments, which also demonstrate disrespect. **Example** A preschool teacher allows only boys to use woodworking tools and allows only girls to bathe dolls.

Showing contempt for any family or cultural group is outrageous and inhumane, and conveys disrespect about a child's family or culture to a child. If it is true that self-esteem develops in a social context, then doing any of these things has the potential for harming children, and this is a violation of the Code of Ethical Conduct for early childhood educators (National Association of the Education of Young Children, 2006).

WORKING *with* **FAMILIES**

THE ROAD TO SELF-ESTEEM STARTS IN INFANCY

Infancy is an important time for developing sense of self. An infant begins to construct ideas about his self as he interacts with responsive parents. Here are practical things that parents can do to help infants build the self.

- **Early infancy.** Make the environment predictable, secure, and gentle. Be flexible, not rigid, about feeding schedules. Make routines predictable and regular. Talk to the baby about what you are doing during diapering and feeding. Pay attention to the baby's cues and respond appropriately; for example, respond to cries quickly.

- **4 to 9 months.** Play games. Traditional games such as "where are baby's toes?" or peek-a-boo help infants distinguish themselves from others. Use routine times to play word games.

  Encourage play with appropriate toys. Offer safe and clean toys. Do not overwhelm the baby with too many toys at one time. Try offering a toy just within and outside the baby's grasp to encourage an infant to reach. Talk with pleasure about individual toys: "Oh! Look at this pretty blue cube." Encourage babies to grasp toys and offer toys that make a sound and then focus on that sound. Remember that adult interaction with a baby is more important than any toy.

- **9 to 15 months.** Create an environment that infants can manage—small groups with a moderate, not overwhelming, amount of stimulation. Provide simple

props for pretend-play: dress-up clothes, pots, pans, and dolls. Play games that help young children develop self-awareness, such as, "Simon says touch *your* nose. Simon says hold *Daddy's* hand").

- **15 to 24 months.** An adult's response to a toddler's struggle for autonomy influences a child's view of herself. Structure the environment and activities to give children as much control as is safe and possible. Short songs, finger plays, or walks around the block are all appropriate. Toys (for example, blocks, play dough, telephones, books with short stories) should encourage active manipulation, problem solving, and talking.

  Decide how to look at the child's struggle for autonomy. You are most likely to foster all dimensions of self-esteem if you approach this period as a healthy and normal time rather than as a contest of wills and a power struggle. For example, do state limits but state them as positively as possible: "Walk in the house," rather than "Don't run!" Be prepared for a child's testing of the new limits.

- **24 to 36 months.** Continue to provide safe and appropriate toys and to encourage children to play. Communicate genuine respect through words and actions. Give fair and honest feedback about a toddler's feelings and actions: "It really is hard to wait for the basket of crackers," or "I can see that you are upset about Mike taking your block. Let's think of some words to use to tell him that you're angry."

ANALYZE A VIGNETTE

Refer to the chapter-opening vignettes and to information in the chapter to respond to the following questions.

1. **Infant-toddler vignette:** The teacher focused on self-_____ with the "point to" game. Explain your choice.
2. **Preschool vignette:** Explain how a discussion about the *kindness rules* can help children learn about the concept of the right thing to do. How is the teacher helping the children develop their *moral identity*?

3. **Primary-grade vignette:**
   a. Explain why the "All about Us" chart is an activity deserving of children's time.
   b. Explain how working cooperatively on projects such as the chart can lead to an increased sense of competence and control, two major elements in self-esteem.

SUMMARY

Children need to develop a stable sense of self in order to live a fulfilling life. A child learns about four different parts of his or her self:

- Self-awareness
- Self-concept
- Self-control
- Self-esteem

There are three components of self-esteem:

- **Competence:** a child learns that she can achieve important goals with effort and work.
- **Control:** children need to learn that they have some control over how things turn out for them and how much effort that they expend on any activity.
- **Worth:** children need to feel that other people like them and that they are worthy of other people's time.

Self-esteem develops as children interact and have relationships with others.

- Children are active in their own development, but adults have a much greater share of the responsibility in relationships with children.
- Adults influence children's self-esteem by reflecting their attitudes about the child to him or her.
- Garbage in, garbage out: This phrase describes the effect of constantly conveying negative attitudes about children to them. Reflected negative attitudes have a negative effect on how children evaluate their self.

Children need to develop a strong moral identity in addition to positive self-esteem. Moral identity deals with understanding the right things to do and why we do them.

Teachers can help children construct positive self-esteem in many ways. Such techniques include using positive guidance strategies; planning appropriate curriculum and learning activities; using appropriate feedback; and showing respect for all children, families, and cultures.

QUESTIONS FOR REFLECTION

1. Many people confuse the terms *self-concept* and *self-esteem*. They treat these two terms as if they were the same. Explain how the two terms are different.
2. Choose the strategy from the list in the text that you consider the single most important way to help a

child develop positive self-esteem. Why does that strategy strike you as most important?
3. True or false? Positive self-esteem means that a child will also be kind and thoughtful. Please explain your response.

APPLY YOUR KNOWLEDGE

1. **Observation.** Observe an adult (parent or teacher) and a young child interacting with each other. Focus on the practices that the adult uses that will likely help the child develop healthy and balanced self-esteem. State specific examples of the appropriate practices and be prepared to present your analysis to your classmates.

2. **Conversation with an expert.** Invite a professional who works with children who are abused to speak to your class. Ask the professional questions that will help you understand why these children are likely to be highly anxious, compulsive, withdrawn, or overly hostile. Explain how abuse helps create negative (unhealthy and unbalanced) self-esteem in children, that is, how abuse affects a child's evaluation of her competence, control, and worth.

3. **Problem for you to solve: Identify a more appropriate practice.** For each situation, state specifically how someone has been demeaned. Describe how the adult could just as easily have used a more appropriate practice to enhance, rather than bruise, the child's self-esteem.

Situation

The baseball coach stared out at his team of 7- and 8-year-old boys and said, "You guys swing the bat like girls! Let me show you one more time how it's done."

How has the coach demeaned the boys?

How has the coach also degraded girls?

What more helpful statement could the coach have directed to the boys when he noticed that they used improper batting technique?

Situation

Five-year-old Matt, pointing to a tree, excitedly said to his grandfather, "Grandpa! Look! An oak tree! I'm learning the names of trees by looking at their leaves." Grandpa pointed to a willow tree and said, "What's the name of that tree?" Matt did not know. Grandpa continued, "Well, you have a lot of learning to do, don't you, young man?"

How has Matt been demeaned?

In your view, what would have been a more appropriate response from Matt's grandfather?

Situation

Sam, the class's pet gerbil, died during the night, and the aide found Peter crying after he heard the news. "Come on, Peter. Stop crying. You know that big boys don't cry."

How has Peter been demeaned?

In what way has this adult been sexist?

How has the adult demeaned girls as well as boys?

What would have been a better thing to say to Peter?

Situation

A teacher asked a first-grade child if she would prefer to go to the math or writing center. The child selected the writing center, and the teacher said, "I think that you should start at the math center."

How has this child been demeaned?

What do you think would have been a more appropriate response from the teacher?

KEY TERMS

Appreciation (*181*)
Bullying (*177*)
Competence (*173*)
Control (*174*)

Moral identity (*178*)
Self (*169*)
Self-awareness (*169*)
Self-concept (*171*)

Self-control (*171*)
Self-esteem (*172*)
Worth (*175*)

WEB SITES

Child Welfare Information Gateway
http://www.childwelfare.gov/index.cfm

Home page of this organization. Part of a federal agency, this organization advocates for protecting children and strengthening families. A very good source for information on *child abuse*, particularly for early childhood teachers, as is the following web site: http://www.childwelfare.gov/pubs/usermanuals/educator/educatorc.cfm. This document outlines the signs and symptoms of child abuse and neglect.

National Association for the Education of Young Children (NAEYC)
http://www.naeyc.org

Home page for the organization. At http://www.naeyc.org/ece/eyly you will find short articles designed for teachers or parents. Excellent for newsletters. Index is easy to use.

National Black Child Development Institute (NBCDI)
http://www.nbcdi.org

Click on Programs, then Parent Empowerment Project (PEP) on the quick menu. NBCDI believes that informed parents can help their children thrive.

National Latino Children's Institute (NLCI)
http://www.nlci.org

This web site focuses on the full and healthy development of Latino/Latina children.

Feelings and Friends
Emotional and Social Competence

"Children who have a strong foundation in emotional literacy are healthier, have more friends, are less impulsive, remain more focused, and demonstrate greater academic achievement."
—Center for the Social and Emotional Foundations of Early Learning (CSEFEL), Handout 21

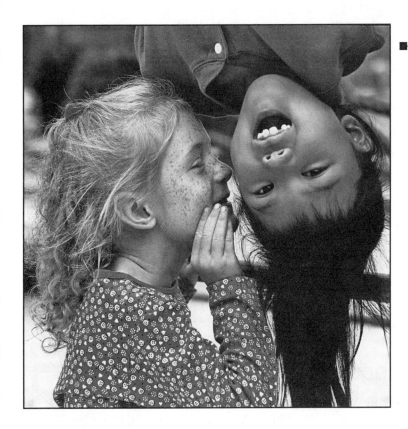

Chapter Contents

Emotional Competence

Social Competence

Guiding Children's Social Emotional Learning

Guiding Questions

- What is emotional competence and why is it important to a child's development?
- How are emotional and social competence linked?
- What can teachers do to guide children's social emotional learning (SEL)?

VIGNETTES

INFANT–TODDLER: COMFORTING THOMAS

Thomas, 8 months old, seemed startled when he heard the loud noise out in the hallway of the center. He cried loudly even after his teacher picked him up. The teacher held him gently and spoke softly and reassuringly to him. Thomas gradually cried more softly, eventually visibly relaxing in the teacher's arms.

PRESCHOOL: LEARNING THAT USING WORDS IS A GOOD THING

"You can't play here, Jerry. You pushed me when we were in line," said Sarah, who was upset with Jerry. He responded by sweeping her small blocks onto the floor. Mrs. Woodward, his teacher, spoke privately with him, and one part of her message was this, "You can use words to tell Sarah that you are upset. Try saying, 'I wanted to play with you. I'm upset because you said no.'" She had Jerry say those words, for practice. Then she said, "Would you like to tell her now?"

PRIMARY: LEARNING TO CALM DOWN

Mr. Sanchez noticed that his primary class was unusually active and even agitated after the fire drill, and the children had difficulty settling back into their routine. Therefore, he gathered them on the carpet, turned on soft music, and led them in deep breathing exercises.

:: INTRODUCTION

The children in the chapter-opening vignettes are learning about feelings and friends, and their teachers are supporting them. The emotional and social domains of development are important all on their own, but never more so than now as teachers face the push for academics in early childhood education and as the expulsion rate for young children in preschools soars (Gilliam, 2005; Gilliam & Shahar, 2006; Ramsey, 2009). Effective teachers understand that they need to focus on the whole child and on a child's development in all areas, not just in the cognitive and intellectual domain. Learning to read and to understand math and science is vitally important, of course. Children learn most effectively, however, when they acquire the emotional and social competence needed for all other learning.

This chapter describes the development of emotional and social competence, a process beginning in infancy, and continuing through childhood. We will explore what it means to be emotionally intelligent and how this relates to specific emotional competencies. We will also describe social competence and examine some of the factors affecting emotional as well as social competence. You will then learn about practical strategies that you can use to help children deal with their feelings well and get along with others. You will learn how to support social emotional learning.

:: EMOTIONAL COMPETENCE

Emotional intelligence refers to how well, overall, a person copes with his or her own feelings and whether the person has empathy for and gets along with others (Salovey & Mayer, 1990; Goleman, 1995, 2007). When we talk about *feelings* in this chapter, we refer to affective states, or **emotions.** Becoming intelligent about one's emotions or feelings is important in a child's development, good mental health, and success in life. Emotionally intelligent children tend to feel more connected to others and they tend to get along with other children better than children who do not have these abilities. They feel competent and capable, both components of positive self-esteem. They experience a general sense of balance in their emotions. Children are in a good position to solve problems and deal with conflicts constructively when they can regulate whirling and swirling emotions and when they can get along well with others.

Howard Gardner reminds us that intelligence comes in many forms, including intrapersonal (knowing oneself well) and interpersonal (being especially good at getting along with others). He notes that everyone has all of the intelligences but that each person seems to be especially gifted in one or two forms (Gardner, 2003). Emotional intelligence is made up of specific abilities linked to feelings or emotions (Brackett, Crum, & Salovey, 2009; Denham, 2006). The combination of the following three abilities results in emotional intelligence:

Perceiving emotions
Expressing emotions
Regulating emotions

Perceiving Emotions

Perceiving emotions refers to noticing your feelings and the emotions of others. It is the least complex emotional competency (Brackett et al., 2009) because we only need to notice but we do not have to interpret, understand, or manage the emotion. It is still an important skill, however, because it requires, in the noticing, that we be aware of two things—our self and others.

Emotional intelligence
How well, overall, a person copes with his or her feelings and whether the person has empathy for and gets along with others

Emotions
Feelings or affective states; they are divided into two groups: basic and complex emotions.

Perceiving emotions
Noticing feelings in oneself and others; the least complex emotional competency

Self-awareness
Being mindful of all
feelings as they occur

Self-awareness

Self-awareness, with respect to emotions, entails being mindful of all feelings, pleasant ones such as happiness or joy as well as more unpleasant emotions like jealously or anger, and being aware of the feelings *as they occur*. A self-aware individual also understands why he is feeling a specific emotion. Mr. Sanchez, for example, admitted to himself that he was surprised, confused, and even a bit afraid at first when he had to deal with a very angry parent. A person who is aware of his emotions has some valuable information necessary in pulling himself together, shaking off a bad mood, and finding a helpful way to cope.

Self-aware children, such as Sarah in the next examples, possess specific and helpful abilities. First, they see themselves as separate from others.

> **EXAMPLE**   Four-year-old Sarah showed the photo of her family, "Look! Dad is here and my Mom is here and I am here."

Sarah is fully aware that she is a person separate from other people. This allows her to look at situations in which she is happy about something or angry with someone else and see that there are at least two separate people involved. This ability will help her learn how to cope with the idea that there are two separate ways of looking at the same situation when she has a disagreement with another person.

Second, self-aware children know that they have some influence over how some things turn out. In self-esteem, this is her healthy sense of control.

> **EXAMPLE**   Sarah and Larry were both working on a large collage. Larry wanted to cut paper, but Sarah favored tearing it. She said, "Okay, we can cut some paper. Maybe we could tear some, too."

Go to the Assignments and
Activities section of Topic 5:
Social Emotional Learning
in the MyEducationLab for
your course and complete
the activity entitled
*Observing an Emotionally
Competent Child*. Note
Emily's enthusiastic
approach to interactions.

Sarah will use this knowledge when emotions are involved. Sarah will be able to see herself and the other person as separate people and will think that she can influence how things turn out.

Children continue to grow in self-awareness during early childhood, enabling them to think even more clearly about themselves. They know, for example, when they are angry or sad and about the things that called forth specific feelings (Denham, 2006; Kuebli, 1994).

Awareness of others
Noticing feelings in other
people and animals;
implies ability to read
emotional cues

Awareness of others

Awareness of others refers to noticing that other's have feelings, and it is a skill that, in turn, requires specific skills. For example, the child must be able to read cues, such as smiling or frowning, in another's face and through another person's body language, such as how a person stands or hold his or her arms (Brackett et al., 2009). The child must also have a hunch about why the other might have that feeling and must understand what the other person is saying regarding feelings. Young children differ in their ability to read emotional cues.

> **EXAMPLE**   Tom, Sarah, and Jerry worked on making patterns with Legos while sharing a large bucket of the Legos. When Jerry accidently bumped Tom's Legos, Tom glared at him, eyes narrowed. Jerry did not seem to notice that Tom was irritated, but Sarah whispered to Jerry, "Uh-oh! Look, Jerry, Tom is really mad. Look at how he's squeezing his eyes almost shut."

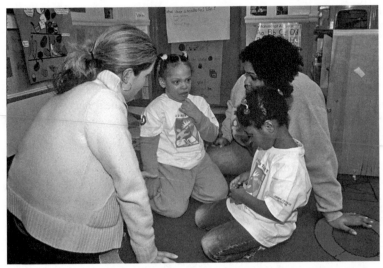

Lela, the child on the left, will develop a theory about why people cry after observing several people who get upset and cry.

Young children learn very gradually to notice feelings in other people. For instance, they are better at recognizing pleasant emotions such as happiness, but they only slowly identify feelings such as anger (Stifter & Fox, 1987). They also create theories after they have several experiences with an emotion. Their theories allow them to group together things that seem to cause a feeling (Denham, 2006). For example, a child might notice that she and others seem to get upset when somebody makes fun of them.

Some children, such as those with autism spectrum disorders (Asperger syndrome or autism, for example), face challenges in discerning emotions, partly because they avoid looking at faces or they look at only part of the face. Thus, they overlook cues from other parts of the face. They tend to look at the lower half of a face, missing information given from the upper half, especially the eyes (Gross, 2004; Hopkins, 2005; Hopkins & Biasini, 2006; Hopkins, Ross, & Biasini, 2005). Recent research shows they can learn to pay attention to a whole face for clues about emotions. The children played an interactive videogame in which they learned to recognize emotions by looking at and following eye movement. Children with Asperger syndrome improved the most, but both groups showed improvement (Hopkins, Perez, & Biasini, 2007). (Watch a video of this approach at http://wearecentralpa.com/content/fulltext/healthcast?cid=6331.)

Similarly, children with nonverbal learning disability (NLD) have difficulty in noticing emotions in others. Children with NLD usually have good verbal skills but they often have difficulty processing nonverbal signals, such as a frown or smile (Foss, 2002; Miller, 2004). They tend not to pay attention to how others react and thus miss important information, which ultimately has a negative effect on their interactions and relationships. Children with NLD do want to have friends, but their inability to process emotional cues presents a problem. If Jerry, in the previous example, does not observe Tom's narrowed eyes or frown, then Jerry will not have that bit of nonverbal information to use in deciding how to proceed.

Let's look more closely at how children notice or perceive one of the most basic emotions—anger – during early childhood.

Anger

A basic emotion present soon after birth; elicited when a person is prevented from attaining a goal

How children perceive anger   Table 8.1 shows that there are two categories of emotions. One category consists of *basic* emotions and the other of *complex*, or *self-conscious*, emotions. **Anger** is one of the basic emotions, which every human possesses at birth or within a few months of birth.

Children tend to notice angry feelings when interacting with another child or adult, when something in the give and take keeps them from attaining any significant goal (Campos & Barrett, 1984). The most common aggravating interactions for young children in classrooms are illustrated next (Fabes, Eisenberg, Smith, & Murphy, 1996).

- **Conflict over possessions:** One of the most common interactions in early childhood classrooms provoking anger is a conflict over possessions, which involves someone taking or destroying the target child's property or invading her space. Most conflicts over possessions take place between two children.
- **Physical assault:** This second, most frequently observed cause of anger in early childhood settings involves something done to a child's body, such as biting or hitting. Children do assault other children, but adults also can physically assault children: Jerry's father often assaults Jerry.
- **Verbal assault:** This involves taunting, teasing, insults, or making degrading or demeaning statements. It blocks a child's goal of psychological safety.

TABLE 8.1	Basic and self-conscious emotions	
Age at Which Children First Feel Emotions	**Basic Emotions**	**Complex, Self-Conscious Emotions**
Birth to 6 weeks	Contentment Distress	
6 weeks to 14 months	Anger Fear Joy	
2 years (24 months) and then continues to evolve through early childhood	Continues to feel all the above basic emotions and now acquires complex emotions	Anxiety Disgust Embarrassment Guilt Hubris (overconfidence or even arrogance) Jealousy Pride Sadness Shame

Source: Saarni, Mumme, and Campos (1998).

- **Rejection:** Other children either ignore or refuse to allow a child to play. Rejection by adults is one of the classic forms of emotional child abuse (Garbarino, Guttman, & Seeley, 1986).
- **Issues of compliance:** This refers to requiring a child to do something that he does not want to do. The child perceives that his teacher's insistence on compliance is blocking his goal for independence. Almost all anger over issues of compliance occurs between an adult and a child

There are different levels of anger. All children get angry, some more than others, but they all experience anger, for example, when someone swipes a toy. Other children have a much deeper reserve of fear, fury, and rage. Someone has aimed anger and aggression directly at these children. An adult has abused them physically, psychologically, emotionally, or sexually or has ignored their most basic need for safety and security. They have not developed trust; they feel insecure and unsafe. It is especially difficult for them to confront the normal, everyday, anger-arousing events in our early childhood classrooms.

Still other children have seen a lot of *background anger*, anger between others but not directed at the child, especially the high levels of anger-based conflict between their parents (Jenkins, 2000). Anger is the center of their emotional life. Consequently, they often develop an antagonist approach to relationships. They are very angry and express anger readily during social interaction, quite often showing aggression in relationships. Like their angry parents, they frequently humiliate and provoke distress in others, mirroring the contempt modeled in their parents' marriages. For example, a child might laugh or smile while saying or doing something cruel to another person or animal.

Expressing Emotions

All children feel emotions: all children express feelings. **Expressing emotions** refers to how a person communicates the feelings that they notice. Infants, for example, notice feelings such as happiness or anger, which they then express with their faces and voices (Stenberg, 1982). Some ways of expressing feelings are helpful and some are far less helpful. An emotionally competent person expresses feelings so that it helps her interact well in daily encounters and in relationships.

Expressing emotions
Communicating a feeling after noticing it

Children can gradually learn how to communicate feelings in social situations if we teach them how. Alternatively, they also observe what works in these situations. For instance, a child might observe how different classmates are assertive when they feel angry—they use words. He sees and hears things such as "No, Pete, that's *my* book," or "*I* was next at the computer!" He also observes that his teacher encourages this way of expressing feelings (Denham, 2006). Let's look at how young children express the unpleasant emotion of anger.

How young children express angry feelings   When you teach, expect the children in your class to express anger in one or more of the following ways (Fabes et al., 1996):

- **Venting** refers to expressing anger through facial expressions, crying, sulking, or complaining. Little is done to try to solve a problem or confront the agitator.

Venting is a way to "blow off steam," but it is an unhealthy approach if the person does nothing to solve the problem that caused the anger.

> **EXAMPLE** Jake and Jim, both 8 years old, were irritated about the number of math homework problems and complained on the way home from school.

- **Active resistance** involves physically or verbally defending one's position, self-esteem, or possessions in nonaggressive ways and is a healthy way to express anger. Teachers encourage active resistance when they tell children to use words to express themselves.

> **EXAMPLE** Luis made a mistake in oral reading and another child called him "dumbbell." Luis used active resistance when he said, "Uh-huh! I made a mistake . . . good observation!"

- **Expressing dislike** involves a child telling the offender that he cannot play or that the victim does not like the offender because of an incident.

> **EXAMPLE** Sarah was angry after Jerry pushed her. Later, in the chapter-opening vignette for preschool, when Jerry wanted to sit at the table to play with his favorite small blocks, Sarah said that she did not want him to play in that area.

- **Aggressive revenge** means that children retaliate, physically or verbally, against the offender with name calling, pinching, hitting, or threatening. Considered a negative way of expressing anger, teachers most often see revenge-like behavior after a physical assault or rejection.

> **EXAMPLE** After snack time the children went to the playground. Jerry, still upset from Sarah's comment at the small blocks table, sang out, "Sarah is stupid. Sarah is stupid."

- **Avoidance** is a way of communicating anger by trying to escape from or avoid the person with whom the child is angry.

> **EXAMPLE** Sarah, mildly irritated by the name calling, walked away and played on the other side of the playground.

- **Adult seeking** involves telling an adult about an incident or looking for comfort from the teacher.

> **EXAMPLE** In the preschool chapter-opening vignette, after Sarah rejected Jerry and he swept her blocks onto the floor, he turned to his teacher and said loudly, "She said to go away!"

Children construct ideas about many things, such as mathematics and art, and they also construct ideas about how to express emotions. How they communicate feelings grows out of what they learn about it and whether they view themselves as having any control over emotion-arousing interactions.

Learning about expressing emotions Children develop and learn in a number of systems that nest within one another, as explained in Chapter 2. All systems affect a child's development, but those closest to the child, such as family and friends, have a more direct effect. Systems farther away, such as a parent's workplace, have a somewhat more indirect effect (Bronfenbrenner, 1979).

Different systems convey messages about expressing emotions. A family system provides direct lessons based on its *rules,* which, in the case of expressing one's feelings, tells each person how that family expresses emotions such as anger (Christian, 2006). Peer groups also teach children how each group expresses feelings, and children learn about expressing emotions by watching television or movies, playing videogames, reading books, and using the Internet. Some systems teach children to express anger by hurting others (Hennessy, Rabideau, Cummings, & Cicchetti, 1994) and then to use aggression when they face normal everyday conflicts at school.

Whether the child feels in control   A significant factor affecting how children express angry feelings is whether they think that they have some degree of control in a conflict (Levine, 1995; Zeman & Shipman, 1996). Children tend to be on an equal footing with other children; both children have about the same amount of power. Therefore, a child's interactions with other children have a far greater give-and-take quality (Piaget, 1970) than do child–adult interactions. Children believe that they have some measure of control in interactions, including anger-arousing situations, with other children. Therefore, a child who feels angry tends to use direct strategies such as active resistance with other children, as Luis did in the examples in the bulleted list above "Uh-huh! I made a mistake . . . good observation!"

Many children can easily detect the difference in power between an adult and themselves. Young children tend to think that they have much less control when a teacher provokes their anger. With adults, children express anger more indirectly, with strategies such as venting (Fabes & Eisenberg, 1992). Curiously, some children express anger toward a popular child who provokes anger in much the same indirect way as they do toward an adult (Fabes et al., 1996). Again, a child's view of his level of power or control is at work here. Children tend to see themselves as having far less control in angry interactions with popular children.

Regulating Emotions

Regulating emotions is the most complex and difficult of the emotional competencies because it goes far beyond merely noticing or expressing feelings. It refers to understanding and managing moods and feelings responsibly (Brackett et al., 2009). An emotionally intelligent and competent person keeps emotions in check; he or she does not let them run wild and restrains feelings when appropriate. For example, Mr. Sanchez was astonished and somewhat anxious when a parent angrily pounded on the table. However, he knew the parent and had figured out that the parent was furious because the school had made a major decision without consulting parents. The teacher could stay calm and regulate his emotions, even though he felt anxious.

Managing one's moods is difficult because it requires some high-level understanding and skills, something that humans develop very slowly. A person has to be able to monitor feelings and to discriminate among emotions accurately, such as

Regulating emotions
The most complex of the emotional competencies; refers to understanding and managing moods and feelings responsibly

recognizing that anger differs from disgust. He must experience feelings clearly and must be able to label them accurately, which requires knowledge of the glossary or lexicon of emotion words. In addition, he must believe in his ability to improve his feelings and must be able to use strategies that will indeed modify the emotions (Brackett et al., 2009; Denham, 2006). All of this makes regulating emotions extremely demanding, especially for young children who are just starting out with this skill.

Children have to learn how to regulate specific groupings of emotions (Denham, 2006), including:

Distressing or unpleasant emotions
Positive but overwhelming emotions
Relevant and helpful emotions
Relevant but *unhelpful* emotions
Irrelevant emotions

Distressing or unpleasant emotions include distress, anger, fear, anxiety, disgust, embarrassment, guilt, jealousy, sadness, and shame (Saarni, Mumme, & Campos, 1998). We will focus on one of these emotions—anger—to illustrate why it is so important to learn to manage it well and responsibly. It is a natural and normal emotion, but chronic, unresolved anger and hostility is a health threat, making a person vulnerable to illness and a weakening of the immune system. Chronic unresolved anger makes pain worse and increases the risk of death from cardiovascular disease (Siew et al., 2005). A child will have a difficult time making and keeping friends if she is chronically angry. *Positive but overwhelming emotions* include joy or pride (but not arrogance). These are pleasant and indicate a sense of well-being or a legitimate feeling of accomplishment. However, children must still learn about regulating such feelings in situations when even a positive emotion can overpower them.

> **EXAMPLE**   Eight year-old Sheri was overcome with joy after she got three baskets in a row during recess and had a very difficult time settling down during the afternoon at school.

Relevant and helpful emotions refer to those feelings that help us in interacting with others. The emotion of disgust, for instance, is usually unpleasant but it is certainly relevant when we observe someone mistreating another person or animal, and it would be helpful to retain or preserve this feeling as we reflect on the incident. Guilt, although very unpleasant, is helpful and relevant when we have violated a moral or ethical code. Our guilt helps us focus on what we have done and make decisions about how to repair any damage that we have caused. In the next example, Eric feels embarrassed but retains the feeling long enough to help him make a plan to stop the teasing.

> **EXAMPLE**   Second-grader Eric, embarrassed when Sid called him "four-eyes" (Eric wears glasses), remembered what his teacher suggested about how to respond to such teasing., "Yes, I wear glasses, so what." This disarms the teaser, literally taking away his ammunition (Freedman, J., 2002).

Relevant but unhelpful emotions are legitimate feelings but might not be very useful in some interactions. Consequently, each culture teaches children how to regulate them. This involves learning complicated rules for expressing emotions. Children must learn, for example, to *mask emotions*, projecting the appearance of one emotion on the outside (pretending to like a gift, for instance) even if they feel something else inside (disliking the gift). The emotion of disappointment on seeing socks as a birthday present is relevant for many children. However, expressing the relevant feeling of disappointment to one's grandmother who gave the gift is not helpful in the relationship. Therefore, a child learns that he is expected to hide the disappointment. Children also learn to regulate how they express an emotion with different people (Denham, 2006), such as the rules for expressing irritation or anger toward a teacher compared to expressing such feelings toward other children.

Irrelevant emotions refer to feelings that are not germane or appropriate to a current discussion or ongoing activity. Children must learn to hold back irrelevant emotions (Denham, 2006), and their failure at doing this is linked to their low-level ability to walk in somebody else's shoes, in other words, take the other person or animal's perspective.

> **EXAMPLE**   Mrs. Woodward was talking to Katy, who was very sad about her father leaving for his military assignment. Mrs. Woodward was surprised to hear Sarah interrupt their discussion with a description of how happy she was about going on a trip. Even though Sarah's happiness was relevant to her, it was *irrelevant* to Katy's distress, and Sarah has to learn when to avoid sharing emotions that would be considered irrelevant.

Children's Development Affects How They Understand Feelings

Children do not understand their feelings (Zeman & Shipman, 1996). **Understanding feelings** refers to reflecting on or evaluating emotions. There are reasonable developmental explanations for why young children can neither evaluate nor interpret how they feel. Three of the major developmental factors contributing to a young child's inability to understand, and therefore to control, how he expresses anger and other emotions are:

Understanding feelings
The ability to reflect on and evaluate emotions

Brain development
Memory
Language

Brain development   Different parts of the brain have important roles in how we perceive, express, and regulate our emotions. Table 8.2 shows the role of two such sections of the brain—the prefrontal cortex and the amygdala—in children's emotional competence. The prefrontal cortex governs the regulation of emotion and helps us rationally process and understand emotion, but it takes years for it to develop fully. An adult, whose prefrontal cortex is fully developed, is equipped to understand and evaluate his emotions. Table 8.2 shows that the prefrontal cortex is immature in young children. It also shows that the amygdala, which often causes us to act before we can think, is almost fully mature at birth. This difference accounts,

TABLE 8.2	Role of amygdala and prefrontal cortex in emotional development			
Part of Brain	**Description, Location, When Developed**	**What This Part of the Brain Does**	**Examples**	**What This Means for Teachers**
Amygdala	Part of the emotional center in brain Located at top of brain stem Almost fully formed at birth	Stores a memory of emotional quality of child's experiences, pleasant or unpleasant Monitors new experiences to spot dangers or joy Reminds children of previously stored memories of episodes of emotion Can seize brain and keep child from thinking	Four-year-old Beth's amygdala preserved her memory of the fear and anxiety during arguments between her parents and times when they hit her Beth observed an argument between two other preschoolers. Reminded Beth about her parent's arguments Upset, Beth ran from the center	Children who are abused are primed to interpret another person's behavior incorrectly. Normal classroom disagreements signal the amygdala that danger is imminent Moves child to action before she can think about things (teachers want children to learn to think before acting)
Prefrontal Cortex	Part of the rational part of the brain; connected to limbic system Located at front part of human brain Shows growth at age 3 or 4 By age 6 has developed further	Receives and processes signals from amygdala Helps humans choose how they respond by analyzing information Balances amygdala's purely emotional response Gives humans a chance to think about emotions sensibly	Mrs. Woodward has helped Beth recognize signs of being upset and to "stop and think" At year's end, Beth did not automatically hit when angry Eight-year-old Tom looked at another child who had called him "dummy" and said, "I am not a dummy"	Expect infants and toddlers to express emotions quickly and not be able to regulate emotions (amygdala fully developed, prefrontal cortex is not) Expect preschool children to show emerging self-control and emotional regulation Expect primary grade children to show more self-control and emotional regulation

Source: Based on Goleman (1995); Marion, (2007).

in large part, for a young child's inability to understand or regulate emotions such as anger, even as the child feels and expresses a wide range of emotions.

Humans need a good pathway or connection between the prefrontal cortex and amygdala so that these two sections of the brain can communicate about what a child feels. The prefrontal cortex has to get information about emotional states from the amygdala in order to make sense of the information. Think of the *prefrontal cortex–amygdala connection* as a cable carrying signals between the two sections of the brain. A weak, underdeveloped, or damaged connection or cable slows or obstructs the passage of signals, placing a child at a disadvantage in managing emotions. His brain is not wired for the prefrontal cortex to communicate with the amygdala. Such a child would very likely misread signals from others and might have a *short fuse,* or be quick to anger. She would rarely use emotion words, would seem unaware of feelings in general, and would get in trouble with other children because of poor social skills.

A strong, well-developed cable or pathway lets those bits of information pass quickly between the amygdala and the prefrontal cortex. This sets the stage for better analysis and management of emotions because the child's brain is wired in a way that allows it to get the information it needs about emotions from one part to another. This child would have the physical characteristics he needs to read signals from others accurately, would be able to learn about emotion words, and would be aware of feelings. Thus, he would have what he needs in order to learn how to work and play well with other children.

Follow Vygotsky's advice on helping children construct ideas, in this case about emotions. We are the "experts" who, along with parents, can help children develop a strong prefrontal cortex–amygdala connection. We install the hardware to build this pathway by paying appropriate attention to a child's emotional needs. At times, teachers make a conscious effort to help a child make these connections. At other times, they might not even realize that supportive interactions are helping a child develop the wiring and connections—the hardware—that is essential in managing his feelings (see Figure 8.1).

FIGURE 8.1	Whoosh! whoosh! connect! installing hardware for emotional intelligence

Help children develop a good strong prefrontal cortex–amygdala connection by taking children's emotional needs seriously. Here are some ideas.

- Let a child know explicitly that her needs are important and worthy of attention. Whoosh, a connection between amygdala and prefrontal cortex!
- Tell a child that hitting somebody hurts the other person—Whoosh! Connection.
- Say to a child who has hit somebody, "Jerry, I want you to use words to tell Sean that you are angry." Whoosh! A connection.
- Give the script, the words. i.e., Do not expect the child to come up with the words. "Jerry, you can say, 'I am using the tape recorder, Sean. It's not your turn, yet.'" Whiz! Another connection.
- Comfort an anxious or fearful child. Connection.
- Help a child calm down when he gets agitated, as Mrs. Woodward did with a child who had had an argument. Connection.
- Incorporate calming activities into the day and prevent agitation. Connection.
- Model self-control. Manage your own emotions well. Connection.
- Help children learn how to manage anger, anxiety, sadness, or even joy. Whoosh! Whoosh! Whoosh!

Memory Memory is a basic cognitive process, and it is part of the foundation enabling children to understand feelings such as anger. Children can understand things only if they can remember them. Memory improves substantially during early childhood (Perlmutter, 1986), which makes it possible for young children to retain information about anger-arousing interactions. This is a slow process. Mrs. Woodward, for example, knew that Jerry needed help managing anger. She started working with him just as soon as she had observed him sufficiently. She used a number of strategies to give him better ways of dealing with his feelings, and after a time, he seemed to understand what she meant.

> **EXAMPLE** Mrs. Woodward showed Jerry how to use words to express anger and then had him practice.

Could Mrs. Woodward expect Jerry to remember her suggestions, or would he regress and use one of his old, unhelpful ways of expressing his anger? Young children such as Jerry remember an *incorrect* perception (unhelpful way to communicate feelings), even when it has been replaced by a more accurate perception of events (more helpful way to express anger) (Freeman, Lacohee, & Coulton, 1995). While a child is learning the new method, his brain can repress an incorrect idea for a short time so that the child can use a new idea. In Jerry's case, it seemed like he really understood Mrs. Woodward because he did remember and he did use words a couple of times to express his anger. However, his previous memories of expressing anger were also very strong, and for the time being, stronger than Mrs. Woodward's help. He went right back to hitting when he was angry.

Jerry retrieved an earlier unhelpful strategy even after his teacher taught him a new, more helpful strategy. This implies that teachers must be unrelentingly positive and remind certain children, often several times, about a less aggressive way of expressing anger. Overcoming old, unhelpful memories takes time. Children with deep reserves of anger need help managing that anger. Getting angry with them when they revert to old methods does not help them; it only adds fear and confusion to their anger.

Language How well a child understands emotions depends somewhat on his overall language skills (Denham, Zoller, & Couchoud, 1994). Children have a much easier time learning to talk about emotions if they have good language development in general. Preschooler Ralph, for example, has very good language skills and a large vocabulary, so Mrs. Woodward was confident that he could tell her what had upset him. One of Vygotsky's major ideas centers on *discussion between teacher and child*. Children glean valuable information from such conversations with an older member of their culture. In terms of managing emotions such as anger, discussions are one of a teacher's most valuable tools. Talking about emotions helps young children understand their feelings and helps them begin to evaluate them. What do children need in order to participate actively in and benefit from such discussions? Emotional development is one domain of child development, but it influences all other domains, such as social development, a topic to which we now turn.

:: SOCIAL COMPETENCE

Children who can regulate their emotions well are better equipped to make and keep friends and to work and play for extended periods with peers. They have what they need to develop skills for positive and ongoing interactions and relationships—including cooperating, searching for help, joining in, listening, and negotiating (Denham, 2006). Therefore, emotional competence is important because it promotes children's social competence and helps children construct school success skills.

Socially competent children share several characteristics, including:

Relating well to other children
Responding agreeably to others
Having developed good social skills

Relating Well to Other Children

Socially competent children relate well to other children at three different levels—interactions, relationships, and with groups of children. They have primarily positive *interactions* with other children under a variety of conditions. John, for example, says hello to other children, interacts positively with classmates in the lunchroom, and gets along with others during both large- and small-group activities. Socially competent children can also start and then maintain a *relationship*, which requires getting along with the same person under a variety of circumstances and over time. John has developed a good relationship with Stephen, who lives next door to him and is in the same class at school. John has the emotional and social skills to maintain this relationship. Socially competent children also get along well in *groups of children*, which refers to how well liked versus disliked a child is, on average, by members of his or her peer group. John's classmates like him. Peer acceptance predicts children's academic readiness and classroom involvement (Ladd, Kochenderfer, & Coleman, 1997); peer rejection is linked with negative attitudes toward and avoiding school, as well as not doing very well academically (Ladd, Birch, & Buhs, 1999).

Responding Agreeably to Others

This involves the concept of sociability. Socially competent children are sociable, pleasant, welcoming, and approachable, whether the other child is a good friend or only an acquaintance (Mize, 1995). They are friendly toward everyone.

> **EXAMPLE** During the morning meeting in his first-grade class, John eagerly sits next to anyone. He plunks himself down and looks to his left and right, greeting whoever sits there with genuine pleasure.

Having Developed Good Social Skills

Socially competent children have also developed good **social skills**, which are observable behaviors through which a child demonstrates that he can regulate his

Socially competent children
Characteristics of socially competent children include relating well to others, responding agreeably to others, and using good social skills

Social skills
Observable behaviors through which a child demonstrates the ability to regulate thoughts and emotions

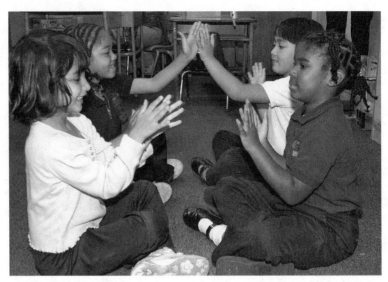

Cecilia (front, right) gets along well with other children. Today, she invited the other three girls to play a game.

thoughts and emotions. Good social skills allow children, for example, to keep themselves from doing something like interrupting a conversation. Good social skills also allow children to initiate appropriate actions, such as carrying on a conversation with a friend who is upset.

Key social skills include the following:

Correctly interpreting another person's actions, for example, why another person would stick out his or her tongue. "Pete was sticking out his tongue at me to show me that the grape juice had made it purple." A less socially competent child might jump to the conclusion that someone sticking out his tongue was rude.
Turn taking
Following directions
Coming up with good solutions to conflicts
Carrying on a conversation
Persisting at tasks

John, our first-grade child, is gradually developing good social skills. He had some trouble with the one of the new sight words, but he persisted at tracing the letters of the word and pronouncing it a couple of times. He demonstrated his ability to take turns when he negotiated his turn with kicking the soccer ball.

Tuning in to the social setting   Tuning in to the social setting refers to how well a child observes others in ongoing activities. Socially competent children are good observers, watch other children at play, and are skillful in assessing the behavior of others (Mize, 1995). Thus, they have information useful in figuring out what they need to do in different situations, as John demonstrates in the next example.

> **EXAMPLE**   John wanted to join the play at the puppet theater, but he observed that all of the puppets were in use. He watched for a little longer, seemed to be thinking, and then volunteered to open and close the curtain to the stage.

Socially competent children do not get too upset when they fail to get what they want. John was successful in his bid to participate in the puppet play, but if the others had rejected his idea, he might have come up with another or might simply have found something else to do.

Children construct ideas about emotional intelligence from models who take the time to give the essential lessons (Corso, 2003; Elias, 2004). It takes many years for children to build knowledge about emotions, controlling themselves, understanding how other people feel, and getting along well with others. Let's look at how teachers can guide children's social emotional learning.

myeducationlab

Go to the Assignments and Activities section of Topic 5: Social Emotional Learning in the MyEducationLab for your course and complete the activity entitled *Observing a Socially Competent Child*. Note Bri'asia's strengths and areas for growth.

:: GUIDING CHILDREN'S SOCIAL EMOTIONAL LEARNING

Social emotional learning (SEL) focuses on helping children gain knowledge about feelings (the emotional domain) and about getting along with others (the social domain). Educating the whole child requires that we focus on all domains and not just cognitive learning (Rimm-Kaufman, 2006). Effective teachers guide children's learning about feelings and friends deliberately and intentionally (CSE-FEL, 2008).

Children, especially those who most need this knowledge, benefit when teachers focus on SEL. One group of children in need of special attention are those neglected by parents because the parents give their children very little help or support in learning about or understanding emotions (Edwards, Shipman, & Brown, 2005). Highlighting SEL seems to encourage school attendance by helping children to feel cheerful about going to school. Teachers see far less challenging behavior, and SEL helps children achieve at a higher academic level. Deliberate instruction about emotions or social relationships actually shapes a child's brain in a positive way by helping to build the brain circuits directly linked to emotions and social development (Goleman, 2007). For example, when teachers consciously teach about emotions and getting along with others, children learn how to deal effectively with anger and other specific emotions. They learn how to compose themselves, stay calm, and control their impulses.

It is important that teachers who want to foster SEL use evidence-based practices, which are practices that teachers can document with well-done, ethical, useful research (Dunst, Trivett, & Cutspec, 2002). We will now look at several of these strategies, grouped into two categories:

> Create supportive SEL environments
> Teach SEL knowledge and skills

Social emotional learning (SEL)
Gaining knowledge about feelings and about getting along with others

Create Supportive SEL Environments

Children flourish in positive, trust-building environments (Day & Kunz, 2009; Greenman, 2005; Perry & Szalavitz, 2007; Pianta & Stuhlman, 2004). For example, they need healthy *interpersonal* environments, or relationships with teachers, where they feel their teacher's respect. Teachers communicate genuine respect with a validating and open style of communication; when they are positive, warm, and caring; and when they are highly responsive to what children need. They also have expectations for children based on a child's level of development (Baumrind, 1996). A healthy interpersonal environment surrounds children with the safety and security (Maslow, 1954) that they need as a base for learning about feelings and for making friends.

Unfortunately, some children experience less supportive interpersonal environments, in which adults model irresponsible emotional management and ineffective social skills. Adults in these environments have "silent" arguments, argue or yell loudly, attack one another physically, and frequently belittle or humiliate others, thus modeling a distorted view of emotions and social skills. A child observing this behavior tends to see anger-arousing situations as a signal that an attack is about to take place. They experience great stress and are on alert, ever ready for a fight or ready to hide. They do not view conflicts as mere problems that reasonable people can solve (Pollak, Vardi, Putzer Bechner, & Curtin, 2005). Therefore, these children truly need a healthy relationship with their teacher.

Children also need a pleasant, productive, and peaceful *physical* environment—the arrangement of space and furniture and materials used for their learning. Teachers show respect for how young children learn and develop by arranging space and materials well. As you read in Chapter 4 such a physical environment conveys a sense of order and provides a place for work and play (Greenman, 2005). The teacher arranges the room well and creates an orderly and organized space. Such a physical environment emphasizes active learning and invites children to make choices and to work with other children, which is essential in learning about how to deal with emotions and social skills.

Children need an appropriate and suitable schedule or *temporal (time) environment*, which conveys a sense of balance between active and quiet periods and between teacher- and child-initiated activities. An appropriate schedule offers children expanded periods for learning and interacting with others (Hopkins, 2007). For example, work periods of longer than 30 minutes result in higher levels of social and cognitive play (Ostrosky, Jung, Hemmeter, & Thomas, 2003). The following subsections describe some practical strategies to use in creating environments that foster SEL (Carlson, 2006; Marion, 2007; Perry, 2000; Tanner, 2005).

Accept feelings and set limits about expressing them   Communicate your acceptance of all feelings. Avoid criticizing children for having any feeling, but set clear, consistent, yet flexible boundaries about how to manage emotions responsibly (Christian, 2006). Let children know that you will help them with learning about emotions. Convey this message simply, firmly, and kindly to children, as the teacher in the next example does.

PEARSON
myeducationlab

Go to the Assignments and Activities section of Topic 5: Social Emotional Learning in the MyEducationLab for your course and complete the activity entitled *The Role of Play in Children's Social Skill Development*. Note how play can help children who need to develop key social skills.

EXAMPLE   Mrs. Woodward watched Larry get ready to hurl a shovel at Ralph after Ralph ran over Larry's sand structure. The teacher quickly grabbed the shovel, and said, "Stop! Throwing a shovel is dangerous. I won't allow you to hurt children when you're mad." From all indications, Ralph destroyed Larry's sand structure accidentally. After Larry had calmed down, the teacher spoke with him briefly about accidents, such as Ralph's unintentional ruining of his sand structure.

Demonstrate respect for children   The interpersonal environment also refers to your role as a trustworthy, respectful adult. Children need to know that you are reliable and that you will help them learn about friends and feelings. Table 8.3 lists several realistic things that you can do to demonstrate your respect for children.

Create a socially responsible classroom   Children need to learn that they have a responsibility in making their classroom work and that they can contribute to

TABLE 8.3	Showing respect creates a safe and secure interpersonal environment		
The Strategy	**What the Teacher Does**	**Example**	**Why This Is Effective**
Walk in the child's shoes (take a child's perspective)	Figure out how things look to children. Look at them when speaking. Get down to their level.	The teacher in the chapter-opening infant–toddler vignette seemed to understand how the loud noise might appear to Thomas.	Changes how you see things. Helps children feel worthy of your attention.
Observe	Watch carefully. Record observations. Reflect on what you see. Use information to plan for children.	Mrs. Woodward has seen that Jerry gets upset when there is a lot of noise in the classroom.	Helps you recognize children's style and temperament. You discover each child's overload point. You can plan to prevent a child from reaching that point.
Communicate caringly	Be unruffled. Speak kindly and avoid loud, stress-inducing speech. Smile and laugh easily. Use *appropriate touch* (hand on shoulder or touch a child's hand). Be unrelentingly positive. Acknowledge each child every day. Use active listening.	Thomas, from the infant–toddler chapter-opening vignette, heard his teacher speak kindly and could feel the teacher holding him gently.	Conveys genuine affection for children; helps children pay attention to you; shows them that you are reliable and will help them figure things out about feelings and friends, even when they make mistakes; listening actively tells children that somebody is finally interested in their problem.
Focus on calming activities	Allow time for quiet reflection. Teach children how to focus and calm themselves— deep or slow breathing, yoga, for example.	Mr. Sanchez encouraged his primary-grade children in the chapter-opening vignette to calm themselves with deep breathing.	Teaches children to concentrate; gives them time to think and reflect by themselves; trains brain circuits that are responsible for focusing and calming.

their classroom and to the world. They need to feel like a valuable member of a cohesive and caring group, that their teachers are friendly and kind, and that they will get to see and work with their friends in school. Teachers create such an environment by encouraging playing and working together in learning because social interaction gives children good opportunities for SEL (Association for Moral Education, 2004; Tolme et al., 2009). Apply democratic principles of self-rule, social equality, and inclusion. Teach children about the concept of *fairness* and applying rules to everyone. Mr. Sanchez used his job chart, for example, to help children understand that everybody had a job. Focus on the benefits of cooperation—that the children will get work done more efficiently and that it is fun to work together, as Mr. Sanchez does in the next example, by teaching the children about negotiating parts of jobs and having fun working together.

> **EXAMPLE**   One classroom job, washing tables, required that two children work together. Jerry started out by telling Alison what to do and she responded by saying, "You're not the boss, Jerry!" Mr. Sanchez said, "This is a two-person job and you have to figure out which parts you each will do. One of you could get the sponges and give one to each of you and maybe the other person could rinse and store the sponges when you're finished. Also, decide which end of the table each of you will wash. You can wash, wash, wash and then meet in the middle."

Model social emotional and social skills   Provide a good model of responsible emotional management and social skills for children by *acknowledging emotions*. Simply accepting your feelings and demonstrating that there is nothing wrong with any emotion is a valuable lesson in emotional intelligence.

> **EXAMPLE**   As the children sat down for a story, they all heard the music blaring from a car in the parking lot. Mrs. Woodward said, "Wow! That's really loud and I feel a little annoyed that it's disturbing our story."

Stay calm and precisely identify emotions so that children observe a composed adult dealing with a real feeling and demonstrating the key social skill of calming oneself, something many children never see. Children benefit from observing a teacher take the time to get that burst of emotional energy under control, as Mr. Sanchez does in the next example. He felt quite upset when two second-grade boys knocked over paint cups and laughed about it.

> **EXAMPLE**   After the teacher and two boys sat down, Mr. Sanchez said, "I am very upset. I want you just to sit here with me until I calm down. No talking while I take some deep breaths."

Choose how to express an emotion so that children will see that they, too, can make choices about expressing feelings. Mr. Sanchez did not simply "blow off steam" because some of the children see enough of that at home or on television and need a different example from teachers. He deliberately decided how to respond. The next example shows that he took responsibility for how he felt. He did not blame the boys for causing his feeling, but he described their part in the incident. His is direct and firm, but also kind. He uses the I-message strategy explained in Chapter 5.

EXAMPLE   Mr. Sanchez said, "I saw your hands hit every paint cup. Each cup fell over and the paint splashed onto the table, the floor, and the wall. I heard your laughing." (Mr. Sanchez simply gave the facts, the data, but did not blame). "Now, we have to spend our time cleaning up, not painting." (He gave the real effects of their behavior). "I am upset and disappointed that two children in my class have wasted paint and created such a mess." (He stated his feeling)

Intentionally Focus on the Language and Skills of SEL

All children need to develop specific knowledge and skills about emotions and social interaction. Specific groups of children, such as those with anxiety disorders, especially need help because their parents do not seem to be able to convey any information about this topic or situation (Suveg et al., 2008). Teachers can help children by planning SEL literacy learning activities. The activities center on showing children how to talk about feelings and friends.

Show children how to talk about feelings and friends   We can help children to become emotionally literate, to be able to express feelings accurately (Weare, 2004). The preschool teacher in the chapter-opening vignettes said, "You can *use words* to tell Sarah that you are upset." It is a supportive strategy because so many young children might never have heard of such an idea and also do not know the words to use. Use Vygotsky's advice and scaffold their understanding.

Help children understand that they have feelings.   Here, you would teach the idea, the concept, that people have feelings. Do this formally with lessons or informally through daily interactions with children. For example, read a book and note that the story involved feelings ("I wonder how Sammy was feeling when it snowed"), or show a picture of a child approaching a group that she wants to enter and ask, "This girl wanted to play with the others but had to ask first. How do you think that she might have felt about asking?"

Teach how to use a word to describe a feeling.   "Sammy was smiling when it snowed. The word *happy* tells us how Sammy felt." "The words we can use to tell how the girl felt about asking to play are *anxious* or *afraid*." Show drawings or photographs of facial expressions of emotions—children tend to be more accurate in decoding drawings (MacDonald, Kirkpatrick, & Sullivan, 1996). "Let's make this face. The word to use when we feel like this is *disgust*."

Build a strong feelings vocabulary.   Emotions are complex, with many levels of emotional energy. For instance, a person can be pleased, happy, thrilled, or even overjoyed. A feeling of anger can range from minor irritation to rage. Help children understand that they might feel "a little happy or a little angry" but at other times feel "very, very happy or very, very angry."

After children have learned one word for a feeling, encourage them to increase the number of labels or words they can use to describe the specific feeling they are experiencing. Many children know or use only one word, *mad*, for example, to

FIGURE 8.2   **Expand the range of emotion words for children**

Younger children

Glad

Cheerful

Happy

Older children

Glad
—Delighted
—Pleased

Cheerful
—Jolly
—Jovial

Happy
—Contented
—Blissful
—Elated

Expanding the Range of Happy

describe angry feelings. Build their feelings vocabulary by adding new words such as *angry, irritated, annoyed, furious, irate, enraged,* and *upset* to the list (Figure 8.2). These new words will help them more accurately describe the level of emotion in different situations, a powerful skill. Make a permanent record, such as a book or chart listing different words for angry feelings, and refer to it when discussing anger. You can do the same thing with other feelings words, too.

> **EXAMPLE**   "I think that the librarian was *pleased* when we were on time for our library period." "I feel *cheerful* when I get to read a story to you." "I noticed that you seemed *very happy* when you got your kitten."

Expand the Range of Emotion Words for Children

Plan discussions about feelings and friends   Teacher–child dialogue is important in children's learning in general (Berk & Winsler, 1995) and when discussing emotions and social skills in particular. Consider treating this topic as you would any other important topic, as something you need to teach. Carry out the instruction in small or large groups, or even with individuals. Here are a few ideas to get you started.

Vignettes.   Make up scenarios or situations, and then encourage children to generate a direct, nonaggressive response: "Somebody sits next to you at snack. What would be a friendly thing to say? An unfriendly thing to do or to say?" "Another child wants to play with you. What is an *unfriendly* thing to do? What is a friendly thing to do?" "What could you do if you were washing your hands and somebody pushed you out of the way?" "Here's a picture of a child who is upset because somebody just called her a stupid girl. Tell me how she can use words to say how she feels."

Thinking puppets.   Puppets help children think about many things, develop reasoning skills, and solve problems that the puppet might be having (Keogh,

Naylor, Simon, Downing, and Maloney, 2006: Quakley, Reynolds, & Coker, 2004). Use puppets to demonstrate friendly versus unfriendly responses, or to demonstrate the use of words to tell somebody that you are angry, and then lead a discussion about how well they managed. Conversely, present a problem about anger through the puppets and help the children work to achieve a positive, responsible solution. A preschool teacher in the next example has observed that some of the children needed to learn how to respond in a healthy way when somebody pushed or pinched them.

EXAMPLE   The teacher intentionally planned a discussion about anger for large-group time. She demonstrated a mild conflict in which one puppet pinched the other. "Harvey (puppet) is *angry* because this other puppet pinched him. Help Harvey think about what he could do. He's not allowed to yell at or hurt the puppet that pinched him."

Books and stories.   Literacy-related activities, such as scripted stories and books, help children develop SEL All children gain when we focus on SEL, but children with communication disorders or challenging behaviors especially need the explicit instruction in a scripted story (Figueora-Sanchez, 2008). Write a scripted story by combining pictures and words focused on teaching specific skills, such as joining a group or using words to express feelings. Consider using clip art or photographs to develop hard copies of the stories or simply develop PowerPoint slides and show stories with a computer. Figure 8.3 shows a how to write a scripted story about skills for joining a group of children for play.

Bibliotherapy
Using books and literature to help children deal with issues that they face

Bibliotherapy refers to using literature to help individuals deal with psychological and mental health issues. Teachers can use books to help children understand feelings and friends (Birckmayer, Cohen, Jensen, & Variano, 2005; Sullivan &

| FIGURE 8.3 | Scripted story for teaching a social skill |

Write sentences that explain situations and answer questions, such as who, what, where, why.

- I like to play with other children at school.
- It is fun to play with others.
- Sometime, I see other children already in a group.
- I have to ask if I can play with my friends if they are already in a group.
- It is okay to ask to play with others.

Write sentences that describe how those involved might feel.

- I feel a little scared about asking to play sometimes.
- The other children like it when I ask to play.
- My teacher likes it when I ask if I can play with others.

Write a sentence or two about what the child might do.

- I will try to remember to ask if I can play.

Source: **Based on** CSEFEL (n.d.). Scripted Stories for Social Situations—Tip Sheet. Retrieved on May 6, 2009, from http://www.vanderbilt.edu/csefel/scriptedstories/tips.pdf

Strang, 2002). When you read books about emotions, for example, children get information about the topic, and they make connections between what they hear about feelings in and out of school. They are more likely to view their own emotions as natural and normal when a teacher plans, reads, and follows up on a story about emotions (Jalongo, 1986).

As an example, choose books about anger that teach one or more of the major concepts about anger management. Some of these concepts are anger is a normal emotion, we can express feelings words, anger can range from mild irritation to rage, and a child should express anger without resorting to aggression. See Figure 8.4.

FIGURE 8.4   **Checklist: Guidelines for choosing books on anger**

Follow selection guidelines from Reading Is Fundamental (RIF) (Reading Is Fundamental, 2004) for choosing any picture book, and then check to be sure that the book meets additional, specific selection criteria for stories about anger. Use this checklist to evaluate a book on anger.

1. **How does this book deal with words/vocabulary for angry feelings?**
   ❑ Uses one word (*mad* or *angry*) exclusively.
   ❑ Uses two different words (such as *mad* and *angry*) or some other combination.
   ❑ Uses several different words, thus demonstrating how to describe anger with different words.

2. **Does this book identify the specific event that seemed to elicit the anger?**
   ❑ Not at all. Anger trigger never mentioned.
   ❑ Identified a trigger for the anger, but was inaccurate.
   ❑ Identified the anger trigger, but in a blaming, accusatory way.
   ❑ Correctly identified the specific thing that brought on the anger, without blaming.

3. **How well does this book convey the idea that feeling angry is a natural and normal experience?**
   ❑ Not at all. It actually blames the child in the story for feeling angry.
   ❑ Not very well. It acknowledges that the child is angry but in a guilt-inducing way.
   ❑ Adequately. It acknowledges anger, but says nothing about it being okay.
   ❑ Very well. It clearly conveys the idea that anger is a normal emotion.

4. **How does this story urge children to manage their anger (goal: present nonaggressive, optimistic strategies)?**
   ❑ With aggressive strategies exclusively (such as, hitting others—an inappropriate strategy).
   ❑ Sometimes aggressively (also an inappropriate strategy).
   ❑ With positive strategies (such as using words—an appropriate strategy).

5. **My decision, based on my checklist analysis:**
   ❑ Reject the book because it advocates aggression or it blames the child.
   ❑ Read the book, but make adjustments to fix minor issues.*
   ❑ Use the book with confidence that it meets most of the selection guidelines.

*It is possible to use a book even if it is less than perfect (assuming it does not advocate aggressive strategies or blame children). Suppose that a book does not identify the event that angered a child. How might you use the book anyway? What might you do to help the children come up with their own ideas about the anger trigger?

Read and use books thoughtfully, and employ a variety of follow-up activities to the story (Hsieh, Hemmeter, McCollum, & Ostrosky, 2009). CSEFEL (no date), for example, has developed the "Book Nook," part of their web site giving specific suggestions about how to use books—and scripted stories—in SEL. They give numerous suggestions for using books such as *Hands Are Not for Hitting*, by Martine Agassi. Suggestions for teaching alternative uses for hands abound in art, music, science, drama, and pretend-play. (Refer to the list of web sites near the end of this chapter to find the URL for the CSEFEL web site.)

myeducationlab

Go to the Building Teaching Skills and Dispositions section of Topic 5: Social Emotional Learning in the MyEducationLab for your course and complete the activity entitled *Teaching Social Skills*. This teaching skill can help teachers facilitate children's social and emotional development.

WORKING *with* FAMILIES	**FAMILIES CAN HELP CHILDREN LEARN ABOUT FEELINGS AND FRIENDS**

Work with parents to help children learn about emotions and social skills. Use the same strategies that you employ when talking with parents about other areas of the curriculum or other concerns. The following list provides examples:

- **Newsletter.** Write a regular column on feelings and friends, and include articles about learning to use words to label anger or about social skills such as taking turns.
- **Group-based parent education.** Teach parents how to structure situations so that a child can succeed. Two examples include (1) limiting the number of playmates at any one time and (2) breaking tasks into smaller steps to decrease a child's frustration and anxiety.
- **Electronic communication.** Create a blog or listserv for parents of children in your class or in a parent education group. These methods use technology for communicating with a whole group.
- **Feelings chart.** Explain how you use the chart with the words for different feelings. Give a handout of the same chart to parents so that they may have a reference.
- **Thinking puppets.** Introduce the thinking puppets to parents, and explain how to use them in discussions about feelings and friends with their children.
- **Web sites.** Some parents like to get information electronically. Help them by suggesting good web sites. See the list of suggestions at the end of the chapter.

RESOURCES FOR PARENTS

Elman, N., & Kennedy-Moore, E. (2003). *The unwritten rules of friendship: Simple strategies to help your child make friends.* New York: Little, Brown, & Company.

Lantieri, L., & Goleman, D. (2008). *Building emotional intelligence: Techniques to cultivate inner strength in children.* Louisville, CO: Sounds True.

Rudd, B. (2009). *Help your child develop emotional literacy: The parent's guide to happy children.* London: Continuum.

myeducationlab

To check your comprehension on the content covered in Chapter 8, go to the Book Specific Resources in the MyEducationLab for your course, select your text, and complete the Study Plan. Here you will be able to take a chapter quiz, receive feedback on your answers, and then access review, practice, and enrichment activities to enhance your understanding of chapter content.

ANALYZE A VIGNETTE

Now that you have read the chapter, analyze the chapter-opening vignette about preschool by answering the following questions.

1. Jerry noticed that he was angry. Which of the types of interactions from the How Children Perceive Emotions section of the chapter would you say fits Jerry's anger?

2. From the section on Expressing Anger, identify the method that Jerry used to express his feeling. Explain your answer.

3. From information in the chapter, explain how Jerry has probably learned to express angry feelings so aggressively.

SUMMARY

Teachers focus on the whole child, including social and emotional competence. Emotionally intelligent individuals cope well with feelings, have empathy for others, and get along well with others. Children who are intelligent about their feelings are competent and capable, feel connected to others, and have a good sense of balance in their emotions. The abilities that make up emotional intelligence and competence are:

- Perceiving emotions
- Expressing emotions
- Regulating emotions

Children who are emotionally competent and intelligent are equipped well for making and keeping friends—for developing social competence. Emotional and social competences are linked because good emotional regulation gives children a good chance at developing good social skills, too. Socially competent children:

- Relate well to other children
- Respond agreeably to others
- Possess developed social skills

Teachers can guide children's learning about emotions and social development—SEL. They can:

- Create supportive SEL environments. Children need a trust-building interpersonal environment in which they interact with warm and supportive teachers. They need supportive physical environments, that is, classrooms conducive to active, collaborative learning, and they need schedules allowing large blocks of time for their learning.
- Focus intentionally on the language and skills of SEL. They can focus on having feelings, helping children develop the vocabulary with which to label and discuss emotions, and discussing the topics of feelings and friends.

QUESTIONS FOR REFLECTION

1. Why is it so difficult for young children to *understand* emotions, especially when they can feel emotions and they certainly do express emotions?

2. Explain why arguing over possessions is the type of interaction most likely to call forth anger in preschool children.

3. A parent asks you this question: "Okay, Tim is only 2 years old. He cannot manage anger on his own. I

understand that. How will I know when he is ready to handle some of his feelings on his own?" What would you say to this parent?

4. Why is it so important to teach children how to use words as labels for their feelings? Why can you expect children to show individual differences in their ability to use word labels for emotions?

APPLY YOUR KNOWLEDGE

1. Analyze one or two books on anger from the list below to decide whether it meets the guidelines for choosing books about emotions/anger. Use the checklist in Figure 8.4 as a guide. Consider adding the completed checklist to your portfolio.

> Bang, M. (2008). *When Sophie Gets Angry—Really, Really Angry*. New York: Scholastic Paperbacks, reprint edition.

> Kroll, S, & Davenier, C. (2002). *That makes me mad!*. San Francisco: CA: Chronicle Books.

> Shannon, D. (2000). *The rain came down*. New York: Blue Sky Press.

2. Read a story to children. Access http://www.vanderbilt.edu/csefel/booknook/hands/hands.html, which opens part of the CSEFEL site for activities related to a children's book, *Hands Are Not for Hitting*, by Margaret Agazzi. (If you are currently at a practicum site, request permission to read the book to the children.) Request permission to carry out one of the activities described on this web page. The activities will help children understand the major concepts in the book. If you cannot read to a whole group, then consider reading to and doing one of the activities with a single child.

KEY TERMS

Anger (*194*)
Awareness of others (*192*)
Bibliotherapy (*211*)
Emotional intelligence (*191*)
Emotions (*191*)

Expressing emotions (*195*)
Perceiving emotions (*191*)
Regulating emotions (*197*)
Self-awareness (*192*)
Social emotional learning (SEL) (*205*)

Socially competent children (*203*)
Social skills (*203*)
Understanding feelings (*199*)

WEB SITES

Center on the Social and Emotional Foundations for Early Learning (CSEFEL)
http://www.vanderbilt.edu/csefel

A federally funded, national resources center. Excellent resources on SEL for teachers, trainers, and parents. See the excellent examples of scripted stories for SEL, complete with pictures or drawings, in the Resources/Practical Strategies section of the web site. These scripted stories are PowerPoint slides that you can use in your teaching.

Edutopia
http://www.edutopia.org/social-emotional-learning

A web site devoted to what works in public education This part of the site deals directly with emotional learning. Watch videos on emotional intelligence.

Second Step Program
http://www.cfchildren.org/programs/ssp/overview

A packaged social skills education program for children of different ages. Follow the links to see video clips and to find additional information.

Resilience and Stress in Childhood

"I think I can, I think I can."

—PIPER and LONG, *The Little Engine That Could*

"If the track is tough and the hill is rough, THINKING you can just ain't enough!"
—SILVERSTEIN, "The Little Blue Engine" (a poem)

Chapter Contents

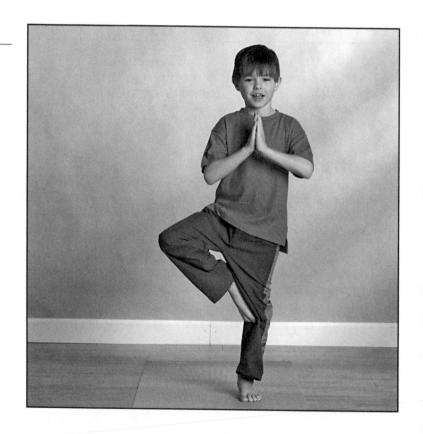

Guiding Questions

- How can we explain how children become resilient?
- What are the major sources of stress and what are the stages that children go through in responding to stress?
- How can I, as a teacher, help children learn to cope with stress effectively?

VIGNETTES

INFANT–TODDLER: SCHOOL IS A COMFORTING PLACE

Mr. Bjornrud realized that 15-month-old Lela's family had moved to a trailer after they lost their house in a flood. Things at home were beginning to settle down, but Lela was still showing signs of stress. The teacher had been working with her and her parents by continuing to make school as predictable as possible. He greeted her warmly every morning, set up interesting and favorite activities and toys, and comforted her as needed. He also invited her parents to spend a little time with Lela in the classroom, and they seem to enjoy this calm and peaceful time together.

PRESCHOOL: THE FIRE ALARM RINGS

Mrs. Woodward and the 4-year-olds had just started their morning meeting when the fire alarm rang out loudly (an unscheduled fire drill). Even though the class had heard the alarm during a practice drill, some of the children were startled. A few showed obvious signs of distress, especially as the sound continued, growing louder and more piercing. The teacher remained calm, called to the children quietly but firmly, and told them to look at her. "That's the fire alarm. We have to leave the building, just as we practiced. Stay with me and watch me." She and the assistant lined up the children and then quickly moved them outside.

PRIMARY: ALDEN GOES TO A NEW SCHOOL

After transferring to his new school, Alden would be in Mr. Sanchez's mixed-age class. The teacher met Alden and his father after school to orient them to 5-year-old Alden's new classroom. The teacher showed them his cubby, took his picture to add to the class pictures, and showed him where he would nap. They toured the room, and Alden learned where things were and how they worked. Mr. Sanchez gave a copy of the daily schedule to Alden's father and gave him a choice of children's books about moving to read to Alden. The next day, the teacher assigned a friend to help Alden through routines. He also explained playground rules.

:: INTRODUCTION

Stress
A child's reaction to psychological or physical threats to safety and security

Children are not immune to stress. They face stress-inducing situations every day, such as those faced by Lela, the preschoolers, and Alden in the chapter-opening vignettes. In this chapter, you will learn about **resilience** in children and about how **stress** affects children. We will examine the stages of responding to stress as well as what it takes to cope effectively. You will add to your understanding of why young children have a difficult time coping with stress on their own.

On a practical level, you will learn several general guidelines for helping children with stress. The guidelines can be used to help children who face a variety of stressors. Then we will apply those guidelines to a specific, potentially stressful event—moving to a new neighborhood or school. Finally, you will have an opportunity, in the end-of-chapter activities, to apply this information to other childhood stressors.

:: RESILIENCE IN YOUNG CHILDREN

Resilience
The ability to weather stress and adversity and not be devastated by it

Many children face adversity in their homes and communities. These are the high-risk children about whom we worry so much. What we know, though, is that many, but not all, children who face multiple and severe risks show great *resilience* as they overcome the odds. **Resilience** is the ability to recover relatively quickly from misfortune without being overwhelmed or acting in dysfunctional ways. This implies that a child, for instance, would adapt optimistically under many stressful conditions (Aldwin & Werner, 2007; Siebert, 2005; Werner, 2004). A person who is resilient is calm under pressure, can solve problems, can reflect critically on issues, is autonomous, and has a sense of purpose.

Resilience Grows in Families, Schools, and Communities

Ecological theory, from Chapter 2, explains that children develop in different systems, each system adding its influence. Many children experience **stress**, a reaction to physical or psychological threats to well-being, and often the stress is traumatic. Some children fare well in spite of very stressful conditions, but others do not. What fosters a good developmental outcome in the face of great stress? Why are some children more resilient than other children?

Children become resilient in the systems in which they grow up—family, peer group, school, neighborhood, and larger society. Those who develop resilience are protected in some way from stress. They still experience stress, but something in the child's systems protects the child from major and potentially negative effects of harmful events. Something or someone buffers or absorbs some of the shock of the stressor, shielding a child and allowing him or her to develop well in the face of adversity (Werner & Smith, 2001).

Protective Factors That Foster Resilience

Systems that help children weather trauma provide safety and security in the midst of a whirlwind of stress. In this textbook, we are interested in what separates families or schools who foster resilience from those who do not. First, adults in these systems have a philosophy or basic core values that put protection of children at the center—the most important thing that they do—over and above their stated role. Your professional code of ethical behavior states that protecting children is the most important thing that teachers do (National Association of the Education of Young Children [NAEYC], 2005a). A resilience-building family or school feels good to children: they like spending time there and understand that the adults really care about them.

Second, resilience-building systems—families or schools—provide a specific type of safeguard called **protective factors**. These protective factors are the key in enabling children to navigate the bumpy road of frustration or adversity and to develop resilience. These three protective factors are (Werner & Smith, 2001; Werner, 2004):

> **Protective factors**
> Key features of caring systems in which children become resilient

A caring relationship.
High expectations.
Opportunities for participation.

Caring relationships Adults in resiliency-building families or schools tend to be authori*tative*, a style fostering resilience. Children learn to understand and manage potentially stressful events in caring and compassionate adult–child relationships. Resilient children have been able to connect with at least one caring and compassionate person, often a teacher, who serves as a good model of confidence and positive action. An authori*tative* teacher, for example, is high in responsiveness, and one of the most important aspects of high responsiveness is a warm and caring attitude toward children. This teacher tries to develop a good and caring relationship with all children in a class. The teacher acknowledges each child's existence, what that child does and creates, and how that child feels. The teacher knows that a good relationship is especially important for children who do not have a close relationship with parents.

High expectations Authori*tative* caregivers, parents, or teachers have reasonable but high expectations for children. This helps children become resilient, partly because of how the expectations affect

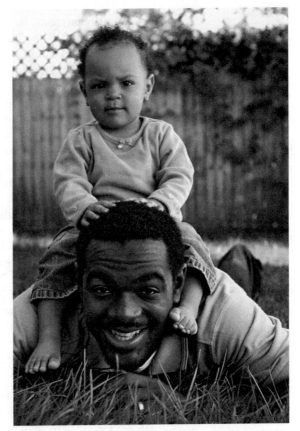

Caring relationships help children build resilience.

a child's self-esteem. Authoritative adults who have high but reasonable expectations help children develop competence, control, and worth, the building blocks of positive self-esteem (see Chapter 7 in this text). Competence, control, and a belief that one is worthy of affection also form the foundation of a resilient spirit.

Opportunities for participation   All humans yearn for validation and group membership. Children have these needs, just as we all do. They require chances to operate as a member of a group, and adults in protective systems make sure that their children get those chances. This can be something as simple as participating in making the limits or rules for a classroom in which caring adults have high expectations. It can also mean participating in family events, activities in one's religious group, Cub Scouts or Brownies, 4-H groups, library reading groups, care and feeding of animals, theater or other arts groups, and athletic teams.

The list of ways for children to participate is long. Children do not need to participate in a large number of activities, only those that give them pleasure and a sense of real belonging. You can do two practical things to help children participate joyfully.

- **Identify interests.** Help a child identify or find those activities that he likes and wants to do. For parents, this might mean spending "registration fees" for activities and letting a child try out the activity. For teachers, this means observing children carefully to discover what they really like to do—not what the teacher thinks a child should like, but what the *child* thinks is interesting and enjoyable. (You will be surprised on occasion!)
- **Encourage participation.** Once a child has found an activity that he likes, make sure that he has opportunities for participating and for feeling like a valued member of the group. For example, Mr. Sanchez knew that second-grader Sonia liked to play jacks. It was simple for him to set up play for jacks during recess. He also knew that Joseph liked to sing, although the 7-year-old would never admit that in front of the other boys. Therefore, Mr. Sanchez made sure that the children sang during most of their morning meetings.

:: TYPES OF STRESSORS

Stressors are forms of excessive stimulation that produce stress. Some of these factors are psychological; others are physical. At times, physical and psychological stressors interact or merge to produce an effect.

Physical Stressors

Physical stressor
Excessive stimulation with potential to damage parts of a child's body

Physical stressors refer to forms of excessive stimulation that injure or can potentially injure the tissue of some part of a child's body. There are several such physical stressors: excessively loud noises, extremely harsh lighting, decreased oxygen or lack of oxygen, extreme heat, extreme cold, injuries, infections, and drugs. Children who experience these stressors usually perceive them as painful or unpleasant.

EXAMPLE   Sarah's family was spending a month on vacation at the beach. Sarah's babysitter failed to put sunscreen on 4-year-old Sarah when the child played outside. Sarah was sunburned and her skin blistered. The stressor was unprotected and excessive exposure to sunlight, which affected Sarah's skin.

Psychological Stressors

Psychological stressors are forms of excessive stimulation with the potential to threaten a child's sense of well-being or to keep a child from developing a sense of well-being. Children might perceive several things as psychologically stressful, and children have varying views about what a psychological stressor is. For example, a child might see the death of a beloved grandparent as extremely stressful. Another child might not view a grandparent's death as stressful at all. Psychological stress, then, is a relationship between a child and his environment. Stress is not an *event*, such as the death of a grandparent, but is instead a relationship between a child and her perception of that event.

Psychological stressor
Excessive stimulation with potential to thwart or damage a child's sense of security

This relationship involves whether a child understands and can evaluate an event as well as a child's ability to cope with the event. A child is most likely to feel psychological stress when she cannot understand, evaluate, or cope effectively with some internal or external event. She then feels overwhelmed by the inability to cope, thus resulting in stress. Children often feel stress when something keeps them from fulfilling any of several fundamental needs—for security, bonding, acceptance, status, meaning, and mastery.

EXAMPLE   Vincent goes to a school in which close to a third of the children were not born in the United States and who have been here for fewer than 4 years. The school district was not prepared to meet the needs of this influx of children with special requirements and is now struggling to do so. Vincent is having a great deal of trouble adjusting to life in a new country, as are his parents. Six-year-old Vincent does not understand and therefore cannot cope with several aspects of his new school. He is very likely to experience psychological stress because he feels overwhelmed in this new environment.

Some people automatically view specific life events as stressful, such as a move, a new school, a parent's death, or parents divorcing. In reality, these are merely life events, which make them only *potentially* stressful. They create stress only if a child does not understand the event, cannot evaluate the event, or does not have the skills for effectively coping with the event.

For example, many people believe that moving is automatically a stressful life event for young children. It would probably be more accurate to call moving a potentially stressful event; it can possible create psychological stress, but whether it does depends on a child's understanding of and ability to cope with the move. Vincent, in the example just given, did view moving as stressful.

Combination of Physical and Psychological Stressors

Often, a child's life includes both physical and psychological stressors that blend. Suppose that somebody hurts a child—a physically stressful event. Then consider what the child might think about this situation: her thoughts about being assaulted tangle with the trauma itself. Therefore, she experiences psychological stress along with the physical stress. Children physically injured in some way might then fear or display anxiety about similar situations.

EXAMPLE   Daniel is a 2-year-old whose father deliberately burned him with a cigarette as punishment for an accident during toilet learning (often called potty training). The physical stressor was the hot tip of the cigarette. Fear and anxiety in the relationship with a parent who uses sadistic punishment provided the psychological stress.

EXAMPLE   An older child on the way to school has punched Jordan several times—has bullied Jordan. Punching is the physically stressful event. However, this is combined with the anxiety and worry that Jordan feels, making such episodes psychologically stressful as well.

:: ACUTE AND CHRONIC STRESS

Suppose that a child has perceived a potential stressor as stressful. He does not understand the stressor or might not have the skills for coping with it. The stress that he experiences can be either **acute** (profound, deep, extreme, intense, short-lived) or **chronic** (persistent, unceasing, continuous) stress.

Acute Stress

Acute stress
Intense strain that occurs rapidly; usually transitory

Acute stress is the most common form of stress. It is intense stress that occurs suddenly. Acute stress can be physical, psychological, or a combination of the two. It occurs quite unexpectedly but tends to subside as abruptly as it arose; for example, a visit to the emergency room to have a broken arm set (physical and psychological stress). How an event affects a child depends, in large part, on how others deal with the event and on how the child appraises it (American Psychological Association, 2004).

EXAMPLE   Six-year-old Jessica stood alone on the front steps of her house, crying. Just minutes before, the fire truck had zoomed into her family's driveway, sirens blaring. The firefighters were at the back of the house in the garage, putting out a fire. Jessica's mother, along with two friends, watched them, looking as though they were at a party, with cigarettes dangling from one hand and drinks in the other. Not one of them explained anything or paid attention to Jessica, other than to tell her to get to and stay in the front of the house. Jessica's apparent upset escalated until she screamed with fear. Her mother strode around the side of the house and angrily regarded her daughter.

Chronic Stress

Chronic stress
Unrelenting, persistent, and ongoing stress

Chronic stress refers to persistent stress, which comes into a person's life and remains for a long period or even forever. Chronic stress is like a chronic disease, such as diabetes, because it is a constant part of a person's life. The children in your classes come from a variety of backgrounds and chances are very good that, in any one year, several of the children will be under chronic stress. They will have experienced grinding poverty, homelessness, illness, child abuse, irresponsible or inept parenting, long-term bitterness after parents divorcing, seemingly never-ending daily hassles, and loneliness or lack of friends. The effects of chronic stress seem to accumulate and to cause problems even for children who are well adjusted (American Psychological Association, 2004).

:: SOURCES OF STRESS

There are two major sources of stress—internal and external (Jackson, 2008; Jewitt & Peterson, 2002). **Internal sources of stress** come from within the child. **External sources of stress** originate outside the child.

Internal sources of stress
Stress originating within a child

Internal Sources of Stress

Internal sources of stress include hunger pangs in a neglected infant or child, shyness, or headaches. Thoughts about real or imagined dangers can be a source of stress, too. Emotions are also potential internal sources of stress. Anxiety, anger, jealousy, guilt, and even joy are potentially stressful for children if parents and teachers do not help them understand and deal with these emotions. Children do not automatically comprehend and know how to manage emotions.

External sources of stress
Stress originating outside a child

> **EXAMPLE**   Matthew just transferred to Mr. Sanchez's kindergarten. In Matthew's former school, his teacher did a morning meeting but it lasted almost one hour, far too long for young children. Matthew experienced a lot of anxiety about going to group and showed signs of the anxiety when he first joined Mr. Sanchez's class.

External Sources of Stress

Other potential sources of stress for children are external; that is, they come from the child's environment. Some of these external sources of stress exist within a child's family, whereas others are in a child's caregiving arrangement. Some external sources of stress exist in schools, others come from peers, and still others have their roots in the interaction of several systems. These stressors include the following:

In a Child's Family
- Overcrowded living conditions
- Moving
- Daily hassles for parents
- Divorce
- Poverty
- Joint custody arrangements

- Lots of background anger in the family, anger that the child hears and observes but is not directed to the child
- Military deployment of a parent

In School
- Going to a new school; leaving the old school
- Developmentally *in*appropriate classrooms, such as those dominated by *in*appropriate practices, including too many transitions, inappropriate instructional strategies, no recesses
- Standardized testing

From Interactions (either at home, in school, or in a child care facility)
- Experiencing child abuse or neglect directly
- Witnessing child abuse but not experiencing it firsthand
- Anger-arousing social interactions
- Developmentally *in*appropriate guidance, such as harsh discipline or inept guidance
- Loneliness or lack of friends

From Other Sources
- Observing violence and aggression in newscasts, movies, cartoons, video or DVD games, in real life, or in any other situation
- Death or injury of a friend or even another child who is not a friend but who goes to the same school; death of a pet; death of a family member
- Experiencing a disaster, for example the December 26, 2004, tsunami in the Indian Ocean or Hurricane Katrina in New Orleans in 2005
- Illness and hospitalization

:: HOW STRESS AFFECTS CHILDREN

Professionals who work with children can fully expect to experience firsthand a child's reactions to stress. You might wonder why one child suddenly has problems focusing on projects, why another behaves aggressively, or why still another is highly anxious. Stress affects children in a variety of ways, just as it affects adults. Stress takes its toll on children physically, behaviorally, and/or psychologically. If a child used words to express the stress that he feels, he might say, "There's something wrong in my life."

Physical Effects of Stress

A racing heart rate, dry mouth, a sick feeling in the stomach, a headache: most adults have experienced such physical reactions to some situation that they perceived as stressful—giving a speech, or seeing the flashing lights of a police car on the interstate. Children can and do experience the same physical effects of stress. Any or a combination of these physical effects usually shows up in cases of acute stress. Given enough stress, as in a chronically stressful situation such as child abuse or a developmentally inappropriate classroom, a child might have even greater physical effects from the stress.

Stress, white blood cells, and resistance to infections Researchers documented years ago that stress could eventually play a major role in disease (Stein, Keller, & Schleifer, 1981; Zegans, 1982). Recent research has found that chronic stress actually worsens some diseases or suppresses a person's immune system (Meagher, 2007; Miller, Cohen, & Richey, 2002). Stress often disrupts a child's immune system response and makes it difficult for the child's body to deal effectively with infections. Here is an example of how it works.

> **EXAMPLE** A child gets a splinter in his foot; the splinter breaks the skin and introduces bacteria. The bacteria multiply (the infection) and white blood cells move through the blood to the site of the infection. White blood cells (leukocytes), which contain digestive enzymes, destroy the bacteria in a process called phagocytosis—literally, "cell eating."

The number of white blood cells changes when an abnormal situation arises. A child's white blood cell count tends to rise when a child is overwhelmed by a stressful event. The child's body is trying to protect itself during a time of stress (Nanda, 2005).

Stress affects a child's brain Evidence has steadily mounted attesting to the unfortunate but preventable outcome of continued abuse and neglect on a child's developing brain (Lowenthal, 1999; Child Welfare Information Gateway, 2008). A major stressor such as abuse signals the child's body to prepare for "fight or flight," in which the body prepares to defend itself from danger. Stress hormones, cortisol and adrenalin, are released and prepare the body to respond to stress by increasing blood pressure and heart rate, for example.

A child under constant threat of abuse is nearly always in this state of readiness. The child's body may then produce an excessive amount of stress hormones, which can kill brain cells and reduce the number of connections among brain cells (the synapses). Adults subjected to long-term abuse as children have brains in which the hippocampus has shriveled, for example, and other parts also responsible for tasks such as memory or regulating emotions are smaller. Therefore, chronic stress causes constant activity of the stress response pathways and thus causes alterations in the brain (Child Welfare Information Gateway, 2008; Gallagher, 2004).

Behavioral and Psychological Effects

Nail biting, bullying, fatigue, aggression, withdrawal, anxiety, fear: all these and others are behavioral or psychological indicators of childhood stress. The psychological distress that children feel, for example, when abused, when they move, or when they are rejected very often shows up in behavior (see Figure 9.1). Some children react to

---

FIGURE 9.1   **Behavioral indicators of stress in young children**

Children show us that they are experiencing stress in a number of ways:
Reactions to stress might be passive.
  Excessive fatigue
  Withdrawing and putting head on table or desk
  Excessive fears
Reactions to stress might be more active with behaviors that involve only the child.
  Nail biting
  Manipulating one's hands or mouth
  Repetitive body movements
Reactions to stress might show up when children interact with others.
  Stuttering
  Bullying, threatening, or hurting others (see Seth in Chapter 9)
  Nervous, inappropriate laughter
Reactions to stress might show up as children work with objects.
  Excessive squeezing or tapping of pencils, markers, or crayons
  Clumsy or fumbling behavior

---

stress with passive behavior, whereas others display a more active approach. You might find that some children react to stress as they play or work with specific objects.

An issue to ponder about behavioral indicators of stress   Oppositional defiant disorder (ODD) is a psychiatric disorder in childhood. It is quite normal for children to test limits at specific junctures during development, for example, during toddlerhood and early adolescence. The psychiatric community believes, however, that "openly uncooperative and hostile behavior becomes a serious concern when it is so frequent and consistent that it stands out when compared with other children of the same age and developmental level," and when it seriously impairs a child's functioning (American Academy of Child & Adolescent Psychiatry [AACAP], 2009; Connor, 2004).

Children diagnosed with ODD have frequent temper tantrums, are touchy, are easily annoyed by others, show a lot of resentment or anger, and argue frequently with adults. AACAP advises that a child labeled as ODD also receive a thorough evaluation to screen for other disorders coexisting with ODD; these other disorders must also be treated.

It is quite possible that some children diagnosed with ODD are also under a great deal of stress. The AACAP even notes that symptoms of ODD tend to increase when a child is "under stress." One of the treatment methods for ODD is training parents. It is possible that parents of some children with ODD have had a major impact on their child's problem with inept or harsh parenting. Inept or harsh parenting is a major psychological stressor for children. Irresponsible parenting is also frequently a physical stressor for children if the parenting includes physical, including sadistically physical, punishment.

The thorough evaluation recommended by the AACAP should not be just an evaluation of the child. It might be more proper and accurate to diagnose a family system as having a problem when a child is given the label *ODD*. We might need a new label for the family system problem. The child would then not be the identified patient; instead, the family system would be the patient.

:: STAGES IN RESPONDING TO STRESS

A child goes through a series of stages in responding to an event that he does not understand and cannot control. Each of the three stages—alarm, appraisal, and searching for a coping strategy—places different demands on a child's body.

Alarm

In the **alarm** stage of stress, a child stops what he is doing and orients toward or focuses on the potentially stressful event. A child is aware of the potentially stressful event for the first time. He might become aware of danger in this new situation or remember danger from similar situations in the past. He will be alarmed.

> **EXAMPLE**   Ben, 7 years old, heard his mother's words and closed his eyes (stage of alarm): "We're moving. You have to help me pack your toys and books tomorrow." He and his mother and brother were moving yet again, putting Ben in another new school, his third in 2 years.

> **EXAMPLE**   David, 6 years old, looked up from his game, startled (stage of alarm), when his mom said, "Your father will be here to pick you up soon." David's parents have joint custody of him after their divorce, and David had come to dread visits with his dad, who had married a woman with an 8-year-old child. This older boy bullies David. David's father knows about it but has not done anything to protect David.

Alarm
First stage in responding to stress in which a child is first aware of a potential stressor

Appraisal

The **appraisal** stage is complex and involves reviewing what this event meant in the past. Ben, for example, thought, "I was scared when I went to the last new school, but the teacher helped me find things." Children also try to figure out how to cope as Ben did: "Maybe the new teacher will help me find things." Several things affect a child's appraisal of a potentially stressful event:

- **Developmental level in terms of memory and perception.** Infants and very young children obviously will not be able to perceive and remember or evaluate a stress-inducing event the way that a much older child or an adult would.
- **Child's experience with adults who have modeled how to look at and evaluate events.** A child whose parents model poor anger management skills, for example, will probably appraise an anger-arousing event differently from a child whose parents show responsible anger management.
- **Self-esteem.** Older children with positive self-esteem have a much more positive view of stress-inducing events and their ability to cope with the stressor. Feeling competent is one of the building blocks of positive self-esteem. Children often express competence with statements such as "I can do it."

Appraisal
Second stage in responding to stress; child assesses what such an event meant in the past

EXAMPLE   Ben is a resilient child who has a positive and realistic view of himself. He appraised the situation and said to himself, "The teacher in my last school told me that I know how to make friends and that other children like me."

Searching for a Coping Strategy

Searching for a coping strategy
Third stage in responding to stress; strategy chosen depends on whether children are familiar with and understand and whether they can generate a helpful way to deal with the event

The third stage in responding to stress involves **searching for a coping strategy**. Children, like all of us, do not always cope effectively with stress-inducing events. We know from some older research that children have a better chance of coping successfully when they believe they can control or master an event (Levine, Weinberg, & Ursin, 1978). Controlling or mastering an event depends, first, on whether the child is familiar with and understands an event, and second, on whether he can generate successful coping strategies. Consider the following possibilities.

First possibility: A child is familiar with an event, has actively dealt with it in the past, and used a good coping strategy   This is the best-case scenario because the child has already successfully dealt with a similar stress-inducing event. This enables him to think that he can master the current event.

EXAMPLE   Tyrell was to get his first barbershop haircut. He had been to the shop on several occasions whenever Dad got haircuts, and Tyrell occasionally sat in the big chair on his own. The barber had demonstrated his haircutting tools, such as a comb, scissors, and towel. Tyrell was thoroughly familiar with the barbershop and, from Dad's observations, seemed not to fear it at all.

Second possibility: A child is familiar with an event, has actively dealt with it in the past, but used an ineffective coping strategy   In this case, the strategy did not work because it was applied incorrectly or was not a good strategy in the first place. This would make a child somewhat wary, or even downright frightened, of the same or a similar stressful event in the future because he has not figured out how to cope.

EXAMPLE   Luke, 7 years old, had been to the emergency room previously when he put his hand through a garage window. The hospital personnel were not mean to him, but they were efficient; their main goal was to stop the profuse bleeding from his hand and arm. They failed to explain procedures and Luke reacted, understandably, with great fear and upset. Now he was going to the emergency room again, but this time for a skin rash that erupted on a Saturday night. Luke's father also remembered the previous visit to the hospital and tried to reassure his son about the current visit. Despite his dad's calm explanation and reassurances, Luke still viewed the hospital as a frightening place because of his first experience there.

Third possibility: A child is familiar with a stressor but has not dealt with it firsthand   The child has only passively dealt with the stressor through secondhand experience; the secondhand source of information made an impact on his level of emotional or physiological arousal.

EXAMPLE   Jake was Ben's friend in Ben's former neighborhood. Jake's family had never moved, but Jake observed Ben's reactions to having to move to another new school. Jake is somewhat familiar with what happens when somebody moves because his teacher read a story about moving before Ben left. In spite of this, Jake has an incomplete understanding of the process.

Fourth possibility: A child is totally unfamiliar with a stressor   In this case, a child who has never dealt with such an event is now thinking about it for the first time and does not yet have a coping strategy. Her degree of anxiety or confusion depends largely on whether adults help her understand the event and whether they help her cope effectively with the stressor.

You can be most helpful to a child who is dealing with a stressful event for the first time in a couple of ways:

- **Change the situation.** You can eliminate the stressful event altogether, as Diana's mother did by taking the new dog from next door back to his own yard after he ambled into Diana's yard.
- **Clarify what the event means.** When the stressor is inevitable and cannot be eliminated, assist a child in comprehending the meaning of an unfamiliar event. Help a child understand as much as he is capable of understanding. If you use this strategy, you will be acting as a buffer to a stressful event. Think of this as *demystifying* the stressful event for a child.

    EXAMPLE   When Tony's family moved (something they had never done before), they did not know anyone in their new neighborhood. Dad took Tony for a get-acquainted walk to meet the new neighbors.

    EXAMPLE   Alden's (from the chapter-opening vignette) first trip to the emergency room had all the earmarks of a stressful event when his parents ran to the car with him seconds after he fell off the swing and broke his arm. In the car, Mom kept her composure so that she could help Alden because she realized how frightened he was. "We are going to the hospital, to a special room called the emergency room. A doctor is waiting for you and she will take a special picture so she can see your arm bone. Then she'll fix the bone. Mom and Daddy will stay with you. Then we'll all come home."

:: COPING EFFECTIVELY WITH STRESS

Suppose that you are working at your computer and your computer freezes; you cannot move the cursor and you cannot type. This has never happened to you before. You sit back and say, "Okay, I have a couple of options. I can get out the manual and try to find out what has happened. I can just turn off the computer and try to reboot it." What you would have done in the process of thinking through your predicament is to have coped. You looked inside yourself and found the knowledge that you needed to get the computer going again and to keep yourself calm.

What Is Coping?

Coping refers to looking for something inside or outside oneself to come to terms with stressors (Canadian Mental Health Association, 2005). In the computer example, you coped by searching within yourself for the resources (knowledge) that

Coping
Searching for internal or external resources to contend with stressors

enabled you to deal with the crisis. At other times, a person looks for something outside herself to deal with a stressor.

> **EXAMPLE**   Another person has the same problem with her computer but calls an 800 number for help. She has coped by looking outside herself for the resources (the 800 number) that she needed.

Our goal in working with children is to help them cope as effectively as possible with the stressors that they face. Remember that coping does not necessarily mean a child will have a happy or successful outcome. Some situations, such as child abuse, make it very difficult for a person to achieve a successful solution.

Different Ways of Coping with Stress

There are many ways of coping with potentially stressful events. There is no one-size-fits-all coping strategy. You will quickly learn to recognize different patterns in different children and in other adults. No single coping method is best for every person, and it is probably wise not to force any specific method on anyone.

Some people cope by getting information about the stressor   Somebody who copes with stress in this way searches his memory for information about how he has dealt with a similar stressor. A person might also look for information outside himself—from other people, self-help groups, a therapist, formal classes, books, pamphlets, movies, television, magazine articles, videos, or the Internet. Bookstores usually stock self-help books that people read for information on almost any stress-inducing event. Early childhood teachers give information on different stressors when they read well-written books to children about specific stressors such as death or moving.

Others cope by taking direct action   Some people take direct action by leaving the scene. Withdrawal can be a healthy way to take direct action and to cope. The withdrawal can be temporary, as when a parent leaves a room to cool off rather than yell at or hurt a crying baby. Such a person chooses either to return to deal with the stressor or to cope by permanently withdrawing. A person who withdraws as a way to cope might either announce his plan to leave or might just leave without notice.

> **EXAMPLE**   Rachel, 5 years old and in Mr. Sanchez's kindergarten class, was tired of hearing Louie tell her and the other girls that they didn't know how to do certain things because they were girls and that they could not play with certain toys. She dealt with the stress by announcing, "You can just play by yourself, Louie. I'm not going to play with you anymore!" She then left the science table.

Others take direct action by asserting their rights. This implies that the person sees an injustice, which is causing him some stress. For example, asserting one's rights by using words to express the emotion is a good way to deal with the stress of anger.

> **EXAMPLE**   Rachel was clearly upset when Louie sat at her place for lunch. She took direct action this time by asserting her rights and using words, as Mr. Sanchez had suggested: "Hey, Louie. That's my chair! Your chair is over here."

Some people cope by restraining movements or actions   A person might control her actions because she understands that it would be the most sensible way to deal with a stressor. For example, a teacher instructed a child who did not have friends in class on how to make friends and taught her how to join a group. Specifically, the teacher showed the child how to control her movements and control her tendency to push her way into the group. The next day she practiced and controlled her actions by waiting and observing what the other children were doing before joining them.

It is also possible for children to control their actions out of fear or anxiety. Children who are abused often try to be as quiet as possible around the abuser. They hope that the abuser will not notice them.

Still others cope with stress by denying or avoiding the problem   As you remember from your study of psychology, denial is a basic defense mechanism that protects people by allowing them not to face certain situations or to remember unpleasant events.

> **EXAMPLE**   Elena, 8 years old, is the fourth child in a family of seven children, and her parents are seasonal farm workers. Elena's parents love their children; nevertheless, they have to move frequently. All of the school-age children in Elena's family change schools frequently as the family moves from one farm to another. Elena, clearly upset by the turmoil of constant moving, has begun to deny that the family is about to move again as a way of coping with the stress.

Denial is evident in abusive families, with abused children often denying that abuse is even occurring. Denial, in fact, is one of the hallmarks of an abusive family system. Denial does not solve problems, however, and people who are in denial often cope with their problem by engaging in some unhealthy or dangerous activity, such as excessive eating, drinking alcohol, taking illegal drugs, or gambling.

Can Young Children Cope Effectively with Stressors?

Children's cognitive, physical, social, and emotional development affects whether they can cope with stressors on their own or whether they need adult guidance in order to cope. This section of the chapter focuses first on the requirements for coping successfully. Then the focus shifts to explaining why young children cannot cope effectively with stressors on their own.

To cope well you have to be able to think about more than one thing at a time   A person who can sift through several options or solutions has one of the abilities that it takes to cope with stressors. Looking at option A as well as option B requires that the person have the basic cognitive ability to consider at least two things at a time. Essentially, the person must be able to look at a problem from different angles. She might have to take a perspective different from her own.

Can young children think about more than one thing at a time? Usually, they cannot. Young children are not as capable as older people of taking different perspectives (see Chapter 2 for a discussion of perspective taking). They tend to focus on only one thing at a time and cannot seem to pay attention to all helpful and relevant facts. A 4-year-old child who gets upset when he slips away from dad at the grocery store and then cannot find his way back would most likely focus on only one thing—that he was lost.

To cope well you must be able to invent alternative ways of solving a problem   First, a person must believe in the concept that "I can move from this problem to a solution to this problem." Second, he must be able to generate creative solutions for the problem, for example, "I'm locked out of my car. How can I solve this problem?" The person must also be able to look at an array of solutions and categorize or classify groups of options.

Can young children invent different ways to solve problems? Usually, they cannot do this on their own. When children are upset, their emotions often overshadow their ability to solve problems. The preschool child lost in the grocery store would not be likely to think about different ways to handle his problem. He would *not* say, "I can go to the manager and ask her to call my dad on the speaker; I can search each aisle; or I can call out to my dad." He would likely focus primarily on the fact that he was lost.

Young children have difficulty seeing how things can change because they tend to focus on the before and then the after, but not on how they can get from before to after. Consequently, young children have difficulty creating solutions because of their inability to deal with the process of change. Young children also have limited classification skills. They are not able to look at a number of solutions and then to classify them into logical groups. For example, they would not say, "I can wait here," or "I can search for dad," or "I can find somebody to help me" (three different groups of things to do).

To cope well you must be able to manage unpleasant emotions   This implies that a person can pay attention to and that she understands emotions such as anxiety, fear, or anger: emotions often associated with stress. She can evaluate what those emotions mean for her: "I'm anxious about giving this speech because the sale depends on how well I present my ideas today." A person who can manage emotions effectively and appropriately has learned good strategies for managing emotions: "I am well prepared for the speech and I know how to do deep breathing prior to beginning to speak."

Can young children manage unpleasant emotions? Young children, even babies, *have* emotions and they certainly *express* them. However, young children tend not to understand their emotions or be able to deal with them. Children learn to understand or deal with anger when their development allows them to, and then only if they have good models and instruction in managing anger.

To cope well you must understand the effect of your reactions   Again, this implies that an individual can think about at least two things at the same time—his reaction and the stressful event. He could also think about the impact of his actions as well as how another person might feel about them. This requires good perspective taking. It also implies that the person has a broad enough knowledge base and enough experiences from which to draw the understanding.

Can young children understand how their reactions affect situations? A young child usually is not able to understand how his reactions to a stressor will affect the situation. The child lost in the grocery store does not understand, for example, that his frantic crying (his reaction to stress) affects his ability to listen to or answer questions from the manager.

Young children in general have a limited knowledge base, and some of the children that we teach have an even more restricted knowledge base than do others their age. Young children have less knowledge and experience from which to draw when they face a stressor such as getting lost.

To cope well you must be able to think purposefully Such a person would be able to think about the obvious in a stressful event but also be able to acknowledge and think about less obvious or hidden factors. Thinking purposefully brings together a person's conscious and preconscious thoughts. Thinking purposefully demonstrates that you know that you have thoughts. You also show that you can think about those thoughts—you can "think about thinking."

Young children do not understand their feelings and have difficulty regulating how they express emotions.

EXAMPLE   Starting college for the first time is perceived as stressful by many students. The ability to think about this stressor purposefully, however, enables an older person to cope successfully. She would be able to think about the obvious, such as where everything is and how to register for courses. She would also be able to think about what is less obvious, such as her anxiety about meeting new people and making friends, because she understands the concept of anxiety and can think about it.

Can young children think purposefully? Young children are not able to consciously reflect—think about thinking—on matters such as how they feel, why others act as they do, or how others feel. Young children tend to focus on the obvious—their own agitation—and cannot reflect on the less obvious psychological aspects of stressful situations.

:: GENERAL GUIDELINES FOR HELPING CHILDREN COPE WITH STRESS

Children gradually learn how to manage stress, but only if we actively teach and encourage them to practice stress management. Many young children live in families that model, teach, and reward poor coping skills. The parents themselves in these families often do not know how to manage stress, so it is nearly impossible for them to teach helpful strategies to their children. These children will come to your classroom having already learned poor coping skills. Other children, fortunately, learn better coping skills.

What follows are general guidelines for encouraging young children to develop good coping skills. After studying the general guidelines, you will have an opportunity to read about a specific experience that is very likely to cause great stress for young children.

Model Good Stress Management

Modeling is a powerful teaching tool. Children observe many models of stress management—parents; teachers; other adults; and people in videos, movies, videogames, and cartoons. These models influence a child's style of stress management. Children need teachers to model calm, thoughtful approaches to dealing with daily hassles. This is particularly important for children who observe a frenzied, inappropriate approach to stress management in their families or on television.

Manage Your Classroom to Be a Low-Stress Environment

It is impossible to create a classroom or any other environment that is completely free from stress. However, taking the time and effort to create a developmentally appropriate physical environment will result in a low-stress (not stress-free) classroom. Develop suitable activities and make sure all materials are appropriate. Use positive guidance strategies when dealing with discipline encounters. Chapter 5 in this text explains how to develop a developmentally appropriate classroom.

PEARSON
myeducationlab

Go to the Assignments and Activities section of Topic 3: Observation in the MyEducationLab for your course and complete the activity entitled *Teachers Can Use Observation to Reflect on their Practices.* Note that teachers can observe both themselves and children.

Acknowledge and Learn about the Variety of Stressors in Children's Lives

This chapter lists several of these stressors and then describes one of them in detail. You will learn the general principles in dealing with stressors, study one or two specific stressors, and then make a commitment to continuing education in this area.

Act as a Buffer between a Child and a Stressor

You can be helpful to children facing a stressor by acting as a buffer if you stand between them and the stressor as you help them. You will shield them even as you teach them. You cannot always make the stressor disappear, nor would you always want to do so. You can soften (buffer) the effect of the stressor by supporting the child in any of several ways as he deals with the stressor.

> **EXAMPLE** The manager of the grocery store acted as a buffer between the 4-year-old and the stressor of getting lost. She squatted down so that she was at the child's level, used a calm and even tone, and assured him that they would find his dad. She did not order him to stop crying but instead continued her soothing talk. He eventually gulped, stopped crying, and stared at her. "I know you're a little scared," she said. "I'll bet that you can tell me your name. Then I can talk on our microphone and tell your dad where we are."

Teach Children How to Relax and to Calm Themselves

Calming oneself and relaxing are essential skills in managing stress. All children must learn these skills, so it is age appropriate to teach them. Children who live in indifferent, chaotic, abusive, or neglectful families need the lessons even more, making it individually appropriate for an adult to teach them.

Calming down or relaxing helps people get the autonomic nervous system under control. The autonomic nervous system, is that part of the nervous system that operates automatically, without our control. The sympathetic nervous system is a part of the autonomic nervous system and puts us in the high-alert stage of alarm when we face a stressor. Learning how to interrupt the action of the sympathetic nervous system is useful in managing stress. You can learn such techniques and you can teach them to children.

Without understanding the biology of the stress response, older preschool, kindergarten, and primary-grade children can learn to control how their bodies react under stress by learning how to relax. Children who can actively control their bodies by deliberately relaxing one or more body parts or by breathing slowly have strategies that they can use when they are under stress. Adults will undoubtedly have to remind them to use the relaxation strategies because children tend to focus on one thing—their problem—and might well forget about relaxing when they face a stressor. Figure 9.2 gives a few practical suggestions on teaching children how to calm themselves and to relax.

| FIGURE 9.2 | Teach children to stay calm and to relax |

Use these ideas to teach older early childhood children to soothe themselves, to calm down, and to relax. Write lesson plans for teaching these relaxation strategies and teach only one at a time. Consider using one of the calming, relaxing techniques that the whole group can do together at open group times. Encourage children to choose the group-time opening relaxation technique. Make sure that you carefully observe your children and know whether they can perform the physical movements in any of the activities. Plan adaptations for children as necessary.

✓ **Rubber band.** Use a real rubber band to demonstrate stretching it s-l-o-w-l-y. Children then stretch one arm up or to the side just as slowly. Hold the stretch and return slowly to the starting point. Try stretching shoulders down slowly and returning to the starting point.

✓ **Gentle waves.** Create gentle waves in the water table or a sealed jar of water as the children watch. Then listen to the recorded sound of gentle waves. Children move their arms in a slow, wavelike way.

✓ **Swim, fish. Swim!** Children quickly learn that watching the fish swimming in the aquarium is relaxing.

Give them permission to pull up a chair and watch. Older children might even enjoy sketching the fish.

✓ **Melting ice cube.** Prepare for this by placing an ice cube in a dish on the science table. Children observe that it melts. At group time, the children become ice cubes, all hard and cold. Then they begin to melt (relax) slowly.

✓ **Yoga stretches.** Teach three or four simple yoga stretches. Place pictures of the poses in the room so children can do the poses whenever they feel the need to relax.

✓ **Paint, sand, and other sensory items.** Remember the power of finger painting (even for primary children) to calm and soothe. The same thing is true for sensory materials such as clean sand or water in a tub or sensory table.

✓ **Let's read!** Reading is a powerful way to deal with stress. We can give good information to children by choosing books that help them deal with stress. An example is A Boy and a Bear: The Children's Relaxation Book written by Lori Lite and illustrated by M. Hartigan (go to http://www.litebooks.net).

Learn and Teach Good Coping Skills

This often involves direct instruction, and specific strategies depend on the particular stressor that a child faces. For example, if a child does not have friends, you might consider teaching him how to approach other children. If a child were under stress because of a lot of anger, you can teach him how to deal with anger and how to do deep breathing. Use books to teach about specific stressors (Needlman, 2004).

Work with Families

myeducationlab

1. Arrival
2. Opening circle
3. Free choice (a.m.)
4. Snack (a.m.)
5. Playground
6. Story time
7. Lunchtime
8. Nap time
9. Snack (p.m.)
10. Free choice (p.m.)
11. Closing circle
12. Departure

Go to the Assignments and Activities section of Topic 7: Schedules and Routines in the MyEducationLab for your course and complete the activity entitled *Key Elements of a Developmentally Appropriate Schedule*. Note that this strategy is a good way to support families.

We are much more effective helping children deal with stress when we also work with their families. Family systems theory is a helpful reminder of just how important the school–family partnership is for children's healthy development and learning. One of the characteristics of a family system that can help you and a family work together to help children deal with stress is equilibrium. This refers to a family's sense of balance. Stress is much like a strong wind at times and can throw a family's sense of balance into turmoil (Christian, 2006).

Teachers and schools can work with families to understand how important it is for children to have consistency when stressors appear, including any of the stressors listed earlier in this chapter. They need to know about the concept of stress. Then they need to learn about how stress affects children. Most of all, they need to gain the knowledge and skills for dealing with current stressors that they and their children face. They might also need to learn that children find things such as overscheduling of activities and not getting enough exercise or sleep to be extremely stressful.

Here are three excellent suggestions from Linda Christian (2006) for helping families maintain equilibrium—balance—in the face of potential stressors:

- Invite an expert to talk with parents about important issues that they face. For example, if there is a major flu outbreak, then parents will find good, timely, and accurate information very helpful. They will have concerns, in this case, about whether the school should remain open and, if it does, about the precautions that the school will take to protect their child's health.
- Provide as much consistency as possible in school. This is important all the time but especially so when a family faces stressful events and the off-balance feeling that goes along with hassles and even trauma. Make your classroom a haven of consistency, where parents and children will be secure in a reliable schedule and with a teacher who is also dependable and trustworthy. Mr. Bjornrud did this is in the chapter-opening infant–toddler vignette.
- Help families figure out how to maintain stability and security. For example, help families deal with military deployment of a parent through each of the phases of deployment, as shown in Figure 9.3.

:: SUGGESTIONS FOR HELPING CHILDREN WHO FACE THE STRESS OF MOVING

Approximately 1 in 5 children in elementary school change schools every year. Some groups, such as the homeless or migrant, urban, low-income, or abused children move even more frequently than others (Branz-Spall, Rosenthal, & Wright, 2003;

FIGURE 9.3	Schools can help military families during deployment

Phase of Deployment	Teacher's Role	Why This Is Appropriate
Predeployment	Communicate: ■ Let parents know that they are welcome to share information about deployment with the school ■ Figure out good ways for deployed parents to communicate with teachers, such as email, text messages, or Twitter	■ Conveys your willingness to listen ■ Creates a partnership with parents ■ Fosters continuity in their child's education
Deployment	■ Observe the child, noting any changes in behavior ■ Create a section on the school web site for military parents who are deployed	■ Teachers are with children many hours; can support parents by noticing changes and discussing them with the parent ■ Deployed parent would have access to information about school
Reunion	■ Be aware of the date of the reunion ■ Listen actively to children's questions and concerns ■ Help children make a welcome-home card or banner ■ Consult the school psychologist or guidance counselor if a child seems quite anxious; the psychologist can plan special session dealing with reunions	■ Listening without judgment encourages children to express feelings without fear ■ A concrete and gentle thing to do ■ Gives information to children and helps them to deal with the stress

Source: Based on Military Child Education Coalition (2003). *How to prepare our children and stay involved in their education during deployment.* Harker Heights, Texas: Author.

Xu, Hannaway, & D'Souza, 2009). In Chicago, in a 3-year period, only about 50% of the children remained in the same school (Kerbow, Azcoitia, & Buell, 2003). The problem of frequent moving also exists in rural areas and contributes to academic achievement gaps (Paik & Phillips, 2002). Recently, the downturn in the economy seems to be making the problem of moving frequently even more of an issue (Allen, 2009).

Teachers today experience frequently and firsthand the effects of a mobile society, just as they have for the last several decades. Teachers start the school year knowing that some of the children will move to a new school and that they are likely to get new students anytime during a year. Teachers witness the stress that moving often produces in children, families, and schools.

Why Moving Is Stressful for Many Young Children

Moving to a new area is among the most stress-inducing experiences a family faces. Moves are especially difficult for preschool and primary-grade children (American Academy of Child & Adolescent Psychiatry, 2002a). For children, moving is a type of loss just as is death or a parent's divorce. A child loses friends, a home, and a school; the losses often result in feelings of sadness and anxiety or even anger. Moving is stressful for many young children for the following reasons (American Academy of Child & Adolescent Psychiatry, 2002a; Steele & Sheppard, 2003).

Moving interrupts friendships and children lose social support   Children who move to a new area or a new school often think that everybody at school or in the new neighborhood is in a group or has a best friend. Children who lose friendships are likely to go through a mourning process for those friendships. Having somebody dismiss or laugh at the loss intensifies the sadness over the loss. If a child is shy or aggressive or has poor social skills, the move and the need to make friends will be even more difficult and stressful. Many children lose the support of older people, too. Moving away from trusted teachers, a Scout leader, religion teacher, relatives, and neighbors means that a child will not have these adults to turn to for support (Pettit, 2000).

Moving elicits unpleasant emotions   Children tend to feel anxious and sad when they move. Young children, however, do not understand their emotions and do not know how to manage them on their own. So added to the already stressful situation of moving is the stress that goes along with emotions that the child cannot manage (American Academy of Child & Adolescent Psychiatry, 2002).

Moving interrupts the separation process   Moving is especially troublesome for children during early childhood because they are in the process of separating from parents and adjusting to adults other than their parents in centers and schools, as well as adjusting to peers. Relocating often pushes young children to return to a more dependent relationship with parents than they might want, thereby interrupting the normal separation process (American Academy of Child & Adolescent Psychiatry, 2002a).

Moving requires children to adjust to a new curriculum in school and different teacher expectations   Children often find that they are behind in some curriculum areas or ahead in others, resulting in boredom or anxiety. Children can withstand the stress if their parents and teachers give them the support that they need (Silver, 2005). However, the children who move most frequently are the least likely to get the help that they need for managing the stress of curriculum changes. Their families and schools are often not prepared to give them the support they require.

Moving interrupts school and social services   Kerbow (1996) reported that some public school systems, such as those in Chicago, went through reforms centering on promoting greater local school autonomy. Greater local autonomy is based on the assumption that children will attend one specific school consistently enough so that the school can make a difference in the child's achievement. Urban low-income children who frequently change schools lose the benefit of any school or social services that go along with such school reform.

Silver (2005) described one district's effort to relieve some of children's stress from moving. The Learning Center for Children in Minneapolis, Minnesota, is a source of stability in the lives of the school district's children who move frequently. Children from anywhere in the district can enroll and they stay put even when they move, which occurs with great frequency. This is a very small school and enrolls only 75 children. It provides a traditional school curriculum. The purpose of this school is to relieve stress from frequent moves by keeping children enrolled despite multiple moves. Executive Director Barbara Novy said that the school's practices were based on the knowledge that three moves before eighth grade can damage a child's scores on standardized tests.

Act as a Buffer between a Child and the Stress of Moving

Schools, teachers, and policy makers can buffer the stress of moving and changing schools for children. Moving and changing schools does not necessarily have to affect children adversely. With proper support, moving can be a positive experience for children (American Academy of Child & Adolescent Psychiatry, 1999a). Teachers, directors, principals, schools, and policy makers must take the first step and make a conscious effort to help children who are about to move away from or who have just transferred to their center or school.

When a child moves *away from* your school or classroom   Consider doing some of the following to help a child deal with the stress of moving *away from* your classroom. Our goal is to acknowledge our regret at his leaving but also to help this child find the strength from within to enable him to deal with his feelings and uncertainties about the move. Another goal is to work with parents so that they can also help their child cope with a move.

- Talk with the child about moving away and help him understand something about his new school. It would help greatly if you took the effort to find out where he is going, the name of his school, and his new teacher. Present this information in a positive way.
- Listen carefully and encourage the child to talk about his feelings about moving away. Avoid being intrusive, however, and do not force a child to talk about feelings.
- Help him say good-bye to his school in a low-key and positive way.
- Give the child a picture of the entire class with him included.
- Make sure that his records are current and accurate and that the records are transferred quickly to the new school.
- Follow your center or school's policy about contacting the new school so that you can give positive information to the new teacher about the child. The goal here is to help the new teacher make the child's transition as smooth as possible.
- Work with the child's parents. Answer their questions and give them information that will enable them to help their child make the move with as little stress as possible (see the Working with Parents feature).

When a child moves *to* your school or classroom   Consider the following suggestions as you welcome a child who is moving *to* your classroom. Your goal is to draw your classroom circle to include this new child. Adding a new member to a family or a classroom involves adjusting the boundaries to include that person.

myeducationlab

Go to the Building
Teaching Skills and
Dispositions section of
Topic 4: Guidance
Techniques/Strategies in
the MyEducationLab for
your course and complete
the activity entitled *Teach
Conflict Resolution*. Note
how this strategy helps
children who are
aggressive.

- Obtain the child's file and read it carefully. Follow your school's policy if you need to contact the previous teacher for clarification on any issues.
- Make a home visit if your school encourages teachers to do so. Home visits are a good way to get to know the child.
- Familiarize the child and family with the new school. Invite them to come to school for a tour so that the new school is not so new on the child's first day.
- Make sure that the child and her family know the schedule in your room. Give them a handout of your schedule and encourage parents to talk about their child's new schedule.
- Create a space for a new child by preparing a locker or cubby, cot for napping, and any other individualized areas or materials. Create her space before she arrives.
- Take a new group picture with the new child included. Do this on the first day that the new child enters your room.
- Walk through the routines in your classroom and your center or school (e.g., bathroom, snack, or lunch; getting on the bus; waiting for parents). Take your class through the fire safety drill so that everyone, including the new child, knows the procedure. Get the child to tell you about how the new routines are different from or similar to those in her old school.
- Talk with the child and find out what she likes to do in school.
- Include the child in the activities of her new room at her pace.
- Request that other children in the class act as guides for the new class member. Be specific in your requests: "Joe, please walk with Robert to the lunchroom. He will be sitting next to you and I thought that you could show him how lunch is served in our school," or "It's time to put the carpet squares down for group time, Cindy. Please help Jean choose her carpet square and then sit next to her during her first group time with us."
- Be sure that every child wears a name-tag so that a new class member can get to know names.
- Read a book about moving with the child or with the class.
- Listen carefully for the feelings that the new class member has about moving. Acknowledge them and avoid commanding her to feel differently.
- Work with parents. See the Working with Parents feature for information that will help parents buffer the effect of moving on their children. Your school might have a formal policy or program in place through which you can help children who are moving. Even if there is no formal program, you can do some things to help parents decrease the stress of moving on their children.

myeducationlab

To check your
comprehension on the
content covered in
Chapter 9, go to the Book
Specific Resources in the
MyEducationLab for your
course, select your text,
and complete the Study
Plan. Here you will be able
to take a chapter quiz,
receive feedback on your
answers, and then access
review, practice, and
enrichment activities to
enhance your
understanding of chapter
content.

IS YOUR FAMILY MOVING? TIPS FOR HELPING YOUR CHILD COPE WITH THE MOVE

- **Explain and listen.** Explain clearly to your child why the move is necessary. Are you being transferred? Are you starting school in another section of the state? Is the home you've been building finally finished? Is your child's school closing? Your child will understand the reason for the move if you state it simply and clearly. Get comments from your child about what you've explained. Listen closely, clarify anything that your child did not seem to understand, and listen for feelings such as fear or anxiety.
- **Read.** Read a book about moving with your child. This will help children understand the process of moving and deal with some of their feelings.
- **Familiarize and describe.** Acquaint your child with the new area as much as possible. Visit the new area and take your child on a tour of the new house and neighborhood. Consider visiting the public library or parks. Familiarize children with their new home by using maps (for older children) of the area or photos of a new house or apartment building. Consider obtaining a copy of the local newspaper early to acquaint your child with the comic section if he has a favorite cartoon. Describe something about the new area that your child might like, such as a pool, a pond with ducks, or an amusement park. Give the information in a positive way but do not force your child to be enthusiastic.
- **Get involved.** After the move, get involved with your children in activities in the new community such as synagogue or church, parent's group at school, YMCA, a family education and support program, and volunteer groups such as the humane society.

Sources: Based on the American Academy of Child and Adolescent Psychiatry (updated 2002). Children and family moves, *AACAP facts for families*, No. 14. Retrieved on May 30, 2009, from http://www.aacap.org.

ANALYZE VIGNETTES: HELPING CHILDREN DEAL WITH STRESS

Refer to the chapter-opening vignettes and information from the chapter. Then answer the following questions.

1. Infant–toddler: Lela is 15 months old. Explain why her teacher's actions are appropriate for a child this age. How do you think that the teacher's actions will help Lela deal with the stress at home? How will the teacher's style help Lela's family maintain equilibrium?

2. Preschool: Explain how Mrs. Woodward has softened the effect of the fire alarm, the stressor, for the children.

3. Primary: Identify the appropriate strategies that Mr. Sanchez has used to help Alden in moving to a new school. Use information from the chapter as your guide.

SUMMARY

A resilient child fares well in spite of stressful events. Protective factors such as caring relationships, high expectations, and chances to participate help children become resilient.

Some stressors are physical and damage a child's body. Other stressors are psychological and harm a child's sense of security. Still other stressors combine a physical and a psychological threat. Some stress is acute, which is an intense but brief stressor, while other stress is chronic or persistent and ongoing.

Children can experience stress from internal sources, such as hunger pains or emotions. Another source of stress is external to the child, such as joint custody. Children experience physical effects from some stress, and stress even has the potential to damage a child's brain.

Children go through three stages in responding to stress:

- Alarm
- Appraisal
- Searching for a coping strategy

Coping involves finding some way, with either outside or internal resources, to come to grips with the stress. There are different ways to cope, and young children need adult help in learning how to cope with stress.

QUESTIONS FOR REFLECTION

1. Describe a *resilient* child. Describe the circumstances under which a child is most likely to experience stress from any life event.
2. "Stress?" asks a friend of yours unfamiliar with early childhood. "What do children have to be stressed about?" Consider this a teachable moment. What would you say to this person?
3. Alarm, appraisal, searching for a coping strategy—all of these are stages of responding to stress. What sorts of behaviors would you look for in a child at each of the stages?
4. What does it mean when we say that a person has *coped* with a stressful event? In addition, why does coping not necessarily mean that a person has come to a happy or successful conclusion?

APPLY YOUR KNOWLEDGE

Get a start on developing expertise in one area that can cause stress for children. Do you want to know more about how death, divorce, hospitalization, child abuse, or neglect results in stress? Do you need to know more about how harsh parenting, not having friends, or loneliness causes stress for some children? Choose a specific stressor and then prepare yourself to help children deal effectively with it by completing the following application activities.

1. **Internet and other resources.** Use a search engine to find information on your chosen stressor. Visit or call the extension office in your county and ask the family or child life specialist for written information on your topic. Collect magazine articles about your stressor. Make copies of the information and organize it in a file for later use.
2. **Children's books.** Develop an annotated bibliography of children's books about the stressor you have chosen. Find and read at least four children's books. Give a brief synopsis of each and then explain how you would use it to help children deal with that specific stressor.
3. **Your portfolio and interview.** Let others know that you have knowledge, skills, and materials for teaching children how to begin to cope with this specific stressor. Decide how to place information in your professional portfolio.
4. **Role-play.** Role-play being interviewed for a teaching position. The director or principal looks over your portfolio, pauses, and says, "I see that you've studied about how children deal with _____ (moving, death, divorce, etc.). How would you see yourself using this information if you're hired to teach in this school?" Be prepared to explain how you would use the material about a specific stress factor to help children and parents.

KEY TERMS

Acute stress (222)
Alarm (227)
Appraisal (227)
Chronic stress (222)
Coping (229)

External sources of stress (223)
Internal sources of stress (223)
Physical stressor (220)
Protective factors (219)
Psychological stressor (221)

Resilience (218)
Searching for a coping strategy (228)
Stress (218)

WEB SITES

Center for Effective Parenting
http://www.parenting-ed.org

This is a collaborative project of the University of Arkansas for Medical Science, the Arkansas Children's Hospital, and the Jones Family Center. This site has numerous links for parent education information. For information on stress, go to the "search site" box and type in *stress*.

National Center for Homeless Education
http://www.serve.org/NCHE/index.php

Find information and resources on working with children who are experiencing homelessness.

National Military Family Association
http://www.nmfa.org

An organization "dedicated to serving the families and survivors of the seven uniformed services through education, information, and advocacy." Provides a wealth of information, fact sheets, and other materials about military families. Refer again to Figure 9.3 for information on helping children whose parent is deployed for military service. (Figure 9.3 is based on information from the National Military Family Association.)

Aggression and Bullying in Young Children

"Bullying is an aggressive behavior intended to cause harm or distress, occurs repeatedly over time, and occurs in a relationship in which there is an imbalance of power or strength."

—(AMERICAN PSYCHOLOGICAL ASSOCIATION, 2005a)

Chapter Contents

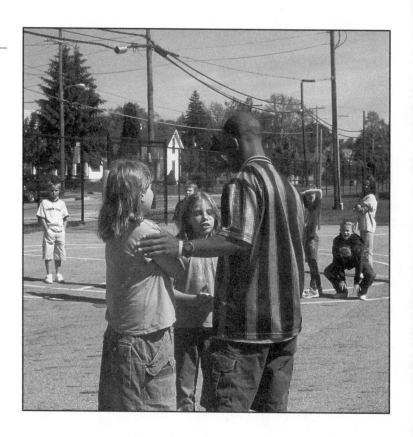

Guiding Questions

- How can I explain the nature, the different forms, and purposes of aggression, including bullying?
- How do children acquire the scripts that tell them how to be aggressive, including how to bully others?
- What can I, as a teacher, do that will prevent or minimize aggression, including bullying?

VIGNETTES

PRESCHOOL: MAYA MOVES IN

Four-year-old Maya wanted to sit on the yellow carpet square at circle time. When she saw that Nadifa was already sitting on the yellow square, Maya sat down right next to Nadifa and started to nudge her. Nadifa shot a look of annoyance at Maya, who kept prodding Nadifa, finally pushing her off the yellow square.

KINDERGARTEN: JESS ATTACKS WITH WORDS

Jess joined his friend Serena in the dress-up center, but she was finished playing and moved on, leaving Jess by himself. When they went out to the playground, Jess kept an eye out for Serena. When she approached the sandbox, Jess did a little singsong chant, "Serena wears glasses, stupid, stupid glasses! Serena wears glasses . . . ," over and over.

PRIMARY: BYSTANDERS CONFRONT THE BULLY

Third-grader Patrick is a bully who calls himself "Number One," and terrorizes other children. Thomas, in the same grade, is his latest target. As usual, Patrick started with name calling but quickly escalated to physical attacks—tripping, shoving, and punching. At first, the other children, afraid of Patrick, stood by and watched, but today they did something very different. At recess, Thomas ran to retrieve the basketball as it rolled into a remote part of the yard. Patrick ran after Thomas calling out, "I'm coming for you, Science Nerd." Thomas was trapped but then saw the other basketball players coming toward him and heard one of the other boys yell at Patrick, "Leave him alone, Patrick!" Another boy chimed in, "Yeah, leave him alone."

:: INTRODUCTION

The chapter-opening vignettes all show some form of aggression. Maya's and Jess's are typical for early childhood, and Patrick's is an example of bullying. Why is it important to understand aggression and bullying? Children often do not feel safe either going to school or while they are at school. This unease or anxiety is often caused by peer abuse, with bullying the most common form (Centers for Disease Control and Prevention, 1995). Deadly violence, a complex issue, grows in part out of a progression of traumatizing events such as bullying, constant teasing, isolation, and rejection. Deadly school violence does have warning signs (Carney, 2000; Hazler, 2000). It is important to understand aggression and bullying because one of the pathways to violence starts in early childhood.

This chapter focuses on the twin topics of aggression and bullying. We will describe and explain different forms and purposes, or goals, of aggression. Then we will focus on bullying *as a type of aggression*. Third, you will study about the ways in which children gather information on how to be aggressive from different systems. Then you will learn several practical strategies for dealing effectively with bullying and other forms of aggression.

:: AGGRESSION

Aggression
Any behavior that a person uses when he or she intends to hurt someone or to destroy or damage property

Aggression is a problem-solving behavior that is learned early in life, is learned well, and is resistant to change. Aggression is any intentional behavior that injures or diminishes a person or animal in some way or damages or destroys property (Gerrig & Zimbardo, 2002).

Forms of Aggression

Aggression takes several forms, causing damage in many ways. It can cause physical, verbal, psychological, or emotional damage. The attack can be direct or indirect, impulsive or well planned (Strauss & Field, 2003; Tremblay et al., 2004).

> **EXAMPLE**   Two adolescents shot and killed 14 classmates and 1 teacher in Columbine High School in Colorado in April 1999 (premeditated, direct, physical aggression).

> **EXAMPLE**   Patrick, from the chapter-opening vignette for the primary grades, squeezes another boy's arm as he takes the child's lunch money (intentional and both psychologically and physically harmful aggression).

> **EXAMPLE**   Sean called his younger brother a "dummy" (verbal, psychologically harmful aggression). He ripped his brother's list of spelling words to shreds (physical, direct aggression that damages property).

Teachers need a common definition of aggression so that they can recognize and then deal with the different forms of aggressive behavior consistently and effectively. The common thread that ties together all acts of aggression is that the behavior, whatever it looks like, *intentionally* injures a person or animal or damages or destroys property.

Aggression is not the same thing as anger. Anger is an emotion, a feeling. Aggression is a behavior. Angry children might behave aggressively, but not always, and children can be aggressive without being angry. John, for example, was very upset about not getting any chocolate milk but was not aggressive. Mary, on the other hand, pinched another kindergarten child, but was not angry with her. Mary was merely showing her power.

Gender Differences in Aggression

There are clear differences in aggression between boys and girls, and these differences are evident during early childhood (Baillargeon, et al., 2007; Cummings, Iannotti, & Zahn-Waxler, 1989). The findings tell us that:

- boys display more aggression than girls do, both physically and verbally.
- boys display more aggression after watching media violence.
- older boys are more likely than older girls to counterattack when physically attacked.
- pairs of boys have more aggressive interactions than a boy/girl or girl/girl dyad (pair).

Researchers document gender differences, but explaining the differences is another thing. One view is that gender differences might result from how we socialize boys and girls (Blakemore, Berenbaum, & Liben, 2009). Our culture has clearly defined attitudes about girls, boys, and aggression, and we can easily observe these attitudes by looking at differing child-rearing tactics used with boys and girls.

Aggression is related to many factors, such as a parent's style of child rearing (Yu, Shi, Huang, & Wang, 2006). Parents' belief systems also affect children's development (Francis & Chorpita, 2009). Some parents expect, permit, and then encourage aggression in boys. Parents tend to use more physical punishment with boys than with girls, and boys might adopt these aggressive methods in interaction with others (Block, 1978). Many parents also manage the environments of boys and girls differently. For example, they choose different toys for girls and boys, and toys often chosen for boys, such as guns or action figures, are aggressive cues, items that seem to elicit aggressive play.

:: PURPOSES OF AGGRESSION

Aggression, as you see from the definition, is the method that some people use to solve problems. They use aggression for different purposes and it helps them meet different goals. Some people have the goal of hurting a person or animal with violent behavior, but others use aggression only as a means of getting something that they want.

Instrumental Aggression

Instrumental aggression
Goal-directed aggression;
meant to get or retrieve an
object or territory; not
anger-based

A child uses **instrumental aggression** when her goal is to obtain or get back some object, territory, or privilege (Hartup, 1974; Rascle, Coulomb-Cabagno, & Delsarte, 2005). This type of aggression usually springs from simple goal blocking; a child who uses instrumental aggression is usually not even angry with the person blocking his goal. He simply wants to remove whatever is blocking his goal and tends to do something offensive to achieve his end. He uses aggression as an instrument, a tool. In the next example, Maya is not angry with the other child. She merely wants something that the other child is using.

> **EXAMPLE**   Four-year-old Maya whined as she watched Nadifa stirring the cake batter, "It's *my* turn." Then she seized the stirring spoon, setting off a wail of protest from Nadifa.

As we know from many decades of research, instrumental aggression is the most common form of aggression during early childhood. Research from the 1930s (Dawe, 1934), the 1970s (Hartup, 1974), and the 1990s (Fabes & Eisenberg, 1992) demonstrated that young children have most of their conflicts over space and resources, such as toys, other equipment, and space, because they are much more egocentric than older children. There tends to be little hostility involved. They push their way into line, grab things from others, yell, "It's my turn!" and even bite. You will read about biting, quite common in very young children, in Chapter 11. Children use instrumental aggression because they want something. At the same time, children cannot take another's perspective because of their egocentricity. Frustrated about not getting the desired object, a very young child uses aggression as a tool, a means to get what he wants.

How to deal with instrumental aggression   Two of the best things that you can do to help young children who use instrumental aggression include the following, both of which focus on the teaching aspect of guidance:

- Do *not* ignore instrumental aggression. Ignoring it rewards a child for being aggressive. Make sure that a child does *not* get what she wants with aggression. Had the teacher allowed Maya to get her turn by swiping the spoon, she would have actually rewarded Maya's aggression.
- Help the child think of a better solution. Acknowledge her frustration and help her think about the situation. This is what she needs from the teacher now, not punishment. Our long-term goal in guidance is to help children build positive ideas about getting what they want.

> **EXAMPLE**   The teacher took the spoon from Maya, saying, "Maya, Nadifa was stirring. You can stir after she finishes. She has to stir 7 more times, so let's count while you wait."

Notice that the teacher did *not* allow Maya to get her way. Maya handed back the spoon. The teacher also focused on the central issue of fairness to others. "Nadifa was stirring," and suggested a solution that helped Maya deal with waiting: "Let's count as Nadifa stirs." This will teach Maya that she can do something at times like this to help herself wait.

Hostile Aggression

Hostile aggression often strikes an observer as nasty, distasteful, vengeful behavior; some forms of hostile aggression are tinged with evil. It is quite different from instrumental aggression.

Hostile aggression
Anger and revenge-based aggression; it is directed at a specific target

Hostile aggression is anger-based   Hostile aggression is bound up with anger aimed directly at a person, animal, or even a country; it is anger-based aggression. The destruction of the World Trade Center in New York City on September 11, 2001; the bombing of the Federal Building in Oklahoma City in 1994; and the Columbine High School tragedy in 1999 are three of our nation's most glaring examples. Hostile aggression is violence clearly intended to hurt someone, a person, or animal, or to destroy something.

> **EXAMPLE**   Keith reached into the gerbil house and grabbed one of the gerbils, picking her up by the tail. He dangled her in midair until Mr. Sanchez intervened. At home, this child intimidates and bullies his dog, laughing as she cowers in fear.

Cruelty toward animals is not a joke; it is outrageous behavior and a warning sign of potential deadly violence. Adults must take it seriously because a young child will not outgrow such cruelty. It is not just a phase (American Academy of Child & Adolescent Psychiatry, 2001). Ignoring such behavior is akin to participating in the cruel behavior. Ignoring a child's cruelty toward an animal is like giving permission for the behavior. Children who are cruel to animals need help, and teachers must have the courage to observe, document, and then report such behavior to protect the animal and to help the child.

Perceived threats to one's ego elicit hostile aggression   A person who is angrily aggressive usually is on guard, has his "antennae up," for any behavior that he perceives as a threat to his ego or any sign that someone is showing him disrespect. He either disregards or is incapable of paying attention to relevant social cues, resulting in his belief that the other person has done something mean-spirited when the other person might well have had no such intention. Mistaken beliefs such as this are starting points for physically or psychologically hostile aggression.

> **EXAMPLE**   Patrick and Theng (pronounced "teng") worked on a science project together. Patrick's brothers have been calling him a "dummy" and so now, Patrick is on guard at school. When Theng offered to help Patrick solve a problem with Patrick's part of the project, Patrick perceived the offer as a sign that Theng thought him incompetent (perceived threat to self-esteem). Patrick's face got red with embarrassment and anger, and he shouted at Theng, "I can do this, Theng! You think you're so smart," as he slammed his fist into Theng's work (hostile aggression).

Hostile aggression shows up in older children   Piaget's theory sheds light on why hostile aggression tends to show up most often in older children, but not young children. A person has to be able to think about what somebody *intended* to do. She must be able to think, for example, that the other person meant to show disrespect. In the previous example, Patrick seemed to think that Theng intended to insult him Children must be able to take the other person's perspective.

Preschool children, usually in the preoperational or second of Piaget's stages of cognitive development, are somewhat egocentric. They are not yet able to understand or take another person's perspective; this explains why their aggression is most often instrumental.

A very young child who cannot take another person's perspective will also not be able to understand what that other person intended to do. An older child, in a different Piagetian stage, becomes less egocentric and is better able to take another child's perspective. Understanding that other perspective also means that older children, such as Patrick, can begin to guess at another person's intentions.

Some older children make mistakes when interpreting social situations   In Chapter 2, we saw that Adlerian theory explains the mistakes that people make in evaluating social interactions. Some older children have deficits in several aspects of social problem solving. For example, in spite of their greater cognitive ability to detect others' intentions, some older, aggressive children are inattentive to relevant social cues or signals. As a result, they frequently presume that another person had some sort of unfriendly plan in mind, even where no bad feeling was intended (Dodge & Frame, 1982). They repeatedly make mistakes about the intentions of other people, as did Patrick with Theng's friendly offer of help in collaborative learning, but it is a person's perception of reality that matters, even if the perception is a faulty one. Patrick acted on his opinion, faulty as it was, and he reacted with hostile aggression.

What About Accidental Aggression?

Accidental aggression is *unintentional injury* (Feshbach, 1970). All teachers observe a certain amount of this sort of unintended injury or damage. Whether unintentionally hurting others is really aggression is a good question. What does happen, though, is that someone accidentally hurts another person or animal or accidentally damages something.

The real problem with accidental aggression   The child who is accidentally hurt or whose work or possession is damaged often responds aggressively in turn. Recall that young children's development influences their behavior.

> **EXAMPLE**   It was crowded in the coatroom of Mr. Sanchez's classroom because he used it as a storage area. When Mitchell stowed his backpack and turned to leave, he crashed into Louie (accidental aggression). Louie reacted by pushing back at Mitchell (aggressive reaction to the *unintentional* injury).

Louie retaliated in a hurtful way. Like most young children, who are not able to see things from Mitchell's perspective, he is also not very good at dealing with more than one idea at a time. For example, Louie would likely *not* be able to think on his own about these three things: "It's crowded here; Mitchell is rushing around; he bumped into me by accident." He does not understand yet the difference between an accidental and an intentional act.

Mitchell also had a part in this interaction. He does not pay attention to what he is doing at times. He is somewhat impulsive. The crowded coatroom was perhaps just too much for him to handle.

How to respond to accidental aggression

- **Teacher's part.** We make guidance mistakes if we always zero in on the behavior first. Practice examining your role and the effect of the environment on behavior. Clearing up issues with how our classroom is set up often clears up accidental aggression.

    EXAMPLE   Mr. Sanchez realized that the cramped coatroom was part of the problem. After removing a table and several boxes, he noticed an immediate change in the children's behavior in this still small but now clutter-free space.

    He worked on one other thing with the children. The teacher and children discussed the issue of crowding, which Mr. Sanchez made into a new vocabulary word. He could simply have limited the number of children who went to the coatroom at any one time, but he decided that the children needed to learn to recognize crowding and to decide whether it was a good idea to enter the coatroom when it was crowded.

- **Children's part.** Avoid problems by teaching skills to children. Mr. Sanchez realized that the boys lacked some skills that he could easily teach. See Figure 10.1 for examples of the things that he did. These lessons are appropriate for older preschool, kindergarten, and first-grade children.

FIGURE 10.1   **Skill development decreases accidental aggression**

Reduce episodes of accidental aggression by teaching specific skills such as paying attention to cues and events, or thinking before acting. Encourage children to practice skills and to take responsibility for lapses in attention.

- **Pay attention.** Demonstration and discussion: use a video, a real-life demonstration, or puppets. One person, in a hurry and not paying attention, does not see the other person and slams into him. Focus the discussion on what it means to pay attention, what happens when you do not, and the idea that you can still hurt somebody in an accident.
- **Self-talk.** Emphasize and encourage this process. Demonstrate the use of self-talk to individuals, small groups, or the whole group. Example: Show how you move from one center to another, deliberately and carefully. The children should see you use self-talk to remind yourself to pay attention: "Okay, I'm done at the easel. I'll go now to the book corner. Whoa! Somebody is in my way. I'd better walk around her."
- **Practice.** Children need to practice new skills, and they benefit from teacher coaching and discussion as they practice. Vygotsky highlighted the need for teacher–child dialogue. "Okay, you want to go to a new center. Go slowly. Let's walk over to the dress-up corner. Watch out for other children." (They arrive at the dress-up corner.) "You were careful. Now, look to see who is playing here before we go in. Tell yourself to stop and look carefully." The child says, "Okay, I have to stop and look. Now I count—one, two, three. Three other kids." Teacher comments, "You paid attention."
- **Acknowledge an accident.** In spite of our best efforts, accidents do happen. Teach children to acknowledge that they might not have paid attention or were rushing around. Use puppets or role-play. Puppet 1 says, after bumping into the other puppet, "Oh, no! I bumped you." Puppet 2 replies, "It looked like an accident. It's Okay." Then demonstrate a straightforward apology, "I'm sorry that I bumped you. I'll be more careful.'"

Source: Based on *Scaffolding children's learning: Vygotsky and early childhood education*, by L. E. Berk and A. Winsler, 1995, Washington, DC: NAEYC; and *second Step: Preventing aggression by promoting social competence*, by K. S. Frey, M. K. Hirschstein, and B. Guzzo, 2000, *Journal of Educational and Behavioral Disorders*, 8(2), 102–112.

▪▪ BULLYING IS AGGRESSION IN ACTION

Bullying
A form of aggression; occurs in a relationship where the power or strength in one party is greater than the other; intention is to cause harm

"**Bullying** is an aggressive behavior intended to cause harm or distress, occurs repeatedly over time, and occurs in a relationship in which there is an imbalance of power or strength" (American Psychological Association, 2005). Bullying is *not* trivial. It is *not* standard or normative behavior. Parents, teachers, administrators, and children are concerned about the intimidation, terrorizing, and harassment in bullying. Pediatricians are also alarmed about bullying because of all of the physical injuries they are treating that are directly related to bullying. Children's physicians also see the connection of bullying in childhood to violence in adolescence (Sege, Wright, & The Committee on Injury, Violence, and Poison Prevention, 2009).

Forms of Bullying

Physical bullying
Bodily contact intended to cause harm

Bullying is aggression and takes many forms. **Physical bullying** refers to any bodily contact intended to hurt another. Examples are pushing, hitting, pinching, and punching. **Emotional or psychological bullying** refers to some nonphysical aggressive behavior. Examples are refusing to let someone play, excluding a child from a work group, spreading rumors, telling other children not to play with them, telling secrets that hurt the person, and withholding information. **Verbal bullying** refers to name calling, making threats, taunting, and mocking (teasing).

Emotional or psychological bullying
Aggressive behaviors that are not physical and are intended to cause distress

Bullying takes place in homes, parks, schools, camps—anywhere we find groups of children. Bullyng also takes place in cyberspace, the place where electronic information exists. **Cyberbullying** refers to bullying with text messaging, tweeting, email messaging, blogs, and any other electronic venue. Adolescents seem to engage in this type of bullying and aggression because of their knowledge and skills with electronic media (Lenhart, 2009).

Verbal bullying
Using words to cause distress

Participants in Bullying

Cyberbullying
Aggression via electronic media

The participants in bullying episodes include the bully, the victim, and bystanders (Olweus, Limber, & Milhalic, 2002). The definitions and explanations in this section are based on the work of Scaglione and Scaglione (2006).

Bully
The person bent on causing harm or distress

Bully   The **bully** is the perpetrator, the person who intends to cause harm or distress and uses aggression to achieve this goal. It is possible for more than one bully to be directly involved in the aggression. Often, there is a main bully and one or more assistants, such as when a group surrounds a child and the bully beats up the child or when a group of girls excludes one girl from the group. One girl in the group leads the bullying.

Pure bully
Someone who bullies; has not been the victim of similar aggression

There are two types of bullies: the pure bully and the bully/victim. They seem to bully for different reasons. The **pure bully** bullies but has never been the victim of bullying. She bullies to establish dominance and power, often has a high view of herself (good self-esteem), and might even be popular. The pure bully likes the power associated with making somebody feel bad. She often is not even angry with the victim; she merely enjoys the power linked to the effect of the intimidation. She chooses victims mainly on how easy it will be to intimidate or harass them.

A **bully/victim** has bullied others but has also suffered bullying. This type of bully tends to feel like a victim but then to behave like a bully. Unlike the pure bully, the bully/victim tends to have a less positive view of himself; he is often very angry about having been bullied. His bullying is seen as more dangerous because of the revenge he needs. This is hostile aggression in action, a child angry about having been intimidated or hurt and turning to bullying others.

Bully/victim
Someone who has been both a bully and a victim

Victim   The **victim** is the person bullied. There are different types of victims: the pure victim and the provoking victim. The bully seeks out the **pure victim** with the simple goal of tormenting her or showing off her bully power. The pure victim does nothing to provoke the bully; however, the pure victim is simply weaker, smaller, and less powerful—an easy target.

Victim
The person who is bullied

The **provoking victim** does something to exasperate others. This type becomes a victim when others strike back. This seemingly strange way of acting is sometimes a child's mistaken idea of how to be a member of a group, an Adlerian concept discussed in Chapter 2. This child might well assume the victim role, the provoking victim, after he makes his bid for attention and membership in the group.

Pure victim
Often smaller and weaker or less powerful; does not provoke bullying

Children with disabilities and special needs might be especially in danger of being victims of a bully, possibly because they are perceived as different. A bully might misinterpret the disability as a weakness. Examples of disabilities and special needs that are sometimes the target of bullying include the following (HRSA [Health Resources and Services Administration], 2009):

Provoking victim
Elicits bullying with own behavior

- **Overweight and obesity.** This is a risk factor for bullying. Girls with this problem are very likely to be teased and physically bullied. When the overweight girl *or* boy is in middle school, she or he is very likely to be excluded from activities, a form of relational bullying.
- **Medical conditions affecting appearance.** Conditions such as spina bifida or muscular dystrophy place children at risk for teasing and name calling. Specific names used most often refer to their medical condition.
- **Attention deficit hyperactivity disorder (ADHD).** A child with ADHD is likely to be a victim of bullying and is more likely than many other children to be a perpetrator, a bully.

Bystander   A **bystander** observes and witnesses bullying. A bystander can be a child or an adult, such as a teacher. Bystanders observe 85% of bullying episodes (O'Connell, Pepler, & Craig, 1999). The bystander is *not* a passive observer. Instead, he is a dynamic part of the bullying and is closely connected to the bullying. Teachers, for example, have a major role in stopping bullying, but their attitude about it influences what they actually do. If a teacher thinks that bullying is a normal part of childhood or that a child would not be bullied if she were assertive, then that teacher would not likely intervene. Teachers who believe that they should do something do separate the children, and the bullying stops (Kochenderfer-Ladd & Pelletier, 2008).

Bystander
Observes the bullying; can have an important role in stopping bullying

All of these children and their teacher observed bullying. They are *bystanders.*
The teacher is helping the children understand how to step in to stop bullying.

Many believe that bullying is a relationship mainly between a bully and the victim. However, the bystander has a significant part to play in the whole process of bullying and in stopping the bullying, as explained next.

Preventing Bullying

Many ways of preventing or intervening in bullying have been proposed and used. The method chosen depends partly on how you look at bullying. Some people view bullying as a two-person issue, something between the bully and the victim, and do not focus on the setting or anyone other than the bully and the victim. This is a dyadic, or two-person, perspective. In this case, prevention usually involves working with individuals, the bully and/or the victim.

Others see bullying in a larger framework, from a systems or ecological perspective (Frey, Hirschstein, Edstrom, & Snell, 2009; Twemlow, Fonagy, & Sacco, 2006). The ecological perspective reflects Bronfenbrenner's perspective on children's development within different systems, as described in Chapter 2. This approach sees bullying with a bigger lens, focusing on a triadic or three-person relationship of bully–victim–bystander. Figure 10.2 illustrates the ecological view that bullying has a larger cast of characters than originally thought.

One of the most effective ways to prevent bullying or to stop it is to take this same approach, a systems or ecological perspective. In this perspective, you go beyond looking only at the bully or at the victim and examine the entire system of the school, if that is where the bullying takes place. Researchers Fonagy, Twemlow, Vernberg, Mize Nelson, Dill, and others (2009) found that an ecological approach was successful in decreasing bullying. The entire school was involved, and the researchers focused on creating a more peaceful school environment.

The role of bystanders was of particular interest. Bystanders learned that they had a role in bullying, even if they did not land the punch, start the gossip, or exclude someone from play. Bystanders, including other children, teachers, or even administrators, learned to monitor things and were given permission to step in rather than stand back and watch. Stepping in takes many forms, and children need to learn different strategies, such as distracting the bully by saying something like "Mrs. Johnson needs to see you" or telling the bully to stop (Davis & Davis, 2007). See the web sites at the end of this chapter for specific bullying prevention programs.

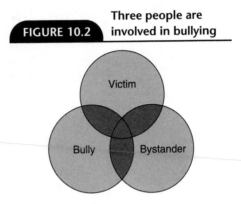

FIGURE 10.2 Three people are involved in bullying

:: HOW CHILDREN LEARN TO BE AGGRESSIVE

The most complete explanation of how children become aggressive is a systems or ecological approach (Bronfenbrenner, 1979). The ecological approach to development was explained in Chapter 2, and Figure 2.1 illustrated the approach. Professionals taking this approach acknowledge that a child is embedded in a variety of social systems and believe that these systems work together to shape a child's development, including aggression (Huesmann, 1988).

We will emphasize three spheres, or three systems, of influence on children's aggression: family, peer, and media (see Figure 10.3). A child frequently first learns about aggression in his *family* system. Almost equal in importance to a family's influence is the *media* system, including television, movies in any format, interactive videogames, and print, in teaching about aggression. The child's *peer group* is a system that teaches and reinforces aggression. Families and peer groups are themselves embedded in a larger setting, the community and culture, and the teachings about aggression from these settings influence what some families learn and pass on to their children.

FIGURE 10.3 Children learn about aggression in different systems

Where do children learn about aggression?

Family
- Model aggression
- Children rehearse aggression here
- Give opportunities to rehearse aggression

Peer Group
- Sets norms
- Teaches and reinforces aggression

Media
- Children: more than 2 hours of screen time/day
- Watching media violence fosters aggression

Scripts for Aggression

Scripts for aggression
Information stored in memory; focused on how to carry out aggression; gleaned from different systems

An actor knows exactly what to say and do onstage because she has a script. Children who behave aggressively, like Patrick in the chapter-opening vignette, also have **scripts for aggression**, files of information that tell them exactly how to hit, punch, kick, grab, insult, extort, threaten, or call names—how to behave aggressively. Other children might not have as many scripts about aggression. They have far less information about how to behave as aggressively as a child who has a large collection of scripts.

Consider the concept of scripts whenever you observe aggressive behavior. Each system *writes* scripts for children. Each system gives children plenty of opportunities to *rehearse* aggressive behavior in the scripts. Children then *store* and *activate* the scripts.

Scripts from Aggression-Teaching Families: Writing, Rehearsing with, and Activating the Scripts

Writing aggressive scripts   Aggression is a learned behavior, and some families teach aggression extremely effectively (Parke & Slaby, 1983). An observer would see parents passing on their knowledge about how to hurt others. They teach hurtful or destructive behavior in a variety of ways, and they teach it very effectively. For example, a child might observe verbal aggression or physical attacks, such as using humor as a weapon, or making fun of someone else.

Families model aggression, demonstrating behaviors for scripts. Children in such families listen to and observe the family's ways of dealing aggressively with one another, with animals, or with people outside the family. This is the scriptwriting step.

> **EXAMPLE**   A stray cat wandered into Patrick's yard, and Patrick watched his oldest brother yell at the cat, sending the animal running for cover. Patrick's new script is called "Yell at Cats".

Rehearsing with scripts   In aggression-teaching families, children use newly acquired scripts to rehearse aggressive behavior. Such families give their children many rehearsal sessions with the aggressive scripts.

> **EXAMPLE**   Patrick listened to a talk show in which a man used a racial slur. Patrick learned a new script called "Use Racial Slurs." Patrick rehearsed the new script, calling forth laughter from two of his brothers. There was no adult around to stop them.

Children who observe these adults arguing will learn a "script" for aggression. Children can also acquire scripts by watching arguments in the media.

Children in aggression-teaching families have many chances to practice using their newly learned aggressive scripts. They practice over and over what they have learned about hurting others (Parke & Slaby, 1983). This is the rehearsal with script step. There is no guarantee, however, that the child will automatically use the script or act it out. Patrick has never used the script that he learned for yelling at cats. In spite of how one of his brothers now treats animals outside the family, Patrick has never rehearsed the lesson.

Therefore, learning does not always mean putting the learning to use. In Patrick's case, something in his personality keeps him from acting out any script for hurting animals. He seems to have also gathered and stored scripts for kind treatment of animals.

Activating the scripts Children store the scripts for aggression in memory and then activate icons for them, just as we store and activate specific files on our computer screens. A child then retrieves and activates the scripts in settings both inside and outside his family. Suppose that Patrick, the child in the chapter-opening vignette, is in your early childhood class. You observe Patrick's behavior and realize quickly that he has a growing number of scripts for aggressive behavior in his memory. Further observation reveals a pattern. Patrick's scripts for fighting and bullying seem to be stored so that he can retrieve and activate them in a flash. We store frequently used folders on our computers as shortcuts. Unfortunately, Patrick's scripts for quick, aggressive responses are stored as shortcuts. He can simply select the shortcut icon that says "shortcut to name-calling."

Three factors induce children to retrieve and activate aggression-packed scripts:

- **Rehearsal:** Children retrieve scripts for aggression if they have rehearsed with scripts. Patrick, our focus child, activates one or more scripts for aggression several times every day; therefore he rehearses the name calling, threatening, and hitting or punching scripts frequently.

- **Cues for aggression, including interactive DVDs:** War toys, guns, or aggressive movies are **cues for aggression**. Playing an aggressive video for a child, for instance, is like showing an actor a cue card. It says, "Here's your cue; time to be aggressive." Children retrieve and activate aggressive scripts after observing specific cues such as war toys or aggressive features on DVDs. Children who play violent videogames observe and participate in these interactive games. They learn and then practice new aggression-related scripts. The scripts are then accessible for real-life conflict situations. The interactive nature of popular, violent videogames puts children right in the middle of the aggression in the video. The child becomes part of the video. Active involvement with violence, even if it is in a video, is still practice. Such practice imprints that script indelibly in the child's memory, giving him a permanent, easily accessed reminder of how to hurt others.

- **Continued exposure to aggression:** This provides even more scripts. Children who already have a large collection of aggressive scripts will very likely continue to observe aggression, increasing even further the number of aggressive scripts in their collection. The brand-new scripts for aggression, in turn, trigger the recall of existing aggression scripts. It is a nasty cycle.

Cues for aggression
Some object, such as a gun, that reminds a person about aggressive acts

Unresponsive Parenting Fosters Aggression

Members of aggression-teaching family systems are not very responsive to each other. Unresponsive parents are often, but not always, insensitive to and do not support their children. This sets the stage for children's increased aggression in a number of ways (Dubow, Heusmann, & Boxer, 2003):

- **Unmet needs.** Unresponsive adults often ignore and fail to meet a child's basic psychological needs for protection, love, affection, nurturance, play, and self-esteem. Unmet needs result in frustration, and frustrated, angry children frequently act aggressively.
- **Failure to teach social skills.** Unresponsive adults do not know that they should or they do not know how to teach specific social skills to their children. Therefore, the parents omit something that their children need. Their children tend to be low in self-control, and children who are not self-controlled are likely to react with aggression under many circumstances.
- **Active teaching of ineffective social skills and rewarding aggression.** On the other hand, unresponsive adults actively teach ineffective social skills, either deliberately or unknowingly. These adults also tend to reward aggressive behavior.
- **Negative or unhelpful discipline strategies.** Using harsh physical discipline, failing to set appropriate limits, disciplining inconsistently, using humor as a weapon, using sarcasm or shame, nattering or nagging, and hurting children with punishment are all unhelpful methods of discipline. Adults in aggression-teaching systems tend to use not just one or two but a whole cluster of negative discipline tactics. Using several negative discipline strategies can increase aggression in children because the strategies demonstrate clearly how to be aggressive. Herrenkohl, Egolf, and Herrenkohl (1997) noted that children whose parents used punitive discipline showed a lot of aggressive behavior when they were adolescents.
- **Providing cues for aggression.** Adults in aggression-teaching systems indirectly influence aggression through their management style. Parents in aggressive systems provide many cues that elicit aggression—media violence in its many forms and toy guns.

  EXAMPLE   Patrick's parents give him free access to all television shows, including sleazy talk and reality shows and entertainment television.

Peers: Children Get Scripts from Other Children

One of the conclusions from many different theoretical perspectives and many years of research is this: A child's behavior is remarkably similar to the behavior of her peer group (Prinstein & Dodge, 2008). Peers teach, maintain, and modify a child's aggression (Parke & Slaby, 1983).

Norm
A standard used by groups to direct a group member's behavior

Peers set norms for aggression   A **norm** is a principle that groups use to guide the behavior of members of the group. Norms tell members of a group what the group considers acceptable behavior. Peer groups influence the aggression of group members by setting norms about a number of things, including the expression of aggression. The norms tell children what the peer group will accept in terms of aggression. Some peer groups, like Patrick's neighborhood friends, have norms permitting and encouraging aggression. Other groups have norms that do not approve of aggression.

Peers model aggression Children learn from many different models, including peers. Observe for levels of aggression in a group of children. If the group approves of and models aggression, it will forecast changes in aggression over time for children in that group (Espelage, Holt, & Henkel, 2003).

> **EXAMPLE** Patrick has observed two friends push their way in line at the bus. The same pair uses aggression to steal lunch money from specific children.

Peers reinforce aggression Paul punches Jeff and says, "Give me your lunch money or I'll punch you again." Being punched is a negative and very unpleasant condition. Jeff gives Paul the lunch money, and Paul does not punch. Jeff has stopped the obnoxious negative condition by giving in to Paul. Jeff, however, has actually *reinforced* the aggression, Paul's punching. Paul is very likely to punch again because he has been reinforced for punching. Paul has learned that Jeff will give him money to *stop* the punching.

We reinforce name calling, bullying, pushing, and other forms of aggression when we give in to them ourselves or when we watch the aggression and do nothing to stop it.

> **EXAMPLE** Patrick discovered that children at school readily gave in to his aggression and bullying to stop the attacks. However, they did not realize that the giving in was actually rewarding Patrick and almost guaranteeing that he would attack them again.

Media: Children Get Scripts from Watching Violence

Children learn from observing different models, including those shown in the media, such as on television and in videogames. **Screen time** refers to the time spent watching a monitor of some sort, such as a television, movies in a theater, DVDs, Internet sources on a computer, and games on any type of device with a screen.

Screen time
Time spent watching action on a monitor of any sort

Children's screen time Children have a lot of screen time (Rideout, Vandewater, & Wartella, 2003). For instance, 74% of children under 2 years old have watched television, and almost 60% of these children watch over 2 hours each day. Thirty percent of infants and toddlers have televisions in their bedrooms, whereas the figure is 59% for children 4 to 6. Young children who watch the most television read less and they learned to read later than children who do not watch television. Some children, such as those with asthma, have even more screen time (Conn, Hernandez, Puthoor, Fagnano, & Halterman, 2008).

Effect of media violence The Kaiser Family Foundation issued a report on the effects of electronic media on children aged 0 to 6 (Center on Media and Child Health, 2005). They documented a variety of health risks to children who watch too much television or play too many videogames. Some of the major health risks are increased aggression from observing so much aggression and obesity connected with inactivity.

Media violence
Hostility shown in DVDs, movies, games, and other screens

Media violence refers to brutality, cruelty, and hostility portrayed on screens. There is an overwhelming consensus in the research, public health, and early childhood communities that watching and participating in media violence threatens the development and well-being of young children. Thirty-five years and well over 1,000 studies show that children watch an excessive amount of media violence. The ability to imitate models is present very early in life; thus, children watching a lot of television have many models to imitate. Imitation is the means through which children show that they comprehend screen action (Calvert, 2006).

Children who watch media violence develop aggressive attitudes, values, and behavior (Anderson et al., 2000; Walma van Der Molen, 2003). Three major risks go along with watching media violence:

- **Increases aggression.** Media violence can and does increase subsequent aggression in children.
- **Allows acceptance of aggression.** Media violence increases a child's passive acceptance of aggression by others. Not only do children themselves become more aggressive, but they also accept violence by others after watching media violence. Children are most likely to relax their standards if they view violence as effective, justified, reinforced, and commonplace.
- **Increases fear.** Media violence often leads children to think that the world is a violent and scary place in which people hurt and degrade each other. It might create and then increase the fear of becoming a victim of violence. Children who are afraid of becoming a victim of violence develop behaviors through which they hope to protect themselves. It also increases mistrust of others.

:: STRATEGIES FOR PREVENTING OR REDUCING AGGRESSION

The combination of aggressive children and media violence offers a challenge to early childhood teachers. Although some aggression, such as taking things from others, is normal as young children learn to live with others, other aggression is much more deeply rooted because the hurtful behavior has developed in an aggression-teaching family.

There are several ways to help all children cope with aggression, including bullying, and with media violence. Some strategies are especially appropriate for children from aggression-teaching families. This section describes a number of strategies through which we can either decrease or prevent aggression.

Set and Clearly Communicate Limits Prohibiting Aggression

Create a nonpermissive atmosphere by establishing limits against hurting or disturbing other people and animals, damaging toys or equipment, and bullying. Lead a discussion with children about why it is important to treat other people and animals with respect. Firmly but kindly enforce limits. You will begin to help children construct the idea that other people and animals have a right to be safe and secure. You will help them develop values and internal controls about the rights of others.

EXAMPLE   When Mr. Sanchez restated a limit, "Lilly, I know that you want to sit in that chair, but I can't just let you push Roxanne," he clearly communicated his refusal to tolerate Lilly's aggression.

Help Children Take Charge of What They Watch in the Media

The main goal is to teach children to make conscious decisions about what they watch, and if they will watch at all. Another goal is to decrease the effect of the power and pull of the media—television, DVD, videogames, and computers—on a child. This is a difficult task because of how well and attractively the media packages shows. The shows have a mesmerizing effect on a number of children, and many have developed habits of tuning in to the screen when they have a few minutes of downtime. They are entertained and do not have to think or exert much energy at all.

Levin (1998) offers excellent ideas on how to help parents and teachers teach children about using media wisely and taking control of what they watch:

- Lead problem-solving discussions with children about the media—for example, about the Power Rangers and all the fighting that they do. Why do they need to fight so much? Is there a way to limit where and when children play Power Rangers on the playground or in the classroom, so that children who do not like the Power Rangers play will not be bothered by it?
- Be clear about limits on imitating certain types of behaviors. Never allow children to imitate hurting animals or other people or damaging property. Talk to them about the reasons, but be firm. This should be a nonnegotiable item.
- Teach children how to make good choices and advance planning about their screen viewing. Help them understand that screen time means a combination of television, DVD, videogames, and computers. Give them specific skills for choosing screen time wisely.
- Help children observe themselves and think about the things that they like doing most. Encourage them to schedule time to do these activities in addition to choosing screen time wisely.

Watch Television with Children and Comment on Aggressive Content

A realistic approach acknowledges that children will have screen time, some much more than others. Teachers and parents can still be proactive. They can gradually decrease the amount of television watched, monitor what children watch, watch with children, and teach them how to understand what they watch (Levin, 1998).

EXAMPLE   While John was watching television, his father said, "Why do you think that man kicked his neighbor's car, John?" . . . "Yes, I think he was mad at him for driving his car over the flowers. That still doesn't make it okay to kick his neighbor's car."

Children who watch media violence with adults and hear a negative evaluation of the violence, as John did, tend to be less aggressive than children who watch the same aggression alone.

Encourage Children to Be Empathic

myeducationlab

Go to the Assignments and Activities section of Topic 5: Social Emotional Learning in the MyEducationLab for your course and complete the activity entitled *Interpersonal Environments Can Support Social Emotional Learning.* This strategy is beneficial for all children, including those who are bullies.

Teach aggressive children by *telling* them how the person they have victimized is feeling. Simply asking a young aggressive child how he thinks that the other might feel is an ineffective approach because young children cannot take the other's perspective. Give them information by telling. The examples that follow are from a preschool classroom for 4-year-olds.

EXAMPLE   "Oh, Susan! You really seem to have scared the gerbils when you banged on the glass. Look. They've run under cover and are hiding."

EXAMPLE   The teacher says to Tahisha, who grabbed the basket of bread at lunch: "Whoa, Tahisha! Let me take the basket back from you. Jordan had it first and looked startled when you grabbed it. Let's sing the basket-passing song while we wait our turns." The teacher then hands the basket back to Jordan.

The adult encouraged Susan and Tahisha to be empathic. Empathic children tend to be more sensitive to another's feelings and to be less aggressive (Feshbach & Feshbach, 1982; Strayer & Roberts, 2004).

Encourage Consequential Thinking

myeducationlab

Go to the Building Teaching Skills and Dispositions section of Topic 5: Social Emotional Learning in the MyEducationLab for your course and complete the activity entitled *Create a Supportive Social Emotional Learning Environment.* This teaching skill can help teachers facilitate children's social and emotional development.

Help children develop a value system that encourages them to treat others with respect and to refrain from hurting others. This is especially important for bullies to learn. One way to help children develop a respectful attitude is to teach them **consequential thinking**, or the understanding that a consequence of aggression is that somebody gets hurt or something is damaged. Focusing on consequential thinking should arouse empathy and that should prevent or decrease aggression. A good way to encourage consequential thinking is to give direct instruction in thinking about consequences, as Mr. Sanchez does in the next example.

EXAMPLE   During the morning meeting, Mr. Sanchez focused on feelings. Using clip art, he presented vignettes and asked questions about how the children might have felt about what happened. "When Pam pinched Rita, Rita cried. How do you think that she was feeling? . . . Right. She was hurt and felt bad."

See the web sites at the end of the chapter for programs and activities that will help you give the bystanders of bullying the knowledge, skills, and courage that they need for intervening in bullying.

Teach More Positive Behavior

Assertiveness, negotiation, cooperation, sharing, helping: all of these behaviors are incompatible with or contrary to aggression. We can essentially prevent or crowd out aggressive behaviors by teaching children how to cooperate or be assertive in place of acting aggressively.

Aggressive children have a limited number of ways to deal with interactional problems. Help children gather scripts for nonaggressive responses to issues. For example, teach children how to ask for and offer help.

> **EXAMPLE** Mr. Sanchez encouraged the children to help each other. He used a puppet that needed help at the computer and asked someone for help. He also taught the children how to offer help.

Recognize and Encourage Cooperative Behavior and Language

Noticing and then encouraging helpful, cooperative behavior (Skinner, Neddenriep, Robinson, Ervin, & Jones, 2002) is an effective way to decrease aggression. The idea

myeducationlab

To check your comprehension on the content covered in Chapter 10, go to the Book Specific Resources in the MyEducationLab for your course, select your text, and complete the Study Plan. Here you will be able to take a chapter quiz, receive feedback on your answers, and then access review, practice, and enrichment activities to enhance your understanding of chapter content.

WORKING *with* **FAMILIES**   **HELP YOUR CHILD TAKE CHARGE OF MEDIA AND SCREEN TIME**

- Slow the pace for and focus on your family. Plan a family night every week. Plan fun activities that do not include screen time, activities that everybody looks forward to and enjoys: playing board games, skating, taking a walk, reading, playing charades, playing music, learning about and looking for birds in your area, anything that family members suggest.
- Help your child take an inventory of favorite activities or new things that she or he would like to try:

  Make a list.

  Refer to the list when planning things to do.

  Refer to the list when a child is bored.

  Revise the list when it seems appropriate.

- Model wise, sensible use of your time, including screen time. Let your child see you, not plunking down in front of a screen, but reading books and magazines, exercising, spending time with family, gardening, sailing, or whatever hobby you enjoy.
- Help your child understand the concept of screen time, which includes television, DVDs, computer time, and videogames.

- Set a reasonable amount of screen time (less than 2 hours) that your child may have each day.
- Teach your child how to plan reading, play, or screen time.
- Write your family's rules for using television. Let children help write the rules. Then post, use, and evaluate the rules. Change them if necessary.
- Make the television set a less prominent piece of equipment. Turn on the television only for specific, planned shows; avoid letting a television run as background noise.
- Have a motto that works for your family. You may choose examples like "homework first," "chores first," "play with and feed dog first," "think first about what I really want to do," or "what are my choices here?"
- Help your child understand "action figure" characters. Talk with your child about why some of the action figures engage in so much fighting.
- If your child wants to imitate the action figures, consider trying to confine the imitation to specific times and places. Consider how "just saying no" might backfire. However, forbid certain things: hurting animals, hurting other people, and damaging property.

is to create a classroom community in which children focus on collaboration and cooperation, not bullying and aggression. The norm, therefore, would be to act cooperatively.

EXAMPLE   Mr. Sanchez's school adopted a plan encouraging children to watch out for and report random acts of cooperation and helpfulness. Two children, in one morning, reported that Patrick had helped them with their math.

ANALYZE VIGNETTES

Use the information in this chapter to answer the following questions about the chapter-opening vignettes.

1. Preschool: Identify the type of aggression that Maya shows. Explain your choice.
2. Kindergarten: What type of aggression does Jess show? What was the root of his aggressive behavior?

3. Primary: What would lead you to think that Patrick might be a *pure bully*?
4. Primary: What has probably happened at the school to change the behavior of the children who intervened in the bullying incident?

SUMMARY

There are many types of aggressive behavior, including physical, verbal, psychological, and emotional. All aggression intends to cause harm or damage. Aggressive people have a goal in mind. The two major goals or purposes are:

- Instrumental: the goal is to get or retrieve an object or privilege.
- Hostile: the goal is to do something harmful based on anger.

Bullying is aggression. It is repeated over time, and there is an imbalance between those involved. Participants in bullying are the:

- Bully
- Victim
- Bystander(s)

Children learn to be aggressive in different systems by acquiring, rehearsing, and activating scripts for aggression. The systems are:

- Family
- Peer group
- Media

Strategies exist for preventing or reducing aggression, such as setting limits on the expression of aggression, teaching, and encouraging more positive and prosocial behavior.

QUESTIONS FOR REFLECTION

1. Reflect on the concept of aggression by answering these true/false questions:
   - True or False? Anger and aggression are the same. Why or why not?
   - True or False? Young children's aggression is usually instrumental in nature. Explain your answer.

   - True or False? Hostile aggression usually shows up in children as they get older. Explain your answer.
   - True or False? There are three forms of violent behavior. Explain your response.
2. Name two specific ways in which aggression-teaching families foster aggression in young children.

3. Explain how a child's peers can teach her to be aggressive, and summarize the influence of media violence on aggression in young children.

4. Why is the bystander's role so important in bullying?

5. Choose at least three of the strategies presented in this chapter for guiding aggressive children, and explain why they would be effective in either stopping or preventing children's aggression.

APPLY YOUR KNOWLEDGE

1. Watch at least 1 hour of television designed specifically for young children. On a sheet of paper, break that hour into 10-minute segments. In each segment, keep a tally of the number of times that you see an act of aggression—any act of aggression—and give a total at the end of the hour. Write a brief description of each act of aggression.

2. Visit a toy store. Find several examples of and describe toys that you think would serve as aggressive cues that would likely bring out aggression in young children. Were these toys designed for a specific gender? If so, state what led you to this conclusion.

3. Review a prevention program. Choose one of the web sites listed at the end of this chapter that is devoted to bullying prevention. Examine one or two of the methods suggested to stop bullying. Say why this method would probably be effective.

KEY TERMS

Aggression (246)
Bully (252)
Bullying (252)
Bully/victim (253)
Bystander (253)
Cues for aggression (257)
Cyberbullying (252)

Emotional or psychological
  bullying (252)
Hostile aggression (249)
Instrumental aggression (248)
Media violence (260)
Norm (258)
Physical bullying (252)

Provoking victim (253)
Pure bully (252)
Pure victim (253)
Screen time (259)
Scripts for aggression (256)
Verbal bullying (252)
Victim (253)

WEB SITES

Coalition for Quality Children's Media
http://www.kidsfirst.org/

A nonprofit organization devoted to developing critical skills in viewing media. They offer many excellent resources for parents, teachers, and children.

National Association for the Education of Young Children (NAEYC)
http://www.naeyc.org

Go to the link for the organization's position statement on media violence in children's lives.

Olweus Bullying Prevention Program
http://www.clemson.edu/olweus/

Main page for this comprehensive, schoolwide program. Used in many different countries. Site contains helpful links that describe and explain the program.

Operation Respect
http://www.dontlaugh.org

Organization focused on social and emotional learning. It developed the *Don't Laugh at Me* antibullying program.

Quit It!
http://www.edequity.org/

A New York–based bullying prevention program for younger children.

Minimizing Challenging Behavior

"Biting is the most common reason children get expelled from child care."
—(American Academy of Child & Adolescent Psychiatry, 2008)

"Adults often underestimate the stress and anguish teasing and name-calling cause children."
—(LEVY, 2004)

Chapter Contents

Guiding Questions

- What is challenging behavior and why are incidents of challenging behavior the "hot spots" in an early childhood classroom?
- Why is it important to understand the roots of challenging behavior?
- How can I use the decision-making model of guiding children to help me support children with challenging behavior?
- How can I support a child with *persistent* challenging behavior?

VIGNETTES

PRESCHOOL: AURELIA SHARES OCCASIONALLY

Mrs. Woodward is concerned about 4-year-old Aurelia's behavior. Here is a small sampling of her anecdotal records about Aurelia in September. She focused on examples of sharing as well as taking things without asking.

1. *Aurelia and Justine worked side by side at a table, sorting plastic squares by color. Aurelia leaned over, picked up three of J's items, and put them in her own pile.*
2. *Angelo yelled, "Give it back Aurelia," referring to a boat that Aurelia had taken from him. Aurelia did not give it back.*
3. *Outside: Four tricycles were available. The sign-up list was near the parking area. Moshe waited for his turn. Angelo finished a turn and then returned the tricycle to the parking area. Aurelia scooted in ahead of Moshe, jumped on the tricycle, and rode away.*
4. *Aurelia, Kim, and Pete painted on a long piece of paper taped to the plastic-covered wall. Aurelia shared the three large pots of paint with the others.*

KINDERGARTEN: EMILY'S EMOTIONS FLARE UP

Emily had been in Mr. Sanchez's class for the last 2 months of kindergarten after moving to the district. Therefore, when school resumed in September, he realized that Emily's angry flare-ups might show up again. The first episode occurred on the third day of school. Emily, now in this teacher's first-grade group, stomped away from the computer center after finding all computers in use. Mr. Sanchez watched the flood of anger in Emily's face, a clear sign of the emotional storm brewing within this 6-year-old. Later that afternoon Emily smacked another first grader.

PRIMARY: SAMIRA FLITTERS AND FLUTTERS

Samira speaks two languages fluently, does well in school, and is well liked by other children. Mr. Sanchez thinks of her as a social butterfly, finishing any work quickly and then flitting off to chat with friends. Samira zips about the room during transitions, too, cheerfully wreaking low-level havoc. During Tuesday's lining-up for lunch, she led the group in a quiet little cheer, "Lunch, lunch, we love lunch!"

:: INTRODUCTION

As you know from earlier chapters, dealing with guidance dilemmas and discipline encounters is a normal part of a teacher's role. This chapter focuses on a different kind of guidance issue—challenging behavior. **Challenging behavior** is a child's behavior that challenges her teacher's ability to guide the child. Many types of behaviors are considered difficult. Most seem out of character for the child or are dangerous, frightening, or anxiety producing. Some teachers refer to challenging behavior as "the times when I want to tear my hair out."

My major goal in this chapter is to help you learn four things about challenging behavior: how to minimize the hot spots of challenging behavior; maximize the calm, cool times in your classroom; feel competent and confident in the process; and learn to support children who persist with challenging behaviors and who do not respond to positive guidance strategies.

Challenging behavior
Behavior that tests an adult's ability to support the child; usually in the eye of the beholder.

:: CHALLENGING BEHAVIOR

Challenging Behavior Is "in the Eye of the Beholder"

Go to the Assignments and Activities section of Topic 8: Challenging Behavior in the MyEducationLab for your course and complete the activity entitled *Challenging Behavior is in the Eye of the Beholder*. This strategy helps teachers clarify their understanding of challenging behavior.

Suppose that 10 teachers in a workshop watch a video or DVD clip. The film shows a 3-year-old child hiding under a table while the teacher reads a story, lagging behind the group of children as they walk to the library, and crying as he slams his fists on the floor when the teacher reminds him that it is cleanup time. "Do you," asks the workshop leader, "think that you have just seen challenging behavior?" Seven participants state that they have definitely observed challenging behavior. The rest have the opposite opinion: that this child's behavior would not fall into the challenging behavior category. How would you have responded? Why?

Challenging behavior is in the eye of the beholder because our perspective determines the behavior we see and label as challenging. In the example, some teachers' perspectives led them to see this 3-year-old child as defiant. A different perspective enabled three of the teachers to realize that the child's behavior was predictable of a very young child feeling insecure in a new setting.

Figure 11.1 shows the frame-by-frame sketch of 5-year-old Jessie's calm and cool times in his kindergarten class. We will also focus on hot spots of challenging behavior in this child's day as the chapter progresses, and you will have a chance to answer a variety of questions. You will reach your own conclusion about whether Jessie's behavior was *challenging*.

Challenging Behaviors Are the Hot Spots in a Classroom

Hot spots
Incidents of challenging behavior in a classroom.

Figure 11.2 shows several hot spots during only part of one morning. Figure 11.3 explains the nature of each of the hot spots. Examine both figures at the same time. **Hot spots** are the times when a teacher might feel less confident about his guidance, anxious, impatient, or even angry or frustrated. He might question his methods of

FIGURE 11.1 Calm and cool times in Jessie's morning in kindergarten

guiding children because the positive methods may not be working with challenging behavior. For example, good limit setting and restating limits well might not work with some challenging behaviors.

Teachers who have an authoritative caregiving style (Chapter 1) are kind as well as firm, understand child development, and use this knowledge when guiding children. However, when faced with situations with no resolution in sight, a teacher could feel irritated and edgy. Then many teachers feel guilty for having been impatient with a child. Anger is then likely to get in the way of clear thinking about the challenging behavior. Unpleasant emotions can affect teachers just as they do anybody else.

Hot spots of challenging behavior are also the times when teachers think that their focus has shifted from teaching to crisis intervention. Jessie's teacher, the cooperating teacher, spends quite a bit of time every day helping Jessie calm down. She likes working with student teachers but thinks that Jessie's challenging behavior might be more than a student teacher can handle. Yet she has found that the student teacher, frustrated and anxious about dealing with Jessie, is slowly learning how to help him and is gaining confidence.

| FIGURE 11.2 | Hot spots of challenging behavior in Jessie's morning in kindergarten |

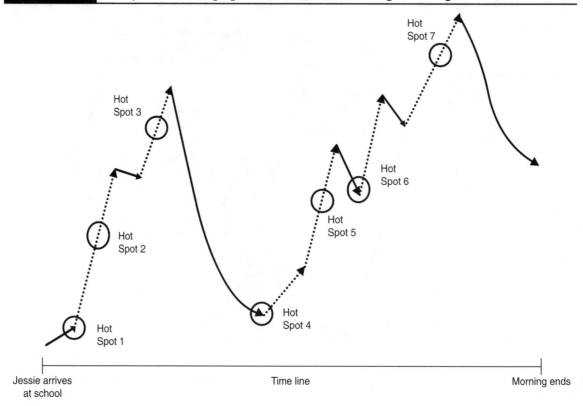

Calm and cool times
Periods of relative peace and serenity in a classroom.

Jessie's teacher wants to increase the **calm and cool times** in the classroom—time for teaching with fewer hot-spot, challenging behaviors. How does she get to this point? How does she help Jessie deal with his anxiety? A good first step would be to consider the origins of his challenging behaviors. We will now examine four of the strongest roots of challenging behavior.

:: ROOTS OF CHALLENGING BEHAVIOR

Voice of challenging behavior
What a child's behavior tells a teacher about what the child needs.

Challenging behavior is complex. Even experienced, competent teachers are astounded at how complicated a challenging behavior can be. They realize that a child's demanding or testing behavior grew out of a number of tightly tangled factors. Jessie's teacher, for instance, knew that helping Jessie would take a lot of time over several months and that she would have to stay focused on his behavior as a complex question with many different answers. The **voice of challenging behavior** speaks through children's actions, their behavior. We begin to help children by listening carefully to what they tell us with their actions.

| **FIGURE 11.3** | Describing Jessie's hot spot challenging behavior |

Hot spot

1. Jessie's father said to the teachers, with Jessie listening, "See if you can do anything with him today!" Jessie seemed agitated as he started his day and ignored his friend Sandi's cheerful greeting.

2. At the listening center, Jessie had a little trouble with the tape recorder. Already agitated, his frustration seemed to increase as he yanked the tape out of the machine.

3. Jessie likes Sandi and they had fun together listening to a tape. Then Sandi went to the math center and Jessie wandered about the room, not stopping anywhere to work. When the student teacher (ST) asked him to choose his next center, Jessie walked away from her without answering. He walked by the sand table, grabbed a corner of the large sign on the table, and ripped the sign in half.

4. When ST started sending children to line up for art class, Jessie went to the library, took a book from the shelf, and buried his face in the book.

5. ST called over to Jessie in the book corner, "Okay, Jessie. Time to line up for art class." "I'm *not* going," he shouted.

6. Jessie looked at ST who asked him if he was now ready to go to art class. He ignored her and hung his head. Jessie's agitation resurfaced.

7. ST placed her hand on Jessie's shoulder as she had seen the cooperating teacher do. Jessie shook off her hand with a violent twist. He now showed even more anger and frustration.

This section targets the four main roots of challenging behavior:

Developmental characteristics
Unmet needs
Lack of skills
Factors in the classroom (contextual problems)

Developmental Characteristics

Memory, perspective taking, social cognition, brain development—these and other **developmental characteristics** are involved in nearly every challenging behavior. Can a 3-year-old, for example, remember to use words when she is angry? How well developed at age 4 is the part of the brain responsible for helping a child calm down? Can a 6-year-old take another person's perspective? The voice of challenging behavior, in this case, says this: "I am still a child and think like a child. I have trouble taking somebody else's perspective. I can't control my emotions yet and it will be a couple of years before I can really control myself."

Some of the major developmental factors explaining challenging behaviors are explained in the subsections that follow.

Brain development A child's brain development is in progress throughout childhood and adolescence. This affects all other areas of development and has special meaning for challenging behaviors. Chapter 8 described and explained the development of the amygdala and prefrontal associative cortex, and the link between the two. To review briefly:

- The amygdala, fully formed at birth, is connected to other brain parts and directs them in emergencies. The amygdala is the specialist for emotional matters. Therefore, the part of a child's brain that takes over after sensing danger operates long before the part responsible for controlling emotions is fully developed.

Developmental characteristics
Factors in a child's growth that contribute to challenging behavior.

Go to the Assignments and Activities section of Topic 5: Social Emotional Learning in the MyEducationLab for your course and complete the activity entitled *The Voice of Challenging Behavior.* This strategy helps teachers clarify the meaning of challenging behavior.

- The frontal lobes, especially the prefrontal associative cortex, help people control themselves and analyze emotions. However, this part of the brain is not fully developed until late adolescence or even early adulthood.
- The calm-down circuit develops between 10 and 18 months. It is responsible for getting signals between the amygdala and the prefrontal cortex so that emotions can be examined. This brain part helps calm agitation. Its development, however, is not automatic. Some children have a very weak circuit but others, fortunately, have a much stronger circuit and can soothe themselves.

In terms of challenging behavior, how do children lose it? We want children to be able to analyze information that, say, makes them angry. A child who hears "You're a dummy," for example, will have to get the data to the prefrontal cortex for analysis. We want the cortex to do its job and analyze the information: "Hmm, looks as if we have some disturbing information here about our child being called a dummy. Wait. Look at who is calling him a dummy. It's Tom, and Tom does not like our child, so we won't let our child get too upset." This part of the brain is not developed well enough in young children for such analysis to occur.

Therefore, young children are far less able to analyze the information than we are. Their amygdala does operate, however, and they say, "Watch out! That Tom is at it again. He called you a dummy! Get him. Smack him." The child does not analyze. He does not use his words. He is more likely to act on the orders of his amygdala and have a fast and sloppy response. His emotions are likely to disrupt thinking and cause neural static. This static makes it difficult for a child to do something as simple and sensible as remembering to use words. The static sabotages the frontal lobe's ability to maintain working memory and makes it difficult for a child to hold essential information in mind for solving problems, even if a teacher has repeated the information several times. Therefore, a child's agitation is likely to last for quite some time.

Other developmental characteristics   We will focus for a moment on four of the numerous developmental characteristics affecting challenging behavior. You have studied these in other chapters in this book.

- Young children tend to think about one thing at a time. They might think about how much they dislike the taste of something, not how the child who brought the treat might feel when she hears a criticism of the treat.
- Young children have difficulty with perspective taking (Chapter 2). Perspective taking is a cognitive developmental skill that develops over time and only if children learn about taking another's perspective and only if they practice this skill.
- Children who have learned an unhelpful way to do something retain powerful images of that incorrect method. Even though a teacher tells them, "Use your words," this child will very likely revert to his old and unhelpful method of hitting when angry, stressed, and agitated.
- Children feel and express anger but they do not understand and cannot manage anger on their own. They cannot contemplate why they feel angry, cannot always generate words for how they feel, and cannot think of how to deal with their irritation.

The girl on the right cannot take the other child's perspective. When she grabs things, she does not think about how the other child feels.

Applying this information to the chapter-opening vignettes   In the chapter-opening preschool vignette, recall that Aurelia is 4 years old and grabs things from other children several times each day. Aurelia's inability to take somebody else's perspective is the developmental root of her challenging behavior.

In the chapter-opening kindergarten vignette, Emily's overly strong emotional responses also reveal a developmental root to her challenging behavior. Emily's inability to focus on more than one thing at a time is one developmental issue. Emily's inability to manage her emotions is another. A third developmental root is that Emily has remembered and used an ineffective way of dealing with angry feelings.

Unmet Needs

The challenging behavior says, "There is something that I really need. Would you help me get it?" The root of some, but certainly not all, challenging behavior is one or more **unmet needs**. Think about a child's basic needs. What does he need before

---

Thinking about Jessie's Challenging Behavior

1. Jessie came to school upset. He stayed agitated throughout the morning in spite of his friend Sandi's and his teacher's help. Explain this in terms of his current level of brain development.

2. How have the other developmental characteristics probably affected Jessie's behavior?

Unmet need
One of a child's basic requirements for healthy development and good mental health that have not been satisfied and that contribute to challenging behavior.

he can behave well? Here are some of any child's most basic needs (you might have additions to the list):

Feeling of being loved and appreciated
Feeling of being safe and secure
Exercise and physical activity
Sound sleep and rest
Adequate nutrition, including enough water
Basic medical and dental care
Play
Classroom structure based on principles of developmentally appropriate practice
Authoritative, constructive guidance

EXAMPLE   Mrs. Woodward knew that it would rain all morning and the children would not go outside. Knowing that the children still needed to move and wanting to forestall problems, she set up an obstacle course in the large group area. During morning meeting, she included quiet jogging in place, and small groups did stretches during center time. The whole class took a walk to the water fountain at the far end of the school to get a drink.

This teacher realized that the children needed exercise. The easy-to-do changes that she made helped meet that need. Highly responsive teachers make a real effort to tune into children's needs by observing carefully. Then, as much as possible, they help children meet their needs.

Applying this information to the chapter-opening vignettes   In the chapter-opening kindergarten vignette, Emily has several angry outbursts. At home, Emily's parents argue frequently and do not argue fairly. They insult and degrade each other. Emily hears and sees this background anger, often in the middle of the night, and has observed her father hit her mother on several occasions. One of Emily's most outstanding unmet needs is a feeling of safety and security. Do you think that she has any other unmet needs?

Lack of Skills

Skill deficit
Lacking a skill for social emotional development and school success that contributes to challenging behavior.

The challenging behavior says, "There is something that I don't know how to do. Will you teach me?" Many children simply do not have the skills they need for getting along with others and for functioning well in school. They have a **skill deficit**. Observing very young children first and then a group of third graders reveals the

---

Thinking about Jessie's Challenging Behavior

Review the hot spots in Figures 11.2 and 11.3. From the information given, what do you think Jessie's most outstanding unmet need might be?

numerous things that children must learn to be successful in relationships and in school, including the following:

Humane treatment of animals
How to get attention appropriately
How to join a group
How to make a friend
How to keep a friend
How to work with others in small and large groups
How a group functions
How to start a project and how to keep it going

EXAMPLE   Aneta, 4 years old, was new to Mrs. Woodward's preschool class. The child had never attended any sort of school and did not know what to do at large-group time. For example, Aneta looked bewildered the first time that the children joined the teacher on the carpet, sat in a circle, and waited for the story to begin.

Applying this information to the chapter-opening vignettes   In the primary-grade vignette, some people might look on Samira's joyful approach to life as challenging behavior. Mr. Sanchez merely wanted to help Samira learn how to organize herself for moving smoothly through the morning. He did not want to stamp out her joy or the happiness that she brought to the class. Mr. Sanchez decided that Samira needed a day planning chart to help her move to the next center. It worked. Samira is still happy and still socializing, but she now has a destination.

Factors in the Classroom (Contextual Issues)

The voice of challenging behavior says, "There's something in our classroom that's making it hard for me to do the right thing. Will you please help me by changing this?" This refers to **contextual factors** that contribute to challenging behavior. Teachers need to examine their own practices when facing ordinary, everyday discipline encounters as well as challenging behaviors.

It is unsettling at times to look at our own practices, but consider thinking about it a different way; that is, consider reframing this process by asking yourself, "How can I make my good classroom even better for every child here? Would a minor change in my classroom support a child with challenging behavior?" It is not

Contextual factors
Environmental issues (physical or interpersonal environment or curriculum) contributing to challenging behavior in classrooms.

Thinking about Jessie's Challenging Behavior

Refer to Figures 11.1, 11.2, and 11.3.

1. Do you think Jessie needs to learn some skill?

2. If you answered yes to the first question, name the skill.

3. If you answered no, what is your reason for saying that Jessie does not need to learn a specific skill?

a matter of finding fault. It is a matter of deliberately examining and thinking about one's own practices, which we know as **reflection**.

Observing and reflecting Effective teachers reflect on their own teaching practices. What matters is an unemotional, dispassionate assessment of classroom structure and processes, which requires observation. Chapter 6 explains the major observational strategies used by early childhood teachers. Observing with anecdotal or running records, for example, will help you get a complete picture about children's behavior. Observing is also a good way to examine how you set up the classroom, your instructional strategies, the materials you use, and how you speak to children.

Figure 11.4 describes three excellent observation instruments that teachers find useful in examining their classroom's environment. They are *rating scales* that yield information only. There is no judgment, only information, which helps teachers learn about the strengths in their classrooms. The main idea is to use the information to build on these strengths. Teachers can also identify areas for growth with these rating scales. Here, the teacher would change something in the classroom to create an even more developmentally appropriate environment.

FIGURE 11.4	Information about ITERS-R, ECERS, and APEEC

OBSERVATION: FOUNDATION OF SELF-REFLECTION FOR ECE TEACHERS
Reflect on program quality with these instruments. Rating scales for programs for infants, preschool, and kindergarten–primary grades.

Infant Toddler Environment Rating Scale—Revised Edition (ITERS–R)
   Developers: Harms, Cryer, and Clifford (2004, revised edition)
   Type of instrument: ready-made assessment tool, rating scale (English or Spanish versions). Training video, video guide, and training workbook available.
   Designed for: assessing program quality, environments for children up to 30 months of age
   Areas of environment assessed:
      Health and safety
      Environment (furniture, equipment, educational materials)
      Educator skill
      Educator behavior
   Scoring: rating scale

Early Childhood Environment Rating Scale—Revised (ECERS–R)
   Developers: Harms, Clifford, and Cryer (1998)
   Type of instrument: ready-made assessment tool, rating scale (English, Spanish versions). Training videos available.

Designed for: assessing program quality, preschool classrooms, children ages 2 1/2 to 5
Areas of program assessed:
   Space and furnishings
   Personal care routines
   Language-reasoning
   Activities
   Interaction
   Program structure
   Parents and staff
Scoring: rating scale through which observers determine the rating for each area assessed based on number of items checked yes or no

Assessment of Practices in Early Elementary Classrooms (APEEC)
   Developers: Hemmeter, Maxwell, Ault, and Schuster (2001).
   Type of instrument: ready-made assessment tool, rating scale.
   Designed for: assessing how well a classroom uses developmentally appropriate practices (DAP) in general-education classes for K–3 children
   Areas assessed (three broad areas assessed):
      Physical environment
      Instructional context
      Social context
   Scoring: either as a rating scale or checklist

Source: **Based on Frank Porter Graham Child Development Center, University of North Carolina's web site: http://www.fpg.unc.edu/~ecers/**

All children in a class benefit when teachers examine the classroom environment. Those whose challenging behavior is linked to inappropriate transitions, overly long group times, a poorly balanced daily schedule, or inappropriate curriculum or guidance strategies benefit even more. Morning meetings, for example, are excellent for early childhood classrooms (Kriete, 2002), but the length of the meeting must be developmentally appropriate.

> **EXAMPLE** A kindergarten's morning meeting started at 8:45 and ended at 9:40, a total of 55 minutes, which was much too long. The teacher was frustrated with all the wiggling and squirming.

> **EXAMPLE** Children in a first grade arrive at 8:15 a.m. They spend the entire morning doing one worksheet after another. Most of the 5-year-olds have great difficulty paying attention and the teacher constantly urges them to pay attention and to stop wiggling.

In the second example, the instructional strategy, along with the schedule, is the root of the children's challenging behavior. First, using worksheet pages is an *in*appropriate instructional strategy for young children. The children were restless because the teacher did not encourage active learning. The children sat at tables and did not get to work in centers, never engaged in sociodramatic play, and did not get to work collaboratively.

Authoritative adults practice what they believe, whatever a child's culture or background. This is difficult to do when children from widely different backgrounds are in the same classroom. Nevertheless, authoritative caregivers are committed to practicing the decision-making model of child guidance. They do not just use the first strategy that pops into their heads. They work at finding a solution. Authoritative caregivers deliberately walk through the systematic process of choosing a strategy. They use the decision-making model of guiding children, the topic we will examine next.

:: DECISION-MAKING MODEL OF CHILD GUIDANCE

The **decision-making model of child guidance** involves making deliberate and intentional decisions when interacting with children, including during discipline encounters. The decision-making model is a way of examining a guidance or discipline encounter and thinking about how to handle it appropriately. Authoritative caregivers make developmentally appropriate guidance plans in a logical and clear-headed manner, avoiding the quicksand of emotional reactions. Authoritative caregivers think purposefully about a problem and then make a decision about discipline encounters—the typical ones as well as those that are more challenging.

Decision-making model of child guidance
Using a four-step process of observing, deciding, taking action, and reflecting to support children with challenging behavior.

Authoritative caregivers consciously think about each child in their care. They know that any child from infancy to age 9 years has a basic style or temperament and a rich personal history of interactions. They understand the impact of families and culture on children. For instance, authoritative caregivers understand that each child's family has its own scripts and rules, its own communication style, its own cultural history, its own view of how children should behave, and its own style of discipline.

They know that some parents feel secure, understand children and children's needs, and know how to communicate legitimate rules and limits. They know how to help children live within limits and know how to demonstrate their love and respect to their children.

Authoritative caregivers also understand that other parents have not had their own needs for nurturance met and *cannot* now, as adults, meet their children's needs for nurturance and security. They know that these parents do not understand how infants and children develop, are angry, and do not know how or refuse to take their children's perspective. They lack empathy for their children. These parents have very poor and ineffective child guidance skills; for example, they do not know how to set limits effectively or how to help children accept limits. Unfortunately, many parents do not know how to demonstrate the love that they feel for their children.

Steps in the Decision-Making Model

There are four logical steps in the decision-making model. As shown in Figure 11.5, they include

Observe
Decide
Take action
Reflect

FIGURE 11.5   **Four steps in the decision-making model of child guidance**

Observe

- **Focus on the encounter as a problem to be solved.**
  Clearly identify the problem. Decide whether the child or the adult "owns the problem." Focus on solving a problem, not on blaming a child.

- **Examine the context of the problem.**
  Ask yourself how the child's age might be affecting her behavior. Ask how the child's family, culture, or the classroom physical environment, activities, or materials have contributed to the problem. Ask how your way of talking with a child might be contributing to the problem. The idea is not to place blame but simply to get a better picture of the context or setting in which the behavior has evolved.

Decide

Your observation will tell you what to change. For example, you might need to:

- **Choose a guidance strategy.**
  Use only positive, developmentally appropriate strategies, not punishment. Consult your list of guidance strategies in the Appendix and in

Chapter 4. Say why the chosen strategy is appropriate for this child at this time.

- **Change the context.**
  You might decide that you have to change the classroom physical environment or the time schedule. You might decide that you should choose more DAP activities, or that materials need to be organized better.

- **Change your own practices.**
  You might decide that you want to change something that you are doing. For instance, you may decide that you want to talk with children about playground rules after you realize that you have never done this.

Take Action

Carry out the guidance strategy, make the contextual change, or change the practice that you want to change.

Reflect

If your approach did not work, then go through the process again.

Note: You will use see this figure again, but in greater detail, in Chapter 13.

In the next section, you will apply information on the roots of challenging behavior to some of the more common guidance issues facing teachers. We will use the decision-making model to choose effective strategies for each challenging behavior.

:: SPECIFIC CHALLENGING BEHAVIORS: USING THE DECISION-MAKING MODEL OF CHILD GUIDANCE

This general framework enables teachers to think clearly and purposefully about a problem. It helps teachers avoid making wild guesses or using the first guidance strategy that pops into their head. Instead, they support children by searching for a solution to challenging behaviors—systematically, logically, and rationally.

You have also studied many different positive guidance strategies in this text, especially in Chapter 5 (they are listed in the Appendix, too). Many chapters focus on using positive guidance strategies for special guidance issues, as you read, for example, in Chapter 8 on social and emotional learning. Now, the focus shifts to applying knowledge of guidance strategies to challenging behaviors. Dealing appropriately with challenging behaviors usually requires that a teacher use more than one positive strategy because challenging behavior usually has more than one root.

This section deals with the following challenging behaviors:

Biting
Disrespectful language (including cursing or swearing)
Teasing

These behaviors illustrate challenges common to three different phases within early childhood. Teachers typically see biting in infant and toddler groups. You will hear disrespectful language, including cursing or swearing, in all age groups but most frequently in preschool children. Teachers notice that the teasing and hostile aggression of bullying increases in frequency in the primary grades (Freedman, 2002; Troop-Gordon & Ladd, 2005).

Information about and possible solutions for each challenging behavior are nested within the decision-making model format. I have emphasized identifying the root of the challenging behavior.

Biting

Observe

- Observe yourself. This is a situation fraught with emotion. Teachers are usually alarmed, and the children are either angry or afraid. The children are also very young and cannot handle their feelings on their own. They need their teacher to support them. You will support children best by staying centered, calm, and objective. Focus on helping the child communicate with others without aggression—without biting.

- Observe the child's challenging behavior systematically. Ask the "W" questions about biting (Osterreich, 1996): Where did the biting incident take place? Who was involved? When did the biting occur? What happened before the biting incident? Why did it occur?

Decide   Use your observations to identify the root(s) of the challenging behavior. Decide and explain which of the four major roots seem to apply in this case (Downs, Blagojevic, Labas, Kendrick, & Maeverde, 2005; National Association of the Education of Young Children, 2003):

- **Developmental issue:** Biting is common in infants and toddlers. They explore by mouthing and chewing. Teething begins at about 4 to 7 months. Chewing on things relieves some pain, but children this young sink their teeth into the arms, legs, and shoulders of other people. A very young child also gradually builds the idea that she can make things happen. For instance, when she bites somebody, she hears, "Ouch!" Children also learn from models; therefore, when a parent bites a child or when that child observes another child biting someone, she has a model of biting. Some biting grows out of imitation of the behavior.
- **Child has an unmet need:** Older toddlers need and want attention and interaction. Some very young children bite to meet this need. A healthy sense of control is central in developing positive self-esteem. Children discover that biting is quite powerful in controlling others, but this is not a healthy way to feel in control.

Take action   Consider saying or doing some of the following:

- For teething and exploring, give children safe items to chew—a clean cloth or teething ring.
- For attention issues, focus on spending enjoyable time together and prevent some of the more stressful interactions.
- Teach a new behavior. Be clear that biting is *not* acceptable. Use the limit-setting strategy. Be firm but kind as you say, "Here, Luke, bite this cloth. It's *not* okay to bite Miosha." To an older toddler, say, "Use words. Say, 'Give it back.'"
- Help children acquire a healthy approach to feeling in control. Give age-appropriate choices. For example, "Do you want orange or grape juice?" "Would you rather play in the sand or with the paints?" "You can decide if you want to show the painting to your dad."

Reflect   How did my decision help this child at this time?

- Was I centered, calm, and kind while I carried out my decision?
- Do I need to repeat any of these steps? If your answer isyes, which would be most helpful?

Disrespectful Language (Including Cursing or Swearing)

Observe

- Observe yourself. Examine your own way of speaking and make sure that you are not the model of disrespectful language. Stay centered, calm, and objective. Focus on helping the child find a better way. Take a slow, deep breath. Say, "I will stay centered. I will not reply angrily."
- Observe the child's challenging behavior systematically. Answer as many of the five "W" questions as possible. Record dates and times about *when* the child curses, *who* else is present, *where* you hear it, and *what* he says. This will give you valuable information.

Decide   Use your observations to identify the root(s) of the challenging behavior. Decide and explain which of the four major roots seem to apply in this case:

- **Developmental issue:** Young children are like little digital voice recorders and might just be imitating language that they have heard—from parents, siblings, or screen time such as in television, movies, and DVDs. They do not take another person's perspective and do not really understand the impact of disrespectful language.
- **Child needs to learn a skill:** Cursing and rude language is often a sign of hostility, or it might be a sign that the child needs to learn to speak to others or to express herself by using words that are more respectful.

Take action   Consider saying or doing some of the following (Faull, 2002):

- If you find that you occasionally lapse into disrespectful talk, adopt words that are more respectful. For example, say, "Wow! I hear a lot of noise near the gerbil's house," in a friendly, nonaccusatory tone. Do *not* say, "Haven't I told you before to be quiet?" The second way suggests a basic lack of respect.
- If the child is angry, acknowledge this emotion: "I can tell that you are upset. Getting upset is okay." Avoid preaching because you will deal with the rude behavior shortly.
- Say, "In our school, we have agreed to respect others. That word is disrespectful and is not allowed."
- Say, "Let's think of a kinder way to tell how you feel." Suggest some words for the child to use and then practice using them (a puppet is helpful). Notice and encourage the child's effort and willingness to make a change: "You thought of a kinder way to say what you felt!"

Reflect

- How did my decision help this child at this time?
- Was I centered, calm, kind, and objective while I carried out my decision?
- Do I need to repeat any of these steps? If your answer is yes, which would be most helpful?

Teasing

Chapter 10 dealt with aggression and bullying. Teasing, unfortunately, is very common during childhood and it can easily turn into bullying (Vessey, Horowitz, Carlson, & Duffy, 2008; Townsend-Butterworth, 2009). Teasing might seem like playful banter or joking to some people, but it can be aggression when the teaser *intends* to hurt another person. Therefore, teachers need to be acutely aware of this challenging behavior and be willing to intervene and stop or prevent the negative effects of teasing. **Teasing** refers to verbal or nonverbal exchanges between children or between a child and an older person—this chapter focuses on child-to-child teasing. There are different views of these interactions. Teasers see their words or actions as funny, but the person or child who is teased most often feels annoyed or humiliated (Vessey, 2006).

It is critical that early childhood teachers understand the real impact of teasing on victims as well as how to help victims protect themselves. The long-term effects of teasing on preadolescent victims include emotional distress, depression, anxiety, and loneliness. Victims of teasing develop negative perceptions about themselves. They also develop negative beliefs about classmates who tease them. For victims, greater negative beliefs about teasers resulted in higher levels of aggression by victims. Teasing can escalate into harassment and bullying, with violent outcomes well documented in the past several years in American schools (Troop-Gordon & Ladd, 2005).

Observe

- Observe yourself. Do not model teasing. Do not joke about things with which children are struggling because it shames a child. For example, it is not appropriate to say, "Caden is not an artist and we all know that!" if the third grader's drawings are primitive.
- Stay centered, calm, and objective. Focus on helping the teaser find a better way. Say to yourself, "I will stay centered. I will not be aggressive with this teaser."
- Systematically observe the child's teasing. Who, when, where, and why does he tease? What does he say?

Decide   Use your observations to identify the root(s) of the challenging behavior. Decide and explain which of the four major roots seem to apply in this case:

- **Developmental issue:** Some teasers are teased by other people. They are victims of teasing and are now just passing it on. They have not yet learned to take another person's perspective and do not really understand the impact of disrespectful language.
- **Child needs to learn a skill:** For example, the child needs to learn how to take another's perspective.
- **Child has an unmet need:** Some children have not gotten attention for their good qualities but get plenty of attention when they tease. A sense of control is part of positive self-esteem, but some children mistakenly construct this sense of control out of making others feel bad. All children need to feel accepted, and some teasers mistakenly believe that teasing is the route to peer acceptance.

- **The teacher needs to change something.** Do you need to change something in the classroom or yourself? Do you need to examine your reactions to teasing as well as whether you have set real limits about teasing?

Take action   Consider saying or doing some of the following (Committee on Injury, Violence, and Poison Prevention, 2009; Freedman, 2002; Townsend-Butterworth, 2009):

- Build a classroom community in which respect is the foundation (Kriete, 2003). "In our school, we have agreed to respect others. Teasing is disrespectful and is not allowed."
- Focus on how the teaser views control, who likely thinks that his or her personal power comes from teasing others. Help a teaser develop a sense of control in a way that does not include aggression. For example, if the teaser is a good runner, have her teach her skills to others. At the same time, set a limit prohibiting teasing while she is teaching.
- Teach perspective-taking skills to teasers. This general approach builds a basic cognitive developmental skill, necessary for acting and speaking with empathy.
- Teach victims of teasing good coping skills. See Figure 11.6.
- Involve the bystanders. Create a classroom and school culture in which teasing is *not* tolerated and where observers step in and tell a teaser to stop.

Reflect

- How did my decision help this child at this time?
- Was I centered, calm, kind, and objective while I carried out my decision?
- Do I need to repeat any of these steps? If your answer is yes, which would be most helpful?

FIGURE 11.6   **A nerf ball and a question: real help for victims of teasing**

Help victims of teasing develop real coping skills. Teach them effective techniques to use when teased. This will help them feel less helpless and that they can control their reactions—that teasers are not in control. Encourage bystanders to use these same techniques because teasers stop teasing when an onlooker steps in. Here are some suggestions:

- **Nerf Ball:** Teach child to visualize taunts as a "Nerf ball" that bounces off them. Teach them to say, "Whoa! A Nerf ball! Bounced right off me!"

- **Agree with the Facts:** One of the most effective ways to stop a teaser in his tracks. A teaser who says, "Hey, four-eyes" to a child wearing glasses, hears this from the victim, "Yes, I wear glasses." To the taunt, "You're so short," the victim replies, "You are correct, I am short." This is a disarming strategy. It literally takes away the teaser's ammunition.

- **Ask a Question:** Teach that one simple word, "So?" will also stop the teaser. It conveys indifference and takes the wind out of a teaser's sails.

- **Self-Talk:** Teach children to value their own opinion when the teaser fires away. Give permission to disregard the teaser's opinion. For example, "John is teasing again; I can handle it," or "I like my curly hair; John's opinion stinks."

- **Reframing:** Teach victims to take charge, avoid anger and frustration, and turn things around. For example, reframe the taunt, "Hey, freckles. Do those spots peel off?" The victim says, "You like to make observations" or "That's a great put-down." This type of response typically confuses the teaser who has to then stop and think. It works because the teaser gets no anger, no frustration, no anxiety from the victim—a far different response than she anticipates.

Source: Freedman, (2002); Poussaint, A. in Cosby (1997).

:: PERSISTENT BEHAVIOR CHALLENGES

Persistent behavior challenges

Behaviors that seem not to respond to normal positive child guidance strategies

By now, you have learned about many positive guidance strategies and you know the value of the decision-making model. Some children, however, continue to show challenging behaviors. Think of such actions as **persistent behavior challenges**. This can be puzzling and frustrating to teachers. It is especially perplexing when the classroom and curriculum are developmentally appropriate and when teachers use instructional strategies appropriate for young children. Persistent behavior challenges do not seem to respond to normally effective positive guidance. Here is an example from Mr. Sanchez's classroom.

> **EXAMPLE**   Seven-year-old Tim has been interrupting the teacher and the student teacher and it has been going on for about 6 weeks. This seems to be a change in behavior. He does this in spite of the teacher having done direct instruction of how to get attention appropriately and in spite of normal reminders. Tim interrupts the teacher so often that many reasonable people would conclude that it is challenging behavior. Mr. Sanchez is worried because he is afraid that this issue will damage his relationship with Tim.

Children with persistent behavior challenges often need additional, intensified support known as *positive behavior support (PBS)*. The information in this section relies on resources in the CSEFEL web site at the end of this chapter (Fox, no date; Fox & Duda, no date). PBS involves observation, making decisions, and developing a plan to support the child. I will illustrate this intense support using Tim as an example.

Mr. Sanchez met with Tim's parents and they discussed the need to help Tim. They decided to record examples of Tim's interruptions. Their goal was to get a bigger picture of the five "W" questions of his behavior, both at home and in school. For example, does Tim interrupt at home? If so, when, who does he interrupt, and where does this behavior take place? This would yield a better perspective on his behavior because of the additional information from home, not just from school alone. This type of observation involves more system parts than just school, a concept from systems theory discussed in Chapter 2. Figure 11.7 shows a portion of the parents' handwritten notes.

myeducationlab

Go to the Building Teaching Skills and Dispositions section of Topic 8: Challenging Behavior in the MyEducationLab for your course and complete the activity entitled *Skills for Dealing with Challenging Behavior*. This skill will help teachers make good decisions about how to deal with challenging behavior.

FIGURE 11.7	Tim's parents observe

March 2

- Tim interrupted Grandma when she cuddled Henry (new baby).
- Grandma was changing baby; Tim followed her into the room; asked her several times to come with him.
- Dad was putting the infant carrier into the car. Tim cried when Dad said that he would help Tim after he finished with the carrier.

March 3

- Dad was feeding the baby. Tim insisted that he needed Dad's help right away; had a full-blown tantrum.
- Dad, Tim, and the baby were in the kitchen; Dad was cooking dinner. When Dad spoke to the baby, Tim immediately chimed in, "Dad, look at my drawing!"

Then the teacher and parents met again and included the school psychologist. This meeting's purpose was to figure out, assess, Tim's purpose when he interrupted. They discovered some helpful information, such as his parents noticing that Tim had begun to interrupt after Grandma moved in to help with the newly adopted infant. Mr. Sanchez realized that Tim's persistent behavior challenge in school started at about the same time that his parents documented increased episodes of interruption at home. They realized that they stopped what they were doing when interrupted and talked to Tim, even if their purpose was to remind him *not* to interrupt.

Tim was definitely getting something by interrupting. The Adlerian approach described in Chapter 2 would say that Tim had a mistaken goal about how to get attention. He, like all humans, deserves attention and recognition, but many children make mistakes about how to get the attention that they need. They do things to get attention when it is inappropriate to do so, such as interrupting a teacher who is helping another child or a parent or grandparent who is taking care of a new baby. The team concluded that Tim was now interrupting in the mistaken belief that this was a good way to get attention. The adults also realized that they had been giving attention when Tim interrupted, thus reinforcing the behavior. Tim was also reinforcing the adults because his challenging behavior stopped after the adults paid attention to him. Thus, the team has done a *functional behavior analysis*.

After the team identified the purpose of Tim's behavior, they developed a *behavior support plan*. Figure 11.8 shows their plan, which includes three steps: making changes to prevent the challenging behavior, teaching or reteaching a new skill, and ensuring that the child shows the new skills. They reflected on the effectiveness of the plan in a subsequent team meeting.

myeducationlab

To check your comprehension on the content covered in Chapter 11, go to the Book Specific Resources in the MyEducationLab for your course, select your text, and complete the Study Plan. Here you will be able to take a chapter quiz, receive feedback on your answers, and then access review, practice, and enrichment activities to enhance your understanding of chapter content.

FIGURE 11.8 Behavior support plan

Part of Plan	What Happened	Why This Was Effective
Modify environment, curriculum, or interactions to *prevent* the challenging behavior	• Parents decided to change themselves and pay attention to Tim as they did before adopting the new baby. • Teacher planned on giving Tim individual attention every day, such as reading together.	Parents, busy with the new baby, simply forgot about how much a young child craves their attention and affirmation. The teacher, now aware of Tim's home situation, understands the child's need for contact.
Teach or reteach a skill	• Teacher revisited classroom rules, including how to get attention appropriately, with whole group. • Teacher reminded Tim on an individual basis when necessary.	Tim had learned the rule at the beginning of the year; reteaching is a good reminder for all the children.
Use strategies to ensure that the child uses the new skill instead of the challenging behavior	• Teacher used a "just one moment" signal when Tim interrupted. • Teacher said, "I'll be right with you. Hold on just a bit." • Teacher then ignored any more interrupting.	The signal for waiting for attention signals Tim that the teacher hears him but that he will need to wait. Tim will not get attention when he should not get it.

WORKING *with* **FAMILIES** **PARENTS NEED RESOURCES**

Parents have questions about challenging behavior just as a teacher does. Help parents get the information that they need to support their child. Here are some suggested resources for helping parents understand biting, disrespectful language, and teasing.

Biting

- Share the center or school's policy on dealing with biting.
- Give a good handout, such as the recently updated document available from the University of Missouri-Columbia, Extension Division (2009) at this site: http://missourifamilies.org/FEATURES/parentingarticles/parenting1.htm.

Disrespectful language (cursing and swearing)

- Again, let parents know the center or school's policy on cursing and swearing.

- Give some specific guidelines, either in a parent meeting, through links to resources, or in hard copies of documents.

Teasing

- Parents might find it useful to discuss this issue with other parents under the guidance of a professional, such as a child psychologist or guidance counselor.
- The relationship of teasing and bullying should be made clear, and parents need information on practical steps to take about this issue.
- Two good resources are Judy Freedman's book *Easing the Teasing*, which is available at http://www.easingtheteasing.com/book.html and a handout written by Beth Levy from the National Association of School Psychologists at http://www.nasponline.org/resources/handouts/revisedPDFs/namecalling.pdf.

SUMMARY

This chapter focused on challenging behavior in children. Some of the main ideas are the following:

- Whether a teacher sees a child's behavior as challenging depends on his or her perspective. We tend to label behavior as challenging when we think we cannot deal effectively with it.
- Challenging behaviors are the hot spots in classrooms, causing both child and teacher great concern. During hot spots, children feel anxious, angry, or afraid, and teachers often feel unpleasant emotions. Our goal is to minimize the hot spots and maximize the calm and cool times for children.

Challenging behavior has different roots, making dealing with it very complex. However teachers can begin to understand challenging behavior by discerning whether it came about because of:

- Developmental characteristics
- Unmet needs

- Lack of skills
- Factors in the classroom (contextual problems)

The decision-making model of child guidance can help teachers deal with a variety of normal, everyday guidance or discipline issues as well as challenging behavior. This model involves four steps:

- Observe
- Decide
- Take action
- Reflect

Use the decision-making model to deal with challenging behaviors such as biting, disrespectful language such as cursing and swearing, and teasing. Support children with *persistent* behavior challenges—behavior that does not respond to normal guidance strategies—with a more intensive level of support. Develop a positive behavior plan to support the child.

QUESTIONS FOR REFLECTION

1. Think about a classroom in which you have seen challenging behavior. Identify the behavior. Then reflect on how the challenging behavior affected this classroom: the teacher, the other children, and the child with the challenging behavior.
2. With another student in your class, discuss your analysis of the roots of Jessie's hot spot challenging behaviors in Figures 11.2 and 11.3. Did you all come to the same conclusions when responding to the questions about Jessie's behavior? If not, explain the other students' perspectives.
3. Biting, disrespectful language (including cursing and swearing), and teasing are all challenging behaviors. Have you observed any of these challenging behaviors firsthand? If so, describe how effectively the adult dealt with the behavior.

APPLY YOUR KNOWLEDGE

1. Jessie's story on the 35th day of the school year. The calm and cool times were slowly increasing. After examining Figure 11.1 and reading this chapter, name three factors that you think most likely account for more calm and cool times in Jessie's day.
2. Be prepared. Choose two or three challenging behaviors that you are likely to face in your classroom.

Search for reader-friendly, brief articles that you can use for your own reference and that you can hand out to parents. The articles should give accurate information about the roots of the challenging behavior and should give developmentally appropriate information for dealing with the behavior.

KEY TERMS

Calm and cool times (270)
Challenging behavior (268)
Contextual factors (275)
Decision-making model of child
  guidance (277)

Developmental characteristics (271)
Hot spots (268)
Persistent behavior challenges (284)
Reflection (276)
Skill deficit (274)

Teasing (282)
Unmet need (273)
Voice of challenging behavior (270)

WEB SITES

Center on the Social and Emotional Foundations for Early Learning (CSEFEL)
http://www.vanderbilt.edu/csefel

A federally funded, national resources center. Excellent resources to help children with challenging behavior.

Frank Porter Graham Child Development Institute, University of North Carolina at Chapel Hill
http://www.fpg.unc.edu/~ECERS

Read more about the environmental rating scales described in this chapter. Information is also available about training and conferences. The chapter described three of the four rating scales available from this site. The fourth rating scale is for family child-care centers.

PBS Parents
http://www.pbs.org/parents/inclusivecommunities/challenging_behavior.html

An excellent site in general. The link will take you to the site's information on challenging behavior.

Apply Your Knowledge of Child Guidance

Chapter 12 Apply Your Knowledge: Guiding Children during Routines and Transitions

This chapter gives you a chance to see that guiding children is an applied process. We use guidance throughout the day, such as in routines and transitions. In Chapter 12, we accentuate a teacher's role in supporting children during selected routines and transitions, including arrival and departure, large-group and small-group routines, as well as transitions. You will learn how to use both direct and indirect guidance during routines and transitions.

Chapter 13 Apply Your Knowledge: Use the Decision-Making Model of Child Guidance

In this last chapter, you come full circle: you will now *use* the decision-making model. This model advocates viewing discipline encounters merely as problems to be solved and argues for making active, conscious decisions about how to solve those problems. There are no quick fixes, no easy answers to some discipline encounters. By this point in the book, you should not be surprised to discover that there is no single right way to deal with any discipline encounter; there are many effective and positive approaches. You will get a chance to consider the eclectic approach, which draws from many theories and strategies.

Apply Your Knowledge
Guiding Children during Routines and Transitions

"Each child is different, and the way any one child reacts to transitions may be influenced by a variety of factors. Planning helps all children."

—DOWNS, BLAGOJEVIC, & LABAS (2006)

Chapter Contents

Guiding Questions

- Why is it important to plan my guidance for everyday routines and transitions?
- How can I use direct and indirect guidance to support children during routines?
- How can I use direct and indirect guidance to support children during transitions?

VIGNETTES

TODDLER: JOSEPH GOES HOME

Joseph, 2½ years old, spied his father at the classroom door and squealed with delight. His father said, "Hey, Joey. Let's get your things. Mom is waiting for us." Joseph retrieved a painting from his locker and showed it to his father, "Look, blue!" After putting on his coat, father and son waved good-bye to the teacher and headed out the door, Joseph holding his father's hand and Dad asking about the painting.

PRESCHOOL: PRESCHOOLERS LEARN ABOUT SMALL GROUP

Early in the school year, Mrs. Woodward sat with six children at a table. She was holding a magnet and passed it over a paper clip, picking up the metal item. "Hmm, what happened here?" (Discussion followed). Then she said as she stood up to retrieve six small baskets, "I have a basket here for each of you. I will hand it to you. Look inside and then you can work with the magnet. You should use things in your own basket but not from anybody else's." (The children worked and discussed magnets for about 5 minutes). Near the end of the activity, the teacher said, "It's time for outside, so put everything back into your basket." Then she gathered the baskets, sending each child to his or her cubby as he or she handed over the basket.

PRIMARY: TEACHERS GREET CHILDREN

The principal, the assistant principal, and an assistant teacher stood outside the arrival door at school as the buses pulled up. Different teachers took turns greeting children; the principal always greeted the children, unless she was ill or out of town. The drivers opened the doors of the buses, and the children scurried down the steps and toward the entry. The principal and teachers waved and spoke quietly to children, "Remember to walk." "Hi Dave. How is the new puppy doing?" "Good to see you, Theresa." Jake gave a high five to the principal, who said "Glad you're here, Jake. Have fun today." The children proceeded to their rooms, having been welcomed to a new day at school by adults who genuinely like and care about them. (Based on Freeman-Loftis, 2009)

:: INTRODUCTION

Teachers show respect for young children by using direct and indirect guidance throughout the day at school, for example, during routines and transitions. You studied direct guidance in Chapter 5 and you learned about each strategy, read how early childhood teachers used it, and practiced using each. You read how indirect guidance, that is, well-designed classrooms, curriculum, activities, and materials, support children's behavior. You had an opportunity to analyze a classroom's physical environment and materials, thus, using your knowledge about indirect guidance. With the two types of guidance, we give children the information and support that they need for cooperative, kind, and compassionate behavior.

Routine
(in a school or center), Part of a school day or a day in a center; the element occurs regularly, every day.

Because of their emerging but still immature physical, cognitive and language, social, and emotional development, children need help in constructing ideas about getting along with others. They need adult support to learn how to control their own behavior and emotions, for example, at different times during the school day. This chapter targets **routines** and transitions or scheduled elements in a school day that occur day after day (Malefant, 2006). We will emphasize a teacher's role in supporting children during selected routines and transitions, including arrival, departure, large group, and small groups as well as transitions. We will focus on three factors about each routine or transition:

What children need during the routine or transition.
How to support children with *indirect* guidance during the routine or transition.
How to support children with *direct* guidance during the routine or transition.

:: ARRIVAL AND DEPARTURE

Arrival
The start of the day at school when children enter the school grounds and their classroom.

Arrival is the beginning of a child's day at school. **Departure** is the time when a child finishes the day at school and goes home. Children go through these routines every day, and it is important that they understand how arrival and departure work. This understanding helps them to feel secure and sets the tone for the day or the tone for the afternoon and evening. A child first arrives at *school* and then arrives in his or her classroom. Arrival and departure are both very good times for building relationships with children. We can send warm and caring messages to children and their families by how we structure both routines.

Departure
The routine dealing with leave taking; children exit their classrooms and the school grounds.

How you structure arrival and departure depends on how children come to school. Some children, especially infants and toddlers and many preschool and kindergarten children, arrive or depart with one of their parents. Many children ride on buses. In some schools, children go directly to their classroom but in others, they go to a gym, cafeteria, or playground first. Then they go to classrooms with their whole class. Several different factors, therefore, affect decisions about structuring arrival. The same holds for departure.

What Children Need during Arrival and Departure

Recalling Maslow and Erikson's theories, we can help children meet their needs for security and help them develop trust, autonomy, or initiative during arrival and departure or any other routine. We can build a trusting relationship through these everyday occurrences (Zero to Three, 2009). We support children by taking their perspective and thinking about what they need during arrival and departure.

- **Steps in the routine.** Children need to know the arrival and departure routines, the order of events, and where thing are located. An example of an arrival routine is: hang up coat and backpack, go into room, sign in, greet my teacher, say hello to my friends, pick a center, and start to play and work. Knowing what to expect during arrival or departure directly contributes to a feeling of security.
- **Expectations.** Children need to know the teacher's expectations for behavior during the routines that begin and end the day. For example, the child needs the answers to the following questions: Can I go to another center after I am done in one area? Do I have to let everybody play who wants to play in a center where I am working? Can I ask for something that I need? Do I have to take everything that I have in my cubby home with me? When do I line up for the bus?
- **Acknowledgment.** For arrival, all children need to know that the teacher recognizes that they have arrived, that they exist. They need their teacher to greet them warmly, in a low-key way. They also need the opportunity at arrival to greet others. They need a soft introduction to the day, even if arrival is used for instruction. Each child needs to hear the teacher say good-bye to them at departure.

Indirect Guidance

Arrival: Soft Landings   The 10 kindergarten teachers in a very large elementary school had observed the negative effects of the school's mandated arrival process on their 5-year-olds. The children got off the buses and waited in the kindergarten gym, lined up in straight rows, sitting on the floor with their coats and backpacks. They waited until the principal made announcements over the loudspeaker. Then all the kindergarten children filed out of the gym and to their classrooms. By this time, there were usually many children crying, angry, or just plainly frustrated with the waiting.

The kindergarten teachers met with the principal and voiced their concerns. They proposed a new arrival strategy and called it *soft landings*, a good descriptor for their approach. The principal agreed to try the new approach for this age group, an approach in which children arrived by bus, not quite all at once, but within a 15-minute span. Therefore, the teachers needed a good way to get the children started on their day without having to wait for everyone. They also wanted arrival to benefit children and not waste their time.

In the new plan, children placed belongings in cubbies in the hall and came into the room. There, they found the learning centers set up for the day's activities. The teacher greeted children warmly, speaking quietly with each child, asking how he or she was. Then the children were free to go to a center of their choice. The teacher asked most children where they would like to start their day, thus giving support for decision making.

The teachers used indirect guidance by how they had set up the rooms for arrival. They also used indirect guidance by structuring the schedule to allow children to start their center time immediately after saying hello and checking in with the teacher. Children started on their learning activities and did not waste their time by having to wait for the other children.

This method was quite effective. The children seemed far less agitated. They also seemed to know and like the new routine, felt safe in making choices, and did not have to wait. They worked and played with others actively and enthusiastically. Even when children came to school upset about something, teachers reported that this arrival procedure gave them time with the adult so that they could deal with feelings as they started on their day. The atmosphere in all 10 classrooms was quiet and productive. By changing the arrival routine, the teachers had created a "respectful, supportive, and challenging learning environment," as recommended by the National Association of the Education of Young Children (2008).

Departure: A Calm Ending   Mr. Sanchez planned a brief large group just before the children went home. They reviewed the day and planned for the next day. Each child had prepared for departure before large group—gathering things needed for homework and for showing to parents, packing up backpacks, tidying up the classroom, and saying good-bye to the two classroom pets. Finally, they said a formal good-bye to another child. At morning meeting, each child greeted another child in the greeting section of the meeting. Mr. Sanchez liked the saying-good-bye ending to their day and the children seemed to like it, too. They were usually calm and reflective as they left for the bus.

Direct Guidance

The kindergarten teachers and Mr. Sanchez used several of the guidance strategies explained in this book (see the Appendix for an overview of the strategies). Here are three examples:

- **Limit setting:** Children knew the routines and the limits. The teacher had spent time teaching the arrival and departure routines at the beginning of the year. This included setting and then reminding children about limits until everyone knew them. One of the kindergarten teachers restated limits about placing all of their belongings in their cubbies for a couple of the children.
- **Calming techniques:** At departure, during their brief meeting, Mr. Sanchez taught and then led the children in a calming and focusing exercise, just before they said their formal good-bye to a friend. His goal was to help them make a psychological transition from their stimulating and busy day at school to the rest of their day at home.
- **Active listening:** One of the children was upset when she could not find the parent letter that she was supposed to take home. Mr. Sanchez identified the problem as belonging to the child (a concept from Rogerian theory, Chapter 2). Therefore, he used active listening to help her start the problem-solving process.

myeducationlab

Go to the Assignments and Activities section of Topic 7: Schedules and Routines in the MyEducationLab for your course and complete the activity entitled *Transitions Affect Children's Development and Behavior.* This strategy is a very effective way to help children learn self-control.

:: LARGE GROUP

Large group refers to gatherings or meetings of all children, along with the teacher, at one time. They participate in a learning experience, all at the same time. Some teachers or programs, such as High/Scope call this large-group circle time (HighScope, 2009) or simply circle time. The Responsive Classroom model uses the term a *morning meeting* (Kriete, 2002).

> **Large group**
> Time when all children and the teacher meet; used for a variety of educational purposes.

Teachers use large groups for many purposes, for example, reflection on how the day went, reading stories, instruction in content areas such as math or science, talking with a guest speaker, dance, drama, or music. Recent research demonstrated that children could learn social skills when teachers embed the skills in a group time (Macy & Bricker, 2007). Some teachers schedule large group for the same time every day. Other teachers might call a large-group meeting to discuss a current topic or problem in their class.

Children benefit greatly from well-managed large-group experiences. They learn academic content, forge friendships, and learn how to be a member of a group. They also practice listening and speaking in a relaxed and natural setting, two important literacy components. Therefore, it is important that teachers learn to manage large group so that it supports children's learning and development. Poorly managed large groups frustrate teachers, cause anxiety for children, inhibit learning, and often contribute to discipline and guidance problems.

What Children Need during Large Group

Put your perspective-taking ability to work when thinking about large group. As the teacher, you will have a goal for each group, and you are responsible for the tone and content of group time. Children will join in eagerly when they discover that gathering with everybody in class is an enjoyable experience. Think about your professional role in managing the large group. What do you need to do to help children participate well? They most often will not know about your goal for learning in any specific group until you tell them, but they will trust you as the leader. Use Vygotsky's theory as a guide to scaffold their understanding of the large-group experience. To participate fully in large group, children need specific knowledge about and skills in participating in large group.

- **Structure of large-group time.** Children need to know about the general organization of large group or flow of this routine. For example, what comes first, second, or third? How does large-group time start? Who talks first? Figure 12.1 shows the general structure for most large-group times. As with all routines, effective teachers actually teach children about large group at the beginning of the year.
- **Expectations.** Large group goes more smoothly when teachers help children understand expectations for this routine. Many groups fail because teachers forget to state expectations or do not state them clearly enough. Children feel much more secure about participating in large group once they understand the rules or limits.

FIGURE 12.1 **General structure for large groups**

Three Main Parts of a Large Group

Beginning

The starting point for the group.

Teacher gets group started as children arrive; do *not* wait until everyone is there.

The content varies with age group.

Use an attention-getting device such as a song, finger play, or poem.

Focus children's attention and then move smoothly into the main content.

Middle

The main content for the large-group time.

Varies, depending on children's needs, learning goals, and the content areas emphasized.

Children should be actively involved.

Directions to children should be clear.

Props make good additions.

End

The conclusion to the group time.

Two main purposes are to close the discussion on the topic and help children make a transition to their next activity.

Summarize content.

Do the transition to the next activity: send individuals or very small groups to their next activity.

Source: Based on *Developmentally Appropriate Curriculum*, 4th edition, by M. Kostelnik, A. Soderman, and A. Whiren. 2007, Upper Saddle River, NJ: Pearson Merrill Prentice Hall.

For example, teach about the signal for beginning a group. Teach children what to do when you give the signal. Teach about how to listen and respond, for example, to questions about a story. Teach large-group social skills, such as waiting for someone to finish speaking before asking a question or responding respectfully to another person's comment. Teach about the transition *out* of the large group. To do this effectively, think through any specific large group that you plan. Identify expectations that will support children's behavior during that particular meeting. You will discover that there are some limits common to all large groups. In addition, it is a very good idea to identify limits for new activities in large group, as Mrs. Woodward has done in the next example.

> **EXAMPLE**   Mrs. Woodward planned to teach a new song in large group, and it would require children to march in place and swing their arms. The children already knew about carpet squares signaling where to sit. For this new activity, the teacher decided to involve the children in thinking about a different limit for safety. After they were sitting, she said, "I have a new song for you, but you're going to have to move around. We are sitting close to each other. What can we do to make sure that everybody is safe?" The children decided that they should move their carpet squares farther apart.

- **Feedback.** Children need information on how they participate in large group. Observe carefully and acknowledge their effort and success in participating well. Mrs. Woodward said to the problem-solving 4-year-olds, "Good thinking. You have come up with a solution to the problem."

Indirect Guidance

Use indirect guidance by setting up well for large group. Be deliberate and intentional in how you set up for the group. Some of the most essential considerations include the following:

- **Content worthy of children's time.** Well-chosen content, presented engagingly, supports children's behavior. Group-time content should be worthy of children's time. Mind-numbing drilling and reciting of information is disrespectful to children and *not* worthy of their time. The Responsive Classroom's Morning Meeting is an excellent example of a large group worthy of children's time (Kriete, 2002). The morning meeting has four parts and teachers can weave math, science, social studies, literacy, and the arts into the meeting.
- **Time.** Think about disastrous large groups that you have observed. One of the most common problems in such meetings is that the teacher has too long a group time. Effective and developmentally appropriate large groups for early childhood should last only about 10 minutes, or even less for the youngest children (HighScope, 2009). The deciding factor, of course, is the age of the children.
- **Seating.** Decide on the best seating arrangement for each particular activity. Figure 12.2 shows several possible arrangements. Some questions to guide your thinking include the following: Will the children sit on the floor or in chairs? Do you need to be able to show an item to each child during the group time? Will some of the children come up to the front of the group? Are you reading a book that everyone should be able to see? Does a child need to be able to see the face of every other person in the group? Do the children need enough space for a movement activity?
- **Arrange seating ahead of time.** This indirect guidance strategy gives a clear signal to children about where to sit. Carpet squares arranged in a semicircle in the large-group area signal children to sit in the semicircle. Children easily figure out the teacher's intention for seating if the teacher arranges the carpet squares in a cluster. Position yourself on the children's level. Sit in a chair if they are sitting on a chair or sit on the floor with them.
- **Materials.** Have *all* materials prepared before large group. Decide where to place the items. This type of preparation allows teachers to concentrate on the activity itself and on assessing children, not gathering materials.

  EXAMPLE Mrs. Woodward needed three items for the large-group story— the book, a puppet, and a basket filled with laminated cards with children's names. She placed all items in a box and behind her chair. She brought them out after the children sat down and sang an introductory song. The puppet came out of the box first to introduce the story. Then the teacher put the puppet back into the box and took out the book. She used the laminated name cards in the closing of the large group. She showed a card and the children read the name. The child whose name was shown went to the next activity.

FIGURE 12.2 Different seating arrangements for large group

Cluster

Teacher

This arrangement works when children are supposed to stay in one spot during the group time. Children can sit farther apart if they will do any movement activities.

Semicircle

Teacher

Use semicircle seating with children facing the teacher.

Circle
Many teachers prefer using a circle for large group.

The teacher sits in the circle with the children. Morning meetings take place in a circle. Many teachers like to sit on the floor with the children.

Contrast her approach with that of another teacher, who set all the items on the floor in front of the children. He got upset when one of the children picked up the puppet during the story. Another child sifted through the cards, excitedly calling out names as he went. The teacher's frustration level increased as he kept telling children to put things down.

It is also important to practice ahead of time. Listen to and practice a new song, watch a DVD or video, practice reading a book. Mrs. Woodward, for instance, practiced a puppet play that she presented to the whole class. She discovered that she had difficulty with one of the puppets and decided to substitute another.

Direct Guidance

Guide directly by using appropriate limits. Reflect on the limits needed for the particular large-group activity. Determine what you need to say to children to support their positive participation.

> **EXAMPLE**   Mrs. Woodward reminded the children about a group-time limit. "Stay on your carpet square so that everybody can see the book."

Restate limits as needed, as one teacher did for Timothy when he scooted forward, blocking Serena's view. The teacher reminded Timothy, by saying, "Stay on your carpet square, Tim".

:: SMALL GROUP

A **small group** refers to a gathering or meeting of only part of the total class, usually up to about six children plus the teacher. All participants in a small group participate in the same learning experience. Small groups take about 10 to 15 minutes to complete. Teachers use small groups with preschoolers, kindergarten, or primary-grade children. Effective teachers use small groups to introduce children to concepts from any of the content areas (math, science, social studies, literacy, and the arts). Children tend to enjoy small groups because they work with other children in a relaxed learning environment and have a chance to socialize with others as they learn (Graves, 2007).

Small group
Time when a fraction of the entire class, about four to six children, meets with the teacher for a variety of educational experiences.

What Children Need during Small Group

Children need the same things during small group that they needed in large group. They should understand the general structure of small groups. They need to know what their teacher expects of them in terms of behavior, and they need feedback.

- **Structure of small-group time.** Children need to know that their small group meeting has a beginning, a middle, and an end. Effective teachers teach children how to navigate small groups at the beginning of the school year. Children need their teacher to be a guide and a facilitator for small group. For example, children need to know that small groups occur in different places, depending on the learning goals. The teacher supports this understanding by telling children about different possible locations for small groups, such as specific tables, the block area, or the science area.

- **Expectations.** Tell children clearly what you expect when they are in small group. One of the functions of this type of group meeting is to provide social interaction for a small number of children. Children need to know about and how to practice social skills for interacting with only a few other children along with the teacher, which is different from the level of large-group participation. Communicate expectations for respectful and polite communication.
- **Acknowledgment and feedback.** Observe children carefully as they participate in small group. Acknowledge and encourage their positive participation. For example, "You held down the paper for Jerry, Sarah, so that he could write his name. That was a helpful thing to do." If the group met in a new location, acknowledge the children's flexibility.

Indirect Guidance

Support children by arranging the small-group activity well. Pay attention to time, seating, location of the group, and materials.

- **Time.** As with large groups, small groups are much more effective if they are brief and engaging. Plan on about 10 to 15 minutes for small groups.
- **Seating.** Consider the specific small-group activity and decide whether children need chairs or whether the activity can be done while standing or sitting. In the chapter-opening preschool vignette, the children found six chairs at one table, indicating that they would be sitting. However, some of the children stood up, not using the chairs. Many of the examples of small group on the HighScope web site show teachers and children at tables, the children using chairs in some of the small groups and standing for others.
- **Location.** Consider where the best location in the classroom might be for specific small groups. Many teachers designate a table for group. For other groups, the floor might be better. Some small groups take place outside the classroom, for example, when children explore the school and yard.

    EXAMPLE Mr. Sanchez decided that the small-group math activity—sending small cars down a ramp, marking, and then graphing how far each went—would work best on the tile part of the floor.

    EXAMPLE The assistant teacher in the kindergarten classroom took a small group to the yard, where they sketched and took photographs of the flowers blooming next to the entryway.

- **Materials.** A major key to successful small groups is planning and preparing for the experience. One element of planning involves gathering *all* needed items. This helps teachers feel calmer about working with the small group. They are not running around gathering materials at the last moment.

    EXAMPLE Mr. Sanchez planned the math activity with racing cars for Tuesday and Wednesday. On Monday afternoon, he gathered everything that he needed: cars, ramp, sheets of paper for graphing, markers, and tape for hanging the graphs. He also placed his digital camera with the materials because he planned to document the activity with photos.

Direct Guidance

Use direct guidance to state expectations for behavior, such as limits on using only materials in one's own basket. After Mrs. Woodward noticed some of the children standing up as they worked with magnets, she said, "If it's easier for you to work standing up, you can just push you chair back a little." She wanted to give children the room that they needed, and she wanted to prevent tipping over chairs. The children readily complied with this simple suggestion. In the next example, the teacher sets and then gives sound reasons for limits.

> **EXAMPLE**   For the small group about racing cars and math, Mr. Sanchez said, "It's very important for our experiment that only one car at a time goes down the ramp. In addition, it is important to start every car at the exact same point on the ramp." Then he touched that starting point.

Choose specific direct guidance or discipline strategies based on the specific small group and the children's needs. For example, when two children squabbled over who was next at the ramp, Mr. Sanchez used the conflict resolution strategy.

:: TRANSITIONS

A **transition** refers to moving from one part of an activity to another or from one activity or part of the room to a different activity or location (Downs, Blagojevic, & Labas, 2006). Transitions are a necessary part of any early childhood program. Some examples of transitions include the following:

Changing from large group to the next activity.
Moving into large group.
Moving from small group back to center time.
Moving from one center to another.
Arriving at or departing from school.
Going from the classroom to work with a specialist.
Moving from the classroom to the gym, lunchroom, or playground.

It is good pedagogical practice to plan transitions. Well-planned and wisely used transitions are comforting to children, helping them understand how to end one activity and start another, not something that children automatically know how to do. Unplanned transitions create great stress for children.

What Children Need during Transitions

Transitions are not an end in themselves, but they are part of the day. Children need as few transitions as possible, they need teachers to plan the necessary transitions, and they need to have transitions contribute to their development and learning.

Transition
The process of shifting from one part of a school day to another or from one activity to another.

myeducationlab

Go to the Assignments and Activities section of Topic 7: Schedules and Routines in the MyEducationLab for your course and complete the activity entitled *Teachers Plan Routines and Schedules.* Note that children derive clear benefits when teachers plan transitions well.

- **As few transitions as possible.** A clear sign of a developmentally *in*appropriate classroom is an excessive number of transitions (Burts, Hart, Charlesworth, Fleege, Mosley, & Thomasson, 1992). While some are necessary, other transitions are *not*. Children need the teacher to reflect on the schedule, making sure that any transition is necessary. Teachers need to eliminate unnecessary transitions.

  EXAMPLE OF *UN*NECESSARY TRANSITIONS.   A kindergarten teacher rotated children in centers, ringing a bell after 10 minutes. The bell told children that it was time to move to a different center, whether they wanted to or not. During the one-hour center time, children experienced at least five transitions. Of course, there were numerous other transitions during the day at school. The teacher was puzzled about the amount of *disruptive behavior* (his term) during centers.

  EXAMPLE   A different kindergarten teacher had the same amount of time scheduled for centers. However, the children chose the centers in which they wanted to work and plan. They went to a different center when they wanted to (a transition). The teacher found that most children worked in about two centers each day.

myeducationlab

Go to the Assignments and Activities section of Topic 7: Schedules and Routines in the MyEducationLab for your course and complete the activity entitled *Schedules Affect Children's Behavior.* This strategy helps children learn to negotiate and cooperate.

The second classroom has a more developmentally appropriate approach to centers and certainly to transitions. Children have some choice and control over their activities as they learn. Having a healthy sense of control is a part of positive self-esteem. Children in this room also have enough time to work and play long enough to try ideas, work productively with others, and redo activities if necessary. They do *not* have to stop one activity, move to another, gear up for something completely different, and try to act interested. The only time that they have a transition during centers is when they choose another center.

- **Transitions that have been *planned*.** Thoughtful, reflective, and effective teachers think through every aspect of their teaching, including transitions. Children need teachers not only to identify necessary transitions, but then to plan them. Mr. Sanchez, for example, planned the general procedure for each major transition one time and then used that plan every time he used the transition. However, he often used a different song, chant, or game. The basic structure of the transition was the same, which the children found reassuring.

- **Transitions that contribute to development and learning.** Consider the amount of time given to transitions. Here is an example. A teacher uses 1 minute to move children from morning meeting (large group) to the next activity. This happens two times each day, for a total of over 6½ hours per school year moving from group to another activity. And this is only one transition. If you combine all the transitions in a school day, it quickly becomes apparent that they consume much time.

Transitions are not trivial. A teacher who manages time well and is committed to activities worthy of children's time strives to use children's transition time effectively. Children need transitions that contribute to their development and learning. Teachers can use transition time to help children meet state learning standards in the different content areas. Figure 12.3 shows several examples of using transitions to foster development and learning.

FIGURE 12.3	Transitions can benefit children's development and learning

Transition Idea	For each transition idea in the left column, state how this transition idea would benefit children's development or learning? (The first one is answered as an example)
Show cards, each with a different child's name. Children read the names and the child whose name is read can move to the next activity. Can also show two cards at one time.	Benefits language arts, specifically reading.
Everyone in the group marches in place. Chant, "March in place . . . 1, 2, 3, 4, 5. Stop. John and Sharon, please go to your cubbies." "March in place . . . ." Continue until every child has left. Change the movement at another group time for variety.	.
Show a list of children's names. Say, "If you have a(n) ___ in your name, you can (go to snack or whatever the next activity is).	
Taking slow breaths: Move a whole group or a small group by helping them focus on the next activity. "We are all going to walk down to the cafeteria. Let's focus. Take in some air through your nose. Breathe in s-l-o-w-l-y. Hold the breath. Now, let it out through your mouth."	
Roll a beach ball or other soft ball to a child in the group. That child goes to the next activity.	
Say, "If your birthday is in the month of ____ (name the month), you may ____ (get your coat or whatever comes next).	
Show a square of colored paper. Say, "If you are wearing ____ (blue, red, etc.), then you can go to snack."	
Sing a song (tune: This is what I can do). "If you're wearing red today, you can leave right now."	
Show a circle (chalkboard, computer screen, or other method). Say, "Everybody draw a circle in the air." When the children are finished, say, " John, Duvall, Jenny, and Sam can get ready for___." Repeat with other shapes until everyone leaves.	

Indirect Guidance

In the case of transitions, teachers use indirect guidance by using the least number of transitions possible, planning the necessary shifts in activity well, as you just read. Indirect guidance also includes having all materials for a transition ready before the teacher and the children need it.

myeducationlab

Go to the Building Teaching Skills and Dispositions section of Topic 7: Schedules and Routines in the MyEducationLab for your course and complete the activity entitled *Use Effective Transitions*. Note the many ways in which this teaching skill fosters children's development and learning.

EXAMPLE   Mrs. Woodward kept a wand that she used occasionally for transitions (for tapping the shoulder of the child who was supposed to move next with the wand) in the large-group area. She also keeps other transition items there—a basket of laminated name cards, a basket of colored squares of paper, and small alphabet cards.

Indirect guidance can also include giving children choices on occasion about which transition song or game to use.

Direct Guidance

There are several ways to use direct guidance during transitions. Think about direct guidance as teaching about the transitions and supporting children in participating cooperatively. Here are a few examples.

- **Set clear limits.** Be clear about the limits involved in transitions. For instance, if you use name cards as the transition aid, tell children that they can leave the group when they see their name. Remind those who forget.
- **Teach expected behavior.** For transitions, it is effective to teach about the general process of transitions during the first few days of school. Children like learning about how things work, including transitions, and they will feel more confident after learning the transition process. In Chapter 2, we saw that John Dewey advocated helping children learn that their individual actions affect others.

myeducationlab

To check your comprehension on the content covered in Chapter 12, go to the Book Specific Resources in the MyEducationLab for your course, select your text, and complete the Study Plan. Here you will be able to take a chapter quiz, receive feedback on your answers, and then access review, practice, and enrichment activities to enhance your understanding of chapter content.

  EXAMPLE   Mr. Sanchez taught the process for transition from playground back to the classroom, including placing soccer balls in the large basket. He led a brief discussion about why they should store the balls out of the way. One of the girls thought that others could have trouble finding the soccer balls if they were left to roll around the playground.

- **Give signals or cues for newly constructed ideas.** After children have learned about transitions, remind them about procedures with appropriate cues or signals.

  EXAMPLE   On the second day of school, *before* going out to the playground, Mr. Sanchez reviewed the transition rules and showed a drawing of soccer balls in the basket, the cue that he would use as a reminder.

ANALYZE A VIGNETTE

Refer to the chapter-opening vignettes to answer the following questions.

1. Toddler: How has the teacher supported Joseph and his parents with *indirect* guidance during the departure routine?

2. Preschool: Explain how the teacher has supported the children with both indirect and direct guidance.

3. Primary: Explain how this arrival routine supports children with *indirect* guidance.

SUMMARY

Routines and transitions are a necessary part of a school day. They are not an end in themselves, but they are part of the fabric of a child's day. They should have a real reason for existing. For all routines and transitions, even for the necessary and unavoidable ones, we should:

- Use children's time wisely.
- Reflect on how routines and transitions are done, changing them when we discover that they really do not benefit children.
- Keep in mind that routines and transitions are meant to support children's learning and development, not to waste children's time and *not* to be used as filler time.

We support children during routines and transitions by:

- Using children's needs as the foundation for developing each routine or transition.
- Having as few transitions as possible.
- Making sure that each necessary transition benefits children's development and learning.
- Planning routines and transitions.
- Supporting children during routines and transitions with direct and indirect guidance.

QUESTIONS FOR REFLECTION

1. Mr. Sanchez has a good relationship with the children in his class. Explain why this will support the children's behavior during any routine or transition.
2. You are a first-grade teacher. One of the parents, arriving for a brief before-school meeting, notices that you are placing items for large group next to your spot on the carpet and that you have materials for small-group guided reading all set up. In addi-

tion, he spots items, arranged and ready for the children, in the writing center. Other centers are prepared, too. He asks, "Do you do this *every* day—the organization?" When you say, "Yes, *every* day," he asks, "Why?" Explain how your method of preparing for the day is a form of guidance and how it supports children.

APPLY YOUR KNOWLEDGE

1. Hand washing is an essential routine and is part of other routines. Explain how you would use *indirect* guidance to support children's learning about hand washing.
2. Explain how you would use *direct* guidance during the hand-washing routine. Use Chapter 4 and the

Appendix as references. To get you started, how would you use the direct guidance strategy of setting limits to support children?

KEY TERMS

Arrival (*292*)
Departure (*292*)

Large group (*295*)
Routine (*292*)

Small group (*299*)
Transition (*301*)

WEB SITES

Zero to Three

http://www.zerotothree.org

A nonprofit organization based at Harvard, Zero to Three focuses on the well-being of infants and toddlers. Reliable and accurate information and excellent resources.

New Horizon Montessori School

http://home.earthlink.net/~aletaledendecker/
newhorizonmontessorischool/id9.html

This is a school based on the theory of Maria Montessori; the web site shows the schedule for the school day. Each segment of the schedule details how teachers support children in the routines and transitions inherent in the program.

'*The teacher must orient his work not on yesterday's development in the child but on tomorrow's*'
—Lev Vygotsky (1987)

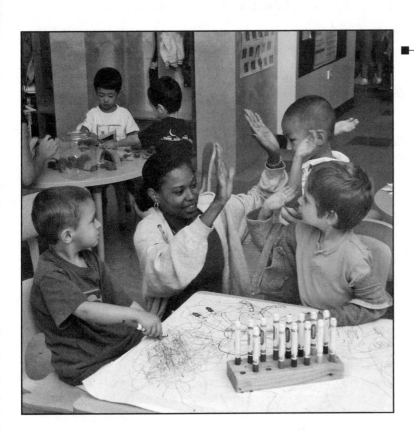

Guiding Questions

- What is the decision-making model, and what are its building blocks?
- Why is it a good idea to adopt an eclectic approach to guiding children?
- What are the benefits of using the decision-making model for both adults and children?
- How can I use the decision-making model to write a guidance plan intended to support a child?

VIGNETTE

WHAT SHOULD WE DO ABOUT THE CURSING?

Mr. Sanchez is Jake's first-grade teacher as well as the cooperating teacher for student teachers Anne and Tony. The teachers are discussing the day's events.

Mr. Sanchez said, "Okay, you've both noticed that Jake curses."

"I suggest time-out," responded Anne.

"His father curses, too. I've heard it. Like father, like son!" added Tony.

"Could be, but let's avoid blaming," said Mr. Sanchez. "This is only a problem, so let's do some decision making. Jake is 6 years old and to him, !*!#! is just another word that he has heard. All I want is for Jake to know that there are different words that he can use in school to express his feelings. So I want you to think about who really has a problem here—Jake or us?"

"Jake, of course!" sputtered Anne.

"Think about that, Anne. What would the P.E.T. [parent effectiveness training] people say?" asked the teacher.

"Let me think," said Anne. Oh, yeah. Figure out who owns the problem. They would probably say that I'm the one with the problem because I get upset when he curses."

Mr. Sanchez. "Probably. So let's help Jake find a different way to say what he feels." He gave each student teacher a list of guidance strategies. "Let's review some guidance strategies," he said. "Do you think we've made it clear that cursing is not permitted here?"

"We've never really talked about it at all," responded Tony, "and we probably need to state a limit about cursing."

"You might be right. Does that sound okay to you, Anne?" responded Mr. Sanchez. She nods. "Okay, limit setting is our first item. Now, what do you think Jake gets from us when he curses?"

"Our attention!" said Anne. "We all laugh."

Mr. Sanchez said, "Attention for inappropriate behavior. What can we do instead?"

Anne looks over the list. "Use substitution; let's give him a different word to use as a substitute and then encourage him for using the new word."

"Good. Substitution *and* encouragement *is item number two in the plan. What if he forgets or even tests our limit and substitution?" asked Mr. Sanchez.*

"Sounds like you don't want to use time-out," said Tony.

"Right," said Mr. Sanchez. "I just don't like using punishment, and anyway, limit setting and noticing the more acceptable word will work in the long run."

Anne said, "I think that we should all just stick to the limit and the substitution and not get all upset if he forgets or tests."

Mr. Sanchez responded, "I agree. We should change ourselves a bit. Item number three in our guidance plan is to be calm and restate substitution. *Let's stop with three ideas and review the plan that we've made."*

Set limits.
Use substitution.
Calmly restate the limits and substitution, if needed.

"We'll evaluate it in two days at the next staff meeting. I like how we made this decision."

:: INTRODUCTION

Tony, Anne, and Mr. Sanchez faced a typical guidance or discipline encounter and solved it by making deliberate and intentional decisions. Notice that they thought things through carefully. You learned about this in the decision-making model in Chapter 11. You will apply your knowledge in this chapter by systematically using the four steps of the model.

This chapter will give you an opportunity to practice making decisions just as Tony and Anne have done with support from Mr. Sanchez, who has scaffolded their learning about child guidance decisions. We will review the decision-making process briefly. Then, we will focus on *using* decision making for four different categories of guidance problems.

:: DECISION-MAKING MODEL OF CHILD GUIDANCE

The **decision-making model of child guidance** is a process. We use it to construct decisions about how to handle a variety of guidance issues with children. This model focuses exclusively on arriving at a developmentally appropriate solution in a logical and clearheaded way. You will avoid being caught up in emotion when faced with a discipline encounter.

Decision-making model of child guidance
Four-step process for making choices about dealing with many different types of guidance issues

Knowledge, Skills, and Respect: The Basis of the Decision-Making Model

Making good decisions about discipline or guidance is more than just common sense. Making good decisions about guidance is not something that people do automatically. Early childhood professionals realize that they have to learn how to make good decisions about guidance, to learn and practice the strategies. Those who use the decision-making model successfully:

Possess a specific knowledge base about guidance.
Have specific child guidance skills.
Respect all children and all families.

Knowledge base about guidance   A good knowledge base about guidance helps adults use the decision-making model effectively. The most essential knowledge needed is information about how children develop. Understanding what children are like at different ages helps teachers clarify their expectations of children. Adults also need information about how a child's family and culture affect her development and behavior.

EXAMPLES

Is it reasonable to expect a 6-month-old infant to stop crying just because someone tells him to stop?

How empathic can you expect an abused toddler to be?

How difficult is it for 3-year-old children to wait in line for the next activity?

How likely is it that a 4-year-old whose dad curses will say the same words?

What effect might witnessing a drive-by shooting have on a 6-year-old?

Are kindergarten children able to understand emotions well enough to manage them responsibly on their own?

Are third-grade children able to understand emotions well enough to manage them responsibly on their own?

Will an aggressive preschool child outgrow her aggression by the time he is 6 or 7 years old?

How likely is it that an 8-year-old child whose parents are permissive will willingly follow classroom rules and limits?

A person who can answer these and other similar developmental questions possesses one of the key elements in using the decision-making model, a knowledge base.

Skills   A professional who uses the decision-making model effectively also possesses specific child guidance skills. He can use any one of a variety of developmentally appropriate child guidance strategies (the same ones presented in several chapters and the Appendix in this text). He has the skills to manage the layout of the classroom well and to manage the schedule, curriculum, activities, and materials. He understands current special topics in child guidance, such as self-esteem, bullying, or stress, and has the skills to help children deal with these issues.

Respect for children and families Professionals who have a deep-rooted respect for children and families are most likely to use the decision-making model well. A person who does not respect children and families and is not culturally competent will have a great deal of difficulty with child guidance.

Professionals using the decision-making model competently understand that they, the adults, have greater responsibility in any interaction between them and children of any age to recognize signals that children of different ages send. For instance, a child who loudly interrupts would undoubtedly annoy many adults, but it is up to the adult to figure out whether this child needs social skill training, limit setting, and/or a different way of getting adult attention. The adult has to understand that it is her responsibility to ponder the problem and think it through. Here is an example from Mr. Sanchez's first-grade class.

> **EXAMPLE** Mr. Sanchez understands that Jake's cursing is an example of imitation but is also probably an attempt to be recognized. Irritating? Yes. However, the teacher understands that it is up to him to recognize Jake's attention seeking. He also knows that only he, the adult, can control how he responds to this discipline encounter. He knows that Jake plays a big part in this interaction, but he also knows that he, the adult, has the greatest share of responsibility for deciding how to handle the situation.

Decision making requires a great deal of active involvement. For example, Mr. Sanchez made an active, conscious, responsible choice about how best to help Jake. He did not just use the first strategy that popped into his head. He did not have an automatic reaction; he had to work at finding a solution. He deliberately walked the student teachers through the systematic process of choosing a strategy. He has encouraged them to recognize their responsibility for choosing the adult behavior most likely to help Jake at this time, that is, to choose individually appropriate strategies. Choosing adult behavior also means consciously rejecting certain strategies that do not fit one's personal philosophy of guidance, as Mr. Sanchez rejected the time-out strategy.

Eclectic—One Strategy Does Not Fit All

Teachers using an **eclectic approach** select what appears to be the best from several different methods and theories. Mr. Sanchez, Tony, and Anne reviewed many strategies before making their final decision. They chose the strategies that would be best for Jake at this time. They also changed their own practices. Tailoring a guidance plan to a specific child's needs is the hallmark of the eclectic approach to decision making. They avoided the one-strategy-fits-all model; they did not automatically put Jake in time-out when he cursed. Instead, they thought about what might be best for Jake. They actively rejected a punishment because there is a great potential for harm when using such an approach (see Figure 13.1).

Eclectic approach
Guiding children with the best ideas from different theories and strategies

Different Children, Different Families Call for an Eclectic Approach

This textbook is about working with real children in the real and complex world. Typical discipline encounters, such as cursing, are relatively easy to handle. We all face such encounters, regardless of where we teach. Examples include children who

FIGURE 13.1   An eclectic approach: what does it mean?

An eclectic approach does *not* mean "go with the flow" or "do whatever works."

An eclectic approach requires:

- Understanding different theoretical approaches, not just one.
- Adults to justify choices in a logical fashion and not defensively.
- Skill with many different guidance strategies.
- A willingness to change the setting or context.

An eclectic approach implies:

- That no single approach is appropriate for every child.
- A willingness to examine and change one's own practices.
- That children exist in several different systems (peer, family, school, community, culture).

The decision-making model can be used with children of different ages.

wiggle around during group time, children who do not clean up after themselves, or those who exclude somebody from a group. They also include children who grab items from others or who impulsively blurt out answers. It would be foolish to think that an adult could possibly prevent all discipline encounters. It is healthier and more productive to acknowledge that you will run up against many everyday discipline encounters and that you must work to deal with them.

Some children, unfortunately, live under conditions that make it difficult for them to learn appropriate behavior. They present teachers with discipline encounters that are tougher to deal with and challenge us as we guide them. They exhibit difficult or challenging behavior as described in Chapters 10 and 11. Examples include the following:

Children who are abused or neglected.

Children whose families move frequently.

Children whose families live in poverty—real poverty.

Children who liven in drug-infested areas.

Children whose neighborhoods ring with the noise of gunfire.

Children who live in permissive homes.

Children whose parents model anger, aggression, and lack of empathy.

Children whose parents are self-centered and ignore their children, in spite of having enough money and resources to care for them.

Children who have a diagnosable mental illness (only a qualified professional can diagnose this type of problem).

When you have your own classroom, you will be energized (exhausted on occasion!) by the often confusing, sometimes exasperating, wildly wonderful differences that make each child truly unique. You will meet a new group of individuals every year that you teach—children, yes, but individuals first. Children in your room will be living in the United States, most immersed in the U.S. culture and all exposed to it through the media. The children will have different ethnic backgrounds, and their race will have an impact on how they and their families have experienced life and how they view it. Consider just two examples. You might have a child in your class whose family has lived in the United States for three generations but who observes many of the customs of their Chinese heritage. Another child, born in the United States, might have an African father and a mother who is from Korea, the parents now both U.S. citizens.

Each child in your class has a unique family system. Every child, whether an infant or a 9-year-old, whatever his heritage, has a basic style or temperament and a rich personal history of interactions that have taught him how to exist in this large world. Children all come from different families, each with its own scripts and rules, its own communication style, its own cultural history, its own view of how children should behave, and its own style of discipline (Christian, 2006).

Some children have parents who feel secure, who understand children and children's needs. These parents know how to communicate legitimate rules and limits and how to help children live within limits. They know how to demonstrate their love and respect to their children.

Other children have parents who perhaps never felt cherished themselves and who cannot, as adults, meet their children's needs for nurturance and security. These parents do not understand how infants and children develop, how they express their anger, or how to take their children's perspective. They lack empathy for their children; they might well be irritable. Often, these parents have very poor and ineffective child guidance skills; for example, they do not know how to set limits effectively or how to help children accept limits. These parents do not know how to demonstrate the love that they feel for their children.

Authoritative teachers realize that the children with whom they work truly are individuals, which is the best reason for adopting as flexible an approach to guiding children as possible. The decision-making model is an individualized, personal model that allows you to determine the course of action most beneficial for a specific child in specific circumstances. The decision-making model is eclectic—flexible—because it draws from many different ideas about children and guidance. The decision-making model provides the means for you to combine your knowledge and personal strengths to deal more effectively with issues facing individual children. You will be using the decision-making model in this chapter to deal with a variety of problems, including:

Everyday discipline encounters.
More difficult behavior and issues.
The need to change the context or setting in some way.
The need for a teacher to examine her own practices.

:: STEPS IN THE DECISION-MAKING MODEL

The decision-making model, as you saw in Chapter 11, has four major steps. The process starts with observation and proceeds to making a decision and then to acting. The process concludes with reflection. See Figure 13.2. Use the steps in the decision-making model to analyze the chapter-opening vignette.

| **FIGURE 13.2** | **Four steps in the decision-making model of child guidance** |

Observe

- **Observe the child's behavior.**
- **Focus on the encounter as a problem to be solved.**
  Clearly identify the problem. Decide whether the child or the adult "owns the problem." Focus on solving the problem, not on blaming the child.
- **Examine the "context" of the problem.**
  Ask how the child's age might be affecting her behavior. Ask how the child's family; culture; or the classroom physical environment, activities, or materials have contributed to the problem. The purpose is not to place blame but simply to get a better picture of the context or setting in which the behavior evolved.

Decide

Your observation will tell you what to change. For example, you might need to:

- **Choose a guidance strategy.**
  Use only developmentally appropriate strategies, not punishment. Consult the list of guidance strategies in the Appendix and in Chapter 5 as well as in the rest of the text. State why the chosen strategy is appropriate for this child at this time.
- **Change the context.**
  You might decide that you have to change the classroom physical environment or the time

schedule. You might decide that you should choose more developmentally appropriate activities or that materials need to be better organized.

- **Change your own practices.**
  You might decide that you should change something that you are doing. For instance, you might decide to talk with children about playground rules after you realize that you have never set the limits. Do you need to restate a limit? Do you need to lower your voice when talking to a child who has done something inappropriate? Do you need to ignore a child's arguing or sulking about a limit instead of getting angry and fighting with the child?

Take Action

- Carry out the guidance strategy, or
- make the contextual change, or
- change the practice that you want to change.

Reflect

Think about how things went after you made a change. Specify what went well. State why you think events turned out well. Are there some factors that you still need to change? Why? If you want to make another change, go through this four-step process again to refine your approach.

Note: Chapter 6 discusses observing children's behavior.

:: USING THE DECISION-MAKING MODEL IN EVERYDAY DISCIPLINE ENCOUNTERS

The purpose of the rest of this chapter is to help you pull together your knowledge from this textbook and use it to practice the decision-making model of child guidance. You will use the model to deal with the following:

Everyday discipline encounters.
More difficult behavior.
Contextual issues, matters related to the setting.
Situations in which teachers must change their own practices.

Outdoor Cleanup Time

This is an example of a normal, everyday discipline encounter. It is time for your kindergartners to go inside for story time, and you notice that Adam and Aziz have left the trucks on the path again instead of putting them in the spot designated for trucks. You and the staff have stated the limits clearly and positively. You have also easily accessible parking spots for the trucks. Adam's parents are permissive by choice and do not set limits. Aziz follows Adam's lead.

Use the steps in the decision-making model

1. Observe:
   a. What is the problem?
   b. Whose problem is it—Adam's, Aziz's, Adam's and Aziz's, or yours? Justify your response.
   c. Examine the context of the problem. What is it about Adam's background that is probably contributing heavily to this encounter? How does Aziz's personality contribute to the encounter?
2. Decide, and
3. Plan on Taking Action:
   In this case, the teachers do not have to change the context. They have set up the truck parking very well. They also do not have to change their own practices very much. This encounter calls for choosing a guidance strategy that will help both Adam and Aziz. Several guidance strategies will help you deal with this encounter effectively. Here are some ideas to get you started.
   a. You have effectively stated the limit. Explain why restating the limit is individually appropriate, especially for Adam, who has never had to follow limits, and for Aziz, who follows Adam's lead. Write the exact words you would use to restate the limit.
   b. Explain how you could use an I-message (Rogerian approach) to help Adam and Aziz understand your position. Write the I-message, including all three elements (see the Appendix).
   c. Explain how you can give helpful feedback to encourage the boys when they do cooperate. Write out the exact statements that you would use. Kohn (2001) makes a very good case when he gives five reasons to stop saying "Good job!" Try to avoid mindless praise as much as possible and, instead, express genuine appreciation for their effort.
   d. Explain how you would use scaffolding, from Vygotsky's theory, to help Adam and Aziz. Write a brief statement outlining your plan for scaffolding their understanding of the need to put items away.
   e. Explain why punishment, such as time or response cost, is not an appropriate choice in this case.
   f. Explain why ignoring this problem is also not appropriate in this case.
4. Reflect:
   a. Which strategy do you feel most comfortable using?
   b. From my perspective, the most effective strategy would be _____.
   c. I deliberately chose not to _____ (name the rejected strategy) because _____.

:: USING THE DECISION-MAKING MODEL WITH CHALLENGING BEHAVIOR

Smashing Pumpkins in a Primary Classroom

This is an example of how to use the decision-making model when you confront what you perceive as challenging behavior, a topic that you studied in Chapter 11. You are a third-grade teacher. Some of the class, including Kobe and Murphy, are working on a project about pumpkins, the interest having arisen after they read a newspaper story about a farmer growing a very large pumpkin.

Both Kobe and Murphy are famous for their temper outbursts, and you keep a close watch on them. They were working together writing a "newspaper story" about their decorated pumpkins when you heard them start to yell at each other. You were on your way to their workstation when Murphy picked up Kobe's pumpkin and slammed it to the floor, jumped on it, and smashed it to bits. Kobe responded by grabbing the pumpkin that Murphy had decorated.

You said firmly but quietly, "Put the pumpkin down, Kobe. Do it now."

Kobe glared at you and, saying nothing, threw the pumpkin at the wall, smashing it into a slimy mess.

This is an anger-management issue. Many people would consider this challenging and/or difficult behavior because of the aggressive throwing of the pumpkin and glaring at the teacher, seemingly defiantly.

Using the steps in the decision-making model

1. Observe:
   a. What is the problem?
   b. Whose problem is it: Kobe's, Murphy's, Kobe's and Murphy's, or yours?
   c. Examine the context of the problem. These are 8-year-old children whose families use harsh discipline and whose lives are chaotic. Kobe is a neglected child, and the human services department is working with his parents. You have been focusing on anger management with both boys, but they occasionally forget your lessons, like today.
2. Decide, and
3. Plan on Taking Action:
   In this case, you will need to decide two issues. One, how will you deal with your own anger about this incident? Second, which guidance strategies will enable you to help Kobe and Murphy with their anger?
   a. You will probably be angry, or at least surprised, immediately after this encounter. How will you get your emotions in check before dealing directly with Kobe and Murphy? State exactly what you would do for yourself.
   b. You realize that this a hot time, with anger flaring. It is not the time to preach or admonish. This is the time to talk with the boys, with teacher–child discourse, and to use scaffolding, both Vygotskian concepts. Before you start, decide whether you would separate the children before you talk to them. Why or why not?

   c. What will you say to each child? What will you say if one of them tries to deflect the topic by accusing the other boy? How will you get him to focus only on his own behavior and reaction to the situation?

   d. How do you think you might follow up this incident; for example, the next day, when the boys have both cooled down a bit? This might be a good time to carry out another anger-management activity by scaffolding. Describe at least two things that you can do.

   e. Why is it highly inappropriate to force the boys to apologize to each other?

   f. Why is it highly inappropriate to use punishment, such as time-out or taking away recess?

   g. Why is it also inappropriate to ignore this incident?

4. Reflect:
   a. Which strategy do you feel most comfortable using?
   b. From my perspective, the most effective strategy would be _____.
   c. I deliberately chose not to use _____ (name the rejected strategy) because _____.

:: USING THE DECISION-MAKING MODEL TO MAKE CONTEXTUAL CHANGES

A Preschool Classroom: Keep the Sand in the Pan, Please

You are the head teacher of a group of 4-year-olds. They are interested in writing, and you provide many materials for their use. Today, in addition to all the usual writing materials, you have placed two shallow cookie sheets (with half-inch sides) of dry sand on the table in the writing center. The table is in the carpeted area and the sand sinks into the carpet.

This was an appropriate activity, with almost all the children using the sand trays to print their names or to print other letters. Nevertheless, you are getting frustrated with having to restate the limit so often, reminding the children "Please keep the sand in the tray." The children unintentionally knocked sand out of the trays and onto the table and floor, which you have to vacuum.

Using the steps in the decision-making model

1. Observe:
   a. What is the problem?
   b. Whose problem is it: the children's or yours?
   c. Examine the context, the setting, of the problem. You see sand spilling out of the tray. How might a 4-year-old child's motor development affect how she uses and moves dry sand around in a large tray the size of a cookie sheet? How has your setup of this activity affected the amount of sand flipped out of the trays (trays with very low sides are on the table; the table is on the carpet).

2. Decide, and

3. Plan on Taking Action:

You have used a good guidance strategy already by stating and then restating the limit of "keeping sand in the pan." Therefore, the solution seems to lie elsewhere, meaning that you do not necessarily need to choose another guidance strategy. You could do so, of course, but there is a better solution.

Simply restating the limit, "Keep the sand in the tray, please," does not seem to be enough. Consider the benefits of changing something about the setting (the context) to be effective.

   a. You are using dry sand. How can you safely make the sand itself more stable and less prone to flying up and over the edge of the pan?

   b. You decide to continue with the dry sand, fully realizing that your 4-year-olds will probably continue flipping it out of the pans. Consider changing the situation by moving the table aside for a moment and placing a large sheet under the table. Then replace the table; gently flick any sand that spills to the center, under the table. At cleanup, gather the edges of the sheet and pick up the spilled sand. How do you think that this simple change in context would affect the situation?

   c. What else can you do about the pans themselves?

   d. Do you have to use the pans at all? Can you think of a different place or piece of equipment for this writing activity? What limits would you still need?

4. Reflect:

   a. Which strategy would you feel most comfortable using?

   b. The contextual change that I think would work best is _____.

   c. I do not think that _____ would be very effective. My reason is _____.

:: USING THE DECISION-MAKING MODEL TO CHANGE AN ADULT'S PRACTICES

Liam and the Math Workbook

In this scenario, a teacher needs to change her own practices. Liam is in kindergarten, and his teacher uses many developmentally inappropriate practices. For instance, she uses workbooks in three curriculum areas every day. She has set up the curriculum so that every child is doing the same workbook pages in a large group in each curriculum area. Today, for example, all the 5-year-olds are doing page 54 in the math workbook.

Liam dreads these workbook sessions. He sat at his rectangular table with six other children, his workbook and pencil in front of him.

"Alright, everybody! Turn to page 54," called out his teacher. She waited only briefly before issuing the next command. "Pick up those pencils and put your fingers on question 1."

Liam blinked but opened his workbook. He cautiously turned pages, all the while looking at the other children, most of whom had found the correct page. He said nothing but dipped his head a little lower.

"Liam," called the teacher. "Pick up that pencil and get to work!"

Liam picked up his pencil and stared at the page. He bit his lip, as he often did when under stress.

"Get to work right now, Liam!" The teacher seemed irritated.

Liam squeezed his pencil and looked desperately at the book belonging to the child next to him.

"Don't look at my book, Liam," whispered the child.

Liam turned his head back to his own, incorrect page. He sat still, gripping his pencil, a tear forming in the corner of his eye.

Use the steps in the decision-making model

1. Observe:
   a. What is the problem?
   b. Whose problem is it—Liam's, the teacher's, or both?
   c. Examine the context of the problem. How do you think that the teaching strategy causes Liam's confusion and distress? The teaching strategy consists of using workbooks, and the whole group sitting for direct instruction, all working on the same pages, for several hours each day.
2. Decide, and
3. Plan on Taking Action:
   In this case, the root of the problem is in her instructional style, which is utterly inappropriate and which has directly caused the problem. Liam has done nothing wrong. The teacher needs to change her own practices in order to help Liam.
   a. Describe this teacher's instructional style. For example, does she encourage active, hands-on learning or does she discourage it? Does she use large-group direct instruction? Does she use workbook pages for kindergarten children?
   b. State how you think that the teacher's method of talking with the children, especially how she issues commands, might be affecting Liam.
   c. What does this teacher need to change about her method of talking with the children?
4. Reflect:
   a. Earlier in this chapter, you read that adults who use the decision-making model of child guidance effectively have an abiding respect for children. What is your opinion of the teacher's degree of respect for her kindergartners? On what do you base your opinion?
   b. Suppose that this teacher goes to a workshop and learns about a more developmentally appropriate way of teaching children. On a scale of 1 to 10 ("1" means that she will not adopt better practices; "10" means that there is a very good chance she will change her style of instruction), how likely is it that she will adopt more appropriate practices because of attending such a workshop? State your reasons for your choice.

:: USING THE DECISION-MAKING MODEL TO CHANGE THE CONTEXT *AND* CHANGE THE TEACHER'S OWN PRACTICES

A Third-Grade Classroom: Joseph and Chloe Will Not "Sit Still" During the Last Large-Group Lesson

This example demonstrates that problems are complex and that we often need to change a couple of factors, not just one. The teacher in the following scenario needs to change both her own practices and the context in which her students work. She has mistakenly focused on punishing Joseph and Chloe instead of looking at other factors contributing to the problem.

A third-grade teacher was upset because she had ordered Joseph and Chloe to go to time-out yet again during her last large-group lesson before lunch. This problem occurs every morning. Here is the morning schedule for this third grade:

Opening group—30 minutes
Reading groups—30 minutes
Seatwork, workbook pages for different curriculum areas each day—30 minutes
Specialist (music, guidance counselor, art, or physical education)—40 minutes (always large group)
Large group—20 minutes (before playground time)—(the trouble spot for Joseph and Chloe)

Using the steps in the decision-making model

1. Observe:
   a. What is the problem?
   b. Whose problem is it: Joseph's and Chloe's, or the teacher's?
   c. Examine the context of the problem. How long are these third graders spending in group work every morning? Are the teacher's instructional methods (everything done as a total group, use of workbook pages for every curriculum area, strict division of curriculum into areas) developmentally appropriate? How do you think that all of this might affect Joseph and Chloe's ability to sit through yet another group lesson at the end of every morning?
2. Decide, and
3. Plan on Taking Action:
   This teacher needs to change her own practices. Time-out, a form of punishment, is an inappropriate strategy. Help her understand that her schedule and her instructional methods are the root of the problem. What would you say to her to make her aware of this problem? Remember to be forthright but kind when you tell her. Hearing this type of information often arouses anxiety. People get defensive if they feel attacked.
4. Reflect:
   a. If you could make only two changes in the schedule, what would they be?

b. Time-out—punishing Joseph and Chloe—was not an appropriate guidance strategy. It has backfired and actually had the opposite effect from what the teacher intended; it seems to have made things worse for Joseph, Chloe, and the teacher. How is this so?

:: DEVELOP GUIDANCE PLANS

You will use the decision-making method to develop a **guidance plan**, a written document. It is your roadmap for supporting children. Appropriate guidance plans based on clear thinking and good decision making empower you to deal effectively with a variety of guidance or discipline encounters—the typical as well as those that are more challenging. It is very helpful if you write your plan and file it in a child's personal file. You can then refer to the plan when reflecting on the child's progress and on any changes that you need to make in your classroom, curriculum, teaching strategies, or way of interacting with children.

Guidance plan
Written document based on the process that is part of the decision-making model; outlines how a teacher will support a child

Guidance plans grow out of the decision-making model's process. The plans are brief, and they distill all of your thinking during the process. You can do some good observation in the decision-making process. You can write your main findings in the guidance plan. If, for example, you found that your schedule was a bit too long, then you would say that. If you found that you were ignoring a child whose behavior irritated you, then you would record that.

After you observed the context, you can observe the child and figure out the purpose of her behavior. Record your main finding in the designated space. Figure 13.3a is an example of a blank guidance plan form. See Figure 13.3b for what Mr. Sanchez wrote in Jake's guidance plan—after they went through the decision-making process.

Next, you would decide, based on your observations, on supportive actions that you can take to support the child. Record your brief statement. Finally, think about how you will help the child continue using the appropriate behavior, and record your idea.

:: COMING FULL CIRCLE: WHAT THE DECISION-MAKING MODEL MEANS FOR CHILDREN

If you started reading this text with Chapter 1, you learned about different styles of caregiving. We will come full circle and end this book by stating what is very likely to happen if you do decide to adopt the authoritative style of caregiving. Authoritative parents and teachers believe that they must create a safe and secure emotional climate for children. They realize that they influence, but do not determine, a child's behavior. By using the decision-making model of child guidance, you will set the stage for many positive outcomes.

Using the decision-making model helps children:

Feel safe and secure.
Develop healthy self-esteem and a strong moral compass.

FIGURE 13.3a **Guidance plan format**

Guidance Plan

Date:
Child:
Behavior:

Observation: Observations revealed the following about the physical environment, curriculum, schedule, my teaching strategies, my interactions with the child or children:

Observation: Answering the five "W" questions about the child's behavior reveals that the purpose or function of his or her behavior seems to be:

What I need to do: Based on observations, the most significant things that I can do to support this child are:

Continuing to support the child: What do I need to do to continue to support the child after she or he learns a different way of behaving?

FIGURE 13.3b **Filled-out guidance plan for Jake**

Guidance Plan

Date: *September 20*
Child: *Jake*
Behavior: *Cursing*

Observation: Observations revealed the following about the physical environment, curriculum, schedule, my teaching strategies, my interactions with the child or children:
We laugh nearly every time Jake curses—we have reinforced this behavior.
Jake's father models cursing.

Observation: Answering the five "W" questions about the child's behavior reveals that the purpose or function of his or her behavior seems to be:
Jake's cursing is simply a part of Jake's way of talking and does not seem to be malicious; he seems to be simply imitating a model.
He now seeks our reaction.

What I need to do: Based on observations, the most significant things that I can do to support this child are:
Change our reaction to the cursing; stop laughing.
Set a limit about cursing.
Use 'substitution'.

Continuing to support the child: What do I need to do to continue to support the child after she or he learns a different way of behaving?
Do not laugh or react when/if Jake tries again to get attention with cursing.
Calmly restate the limit and substitution if needed.

PEARSON
myeducationlab

To check your
comprehension on the
content covered in
Chapter 13, go to the
Book Specific Resources in
the MyEducationLab for
your course, select your
text, and complete the
Study Plan. Here you will
be able to take a chapter
quiz, receive feedback on
your answers, and then
access review, practice,
and enrichment activities
to enhance your
understanding of chapter
content.

Honor and respect themselves and others.

Develop healthy self-control.

Learn how to deal with a variety of stressors.

Understand and deal effectively with a variety of feelings: anger, sadness, love, jealousy, etc.

Walk a mile in another person's shoes—or an animal's tracks—to be empathic.

Be cooperative, helpful, and generous.

Learn when to be assertive.

Become self-responsible.

Become compassionate and caring individuals.

ANALYZE A VIGNETTE: WHAT SHOULD WE DO ABOUT THE CURSING?

Use Figure 13.2, the steps in the decision-making model, to evaluate how Mr. Sanchez and the student teachers used the decision-making model of child guidance.

1. Describe how Mr. Sanchez, Tony, and Anne carried out each step. What leads you to think that they observed Jake's behavior? Identify evidence that they viewed the issue simply as a problem to be solved. Who did and who did not—at first? How and when did they examine the context of the problem?

2. Explain what the group decided to do to help Jake. They chose specific guidance strategies. Did they also decide to change the context? If they did, how were they going to do this? Did they decide to change their own practices? If they did, explain. When did they plan to take action and reflect on their decisions?

3. Name one or two things that you might have done differently. From your perspective, how likely is it that the teachers will deal effectively with this typical discipline encounter? State the reasons for your view.

SUMMARY

We can use the decision-making model of child guidance to get information and to make deliberate decisions aimed at supporting children. This model gives teachers an eclectic approach for supporting children The building blocks of this process include the following:

- A knowledge base about guidance.
- Specific child guidance skills.
- Respect for families and children.

The four steps in the decision-making model include observe, decide, take action, and reflect. We can use this process for a variety of guidance or discipline encounters, including:

- Everyday discipline encounters.
- More difficult behavior.
- Contextual issues, matters related to the setting.
- Situations in which teachers must change their own practices.

After using the decision-making process, a teacher develops a written guidance plan, a guide for supporting the child. This plan is a logical outgrowth of the decision-making process.

QUESTIONS FOR REFLECTION

1. Suppose that a new teacher has a lot of respect for children and families. He has studied child development and has a good knowledge base. His major deficit is in child guidance skills; he knows no strategies other than time-out. What are the chances of this new teacher using the decision-making model well? Explain your response.

2. You have learned about many positive child guidance strategies in this textbook. Suppose that somebody says to you, "Why do you need to know so many ways of dealing with discipline issues?" How would you answer that person?

APPLY YOUR KNOWLEDGE

Self-Test: Create a Guidance Plan

Use Figure 13.2 to write a guidance plan for at least three of the following discipline encounters. Go through the steps, just as you did for the discipline encounters that you practiced in this chapter.

- An abused toddler bites other children.
- Five-year-olds in a multiple-age group get younger children to do inappropriate things, such as swearing or throwing objects.
- Third graders push and shove each other while waiting in line for the school bus. They have been waiting for 20 minutes.

- Three- to 5-year-olds push other children while changing activities, such as going outdoors.
- A 4-year-old spits at other people.
- A 4-year-old comes from a family that consistently uses physical discipline such as hitting and pinching. This same 4-year-old hits the teacher when the teacher tries to use even a positive strategy such as restating a limit.
- A 7-year-old tattles several times each day.
- Third graders deface library books.

KEY TERMS

Decision-making model of child guidance (*309*)

Eclectic approach (*311*)

Guidance plan (*321*)

WEB SITES

National Association for the Education of Young Children
http://www.naeyc.org

This is the main page for this professional organization. Look through the electronic catalogue for resources on guidance in general as well as on specific aspects of guidance.

Scientific American
http://www.scientificamerican.com

Organization devoted to publishing information about science. Here is an article about the effect of making tough decisions on your brain:
http://www.scientificamerican.com/article.cfm?id=tough-choices-how-making

Appendix

Review: Major Positive Discipline Strategies

This Appendix reviews the major positive discipline strategies described in this text. First, you will read a list of the major strategies. Then each strategy is presented in outline form, along with suggestions of points to remember and to avoid when using the strategy.

Every strategy outlined here is described in more detail in other chapters, mainly Chapters 5 and 13.

LIST OF MAJOR STRATEGIES

1. Help children save face and preserve their dignity.
2. Set limits well.
3. Teach more helpful behavior.
4. Set up practice sessions and give on-the-spot guidance.
5. Give signals or cues for newly constructed behavior.
6. Change something about a context or setting.
7. Identify problem ownership.
8. Give meaningful feedback to children.
9. Identify mistaken goals and use encouragement.
10. Ignore behavior (only when it is appropriate to do so).
11. Redirect very young children: Divert and distract.
12. Redirect older children: Use substitution.
13. Listen actively.
14. Deliver I-messages.
15. Teach conflict resolution (problem solving).
16. Recognize signs of stress, anxiety, or strong emotion; prevent overstimulation; teach calming techniques.
17. Manage strong emotions responsibly.

1. Help Children Save Face and Preserve Their Dignity

Purpose of the strategy: To treat children respectfully no matter what positive strategy is used. Children are likely to feel embarrassed in spite of well-done positive guidance.

How can adults do this?

- Show respect for children by taking their perspective. Think about how you would want somebody to handle matters if they had just told you to calm down or that you had done something wrong.
- Once you are finished with the positive discipline strategy, let the episode fade into the past and allow the child to move on. Avoid the urge to keep explaining.
- Do not flaunt your power. Avoid saying "I told you so."
- End the interaction quickly, simply, and gracefully. Quietly tell the child, especially if you've helped her calm down, "Let's go back and play now."
- Help the child deal with the root of the upset. Some children might be ready to talk about an emotion-arousing incident, but others need to wait before discussing it. Either way, schedule a time for talking about the original problem with the child. Do what is developmentally appropriate for this child at this time.

2. Set Limits Well

Purposes of the strategy: State expectations for desired behavior. Clarify boundaries or limits.

Appropriate limits: Never arbitrary, limits focus on important matters and are developmentally appropriate.

Points to remember about stating limits:

- Involve children in developing some limits in a classroom or other setting.
- Tune in, help children focus on the task, and give good cues.
- Speak naturally but slowly enough so that a child hears the limit clearly.
- Use concrete words and short, natural, and normal sentences. For example, "It's time to put the teacups away."
- Tell a child exactly what to do, for example, "Take small bites of your bread."
- Be as positive as possible.
- Give choices when appropriate.
- Give short, clear, fair reasons for limits.
- Issue only one or two suggestions at a time.
- Give children enough time to carry out the limit or to complete something else before they carry out the limit.
- Restate limits appropriately. Restate limits when it is necessary to do so.

Avoid the following when stating limits:

- Avoid giving choices when children really do not have a choice. For example, "Do you want to go to the library?" when the whole class goes to the library.
- Avoid giving a chain of limits.
- Avoid using cute reasons. For example, avoid saying, "I think that the teacups want to be put away now." This makes a teacher sound silly.
- Avoid telling children only what not to do. For example, "Don't take such big bites of your bread!"
- Avoid vague limits. For example, "I'm not sure you should be doing that."
- Avoid stating arbitrary or trivial limits.

- Avoid arguing or playing the "why game" about limits.
- Avoid complex or excessive reasoning about limits.

3. Teach More Helpful Behavior

Purposes of the strategy: Teach helpful behaviors. For example, using words to express anger. Adults must pinpoint the more helpful behavior.

Method used: Several methods can be used. With young children, modeling is effective (demonstrating desired behavior, such as hand-washing and table manners; social skills, such as introducing oneself; using words instead of hitting to express anger.

Steps in teaching more helpful behavior:

- Observe the child to figure out what it is that he needs to know.
- Identify the behavior causing problems for the child, for example whining.
- Identify a skill that would be more helpful for the child , for example, asking for items in a normal voice.
- Model more appropriate behavior, for example, model a normal voice for the child.

4. Set Up Practice Sessions and Give On-the-Spot Guidance

Purpose of the strategy: To give the child a chance to practice a newly learned skill with expert guidance (from the adult or from a more skilled child).

How to do this:

- Teach the new skill first, for example, using a normal voice instead of whining.
- Practice the skill with the child. Do this privately if he has just learned the skill, for example, let him ask you for something in a normal voice.
- Give appropriate feedback. For example, tell the child that he seems to know how to use a normal voice when asking for something, or give him hints on how to demonstrate the skill if he makes mistakes in practice.
- Observe the child as he works with other children. Be ready to give on-the-spot guidance if it is needed. For example, Jessie starts to whine when he wants to paint and you step in to say, "Remember, Jessie, use your normal voice for asking."

These reminders from you, the expert, are essential in helping a child strengthen a newly learned skill.

5. Give Signals or Cues for Newly Constructed Behavior

Purpose of the strategy: To help children remember to use the appropriate behavior, part of effective on-the-spot guidance.

Steps in giving signals or cues:

- Identify the skill for which you will use a signal or cue, for example asking for something in a normal voice.
- Figure out what would be a logical signal such as a quiet verbal reminder. For example, "Normal voice, please," or a hand signal.
- Observe the child to discover when the appropriate skill should be used, for example, asking to join other children.
- Whenever possible, give the signal just before the new behavior should occur and not after the child has forgotten, for example, just before the child asks for something.

6. Change Something about a Context or Setting

Purpose of the strategy: Figure out what you can do about a situation that will help a child be safe or to enable the child to use a more helpful behavior.

Ways to change something about a situation:

- Change the physical environment or time schedule.
- Increase options available to a child: prevent predictable problems, introduce new ideas, introduce new materials.
- Decrease options available to a child: limit choices, change activities.

7. Identify Problem Ownership

Purpose of the strategy: Determine whether an adult or a child has a problem so that appropriate follow-up can be used.

- When an adult owns a problem: Use strategies focusing on self-responsible, nonaccusatory skills, such as, I-messages, restating reasonable limits.
- When a child owns a problem: The child's needs are the ones thwarted. Use active listening.

8. Give Meaningful Feedback to Children

Purpose of the strategy: Give the child helpful information. Feedback is critical to constructing skills and competencies. Good feedback can also help children make changes.

Suggestions for giving meaningful feedback:

- Avoid empty praise as feedback. Phrases such as "Good job!" are empty praise.
- Give positive feedback and suggestions for change when appropriate.
- Give positive unconditional feedback, positive information independent of anything the child has done. One example, "I like being your coach."
- Express appreciation, meaningful positive feedback directly related to a child's effort or interest. For example, "You remembered to use words to tell Rachel that you wanted a turn," or "Tom, Larry, and Rob designed the cover for the class photo album."

- Give feedback that helps children construct more helpful skills. Use your expert knowledge and skills to give information so that a child can make a better choice about how to do something. For example, "Lauren got real angry when you hit her. Let's figure out how to use words to tell Lauren that you were upset with what she did to you."

9. Identify Mistaken Goals and Use Encouragement

Purposes of the strategy: Identify a child's faulty perception of how to fit into a group. Be aware of what a child does to accomplish a mistaken goal (seeks undue attention, power, or revenge, or demonstrates inadequacy. Explain how an adult usually feels and reacts. Outline a better way to deal with a child who has any of the four mistaken goals.

Steps in changing how you react to demands for undue attention:

- Ignore the impulse to give in to the attention-seeking behavior.
- Acknowledge the child's request, but let her know that she can complete the task. Leave the area, if necessary, so that she can finish the job.
- Give the child attention at times when her behavior is more appropriate.
- Encourage a child to take the perspective of others by telling her about their perspective and by helping her learn to cooperate.

Steps in changing how you react to a child who seeks power:

- Resist the impulse to fight back.
- Decide to respond differently. (You do not have to be drawn into a power struggle. You can choose to respond differently.)
- Decline the child's invitation to argue or fight. This will surprise a child, particularly if you have previously been locked in power struggles with her. A useful technique is to label the interaction as a power struggle.

Steps in changing how you react to a child who seeks revenge:

- Resist the impulse to retaliate or give sermons.
- Focus on helping this child change her view of herself from a person who she thinks is not valued to the view that she is a good, worthwhile person. The goal is to encourage development of self-esteem, the missing ingredient.

Steps in changing how you react to a child who demonstrates inadequacy:

- Focus on what a normal child of this age should be able to do. For instance, should a 3-year-old be able to put on her own coat?
- Refrain from performing the age-appropriate task for her.
- Encourage a child who mistakenly believes she has to act like she is incompetent demonstrate how she can do it, encourage her to try.

10. Ignore Behavior (Only When It Is Appropriate to Do So)

Purpose of the strategy: To change the adult's behavior, that is, to change the way that an adult reacts to a child; to help the adult stop paying attention to a child's unhelpful behavior.

Do not ignore certain behaviors. I usually like to state things in a positive way, but I find that saying "Do not . . ." seems to be appropriate for this issue.

- Do not ignore behavior that endangers anyone, including the child himself.
- Do not ignore behavior that damages or destroys property or that could potentially damage or destroy property.
- Do not ignore rude, embarrassing, intrusive, or unduly disruptive behavior.

Guidelines for ignoring behavior:

- Pinpoint the behavior to which you have been giving inappropriate attention.
- Explain briefly to the child that you will stop paying attention to the behavior.
- Be prepared. You have paid attention in the past to the behavior and it will be difficult to stop giving attention. A child will likely try even harder to get you to pay attention to the same behavior, so be prepared for a "bigger and better whine" before it decreases.
- Decide to thoroughly ignore the behavior—don't mutter to yourself under your breath; don't make eye contact; don't communicate with the child verbally or with gestures.
- Teach and encourage a more helpful skill along with the ignore strategy.

11. Redirect Very Young Children: Divert and Distract

Purpose of the strategy: To distract a very young child from a forbidden or dangerous activity and then to divert her to a different activity.

Factors to keep in mind:

- Responsible caregivers understand that they must perform most of an infant's or a young toddler's ego functions, such as, remembering to keep an infant away from outlets because she does not understand the danger.
- Avoid a power struggle when stopping dangerous behavior.
- Be prepared to act quickly when working with infants and toddlers. This requires constant supervision and observation, even in a baby-proofed area.

Steps in using diversion and distraction:

- Identify for yourself what you do not want a baby or toddler to do because the activity is dangerous. An example is playing with an electrical outlet, even if it is covered. We do not want children to do this because it is dangerous.
- Immediately do something to distract an infant or toddler from the forbidden activity, for example, roll a ball to Sari the instant you see her near the outlet.
- Decide whether to tell an infant or toddler not to do whatever it is that is dangerous, for example, "No playing with the outlet, Sari."

12. Redirect Older Children: Use Substitution

Purpose of the strategy: Form of redirection in which an adult shows a somewhat older child (over age 2½ to 3) how to perform the same activity or type of activity but in a more acceptable and safer way.

Steps in using substitutions:

- Specify the activity needing a substitution. For example, while outdoors, zigzagging through the sandbox when others are playing there.
- Develop a substitution: a similar activity or the same activity done more safely, for instance, zigzagging through a set of tires laid flat on the ground.
- Present the substitution to the child. For example, "Looks like you want to do an obstacle course, but please do not zigzag in the sandbox. Try zigzagging through these tires."
- Be prepared for the child to test your substitution. Resist getting drawn into a fight or power struggle. Respond to testing with positive discipline; continue to state the substitution calmly and with goodwill. If two children run back through the sandbox, for example, consider saying, "Tom and Jim, the obstacle course is the set of tires, not the sandbox."

13. Listen Actively

Purposes of the strategy: Careful, accurate listening to child's feelings. Use when a child owns a problem. Conveys adult's recognition and acceptance of the child and his feelings. Communicates the adult's trust in the child's ability to work through the problem.

What to remember about active listening:

- Listen carefully.
- Wait until the child finishes speaking; do not interrupt.
- Try to understand what the message means.
- Listen for what the child is feeling.
- Suspend judgment.
- Avoid preaching, giving advice, or trying to persuade the child to feel differently.
- Merely reflect your perception of the child's feelings.

14. Deliver I-Messages

Purposes of the strategy: Used when the adult owns the problem. Give information; communicate feelings in a respectful way; give the child a chance to change her behavior (a Rogerian concept).

Steps in constructing a good I-message:

- Name the exact behavior causing the problem. Give observable data about the child's behavior—what you see, hear, touch, smell, taste, for example, "Adam, I see that the puzzles you used are still on the table."
- Tell the child how his behavior tangibly affects you. Did it cost you time, money, effort to do the job he should have done? (". . . And that meant I had to put the puzzles away just before snack").
- Tell the child how you felt but do not accuse the child of causing your feeling, for example, "I feel annoyed if I have to do somebody else's work."

- Tell the child how to change the situation, for example, "I want you to do your own work and put the puzzles on the shelf."

What to avoid in constructing I-messages:

- Avoid accusing and blaming the child.
- Do not induce guilt.
- Avoid telling the child that he caused your feeling.

15. Teach Conflict Resolution (Problem Solving)

Purposes of the strategy: Achieve a mutually agreeable solution to a problem without resorting to the use of power. Support creative conflict resolution rather than punishing behavior accompanying conflict between children. For example, teach children who are arguing how to resolve the conflict rather than punishing them for fighting.

Steps in using the no-lose method of conflict resolution:

- Identify and define the conflict in a nonaccusatory way, for example, "Vinnie and Reese, you have a problem. You both want the green paint."
- Invite children to participate in fixing the problem. For example, "Let's think of how to solve the problem."
- Generate possible solutions with the children. Accept a variety of solutions and avoid evaluating them, for example, "Yes, you could both use the same paint cup. You could take turns."
- Examine each idea for merits and drawbacks. With the children, decide which to try. Thank the children for thinking of solutions. For example, "Both of you want to use the green paint at the same time."
- Put the plan into action, for example, "You might have to take turns dipping your brushes into the paint. Try your idea."
- Follow up. Evaluate how well the solution worked (teacher comes back in a few minutes: "Your idea of how to solve your green paint problem really worked."

16. Recognize Signs of Stress, Anxiety, or Strong Emotion; Prevent Overstimulation; Teach Calming Techniques

Purposes of the strategy: To look beyond the visible behavior. To detect an underlying cause, such as stress or anxiety, for a behavior. To get the autonomic nervous system under control.

Suggestions:

- Observe carefully, noting signs of stress (Figure 9.1) or anxiety.
- Decide whether to use active listening, to decrease stimulation, or to teach/carry out a calming technique (Figure 5.1).
- Decide whether to change something about the classroom to decrease stress. For example, decide to minimize the number of transitions.

17. Manage Strong Emotions Responsibly

Purposes of the strategy: To support children in recognizing and learning responsible ways to manage strong emotions such as anger. To avoid simply punishing children for behavior resulting from strong emotions.

Steps in teaching responsible anger management:

- Model responsible anger management.
- Create a safe emotional climate. Allow and encourage children to acknowledge all feelings while firmly but kindly not permitting them to hurt anybody because of those feelings.
- Help children understand their anger triggers.
- Help children understand the body's reaction to anger.
- Teach children how to deal with the stress of anger.
- State your expectations for responsible anger management.
- Help some children learn to use words to describe angry feelings, and help others to expand their vocabulary about feelings.
- Use appropriate books and stories about anger management.

References

Aldwin, C. (author), & Werner, E. (foreword) (2007). *Stress, coping, and development, second edition: An integrative perspective.* New York: Guilford Press.

Alexander, N. (1996). How to organize your classroom. *Early Childhood News, 8*(4), 28–30.

Allen, J. (2009, May 31). Uprooting takes an emotional toll on children. *Associated Press.* Retrieved June 1, 2009, from http://www.floridatoday.com/article/20090531/LIFE/905310311/-1/SEVENDAYS

Alward, K. R. (1973). *Arranging the classroom for children.* San Francisco: Far West Laboratory for Educational Research and Development.

American Academy of Child & Adolescent Psychiatry. (2009). Children with oppositional defiant disorder. *AACAP Facts for Families,* No. 72. Retrieved September 28, 2009, from http://www.aacap.org/publications/factsfam/72

American Academy of Child & Adolescent Psychiatry. (2001). Understanding violent behavior in children and adolescents. *AACAP Facts for Families,* No. 55. Washington, DC: Author.

American Academy of Child & Adolescent Psychiatry. (2002a). Children and family moves. *AACAP Facts for Families,* No. 14. Retrieved on December 17, 2009 from http://www.aacap.org/page.ww?section=Facts%20for%20Families&name=Children%20And%20Family%20Moves

American Academy of Child & Adolescent Psychiatry. (2002b). Children's threats: When are they serious? *AACAP Facts for Families,* No. 65. Washington, DC: Author.

American Academy of Child & Adolescent Psychiatry. (2004). Being prepared: Knowing where to find help for your child. *AACAP Facts for Families,* No. 25. Washington, DC: Author.

American Academy of Child & Adolescent Psychiatry. (2004a). Children of parents with mental illness. *AACAP Facts for Families,* No. 39. Washington, DC: Author.

American Academy of Child & Adolescent Psychiatry. (2004b). Children who cannot pay attention. *AACAP Facts for Families,* No. 6. Washington, DC: Author.

American Academy of Child & Adolescent Psychiatry. (2008). Fighting and biting. *AACAP Facts for Families,* No. 81. Retrieved June 14, 2009, from http://www.aacap.org/publications/factsfam/81.htm

American Psychological Association. (2004). *The different kinds of stress.* Retrieved March 24, 2006, from www.apahelpcenter.org/articles/pdf.php?id=21

American Psychological Association. (2005a). *Briefing sheet on bullying.* Retrieved June 22, 2009, from http://www.apa.org/ppo/issues/bullying.html

American Psychological Association. (2005b). What makes kids care? Teaching gentleness in a violent world. *APA Online: Public Affairs.* Retrieved January 6, 2006, from http://www.apa.org/pubinfo/altruism.html

Anderson, C. (2004). An update on the effects of playing violent video games. *Journal of Adolescence, 27,* 113–122. Retrieved January 7, 2006, from http://www.sciencedirect.com

Anderson, E., Cook, D., Honaker, L., & Kestenbaum, C. (2000, July 26). *Joint statement on the impact of media violence on children.* Presented at the Congressional Public Health Summit on Media Violence, Washington, DC.

Anderson, G., Hilton, S., & Wouden-Miller, M. (2003). A gender comparison of the cooperation of 4-year-old children in classroom activity centers. *Early Education and Development, 14*(4), 441–451.

Anderson, K. G., Smith, G.T., McCarthy, D.M., Fischer, S.F., Fister, S., Grodin, D., Boerner, L.M., & Kearfott Hill, K. (2005). Elementary school drinking: The role of temperament and learning. *Psychology of Addictive Behaviors, 19*(1), 21–27.

Association for Moral Education. (2004). *Promoting social responsibility in children and early adolescents.* Paper presented at the AME Symposium, Dana Point, CA. November 12.

Bafile, C. (2004). The prop box: Setting the stage for meaningful play. *Education World.* Retrieved July 10, 2009, from http://www.education-world.com/a_curr/profdev/profdev101.shtml

Baillargeon, R., Zoccolillo, M., Keenan, K., Cote, S., Perusse, D., Wu, H.-X., et al. (2007). Gender differences in physical aggression : A prospective population-based survey of children before and after 2 years of age. *Developmental Psychology, 43*(1), 13–26.

Baker-Ward, L., Gordon, B. N., Ornstein, P. A., Larus, D. M., & Clubb, P. A. (1993). Young children's long-term retention of a pediatric examination. *Child Development, 64,* 1519–1533.

Ballas, P. (2009). Medical encyclopedia: Attention deficit hyperactivity disorder (ADHD). Retrieved June 23, 2009, from http://www.nlm.nih.gov/medlineplus/ency/article/001551.htm

Bandura, A. (1971). Analysis of modeling processes. In A. Bandura (Ed.), *Psychological modeling*. Chicago: Aldine-Asherton.

Bank Street (2009). *Bank street school for children curriculum guide*. New York: Bank Street College of Education. Retrieved July 9, 2009, from http://webstaging.bankstreet.edu/gems/sfc/CurriculumGuide.pdf

Barbour, A., & Desjean-Perrotta, B. (2002). *Prop box play*. Lewisville, NC: Gryphon House.

Barnard, K. E., & Solchany, J. E. (2002). *Mothering*. Mahwah, NJ: Erlbaum.

Baumeister, R. (1996). Should schools try to boost self-esteem? Beware the dark side. *American Educator, 20*(2), 14–19, 43.

Baumeister, R. F., Campbell, J. D., Kreuger, J. I. & Vohs, K.D. (2003). Does high self-esteem cause better performance, interpersonal success, happiness or healthier lifestyles? *Psychological Science in the Public Interest, 4*(1), 1–44. Retrieved June 10, 2009, from http://www.csom.umn.edu/Assets/71496.pdf

Baumrind, D. (1967). Child care practices anteceding three patterns of preschool behavior. *Genetic Psychology Monographs, 75*, 43–88.

Baumrind, D. (1971). Current patterns of parental authority. *Developmental Psychology Monograph, 4*(1, Pt. 2).

Baumrind, D. (1977, March). *Socialization determinants of personal agency*. Paper presented at the meeting of the Society for Research in Child Development, New Orleans, LA.

Baumrind, D. (1979). *Sex-related socialization effects*. Paper presented at the meeting of the Society for Research in Child Development, San Francisco, CA.

Baumrind, D. (1993). The average expectable environment is not good enough: A response to Scarr. *Child Development, 64*, 1299–1317.

Baumrind, D. (1996). Parenting: The discipline controversy revisited. *Family Relations, 45*, 405–414.

Baumrind, D., & Black, A. E. (1967). Socialization practices associated with dimensions of competence in preschool boys and girls. *Child Development, 38*, 291–327.

Becker, W. C. (1954). Consequences of different kinds of parental discipline. In M. L. Hoffman & L. S. Hoffman (Eds.), *Review of child development research* (Vol. 1). New York: Russell Sage Foundation.

Becker-Blease, K., & Freyd, J. (2008). A preliminary study of ADHD symptoms and correlates: Do abused children differ from nonabused children? *Journal of Aggression, Maltreatment & Trauma, 17*(1), 133–140.

Bedrova, E. & Leong, D. (2005). Self-regulation. *Principal*, September/October, 30–33.

Bell, R. Q. (1968). A reinterpretation of the direction of effect in studies of socialization. *Psychological Review, 75*, 81–95.

Bell, R. Q., & Harper, L. V. (Eds.). (1977). *Child effects on adults*. Hillsdale, NJ: Erlbaum.

Belsky, J., Sligo, J., Jaffee, S. R., Woodward, L., & Silva, P. (2005). Intergenerational transmission of warm, sensitive, stimulating parenting: A prospective study of mothers and fathers of 3-year-olds. *Child Development, 76*(2), 384–396.

Bengtsson, H., & Johnson, L. (1992). Perspective taking, empathy, and prosocial behavior in late childhood. *Child Study Journal, 22*(1), 11–22.

Benson, T. (2004). The importance of dramatic play Online article, *PBS Teachers*. Retrieved July 6, 2009, from http://www.pbs.org/teachers/earlychildhood/articles/dramaticplay.html

Berk, L. E., & Winsler, A. (1995). *Scaffolding children's learning: Vygotsky and early childhood education*. Washington, DC: NAEYC.

Birckmayer, J., Cohen, J., Jensen, I., & Variano, D. (2005). Kyle lives with his grandmother—Where are his mommy and daddy? *Young Children, 60*(3), 100–104.

Blakemore, J., Berenbaum, S., & Liben, L. (2009). *Gender development*. New York: Psychology Press.

Block, H. (1978). Another look at sex differentiation in the socialization behaviors of mothers and fathers. In J. Sherman & F. L. Denmark (Eds.), *The future of women: Future directions of research*. New York: Psychological Dimensions.

Bohnert, A., Crnic, K., & Lim, K. (2003). Emotional competence and aggressive behavior in school-age children 1. *Journal of Abnormal Child Psychology*. Retrieved January 2, 2006, from http://www.findarticles.com/p/articles/mi_m0902/is_1_31/ai_97891764

Bolger, K., Patterson, C., & Kupersmidt, J. (1998). Peer relationships and self-esteem among children who have been maltreated. *Child Development, 69*(4), 1171–1197.

Bottini, M., & Grossman, S. (2005). Center-based teaching and children's learning: The effects of learning centers on children's growth and development. *Childhood Education. 81*(5), 274–277.

Boyatzis, C., Matillo, G., & Nesbitt, K. (1995). Effects of "the Mighty Morphin Power Rangers" on children's aggression with peers. *Child Study Journal, 25*(1), 45–57.

Bracken, C. C., & Lombard, M. (2004). Social presence and children: praise, intrinsic motivation, and learning with computers. *Journal of Communication, 54*(1), 22–37.

Brackett, M. A., Crum, A., & Salovey, P. (2009). Emotional intelligence. In S. J. Lopez (Ed.), *Encyclopedia of Positive Psychology*. New York: Blackwell, pages 310–315.

Branz-Spall, A., Rosenthal, R., & Wright, A. (2003). Children of the road: Migrant students, our nation's most mobile population. *Journal of Negro Education, 72*(1), 55–62.

Brassard, M., & Boehm, A. (2007). *Preschool assessment: Principles and practices*. New York, NY: Guilford Press.

Bredekamp, S. (Ed.). (1987). *Developmentally appropriate practice in programs serving children from birth through age 8*. Washington, DC: NAEYC.

Bredekamp, S., & Copple, C. (1997). *Developmentally appropriate practice in early childhood programs* (Rev. ed.). Washington, DC: NAEYC.

Bredekamp, S., & Rosegrant, T. (Eds.). (1992). *Reaching potentials: Appropriate curriculum and assessment for young children* (Vol. 1). Washington, DC: NAEYC.

Brems, C., & Sohl, M. A. (1995). The role of empathy in parenting strategy choices. *Family Relations, 44*, 189–194.

Bronfenbrenner, U. (1979). *The ecology of human development*. Cambridge, MA: Harvard University Press.

Brown University Child & Adolescent Behavior Letter. (1999). Commentary: The wellsprings of anger. *Brown University Child & Adolescent Behavior Letter, 15*(7), 8.

Brown, A. L., & Campione, J. C. (1990). Communities of learning and thinking, or a context by any other name. In D. Kuhn (Ed.), *Developmental perspectives on teaching learning and thinking skills*. Basel: Karger.

Brown, G., Mangelsdorf, S., Neff, C., Schoppe-Sullivan, S., & Frosch, C. (2009). Young children's concepts: Associations with child temperament, mothers' and fathers' parenting, and triadic family interaction. Report. *Merrill-Palmer Quarterly, 55*(2), 184–216.

Brown, P., & Elliot, R. (1965). Control of aggression in a nursery school class. *Journal of Experimental Child Psychology, 2*, 103–107.

Bryan, J. H., & Walbek, N. H. (1970). Preaching and practicing generosity: Children's actions and reactions. *Child Development, 41*, 329–353.

Burts, D., Hart, C., Charlesworth, R., Fleege, P., Mosley, J., & Thomasson, R. (1992). Observed activities and stress behaviors of children in developmentally appropriate and inappropriate kindergarten classrooms. *Early Childhood Research Quarterly, 7*, 297–318.

Calvert, S. (2006). Media and early development. In K. McCartney & D. Phillips (Eds.), *The Blackwell handbook of early childhood development* (pp. 508–531). Malden, MA: Blackwell Publishing.

Cameron, C., Connor, C., & Morrison, F. (2005). The effects of variation in teacher organization on classroom functioning. *Journal of School Psychology, 43*(1), 61–85.

Campos, J., & Barrett, K. (1984). A new understanding of emotions and their development. In C. Izard, J. Kagan, & R. Zajonc (Eds.), *Emotions, cognition, and behavior*. New York: Cambridge University Press.

Canadian Mental Health Association. (2005). Coping with stress. Retrieved December 5, 2005, from http://www.cmha.ca/English/coping_with_stress/index.htm

Caples, S. (1996). Some guidelines for preschool design. *Young Children, 51*(4), 14–21.

Carlson, F. M. (2006). *Essential touch*. Washington, DC: National Association for the Education of young Children.

Carlsson-Paige, N., & Levin, D. (1998). *Before push comes to shove: Building conflict resolution skills with children*. St. Paul, MN: Redleaf Press.

Carney, J. V. (2000). Bullied to death: Perceptions of peer abuse and suicidal behavior during adolescence. *School Psychology International, 21*(2), 44–54.

Case, R. (1992). *The mind's staircase: Exploring the conceptual underpinnings of children's thought and knowledge*. Hillsdale, NJ: Erlbaum.

Center on Media and Child Health. (2005). *The effects of electronic media on children ages zero to six: A history of research*. Report for the Henry J. Kaiser Family Foundation. Retrieved June 22, 2009, from http://www.kff.org/entmedia/upload/The-Effects-of-Electronic-Media-on-Children-Ages-Zero-to-Six-A-History-of-Research-Issue-Brief.pdf

Centers for Disease Control and Prevention. (1995, March). CDC surveillance summaries. *Morbidity Weekly Report, 44*(ss–1).

Chalmers, J. B., & Townsend, M. A. (1990). The effects of training in social perspective taking on socially maladjusted girls. *Child Development, 61*, 178–190.

Chang, C. (2003). A learning space that works. *Instructor, 113*(2), 32–34.

Charlesworth, R. (1985). Readiness: Should we make them ready or let them bloom? *Daycare and Early Education, 12*(3), 25–27.

Charlesworth, R., Hart, C., Burts, D., & DeWolf, M. (1993). The LSU studies: Building a research base for developmentally appropriate practice. In S. Reifel (Ed.), *Advances in Early Education and Day Care: Perspectives on Developmentally Appropriate Practice, 5*, 3–28.

Child Welfare Information Gateway. (2008). Long-term consequences of child abuse and neglect. Factsheet. Washington, DC: Children's Bureau/ACYF. Retrieved May 10, 2009, from http://www.childwelfare.gov/pubs/factsheets/long_term_consequences.cfm

Child Welfare Information Gateway. (2008). Long-term consequences of child abuse and neglect. *Factsheet*. Washington, DC: Children's Bureau/ACYF.

Christian, L. (2006). Applying family systems theory to early childhood practice. *Young Children: Beyond the Journal.* Retrieved April 25, 2009, from http://www.journal.naeyc.org/btj/200601/ChristianBTJ.asp

Christian, L.G. (2006). Applying family systems theory to early childhood practice. *Beyond the Journal: Young Children on the Web,* 8 pages. Retrieved June 3, 2009, from http://www.journal.naeyc.org/btj/200601/ChristianBTJ.pdf

Church, R. M. (1963). The varied effects of punishment on behavior. *Psychological Review, 70,* 369–402.

Ciairano, S., Kliewer, W., Bonino, S., & Bosma, H. A. (2008). Parenting and adolescent wellbeing in two European countries. *Adolescence, 43,* 99–117.

Clark, J. I. (1999). *Time-in: When time-out doesn't work.* Seattle, WA: Parenting Press.

Clark, P., & Kragler, S. (2005). The impact of including writing materials in the early childhood classrooms on the early literacy development of children from low-income families. *Early Child Development and Care, 175*(4), 285–301.

Cohen, J., Bowes, J., Ungerer, J., Sanson, A., Wise, S., Harrison, L., et al. (2003). Multiple child care arrangements, temperament, and children's behaviour in the first three years. *Australian Journal of Psychology, 55,* 172.

Cohn, J. F., Campbell, S. B., Matias, R., & Hopkins, J. (1990). Face-to-face interactions of postpartum depressed and nondepressed mother-infant pairs at 2 months. *Developmental Psychology, 26,* 15–23.

Colbert, J. (1997). Classroom design and how it influences behavior. *Early Childhood News, 9*(3), 22–30.

Coles, R. (1986). *The moral life of children.* New York: Atlantic Monthly Press.

Coles, R. (1997). *The moral intelligence of children.* New York: Penguin.

Committee on Injury, Violence, and Poison Prevention (2009). Policy statement role of the pediatrician in youth violence prevention. *Pediatrics, 124*(1), 392–403.

Community Playthings. (2009). *Pre-K spaces: Designs for a quality classroom.* Rifton, New York: Author. Retrieved July 1, 2009, from http://www.scribd.com/doc/15899428/PreK-Spaces-Design-for-a-Quality-Classroom. *Principles of development and learning that inform developmentally appropriate practice. A position paper.* Washington, DC: Author. Retrieved July 1, 2007, from http://www.naeyc.org.about/positions/

Conn, K., Hernandez, T., Puthoor, P., Fagnano, M., & Halterman, J. (2008). Screen time use among urban children with asthma. *Academic Pediatrics, 9*(1), 60–63.

Connor, D. (2004). *Aggression and antisocial behavior in children and adolescents.* New York: Guilford Press.

Coopersmith, S. (1967). *The antecedents of self-esteem.* San Francisco: W. H. Freeman.

Copple, C., & Bredekamp, S. (2009). *Developmentally appropriate practices in early childhood programs serving children from birth through age 8.* Washington, DC: NAEYC.

Cornille, T. (1993). Support systems and the relocation process for children and families. *Marriage & Family Review, 19*(3–4), 281–298.

Corso, R. (2003). The center on the social and emotional foundations for education. *Young Children, 58*(4), 46–47.

Cotton, K. (2001). Developing empathy in children and youth. *School Improvement Research Series,* Portland, OR: Northwest Regional Educational Laboratory. Retrieved January 7, 2006, from http://www.nwrel.org/scpd/sirs/7/cu13.html

Cross, A. F., & Dixon, S. D. (2004). *Adapting curriculum and instruction in inclusive early childhood classrooms.* Bloomington, IN: Institute for the Study of Developmental Disabilities.

CSEFEL (Center on the Social and Emotional Foundations for Early Learning) (2008). Practical strategies. Retrieved May 1, 2009, from http:// www.vanderbilt.edu/csefel/practicalstrategies.html

CSEFEL (n.d.). Book nook: Ideas for using books to support social emotional development. Retrieved May 1, 2009, from http://www.vanderbilt.edu/csefel/booknook/hands/hands.html

Cummings, E. M., Iannotti, R. J., & Zahn-Waxler, C. (1989). Aggression between peers in early childhood: Individual continuity and developmental change. *Child Development, 60*(4), 887–895.

Cummings, E., & Cummings, J. (1988). A process-oriented approach to children's coping with adults' angry behavior. *Developmental Review, 8,* 296–321.

Curry, N., & Johnson, C. (1990). Beyond self-esteem: Developing a genuine sense of human value. *Research Monograph* (Vol. 4). Washington, DC: NAEYC.

Damon, W. (2004). Studies in the nature of character revisited: Moral identity and its development. Lecture given at Williams College, April 5.

Damon, W. (2009). The path to purpose: How young people find their calling in life. New York: Free Press.

Davis, S., & Davis, J. (2007). *Empowering bystanders in bullying prevention.* Champaign, IL: Research Press.

Dawe, H. C. (1934). An analysis of two hundred quarrels of preschool children. *Child Development, 5,* 139–157.

Day, T., & Kunz, J. T. (2009). *Guidance based on developmental theory.* Unpublished manuscript, Weber State University, Ogden, Utah.

Deal, J., Halverson, C., Havill, V., & Martin, R. (2005). Temperament factors as longitudinal predictors of young adult personality. *Merrill Palmer Quarterly: Journal of Developmental Psychology, 51*(3), 315–334.

Denham, S. (2006). The emotional basis of learning and development in early childhood education. In B. Spodek & O. Saracho (Eds.). *Handbook of Research on the Education of Young Children*, 2nd ed. New York: Routledge.

Denham, S. A., Zoller, D., & Couchoud, E. Z. (1994). Socialization of preschoolers' emotion understanding. *Developmental Psychology, 30*(6), 928–937.

Department of Education (Migrant Education Program). (1994). *Elementary school children: Many change schools frequently, harming their education*. Report to the Honorable March Kaptur, House of Representatives. Washington, DC: Author. (ERIC No. EC369526)

DeVoe, J., Peter, K., Kaufmann, P., Miller, A., Noonan, M., Snyder, T., et al. (2004). *Indicators of school crime and safety: 2004, 7th Edition*. Retrieved January 9, 2006, from the Honorable March Kaptur http://nces.ed.gov/pubs2005/crime_safe04/foreword.asp

DeVries, R. & Zan, B. (1994). Moral classrooms, moral children: Creating a constructivist atmosphere in early education. New York: Teacher's College Press.

Dewey, J. (1897). My pedagogic creed. *The School Journal, LIV*(3), 77–80.

Dinkmeyer, B., & McKay, G. D. (1988). *Systematic training for effective parenting*. Circle Pines, MN: American Guidance Service.

Discipline (2009). In Merriam-Webster Online Dictionary. Retrieved on December 17, 2009, from http://www.merriam-webster.com/dictionary/discipline.

Dixon, J. A., & Soto, C. F. (1990). The development of perspective taking: Understanding differences in information and weighting. *Child Development, 61*, 1502–1513.

Dodge, K. A., & Frame, C. L. (1982). Social cognitive biases and deficits in aggressive boys. *Child Development, 53*, 629–635.

Donfrancesco, R., Mugnaini, D., & Dell'Uomo, A. (2005). Cognitive impulsivity in specific learning disabilities. *European Child and Adolescent Psychiatry, 14*(5), 270–275.

Downs, J., Blagojevic, B., Labas, L. (2006). Daily Transitions - Time for a Change. The University of Maine Center for Community Inclusion and Disability Studies. Retrieved July 13, 2009, from http://www.ccids.umaine.edu/ec/growingideas/transitionstip.htm

Downs, J., Blagojevic, B., Labas, L., Kendrick, M., & Maeverde, J. (2005). Ouch! That hurts!—Biting. In *Growing ideas toolkit* (pp. 35-36). Orono, ME: The University of Maine Center for Community Inclusion and Disability Studies. Retrieved June 18, 2009, from http://www.ccids.umaine.edu/ec/growingideas/bitingtip.htm

Dreikurs, R. (1958). *The challenge of parenthood*. New York: Hawthorne Books.

Dubow, E., Huesmann, L., & Boxer, P. (2003). Theoretical and methodological considerations in cross-generational research on parenting and child aggressive behavior. *Journal of Abnormal Child Psychology, 31*(2), 185–192.

Dunst, C. J., Trivett, C. M., & Cuspec, P. A. (2002). Toward an operational definition of evidence-based practice. *Cneterscope, 1*(1), 1–10.

Dweck, C., & Leggett, E. (1988). A social-cognitive approach to motivation and personality. *Psychological Review, 95*(2), 256–273.

Dweck, C., & Molden, D. (2005). Self theories: Their impact on competence motivation and acquisition. In A. Elliot & C. Dweck (Eds.), *Handbook of competence and motivation* New York: The Guilford Press.

Educational Productions. (1998). *Reframing discipline: Dealing with difficult behavior*. Portland, OR: Author.

Educators for Social Responsibility. (2003). Building character and social skills through classroom instruction. Retrieved January 4, 2006, from http://www.esrnational.org/es/skills.htm

Edwards, A., Shipman, K., & Brown, A. (2005). The socialization of emotional understanding: A comparison of neglectful and nonneglectful mothers and their children. *Child Maltreatment, 10*(3), 293–304.

Eisenberg, N., Spinrad, T., Fabes, R., Reiser, M., Cumberland-Li, A., Shepard, S., et al. (2004). The relations of effortful control and impulsivity to children's resiliency and adjustment. *Child Development, 75*(1), 25–46.

Eisenberg, N., Wolchik, S., Goldberg, L., & Engel, I. (1992). Parental values, reinforcement, and young children's prosocial behavior: A longitudinal study. *Journal of Genetic Psychology, 153*(1), 19–37.

Elias, M. (2004). The connection between social-emotional learning and learning disabilities: Implications for intervention. *Learning Disability Quarterly, 27*(1), 53.

Elliott, E., & Dweck, C. (1988). Goals: An approach to motivation and achievement. *Journal of Personality and Social Psychology, 54*(1), 5–12.

Erikson, Erik H. (1958). *Young man Luther: A study in psychoanalysis*. New York: Norton.

Espelage, D., Holt, M., & Henkel, R. (2003). Examination of peer group contextual effects on aggression during early adolescence. *Child Development, 74*, 205–220.

Eysenck, M. W. (2004). *Psychology: An international perspective*. East Sussex, United Kingdom: Psychology Press.

Fabes, R., & Eisenberg, N. (1992). Young children's coping with interpersonal anger. *Child Development, 63*, 116–128.

Fabes, R., Eisenberg, N., Smith, M., & Murphy, B. (1996). Getting angry at peers: Association with liking of the provocateur. *Child Development, 67*(3), 943–958.

Fagan, J. F. (1984). Infant memory: History, current trends, and relations to cognitive psychology. In M. Moscovitch (Ed.), *Infant memory: Its relation to normal and pathological memory in humans and other animals.* New York: Plenum.

Fantz, R. L. (1966). Pattern discrimination and selective attention as determinants of perceptual development from birth. In A. H. Kidd & J. L. Rivoire (Eds.), *Perceptual development in children.* New York: International Universities Press.

Faull, J. (2002). *Responding to disrespectful talk.* Seattle, WA: Comprehensive Health Education Foundation.

Fawcett, L. M., & Garton, A. F. (2005). The effect of peer collaboration on children's problem-solving ability. *British Journal of Educational Psychology, 75*(2), 157–169.

Feshbach, N. D., & Feshbach, S. (1982). Empathy training and the regulation of aggression: Potentialities and limitations. *Academic Psychology Bulletin, 4,* 399–413.

Feshbach, S. (1970). Aggression. In P. Mussen (Ed.), *Carmichael's manual of child psychology* (Vol. 2). New York: Wiley.

File, N. (1993). The teacher as guide of children's competence with peers. *Child and Youth Care Forum, 22,* 351–360.

Filipek, P. (2008). *Typical and atypical infant development: When should we be concerned?* Presentation at the 2nd International Conference Signs of Autism in Infants, Yorba Linda, CA, Saturday, October 11.

Fiqueora-Sanchez (2008). Building emotional literacy: Groundwork to early learning. *Childhood Education, 84*(5), 301–304.

Flavell, J. H., Miller, P. H., & Miller, S. A. (1993). *Cognitive development* (3rd ed.). Upper Saddle River, NJ: Prentice Hall.

Fogel, A. (1984). *Infancy: Infant, family, and society.* St. Paul, MN: West.

Fonagy, P., Twemlow, S., Vernberg, E., Mize Nelson, J., Dill, E., Little, T., & Sargent, J. (2009). A cluster randomized controlled trial of child-focused psychiatric consultation and a school systems-focused intervention to reduce aggression. *Journal of Child Psychology and Psychiatry, 50*(5), 607–616.

Forni, P. M. (2002). *Choosing civility.* New York: St. Martin's Press.

Foss, J. (2002). Nonverbal Learning Disability: How To Recognize It and Minimize Its Effects. ERIC Digest. ED461238. Retrieved on December 17, 2009 from http://www.eric.ed.gov/ERICDocs/data/ericdocs2sql/content_storage_01/0000019b/80/29/cd/fa.pdf

Fox, L. (n.d.). Positive behavior support: An individualized approach to address challenging behavior. *What works brief #10.* University of North Carolina-Chapel Hill, CSEFEL.

Fox, L., & Duda, M. (n.d.). What are children trying to tell us?: Assessing the function of their behavior. *What works brief #9,* University of North Carolina-Chapel Hill, CSEFEL.

Francis, S., & Chorpita, B. (2009). Parental beliefs about child anxiety as a mediator of parent and child anxiety. *Cognitive Therapy and Research,* doi: 10.1007/s10608-009-9255-9

Freedman, (2002). *Easing the teasing: Helping your cope with name-calling, ridicule, and verbal bullying.* Chicago: McGraw-Hill Contemporary.

Freedman, J. (2002). *Easing the teasing.* New York: McGraw Hill.

Freeman, N., Lacohee, H., & Coulton, S. (1995). Cued-recall approach to 3-year-olds' memory for an honest mistake. *Journal of Experimental Child Psychology, 60*(1), 102–116.

Freeman-Loftis, B. (2009). An administrator shares: A welcoming routine for arrival time. *Responsive Classroom Newsletter, 21*(1), 2 pages.

Frey, K. S., Hirschstein, M. K., & Guzzo, B. (2000). Second step: Preventing aggression by promoting social competence. *Journal of Emotional & Behavioral Disorders, 8*(2), 102–112.

Frey, K., Herschstein, M., Edstrom, L., & Snell, J. (2009). Observed reductions in school bullying, nonbullying aggression, and destructive bystander behavior: A longitudinal evaluation. *Journal of School Psychology, 101*(2), 466–481.

Fu, V. (1984). Infant/toddler care in centers. In L. Dittmann (Ed.), *The infants we care for.* Washington, DC: NAEYC.

Fujiki, M., Brinton, B., Morgan, M., & Hart, C. (1999). Withdrawn and sociable children with language impairment. *Language, Speech, & Hearing Services in Schools, 30,* 183–195.

Gallagher, E. (2004). *Abuse, attachment, and animal assisted activities.* Unpublished honors paper, Lynch School of Education.

Gallagher, J. & Reid, K. (2002). *The learning theory of Piaget and Inhelder.* Bloomington, IN: IUniverse.

Gandini, L. (1993). Fundamentals of the Reggio Emilia approach to early childhood education. *Young Children, 49*(1), 4–8.

Garbarino, J., Guttman, E., & Seeley, J. (1986). *The psychologically battered child.* San Francisco: Jossey-Bass.

Garbarino, J., Guttman, E., & Seeley, J. (1986). *The psychologically battered child.* San Francisco: Jossey-Bass.

Gardner, H. (2003). *Multiple intelligences after twenty years.* Paper presented at the American Educational Research Association, Chicago, IL: April 21.

Geist, E., & Baum, A. (2005). Yeah, but's that keeps teachers from embracing an active curriculum: Overcoming the resistance. *Young Children, 60*(4), 28–34, 36.

Gerrig, R., & Zimbardo, P. (2002). *Psychology and life* (16th ed.). Boston, MA: Allyn & Bacon/Pearson Education.

Gilliam, W, (2005). Prekindergarteners Left Behind: Expulsion Rates in State Prekindergarten Systems, New Haven, CT: Yale University Child Study Center, May 4, 2005.

Gilliam, W., & Shahar, G. (2006). Preschool and child care expulsion and suspension. *Infants and Young Children, 19*(3), 228–245.

Gilligan, C. (1993, originally published 1982). *In a different voice: Psychological theory and women's development.* Cambridge, MA: Harvard University Press.

Gilligan, C. (2008). Always in a different voice. Lunch plenary address at the PEN Annual Conference, 25 Years of Local Education Funds, November 17, San Francisco.

Goleman, D. (1995). *Emotional intelligence.* New York: Bantam Books.

Goleman, D. (2001). Daniel Goleman on emotional intelligence [Documentary/interview]. *Edutopia,* The George Lucas Foundation. Retrieved January 9, 2006, from http://www.edutopia.org.php/interview.php?id=Art_699&key=020

Goleman, D. (2007). Selling SEL: An Interview with Daniel Goleman. CASEL Forum, New York City, December 10. Retrieved on March 18, 2009 from http://www.edutopia.org/daniel-goleman-sel-video

Gomez, C., & Baird, S. (2005). Identifying early indications of autism in self-regulation difficulties. *Focus on Autism and Other Developmental Disabilities, 20*(2), 106–116.

Gordon Training International. (2005). *Our classroom philosophy.* Retrieved October 27, 2005, from http://www.gordon-training.com/schoolphilo.html

Gordon, T. (1974). *T.E.T.: Teacher Effectiveness Training.* New York: David McKay.

Gordon, T. (1978). *P.E.T. in action.* Toronto: Bantam.

Graves, M. (2007). Explore and Learn Quick Cards: 80 Activities for Small Groups. Ypsilanti, MI: HighScope.

Greenberg, A., & Berktold, J. (2006). Holiday stress. Greenberg Quinlan Rosner Research, American Psychological Association. Retrieved May 16, 2009, from http://www.gqrr.com/articles/1843/2603_HolidayStress.pdf

Greener, S. (1998). The relationship between emotional predispositions, emotional decoding, and regulation skills and children's prosocial behavior. *Dissertation Abstracts International, 59,* No. 08B.

Greenman, J. (2005). *Caring space, learning places children's environments that work.* Redmond, WA: Exchange Press, Inc.

Gross, T. (2004). The perception of four basic emotions in human and nonhuman faces by children with autism and other developmental disabilities. *Journal of Abnormal Child Psychology.* Retrieved April 2, 2009, from http://findarticles.com/p/articles/mi_m0902/is_5_32/ai_n6234461/

Grusec, J. E., & Lytton, H. (1988). *Social development: History, theory, and research.* New York: Springer-Verlag.

Hackman, D., & Farah, M. (2009). Socioeconomic status and the developing brain. *Trends in Cognitive Science, 13*(2), 65–73.

Hamre, B. K., & Pianta, R. C. (2005). Can instructional and emotional support in the first-grade classroom make a difference for children at risk of school failure? *Child Development, 76*(5), 949–967.

Harms, T., Clifford, R. M., & Cryer, D. (1998). *Early childhood environment rating scale* (Rev. ed.). New York: Teachers College Press.

Hart, C., Burts, D., & Charlesworth, R. (1997). Integrated developmentally appropriate curriculum. In C. Hart, D. Burts, & R. Charlesworth (Eds.), *Integrated curriculum and developmentally appropriate practice: Birth to age 8.* Albany: State University of New York Press.

Hart, C., Burts, D., Durland, M. A., Charlesworth, R., DeWolf, M., & Fleege, P. (1998). Stress behaviors and activity type participation of preschoolers in more and less developmentally appropriate classrooms: SES and sex differences. *Journal of Research in Childhood Education,* 176–196.

Hart, C., DeWolf, M., Wozniak, P., & Burts, D. (1992). Maternal and paternal disciplinary styles: Relations with preschoolers' playground behavioral orientations and peer status. *Child Development, 63,* 879–892.

Hart, K., Fujiki, M., Brinton, B., & Hart, C. (2004). The relationship between social behavior and language impairment. *Journal of Speech, Language, and Hearing Research, 47*(3), 647–662.

Harter, S. (2006). The self. In N. Eisenberg (Ed.), *Handbook of child psychology: Vol. 3. Social, emotional, and personality development* (6th ed., pp. 505–570). Hoboken, NJ: Wiley.

Hartup, W. W. (1974). Aggression in childhood: Developmental perspectives. *American Psychologist, 29,* 336–341.

Hastings, P., Rubin, K., & DeRose, L. (2005). Links among gender, inhibition, and parental socialization in the development of prosocial behavior. *Merrill Palmer Quarterly, 51*(4), 467–493.

Haswell, K., Hock, E., & Wenar, C. (1981). Oppositional behavior of preschool children: Theory and intervention. *Family Relations, 30,* 440–446.

Haupt, J. J., Larsen, J. M., Robinson, C. C., & Hart, C. H. (1995). The impact of DAP inservice training on the beliefs and practices of kindergarten teachers. *Journal of Early Childhood Teacher Education, 16*(2), 12–18.

Hawes, D., & Dadds, M. (2005). The treatment of conduct problems in children with callous-unemotional traits. *Journal of Consulting and Clinical Psychology, 73*(4), 737–741.

Hazler, R. J. (2000). When victims turn aggressors: Factors in the development of deadly school violence. *Professional School Counseling, 4*(2), 105–113.

Health Resources and Services Administration/HRSA. (2009). Bullying among children and youth with disabilities and special needs. Retrieved September 28, 2009, from http://stopbullyingnow.hrsa.gov/HHS_ PSA/pdfs/SBN_Tip_24.pdf

Healy, J. M. (2004). *Your child's growing mind: Brain development and learning from birth to adolescence* (3rd ed.). New York: Doubleday/Broadway Books.

Healy, J. M. (2005). Helping children learn to pay attention. *Parents League Review.* Retrieved November 8, 2005, from www.parentsleague.org/attention.html

Heath, M., Sheen, D., Leavy, D., Young, E., & Money, K. (2005). Bibliotherapy: A resource to facilitate emotional healing and growth. *School Psychology International, 26*(5), 563–580.

Heide, K. M. (1999). *Young killers: The challenge of juvenile homicide.* Thousand Oaks, CA: Sage.

Helm, J. H., & Katz, L. G. (2001). *Young investigators: The project approach in the early years.* Published simultaneously by New York: Teachers College Press; and Washington, DC: NAEYC.

Hemmeter, M. L., Maxwell, K., Ault, M., & Schuster, J. (2001). *Assessment of practices in early elementary classrooms.* New York: Teachers College Press.

Hennessy, K., Rabideau, G., Cummings, E. M., & Cicchetti, D. (1994). Responses of physically abused and nonabused children to different forms of interadult anger. *Child Development, 65*(3), 815–829.

Hennessy, K., Rabideau, G., Cummings, E. M., & Cicchetti, D. (1994). Responses of physically abused and nonabused children to different forms of interadult anger. *Child Development, 65*(3), 815–829.

Herr, J., & Swim, T. (2002). *Creative resources for infants and toddlers.* Albany, NY: Delmar.

Herrenkohl, R. C., Egolf, B. P., & Herrenkohl, E. C. (1997). Preschool antecedents of adolescent assaultive behavior: A longitudinal study. *American Journal of Orthopsychiatry, 67*(3), 422–432.

Heyman, G., Dweck, C., & Cain, K. (1992). Young children's vulnerability to self-blame and helplessness: Relationship to beliefs about goodness. *Child Development, 63*(2), 401–415.

Hicks, D. J. (1965). Imitation and retention of film-mediated aggressive peer and adult models. *Journal of Personality and Social Psychology, 2*, 97–100.

HighScope. (2009). Introduction to large group time. Retrieved July 12, 2009, from http://www.highscope.org/content.asp?ContentId=381

Hildebrandt, C., & Zan, B. (2008). Constructivist approaches to moral education in early childhood. In L. Nucci & D. Narvaez (Eds.), *Handbook of character and moral education* (pp. 352–369). London: Routledge.

Hildyard, K. (2005). An investigation of cognitive mechanisms and processes underlying neglectful caregiving. *Dissertation Abstracts International: Part B The Sciences and Engineering, 66*(2-B), 1172.

Hoffman, M. (2005). Empathy is fickle, but beneficial. *APA Online: Public Affairs.* Retrieved January 6, 2006, from http://www.apa.org/science/ed-hoffman.html

Hoffman, M. L. (1975). Developmental synthesis of affect and cognition and its interplay for altruistic motivation. *Developmental Psychology, 11*, 607–622.

Hoffman, M. L. (1987). The contribution of empathy to justice and moral judgment. In N. Eisenberg & J. Strayer (Eds.), *Empathy and its development* (pp. 47–80). Cambridge: Cambridge University Press.

Honig, A. (1998, April 23). *Create a prosocial plus cognitive curriculum for young children.* Paper presented at the Early Childhood Branch of the New York Public Library, New York.

Honig, A., & Wittmer, D. (1991). *Helping children become more prosocial: Tips for teachers.* (ERIC Document Reproduction Service No. ED343693)

Honig, A., & Wittmer, D. (1996). Helping children become more prosocial: Ideas for classrooms, families, schools, and communities (Part 2). *Young Children, 51*(2), 62–70.

Hopkins, G. (2007). The school day: It's not a race. *Education World,* interview with Chip Wood. Retrieved on December 17, 2009 from http://www.educationworld.com/a_issues/issues058.shtml

Hopkins, M., & Biasini, F. (2006). Children with Fragile x Syndrome and Children with Autism Show Distinct Impairments in Emotional Understanding. Presented at the 18th Annual Convention for the Association for Psychological Science, New York.

Hopkins, M. (2005). An investigation of children with fragile x syndrome and/or autism and their ability to recognize facial expressions of emotions. The Foundation Quarterly, 21.

Hopkins, M., Perez, T., & Biasini F. (2007). *Children with Autism Spectrum Disorders Show Improvements in Emotion and Facial Recognition Abilities Following Interactive Computer Games.* Presented at the 19th Annual Convention for the Association for Psychological Science, Washington, D.C.

Hopkins, M., Ross, L., & Biasini, F. (2005). *Understanding Facial Expressions: A Comparative Study of Typical Children and Children with Autism or Fragile x Syndrome.* Presented at the 38th Annual Gatlinburg Conference On Research and Theory in Intellectual and Developmental Disabilities, Annapolis, MD

Howe, M. L., & Courage, M. L. (1993). On resolving the enigma of infantile amnesia. *Psychological Bulletin, 113*, 305–326.

Howes, C. (1991). Caregiving environments and their consequences for children: The experience in the United States. In E. Melhuish & P. Moss (Eds.), *Day care for young children*. New York: Routledge.

HRSA. (2009). Bullying among children and youth with disabilities and special needs. *Fact sheet from stop bullying now*, Washington, DC: US Department of Education. Retrieved June 12, 2009, from http:// stopbullyingnow. hrsa.gov/HHS_PSA/pdfs/SBN_Tip_ 24.pdf

Hsieh, W., Hemmeter, M., McCollum, J., & Ostrosky, M. (2009). Using coaching to increase preschool teachers' use of emergent literacy teaching strategies, *Early Childhood Research Quarterly,* available online April 17, 2009. http://dx.doi.org/10.1016/j.ecresq.2009.03.007 http://educ.ubc.ca/research/ksr/AMEsymposium2004-final.ppt

Huesmann, L. (1988). An information processing model for the development of aggression. *Aggressive Behavior, 14*(1), 13–24.

Huffman, L. R., & Speer, P. W. (2000). Academic performance among at-risk children: The role of developmentally appropriate practices. *Early Childhood Research Quarterly, 15*(2), 167–184.

Hurley, S., & Chater, N. (eds.) (2005). Introduction: The importance of imitation. In *Perspectives on imitation: From neuroscience to social science. Volume 2: Imitation, human development, and culture*. Boston: MIT Press, 1–51.

Hyson, M. (Ed.). (2003). *Preparing early childhood professionals: NAEYC's standards for programs*. Washington, DC: NAEYC.

Iannelli, V. (2004). Parenting styles. Retrieved on September 7, 2009 from http://pediatrics.about.com/od/infantparentingtips/a/04_pntg_styles.htm

Illinois State University. (n.d.). *Visual supports*: A Fact Sheet. Online. Retrieved May 16, 2009, from http://autism. pbsillinois.org/iattap_Visual_ Supports_Fact_Sheet_ 1_.pdf

Jackson, S. (2008). *Stress management for health course*. An online health course. Retrieved May 15, 2009, from http://stresscourse.tripod.com/index.html

Jalongo, M. (1986). Using crisis-oriented books with young children. In J. B. McCracken (Ed.), *Reducing stress in young children's lives*. Washington, DC: NAEYC.

Jalongo, M. (1986). Using crisis-oriented books with young children. In J. B. McCracken (Ed.), *Reducing stress in young children's lives*. Washington, DC: NAEYC.

Jason, L., & Fries, M. (2004). Helping parents reduce children's television viewing. *Research on Social Work Practice, 14*(2), 121–131.

Jenkins, J. (2000). Marital conflict and children's emotions: The development of an anger organization. *Journal of Marriage and the Family, 62*(3), 723–736.

Jewitt J., & Peterson, K. (2002). Stress and young children. ERIC Digest. Retrieved March 24, 2006, from www. ericdigests.org/2003-4/stress.html

Johnson, C., Myers, S., & Council on Children with Disabilities. (2007). Identification and evaluation of children with autism spectrum disorders. *Pediatrics, 120*, 1183–1215.

Johnson, G., Poliner, R., & Bonaiuto, S. (2005). Learning throughout the day. *Educational Leadership, 63*(1), 59–63.

Johnson, L., & Duffek, K. (2008). *Creating outdoor classrooms*. Austin, Texas: University of Texas Press.

Jones, E., & Prescott, E. *Environments for young children*. Washington, DC: NAEYC, Film #806.

Kagan, J., Reznick, J., Snidman, N., Gibbons, J., & Johnson, M. D. (1988). Childhood derivatives of inhibition and lack of inhibition to the familiar. *Child Development, 59*, 1580–1589.

Kaiser, J. (1995). Adult choice of toys affects children's prosocial and antisocial behavior. *Early Child Development and Care, 111*, 181–193.

Kantrowitz, E., & Evans, G. (2004). The relation between the ration of children per activity area and off-task behavior and type of play in child care centers. *Environment and Behavior, 36*(4), 541–557.

Katz, L. (1993). *Self-esteem and narcissism: Implications for practice*. (ERIC Digest ED358973)

Keogh, B., Naylor, S., Simon, S., Downing, B., & Maloney, J. (2006). The puppets project: Puppets February 22.

Kerbow, D. (1996). *Patterns of urban student mobility and local school reform*. (ERIC No. ED402386)

Kerbow, D., Azcoitia, C., & Buell, B. (2003). Student mobility and local improvement in Chicago. *Journal of Negro Education, 72*(1), 158–164.

Kernis, M., Brown, A., & Brody, Gene. (2000). Fragile self-esteem in children and its associaions with perceived patterns of parent-child communication. *Journal of Personality, 68*(2), 225–252.

Kids Health. (2005). *School violence and the news*. Kid's Health for Parents. Retrieved January 9, 2006, from http://kidshealth.org/parent/emotions/feelings/school_violence.html

Kim-Cohen, J., Moffitt, T., Caspi, A., & Taylor, A. (2004). Genetic and environmental processes in children's resilience and vulnerability to socioeconomic deprivation. *Child Development, 75*(3), 651–668.

King, C. A., & Kirschenbaum, D. S. (1992). *Helping children develop social skills: The social growth program.* Pacific Grove, CA: Brooks/Cole Publishing Company.

King, C. A., & Kirschenbaum, D. S. (1992). *Helping young children develop social skills.* Pacific Grove, CA: Brooks/Cole.

King, C., & Kirschenbaum, D. (1992). *Helping young children develop social skills.* Pacific Grove, CA: Brooks/Cole.

King, M., Oberlin, A., & Swank, T. (1990). Supporting the activity choices of 2-year-olds. *Day Care and Early Education, 17*(2), 9–13, 67–70.

Kishiyama, M., Boyce, W., Jiminez, A., & Knight, R. (2009). Socioeconomic disparities affect prefrontal function in children. *Journal of Cognitive Neuroscience, 21*(6), 1106–1115.

Klinzing, H. (2003). *Improving accuracy of decoding emotions from facial expressions by cooperative learning techniques.* Paper presented at the annual meeting of the American Educational Research Association, Chicago, April 21–25.

Kochanska, G., Aksan, N., & Carlson, J. (2005). Temperament, relationships, and young children's receptive cooperation with their parents. *Developmental Psychology, 41*(4), 648–660.

Kochenderfer-Ladd, B., & Pelletier, M. (2008). Teachers' views and beliefs about bullying: Influences on classroom management strategies and students' coping with peer victimization. *Journal of School Psychology, 36*(4), 431–453.

Kohlberg, L. (1958). The Development of Modes of Thinking and Choices in Years 10 to 16. Unpublished doctoral dissertation, Chicago: University of Chicago.

Kohlberg, L. (1981). *The philosophy of moral development. Moral stages and the idea of justice* (1st ed.). Cambridge, MA: Harper & Row.

Kohn, A. (1996). *Beyond discipline.* Alexandria, VA: Association for Supervision and Curriculum Development.

Kohn, A. (2001). Five reasons to stop saying "Good job." *Young Children, 56*(5), 24–28.

Kopp, C. (1989). Regulation of distress and negative emotions: A developmental view. *Developmental Psychology, 25,* 343–354.

Kopp, C. B. (1981). *The antecedents of self-regulation: A developmental perspective.* Unpublished manuscript, University of California, Los Angeles.

Kostelnik, M., Purcell, S., Krumbach, E., & Bosch, K. (2005). Helping children resolve conflict: Aggressive behavior of children. *Nebraska Cooperative Extension NF630.* Retrieved on December 17, 2009 from http://elkhorn.unl.edu/epublic/pages/publicationD.jsp?publicationId=150.

Kotchemidova, C. (2005). From good cheer to drive-by smiling: A social history of cheerfulness. *Journal of Social History, 39*(1), 5–37.

Kozey, M., Merkel, C., & Ford, L. (2006). *What does it all mean? A guide to common measures of social emotional development.* Power point slides for presentations. Vancouver, BC: University of British Columbia, Department of Educational and Counseling Psychology and Special Education.

Kriete, R. (2002). *The morning meeting book.* Greenfield, MA: Northeast Foundation for Children.

Kriete, R. (2003). Start the day with community. *Educational Leadership, 61*(1), 68–70.

Kuebli, J. (1994). Research in review: Young children's understanding of everyday emotions. *Young Children, 50*(3), 36–47.

Kuebli, J. (1994). Research in review: Young children's understanding of everyday emotions. *Young Children, 50*(3), 36–47.

Kuebli, J. (1994). Young children's understanding of everyday emotions. *Young Children, 49,* 36–47.

Ladd, G. W., Birch, S. H., & Buhs, E. S. (1999). Children's social and scholastic lives in kindergarten: Related spheres of influence? *Child Development, 70,* 1373–1400.

Ladd, G.W., Kochenderfer, B. J., & Coleman, C. C. (1997). Classroom peer acceptance, friendship, and victimization: Distinct relational systems that contribute to children's school adjustment? *Child Development, 68,* 1181–1197.

Laliberte, R. (1997). Inside your baby's brain. *Parents, 72*(9), 48–53.

Lamborn, S., Mounts, N., Steinberg, L., & Dornbusch, S. (1991). Patterns of competence and adjustment among adolescents from authoritative, authoritarian, indulgent, and neglectful families. *Child Development, 62*(5), 1049–1065.

Lang, S. (1996). Maltreated children move more often, do worse in school. *Human Ecology Forum, 24*(3), 24.

Lapsley, D. (2008). Moral self-identity as the aim of education. In L. Nucci & D. Narvaez (Eds.), *Handbook of moral and character education* (pp. 30–52). London: Routledge.

Lavallee, K. L., Bierman, K. L., & Nix, R. L. (2005, June). The impact of first-grade "friendship group" experiences on child social outcomes in the Fast Track program. *Journal of Abnormal Child Psychology, 33,* 307–324.

Lenhart, A. (2009). Cyberbullying: What the research is telling us . . . *Presentation at the National Association of Attorneys General Year of the Child Conference,* Philadelphia, PA, May 13.

Lerner, B. (1996). Self-esteem and excellence: The choice and the paradox. *American Educator, 20*(2), 9–13, 41–42.

Levin, D. (1998). *Remote control childhood? Combating the hazards of media culture.* Washington, DC: NAEYC.

Levine, L. (1995). Young children's understanding of the causes of anger and sadness. *Child Development, 66*(3), 697–710.

Levine, S., Weinberg, J., & Ursin, H. (1978). Definition of the coping process and statement of the problem. In H. Ursin (Ed.), *Psychobiology of stress.* New York: Academic.

Levy, B. (2004). Name-calling and teasing: Information for parents and educators. *Helping Children at Home and School II: Handouts for Families and Educators.* Bethesda, MD: National Association of School Psychologist.

Lewis, M. L., & Ippen, C. G. (2007). Rainbows of tears, souls full of hope: Cultural issues related to young children and trauma. In Joy Osofsky (Ed.), *Young children and trauma: Intervention and treatment* (pp. 11–46). New York: Guilford Press.

Linan-Thompson, S., & Vaughn, S. (2007). *Research based methods of reading instruction for English language learners grades K-4* Alexandria, VA: ASCD.

Lindner, J., & Rosen, L. (2006). Decoding of emotion through facial expression, prosody and verbal content in children and adolescents with Asperger's Syndrome. *Journal of Autism and Developmental Disorders, 36*(6), 769–777.

Lowenthal, B. (1999, Summer). Effects of maltreatment and ways to promote children's resiliency. *Childhood Education,* 204–209.

Lupinetti, L. (1999). Perspective-taking, social competence, gender, and prosocial behavior of suburban preschool children. *Dissertation Abstracts International, 61,* No. 02B.

Ma, H. K. (2003). The relationship of family social environment, peer influences, and peer relationships to altruistic orientation in Chinese children. *Journal of Genetic Psychology, 164*(3), 267–274.

Maccoby, E., & Martin, J. A. (1983). Socialization in the context of the family: Parent-child interaction. In P. Mussen (Ed.), *Handbook of child psychology* (Vol. 4). New York: Wiley.

MacDonald, P., Kirkpatrick, S., & Sullivan, L. (1996). Schematic drawings of facial expressions for emotion recognition and interpretation by preschool-aged children. *Genetic, Social, and General Psychology Monographs, 122*(4), 373–388.

Macy, M., & Bricker, D. (2007). Embedding individualized social goals into routine activities in inclusive early childhood classrooms. *Early Child Development and Care, 177*(2), 107–120.

Malefant, N. (2006). *Routines and transitions: A guide for early childhood professionals.* St. Paul, MN: Redleaf Press.

Mansager, E. (2004). Parents' prism: Three dimensions of effective parenting. *Journal of Individual Psychology, 60*(3), 277–293.

Marcon, R. (1993). Socioemotional versus academic emphasis: Impact on kindergartners' development and achievement. *Early Child Development and Care, 96,* 81–89.

Marcon, R. (1994). Doing the right thing for children: Linking research and policy reform in the District of Columbia public schools. *Young Children, 50*(1), 8.

Marion, M. (1994). Supporting the development of responsible anger management in children. *Early Child Development and Care, 97,* 155–163.

Marion, M. (1997). Research in review: Guiding children's understanding and management of anger. *Young Children, 52*(7), 62–68.

Marion, M. (1999). *Guidance of young children* (5th ed.). Upper Saddle River, NJ: Merrill/Prentice Hall.

Marion, M. (2003). *Guidance of young children* (6th ed.). Upper Saddle River, NJ: Merrill/Prentice-Hall.

Marion, M. (2004). *Using observation in early childhood education.* Upper Saddle River, NJ: Merrill/PrenticeHall.

Marion, M. (2005). *From hot spot challenging behaviors to calm and cool times in your classroom.* Seminar presented at the National Conference of the National Association for the Education of Young Children, December, Washington, DC.

Marion, M. (2007). *Guidance of young children, 7th Edition.* Upper Saddle River, NJ: Pearson Merrill/Prentice Hall.

Marion, M., Swim, T., & Jenner, L. (2000). Preconference session, National Association for the Education of Young Children, Atlanta, November.

Maslow, A. (1954). *Motivation and personality.* New York, NY: Harper.

Maslow, A. (1987, originally published 1954). *Motivation and personality.* Hong Kong: Longman Asia Limited.

Matlock, J., & Green, V. (1990). The effects of day care on the social and emotional development of infants, toddlers, and preschoolers. *Early Child Development and Care, 64,* 55–59.

McClellen, D. E., & Katz, L. G. (2001). Assessing children's social competence. *ERIC Digest* [Online]. Retrieved September 1, 2009, from http://wps.prenhall.com/wps/media/objects/486/497735/ObservationFiles/OT17.PDF

McComas, J., Johnson, L., & Simons, F. (2005). Teacher and peer responsivity to pro-social behaviour of high aggressors in preschool. *Educational Psychology, 25*(2–3), 223–231.

McCracken, J. B. (1986). *Reducing stress in young children's lives.* Washington, DC: NAEYC.

McKinnon, R., & Wallerstein, J. (1987). Joint custody and the preschool. *Conciliation Courts Review, 25*(2), 39–47.

McMullen, M., Elicker, J., Wang, J., Erdiller, Z., Lee, S., Lin, C., et al. (2005). Comparing beliefs about appropriate practice among early childhood education and care professionals from the U.S., Taiwan, Korea, and Turkey. *Early Childhood Edcuation Research Quarterly, 20*(4), 451–464.

Meagher, M. (2007). *Severe or traumatic stress and inflammation in multiple sclerosis*, a presentation at the symposium Traumatic Stress, Cardiovascular Disease, Metabolic Syndrome, and Neurodegenerative Disease, Annual APA Convention, August 17, San Francisco.

Medical News Today. (2004). ADHD affects 3 to 5% of the American population. Retrieved January 4, 2006, from http://www.medicalnewstoday.com/medicalnews.php?ne wid=7185

Mehana, J., & Reynolds, A. (1995). *The effects of school mobility on scholastic achievement*. Paper presented at the Biennial Meeting of the Society for Research in Child Development, Indianapolis, IN (March 30–April 2).

Merriam-Webster Online http://www.m-w.com/dictionary/ discipline. Retrieved March 19, 2006.

Midlarsky, E., & Bryan, J. H. (1972). Affect expressions and children's imitative altruism. *Journal of Experimental Research in Personality, 6,* 195–203.

Mikulincer, M., Shaver, P., Gillath, O., & Nitzberg, R. (2005). Attachment, caregiving, and altruism: Boosting attachment security increases compassion and helping. *Journal of Personality and Social Psychology, 89*(5), 817–839.

Miller, G., Cohen, S., & Richey, A. (2002). Chronic psychological stress and the regulation of pro-inflammatory cytokines: A glucocorticoid-resistance model. *Health Psychology, 21*(6), 531–541.

Miller, K. (2004). When Asperger's Syndrome and a Nonverbal Learning Disability look alike. *Pediatrics, 114*(5), 1458–1463.

Miller, P., & Sperry, L. (1987). The socialization of anger and aggression. *Merrill-Palmer Quarterly, 33*(1), 1–31.

Milner, J. S., Robertson, K. R., & Rogers, D. L. (1990). Childhood history of abuse and adult child abuse potential. *Journal of Family Violence, 5*(1), 15–34.

Miranda, M. (2004). The implications of *developmentally appropriate* practice for the kindergarten general music program. *Journal of Research in Music Education, 52*(1), 43.

Mirenda, P., MacGregor, T., & Kelly-Keough, S. (2002). Teaching communication skills for behavioral support in the context of family life. In J. M. Lucyshyn, G. Dunlap, & R. W. Albin (Eds.), *Families and positive behavior support: Addressing problem behavior in family contexts* (pp. 185–207). Baltimore: Brookes.

Mize, J. (1995). Coaching preschool children in social skills: A cognitive-social learning curriculum, In C. Carledge, & J. F. Milburn (Eds.). *Teaching social skills to children and youth: Innovative* approaches (3rd ed., pp. 237–261), Boston, MA: Allyn & Bacon.

Moely, B. E., Hart, S. S., Leal, L., Santulli, K. A., Rao, N., Johnson, T., et al. (1992). The teacher's role in facilitating memory and study strategy development in the elementary school classroom. *Child Development, 63,* 653–672.

Morrison, G. M., Brown, M., D'Incau, B., O'Farrell, S., & Furlong, M. J. (2005, December). Understanding resilience in educational trajectories: Implications for protective possibilities. *Psychology in the Schools, 43*(1), 19–31.

Mruk, C. (2006). *Self-esteem research, theory, and practice: Toward a positive psychology of self-esteem,* (3rd ed.). New York: Springer Publishing.

Myhre, S. (1993). Enhancing your dramatic play area through the use of prop boxes. *Young Children, 48*(5), 6–19.

Namka, L. (2004). Emotional intelligence: How these interactive exercises work. *Talk, Trust, and Feel Therapeutics.* Retrieved January 10, 2006, from http://www.angriesout.com/namka.htm

Nanda, R. (2005). White blood cell count. *Medline Plus.* Retrieved June 3, 2009, from http://www.hsc.wvu.edu/som/cmed/c8/results/laboratoryTests/pdfs/WBC%20 Summary.pdf

National Association for the Education of Young Children. (2003). *Early learning standards: Creating the conditions for success.* A Joint Position Statement of the National Association of the Education of Young Children and the National Association of Early Childhood Specialists in State Departments of Education (NAECS/SDE). Retrieved May 14, 2009, from http://www.naeyc.org/about/positions/pdf/position_statement.pdf

National Association for the Education of Young Children. (2005a). *Code of ethical conduct and statement of commitment.* Retrieved September 28, 2009, from http://faculty.weber.edu/tlday/2610/code05.pdf

National Association for the Education of Young Children. (2005b). *Screening and assessment of young English language learners. Supplement to the NAEYC position statement on early childhood curriculum, assessment, and program evaluation.* Retrieved May 18, 2009, from http://www.naeyc.org/about/positions/ELL_ Supplement.asp

National Association for the Education of Young Children. (2007). *NAEYC kicks off national week of the young child with senate resolution.* Retrieved May 11, 2009, from http://www.naeyc.org/about/releases/20070424.asp

National Association for the Education of Young Children. (2009). *Developmentally appropriate practice in early childhood programs serving children from birth through age 8.* A Position Statement. Washington, D.C. Retrieved May 5, 2009, from http://www.naeyc.org/about/positions/pdf/PSDAP.pdf

National Association for the Education of Young Children. (2001). *NAEYC guidelines revision. NAEYC standards for early childhood professional preparation: Initial level.* Washington, DC: Author.

National Association for the Education of Young Children. (2003). Early childhood curriculum, assessment, and program evaluation: Building an effective, accountable system in programs for children birth to age 8 [Position statement]. Washington, DC: Author.

National Association for the Education of Young Children. (2003). What to do about biters. *Early Years Are Learning Years.* Washington, DC: Author.

National Association for the Education of Young Children. (2005, April; amended 2006). *Code of ethical conduct and statement of commitment.* Retrieved June 7, 2009, from http://www.naeyc.org/about/positions/PSETH05.asp

National Association for the Education of Young Children. (1998). Self-esteem and young children: You are the key. *Early Years are Learning Years.* Retrieved from http://www.naeyc.org/pubs

National Association for the Education of Young Children. (reaffirmed 1994; original statement, 1990). NAEYC position statement on media violence in children's lives. Washington, DC: NAEYC.

National Clearinghouse on Child Abuse & Neglect Information. (2003, updated 2005). *Recognizing child abuse and neglect: Signs and symptoms.* Retrieved January 2, 2006, from http://nccanch.acf.hhs.gov/pubs/

National Institute of Mental Health. (2009). *Autism spectrum disorders.* Bathesda, MD: National Institute of Mental Health–Science Writing, Press and Dissemination Branch.

Needlman, R. (2004). *Children's books to soothe worries and fears.* Retrieved from http://www.drspock.com

Needlman, R. (2004). *Emotional intelligence: What is it, and why is it important?* Retrieved January 9, 2006, from http://www.drspock.com/article/D,1510,24353+cbx_behavior,00.html

Neuberger, J. J. (1997). Brain development research: Wonderful window of opportunity to build public support for early childhood education. *Young Children, 52,* 4–9.

Nicholson, E. (2005). The school building as a third teacher. In M. Dudek (Ed.), *Children's spaces,* pp. 44–65. Burlington, MA: Architectural Press.

O'Connell, P., Pepler, D., & Craig, W. (1999). Peer involvement in bullying: Issues and challenges for intervention. *Journal of Adolescence, 22,* 437–452.

O'Moore, M., & Kirkham, C. (2001). Self-esteem and its relationship to bullying behavior. *Aggressive Behavior, 27*(4), 269–339.

Oklahoma State Department of Education. (2003). *Oklahoma pre-kindergarten curriculum guidelines.* Oklahoma City, OK: Author.

Olds, A. R. (1977). Why is environmental design important to young children? *Children in Contemporary Society, 11*(1), 58.

Oliner, S. P., & Oliner, P. M. (1988). *The altruistic personality: Rescuers of Jews in Nazi Europe.* New York: Free Press.

Olweus D., Limber S., & Mihalic, S. F. (2002). Blueprints for Violence Prevention, Book Nine: Bullying Prevention *Program.* Boulder, CO: Center for the Study and Prevention of Violence, Institute of Behavioral Science, University of Colorado.

Osterreich, L. (1996). *Understanding children: Biting.* Ames: Iowa State University, University Extension.

Ostrosky, M. M., Jung, E. Y., Hemmeter, M. L., & Thomas, (2003). *What works brief 3: Helping children understand classroom schedules and routines.* Champaign, IL: University of Illinois at Urbana-Champaign. Retrieved May 1, 2009, from Http://www.vanderbilt.edu/csefel/briefs/wwb3.pdf

Paik, P., & Phillips, R. (2002). *Student mobility in rural communities: What are the effects on student achievement?* Naperville, IL: North Central Regional Educational Laboratory (NCREL).

Parke, R. D., & Slaby, R. G. (1983). The development of aggression. In P. Mussen (Ed.), *Handbook of child psychology* (Vol. 4). New York: Wiley.

Parten, M. (1932). Social participation among preschool children. *Journal of Abnormal and Social Psychology, 27,* 243–269.

Patterson, G. R. (1982). *Coercive family processes,* Eugene, OR: Castilia Press.

Patterson, J., Mockford, C., & Stewart-Brown, S. (2005). Parents' perceptions of the value of the Webster-Stratton Parenting Programme: A qualitative study of a general practice based initiative [Electronic version]. *Child: Care, Health and Development, 31*(1), 53–64.

Pawlak, J., & Klein, H. (1997). Parental conflict and self-esteem: The rest of the story. *Journal of Genetic Psychology, 15*(3), 303–313.

Pelander, J. (1997). My transition from conventional to more developmentally appropriate practices in the primary grades. *Young Children, 52*(7), 19–25.

Perlmutter, M. (1986). A life-span view of memory. In P. B. Baltes, D. L. Featherman, & R. M. Lerner (Eds.), *Life-span development and behavior* (Vol. 7). Hillsdale, NJ: Erlbaum.

Perlmutter, M. (1986). A life-span view of memory. In P. B. Baltes, D. L. Featherman, & R. M. Lerner (Eds.), *Life-span development and behavior* (Vol. 7). Hillsdale, NJ: Erlbaum.

Perry, B. (2000). Emotional development: Creating an emotionally safe classroom. *Early Childhood Today.* Retrieved May 9, 2009, from http://www2.scholastic.com/browse/article.jsp?id=3745868

Perry, B., & Szalavitz, M. (2007). *The boy who was raised as a dog.* New York, NY: Basic Books.

Petrakos, H., & Howe, N. (1996). The influence of the physical design of the dramatic play center on children's play. *Early Childhood Research Quarterly, 11*, 63–77.

Pettit, B. (2000). Moving and children's social connections: The critical importance of context. *Center for Research on Child Wellbeing Working Paper #98-04.* Retrieved June 10, 2009, from http://crcw.princeton.edu/workingpapers/WP98-04-Pettit.pdf

Piaget, J. (1952). *The origins of intelligence in children.* New York: International Universities Press.

Piaget, J. (1952). *The origins of intelligence in children.* New York: W. W. Norton.

Piaget, J. (1965). *The moral judgment of the child* (M. Gabain, Trans.). New York: Free Press.

Piaget, J. (1968). *Six psychological studies.* New York: Random House.

Piaget, J. (1970). Piaget's theory. In P. Mussen (Ed.), *Carmichael's manual of child psychology.* New York: Wiley.

Piaget, J. (1976a). *The grasp of consciousness: Action and concept in the young child.* Cambridge, MA: Harvard University Press.

Piaget, J. (1976b). The stages of intellectual development of the child. In N. Endler, L. Boulter, & H. Osser (Eds.), *Contemporary issues in developmental psychology* (2nd ed.). New York: Holt, Rinehart & Winston.

Piaget, J. (1983). Piaget's theory. In P. Mussen (Ed.), *Handbook of child psychology* (Vol. 1). New York: Wiley.

Pianta, R., & Stuhlman, M. (2004). Teacher-child relationships and children's success in the first years of school. *School Psychology Review, 33*, 444–458.

Pierce, J., & Wardle, J. (1997). Cause-and-effect beliefs and self-esteem of overweight children. *Journal of Child Psychology and Psychiatry and Allied Disciplines, 38*(6), 645–650.

Pollack, S. D., Vardi, S., Bechner, A., and Curtin, J. (2005). Maltreated children's regulation of attention in response to anger.*Child Development, 76*, 968–977.

Pollak, S., Vardi, S., Putzer Bechner, A., & Curtin, J. A. (2005). Physically abused children's regulation of attention in response to hostility. *Child Development, 76*(5), 968–977.

Poussaint, A. (1997). Letter to parents. In B. Cosby, *The meanest thing to say.* New York: Scholastic.

Power, F. C., Higgins, A., & Kohlberg, L. (1989). Lawrence Kohlberg's Approach to Moral Education. New York: Columbia University Press.

Prestine, J. (1997). *Helping children cope with moving: A practical resource guide for "Moving is hard."* Parsippany, NJ: Fearon Teacher Aids.

Prewitt Diaz, J. (1989). *The effects of migration on children: An ethnographic study.* (ERIC No. ED327346)

Prinstein, M., & Dodge, K. (2008) Current issues in peer influence research. In M. Prinstein & K. Dodge (Eds.), *Understanding peer influence in children and adolescents* (pp. 3–16). New York: Guilford Press.

Quakley, S., Reynolds, S., & Coker, S. (2004). The effect of cues on young children's abilities to discriminate among thoughts, feelings and behaviours. *Behaviour Research and Therapy, 42*, 343–356.

Radke-Yarrow, M., & Zahn-Waxler, C. (1984). Roots, motives, and patterns of children's prosocial behavior. In E. Staub, D. Bar-Tel, J. Karylowski, & J. Reykowski (Eds.), *Development and maintenance of prosocial behavior.* New York: Plenum Press.

Raffaelli, M., Crockett, L. J., & Shen, Y. L. (2005). Developmental stability and change in self-regulation from childhood to adolescence. *Journal of Genetic Psychology, 166*(1), 54–75.

Ramsey, C. (2009). Analysis of Preschool Expulsion in California. San Francisco, CA: Child Care Law Center. Retrieved March 30, 2009, from http:// www.childcarelaw.org

Rapee, R., Kennedy, S., Ingram, M., Edwards, S., & Sweeney, L. (2005). Prevention and early intervention of anxiety disorders in inhibited preschool children. *Journal of Consulting and Clinical Psychology, 73*(3), 488–497.

Rascle, O., & Coulomb-Cabaqno, G. (2005). Perceived motivational climate and observed aggression as a function of competitive level in youth male French handball. *Journal of Sports Behavior, 28*(1), 58–67.

Rascle, O., Coulomb-Cabagno, G., & Delsarte, A. (2005). Perceived motivational climate and observed aggression as a function of competitive level in youth male French handball. *Journal of Sport Behavior, 28*, 51–67.

Reading is Fundamental, 2004. *RIF's guide to choosing good books for children of all ages.* Washington, DC: RIF. Retrieved February 8, 2009, from http:// www.rif.org/assets/Documents/parents/choosing_ books.pdf

Rholes, W. S., Jones, M., & Wade, C. (1988). Children's understanding of personal disposition and its relationship to behavior. *Journal of Experimental Child Psychology, 45*, 1–17.

Rideout, V. J., Vandewater, E. A., & Wartella, E. A. (2003). *Zero to six: Electronic media in the lives of infants, toddlers, and preschoolers.* Menlo Park, CA: The Henry J. Kaiser Family Foundation.

Rimm-Kaufman. S. (2006). Social and academic learning study on the contribution of the *Responsive Classroom* approach. Retrieved May 4, 2009, from Http://www.responsiveclassroom.org

Robins, R., & Trzesniewski, K. (2005). Self-esteem development across the lifespan. *Current Directions in Psychological Science, 14*(3), 158–162.

Rogers, C. (1957). The necessary and sufficient conditions of therapeutic personality change. *Journal of Consulting Psychology, 21,* 95–103.

Rollins, B. C., & Thomas, D. L. (1979). Parental support, power, and control techniques in the socialization of children. In W. R. Burr, R. Hill, F. Nye, & I. Reiss (Eds.), *Contemporary theories about the family* (Vol. 1). New York: Free Press.

Rosenkoetter, L. (1999). The television situation comedy and children's prosocial behavior. *Journal of Applied Social Psychology, 29*(5), 979–993.

Rovenger, J. (2000). Fostering emotional intelligence: A librarian looks at the role of literature in a child's development. *School Library Journal, 46*(12), 40–41.

Rubin, R. (1997). The biochemistry of touch. *U.S. News & World Report, 123*(18), 62.

Rushton, S., Eitelgeorge, J., & Zickafoose, R. (2003). Connecting Brian Cambourne's conditions of learning theory to brain/mind principles: Implications for early childhood educators. *Early Childhood Education Journal, 31*(1), 11–21.

Russell, J. A. (1989). Culture, scripts, and children's understanding of emotion. In C. Saarni, & P. L. Harris (Eds.), *Children's understanding of emotion.* Cambridge, England: Cambridge University Press.

Saarni, C., Mumme, D. L., & Campos, J. J. (1998). Emotional development: Action, communication, and understanding. In W. Damon & N. Eisenberg (Eds.), *Handbook of child psychology, 5th Edition, Volume III: Social, Emotional, and personality development* (pp. 237–309). New York: John Wiley & Sons.

Sagi, A., & Hoffman, M. L. (1976). Empathic distress in the newborn. *Developmental Psychology, 12,* 175–176.

Salovey, P., & Mayer, J. D. (1990). Emotional intelligence. *Imagination, Cognition, and Personality, 9,* 185–211.

Scaglione, J., & Scaglione. (2006). *A Bully-proofing children: A practical hands-on guide to stopping bullying.* Lanham, MD: Rowman and Littlefield Education.

Schaffer, H. R., & Crook, C. K. (1980). Child compliance and maternal control techniques. *Developmental Psychology, 16,* 54–61.

Schneider, W., & Pressley, M. (1989). *Memory development between 2 and 20.* New York: Springer-Verlag.

Scott-Little, C., Kagan, S. L., & Frelow, V. S. (2006). Conceptualization of readiness and the content of early learning standards: The intersection of policy and research? *Early Childhood Research Quarterly, 21*(2), 153–173.

Sears, R. R., Maccoby, E. E., & Levin, H. (1957). *Patterns of child rearing.* Evanston, IL: Row Peterson.

Seefeldt, C. (1993, May 23). Parenting. *St. Paul Pioneer Press.*

Sege, R., & Wright, J. (lead authors) and The Committee on Injury, Violence, and Poison Prevention (2009). Policy statement on the role of the pediatrician in youth violence prevention. *Pediatrics, 124*(1), 393–402.

Selman, R. L. (1976). Social-cognitive understanding: A guide to educational and clinical practice. In T. Lickona (Ed.), *Moral development and behavior.* New York: Holt, Rinehart & Winston.

Shek, D. (2007). Perceived parental behavioral control and psychological control in Chinese adolescents in Hong Kong: A replication, *Adolescence, 42*(167), 569.

Shepard, L., Kagan, S. L., & Wurtz, E. (1998). *Principles and recommendations for early childhood assessments.* Washington, DC: national Educational Goals Panel.

Sheslow, D., & Stehl, M. (Reviewers). (2005). Childhood stress. *Kid's Health.* Retrieved December 13, 2005, from http://www.kidshealth.org/parent/emotions/feelings/stress.html

Siebert, A. (2005). *The resiliency advantage.* Portland, OR: Practical Psychology Press.

Siew, M., Bishop, G., Enkelmann, H., Tong, E., Yong, P., Ang, J., et al. (2005). Anger, stress, coping, social support, and health: Modeling the relationships. *Psychology and Health, 20*(4), 467–495.

Siew, M., Bishop, G., Enkelmann, H., Tong, E., Yong, P., Ang, J., et al. (2005). Anger, stress, coping, social support, and health: Modeling the relationships. *Psychology and Health, 20*(4), 467–495.

Silver, B. (2005, December 11). Small school, big provider. *St. Paul Pioneer Press,* p. 2A.

Skinner, C. H., Neddenriep, C. E., Robinson, S. L., Ervin, R., & Jones, K. (2002). Altering educational environments through positive peer reporting: Prevention and remediation of social problems associated with behavior disorders. *Psychology in the Schools, 39,* 191–202.

Smith, C. A., & Farrington, D. P. (2004). Continuities in anti-social behavior and parenting across three generations. *Journal of Child Psychology and Psychiatry and Allied Disciplines, 45*(2), 230–247.

Smith, M., Jaffe-Gill, E., Segal, R., & Segal, J. (2008, last updated). Diagnosing ADD and ADHD. [online]. Retrieved May 10, 2009, from http://www.helpguide.org/mental/adhd_add_diagnosis.htm

Snall, M. (2007). Conversation with Carol Gilligan. Interview at the Women, Power, and Peach Conference, September 15. Retrieved May 27, 2009, from http://www.feminist.com/resources/artspeech/interviews/carolgilligan.html

Snow, C.E., & Van Hemel, S. (Eds.) (2008). *Early childhood assessment: Why, what, and how.* Washington, DC: New Academy Press.

Socolar, R. (1995, January 15). Spanking children is in even though it's out. *The New York Times, 144,* Sec. 1, p. 26.

Sorin, R. (2004). Understanding children's feelings: Emotional literacy in early childhood. *Research in Practice Series, 11*(4). Watson, Australia: Early Childhood Australia.

Stallings, J. (1975). Implementation and child effects of teaching practices in follow-through classrooms. *Monographs of the Society for Research in Child Development, 40*(78).

Stanger, C., Dumenci, L., Kamon, J., & Burstein, M. (2004). Parenting and children's externalizing problems in substance-abusing families. *Journal of Clinical Child & Adolescent Psychology, 33*(3), 590–600.

Stayton, D. J., Hogan, R., & Ainsworth, M. D. S. (1971). Infant obedience and maternal behavior: The origins of socialization reconsidered. *Child Development, 42*, 1057–1069.

Steele, W., & Sheppard, C. (2003). Moving can be traumatic. *Trauma and Loss: Research and Interventions, 3*(1), 1–2.

Stein, M., Keller, S., & Schleifer, S. (1981). The hypothalamus and the immune response. In H. Weiner, M. Hofer, & A. Stunkard (Eds.), *Brain, behavior and bodily disease*. New York: Raven.

Steinhauer, J. (2005, May 22). Only 4 years old and expelled. Maybe preschool is the problem. *The New York Times, 154*, sec. 4, p. 1, col. 1. Available from http:www.nytimes.com/2005/05/22/weekinreview/22stem.html

Stenberg, C. (1982). *The development of anger facial expressions in infancy*. Unpublished doctoral dissertation, University of Denver.

Stifter, C.A. & Fox, N.A. (1987). Preschool children's ability to accurately identify emotions. *Journal of Non-Verbal Behavior, 11*, 34–45.

Stone, M. (1978) *Data Processing: An introduction*. Wheaton, IL: Hitchcock Publishing Co.

Strauss, M., & Field, C. (2003, November). Psychological aggression by American parents: National data on prevalence, chronicity, and severity. *Journal of Marriage and the Family, 65*, 795–808.

Strayer, J., & Roberts, W. (2004). Empathy and observed anger and aggression in five-year-olds. *Social Development, 13*(1), 1–13.

Stuber, M., Nadar, K., Yasuda, P., & Pynoos, R. (1991). Stress responses after pediatric bone marrow transplantation: Preliminary results of a prospective longitudinal study. *Journal of the American Academy of Child & Adolescent Psychiatry, 30*(6), 952–957.

Sullivan, A., & Strang, H. (2002). Bibliotherapy in the classroom: Using literature to promote the development of emotional intelligence. *Early Childhood Education, 79*(2), 74–80.

Surgeon General. (2000). *Youth violence: A report of the Surgeon General*. Retrieved from http://surgeongeneral.gov/library/youthviolence/report

Suveg, C., Barmish, A. Tiwari, S., Hudson, J. L., & Kendall, P. C. (2008). I'd rather not talk about it: Emotion parenting in families of children with an anxiety disorder. *Journal of Family Psychology, 22*(6), 875–884.

Szegal, B. (1985). Stages in the development of aggressive behavior in early childhood. *Aggressive Behavior, 11*(4), 315–321.

Tafarodi, R., & Swarm, W. (1995). Self-liking and self-competence as dimensions of global self-esteem: Initial validation of a measure. *Journal of Personality Assessment, 65*, 322–342.

Tafarodi, R., & Vu, C. (1997). Two-dimensional self-esteem and reactions to success and failure. *Personality and Social Psychology Bulletin, 23*(6), 626–636.

Tajima, E. A., & Harachi, T. W. (2006). *Parenting in the context of immigration: Parenting beliefs and discipline practices of Vietnamese and Cambodians in the U.S.* Presented at the meeting of the Society for Social Work and Research (SSWR), San Antonio, TX, January 14, 2006.

Tanner, B. (2005). Keeping children safe is integral to their health. *Parents Together Primer*, Fall. Retrieved May 1, 2009, from http://parentstogetherct.org/PTPrimerFall 2005.pdf

Tarr, P. (2001). Aesthetic codes in early childhood classrooms: What art educators can learn from Reggio Emilia. Retrieved on December 9, 2009 from http://www.designshare.com/

Terr, L. C. (1991). Childhood traumas: An outline and overview. *American Journal of Psychiatry, 148*, 10–20.

The New York Times. (1997, April 28). Nurturing development of the brain. *The New York Times, 146*, p. A14.

Thomas, A., & Chess, S. (1986). The New York Longitudinal Study: From infancy to early adult life. In R. Plomin & J. Dunn (Eds.), *The study of temperament: Changes, continuities, and challenges*. Hillsdale, NJ: Erlbaum.

Thomas, R. (1992). *Comparing theories of child development* (3rd ed.). Belmont, CA: Wadsworth.

Tolme, A. K., Topping, K., Christie, D., Donaldson, C., Howe, C., Jessiman, E., et al. (2009). Social effects of collaborative learning in primary schools. *Learning and Instruction*. Retrieved from http://dx.doi.org/10.1016/j.learninstruc.2009.01.005

Torelli, L, & Durrett, C. (n.d.). Spaces for children's resources. Retrieved July 11, 2009, from http://www.spacesforchildren.com/critera.html

Torelli, L. & Durrett, C. (1996). Landscape for learning: The impact of classroom design on infants and toddlers. *Early Childhood News, 8*(2), 12–17.

Towle, P. (2009). *Autism spectrum disorder in young children: A visual guide. Volume 1: An overview: Learning to observe across the three symptom domains*. Valhalla, NY: Westchester

Institute for Human Development. Retrieved from http://childdevelopmentmedia.com/assessment-planning/02001a.html

Townsend-Butterworth, D. (2009). Teasing and bullying: No laughing matter. Retrieved on June 19, 2009 from http://www2.scholastic.com/browse/article.jsp?id=1438

Tremblay, R., Nagin, D., Seguin, J., Zoccolillo, M., Zelazo, P., Boivin, M., et al. (2004). Physical aggression during early childhood: Trajectories and predictors. *Pediatrics, 114*(1), e43–e50. Retrieved June 22, 2009, from http://pediatrics.aappublications.org/cgi/content/full/114/1/e43

Trepanier, M., & Romatowski, J. (1981, April). *Classroom use of selected children's books to facilitate prosocial development in young children.* Paper presented at the annual meeting of the American Educational Research Association, Los Angeles.

Trickett, P., & Kuczynski, L. (1986). Children's misbehaviors and parental discipline strategies in abusive and nonabusive families. *Developmental Psychology, 22,* 115–123.

Troop-Gordon, W., & Ladd, G. W. (2005). Trajectories of peer victimization and perceptions of the self and schoolmates: Percursors to internalizing and externalizing problems. *Child Development, 76*(5), 1072–1091.

Tsujimoto, S., Yamamoto, T., Kawaguchi, H., Koizumi, H., & Sawaguchi, T. (2005). Working memory in adults and pre-school children: An event-related optical topography study. *Oxford Journals: Cerebral Cortex, 14*(7), 703–712.

Twemlow, S., Fonagy, P., & Sacco, F. (2006 published online January 12; 2004 originally published). The role of the bystander in the social architecture of bullying and violence in schools and communities. *Annals of the New York Academy of Sciences, 1036, Youth Violence: Scientific Approaches to Prevention,* (pp. 215–232). Retrieved June 15, 2009, from http://www3.interscience.wiley.com/journal/118766611/abstract

University of Missouri Extension (2009). What to do about biting. *Parenting.* Retrieved October 10, 2009, from http://missourifamilies.org/FEATURES/parentingarticles/parenting1.htm

Valentine, V. (2008). The best type of play for kids. Interview with Adele Diamond and Deborah Leong. National Public Radio, February 27. Retrieved June 6, 2009, from http://www.npr.org/templates/story/story.php?storyId=73598288

Varela, R. E., Sanchez-Sosa, J. J., & Riveros, A. (2004). Parenting style of Mexican, Mexican American, and Caucasiannon-Hispanic families: Social context and cultural influences. *Journal of Family Psychology, 18*(4), 651–657.

Venn, E. C., & Jahn, M. C. (2004). *Teaching and learning in preschool: Using* individually *appropriate practices in early childhood literacy instruction.* Newark: DE: International Reading Association.

Verschueren, K., Marcoen, A., & Buyck, P. (1998). Five-year-olds' behaviorally presented self-esteem: Relations to self-perceptions and stability across a 3-year period. *Journal of Genetic Psychology, 159*(9), 273–279.

Vessey J. (2006). ". . . of sticks and stones:" Recognizing and helping kids at psychosocial risk from teasing and bullying. *Program and abstracts* of The National Association of Pediatric Nurse Practitioners (NAPNAP), 27th Annual Conference; March 30–April 2, 2006; Washington, DC.

Vessy, J., Carlson, J., Horowitz, K., & Duffy, M. (2008). Psychometric evaluation of the child-adolescent teasing scale. *Journal of School Health, 78*(6), 344–350.

Vogotsky, L. S. (1978). *Mind in society: The development of higher psychological processes.* Cambridge, MA: Harvard University Press.

Vygotsky, L. (1978). *Mind in society: The development of higher psychological processes.* In M. Cole, V. John-Steiner, S. Scribner, & E. Souberman (Eds. and Trans.). Cambridge, MA: Harvard University Press.

Vygotsky, S. L.(1987). Thinking and speech. In R.W. Riber & A.S. Carton (eds.), *The collected works of S.L. Vygotsky, Volume 1: Problems of general psychology.* New York: Plenum.

Walker, J. (2008). Looking at teacher practices through the lens of parenting style, *Journal of Experimental Education, 76*(2), 218–240.

Walma van Der Molen, J. (2003). "Direct fright or worry? A survey of children's fear reactions to violence in fiction and news" *Paper presented at the annual meeting of the International Communication Association,* Marriott Hotel, San Diego, CA, May 27.

Weare, K. (2004). *Developing the emotionally literate school.* _____: Paul Chapman Educational Publishing/ Sage Publiations.

Werner, E. (2004). Commentary, journeys from childhood to midlife: Risk, resilience, and recovery. *Pediatrics, 114*(2), 492.

Werner, E., & Smith, R. (2001). *Journeys from childhood to midlife: Risk, resilience, and recovery* (paperback). Ithaca, NY: Cornell University Press.

White, R. W. (1959). Motivation reconsidered: The concept of competence. *Psychological Review, 66,* 297–323.

Williams, D. L., Goldstein, G., & Minshew, N. (2006). The profile of memory function in children with autism. *Neuropsychology, 20*(1), 20–29.

Williams, L. (1994). Developmentally appropriate practice and cultural values: A case in point. In B. L. Mallory & R. S. New (Eds.), *Diversity and developmentally appropriate practices* (pp. 155–165). New York: Teachers College Press.

Wilson, D. (2009, May/June). Developmentally appropriate practice in an age of testing. *Harvard Education Letter.* Retrieved May 14, 2009, from http://www.edletter.org/insights/ageoftesting.shtml

Wilson, L. C. (1990). *Infants and toddlers* (2nd ed.). New York: Delmar.

Xu, Z., Hannaway, J., & D'Souza, S. (2009). Student transience in North Carolina: The effect of student mobility on student outcomes using longitudinal data. *CALDER Working Paper No. 22.* Retrieved May 22, 2009, from http://www.caldercenter.org/PDF/1001256_student_transience.pdf

Yu, Y., Shi, J., Huang, Y., & Wang, J. (2006). Relationship between family characteristics and aggressive behaviors of children and adolescents. *Journal of Huazhong University Science and Technology, Medical Sciences, 26*(3) 380–383.

Zahn-Waxler, C., Radke-Yarrow, M., Wagner, E., & Chapman, M. (1992). Development of concern for others. *Developmental Psychology, 28*(1), 126–136.

Zegans, L. (1982). Stress and the development of somatic disorders. In L. Goldberger & S. Breznitz (Eds.), *Handbook of stress: Theoretical and clinical aspects.* New York: Free Press.

Zeman, J., & Shipman, K. (1996). Children's expression of negative affect: Reasons and methods. *Developmental Psychology, 32*(5), 842–850.

Zeman, J., & Shipman, K. (1996). Children's expression of negative affect: Reasons and methods. *Developmental Psychology, 32*(5), 842–850.

Zero to Three (2009). *Love, learning, and routines. Retrieved on July 12, 2009 from* http://www.zerotothree.org

Zhou, C., Liu, X., & Zhang, M. (2004). Characteristics of metamemory monitoring and control of children with learning difficulties. *Acta Psychologica Sinica, 36*(1), 65–70.

Name Index

Subject Index

357